Race and Ethnic Relations

Race and Ethnic Relations: The Social and Political Experience of Minority Groups

REID LUHMAN
Eastern Kentucky University

STUART GILMAN
University of Richmond

Wadsworth Publishing Company,
Belmont, California

A division of Wadsworth, Inc.

To Sue and Connie

Sociology Editor: Curt Peoples
Production Editor: Scott Lowe
Designer: Robert Hu
Copy Editor: Carolyn Davidson
Technical Illustrator: Evenelle Towne

Printed in the United States of America
1 2 3 4 5 6 7 8 9 10—84 83 82 81 80

**Library of Congress Cataloging in
Publication Data**

Luhman, Reid.
    Race and ethnic relations.

    Bibliography: p.
    Includes index.
        1.   Minorities—United States.   2.   United
States—Social conditions—1945-   3.   United
States—Politics and government—1945-
I.   Gilman, Stuart, joint author.   II.   Title.
E184.A1L83   301.45'0973   79-18352
ISBN 0-534-00795-3

Among these widely different people [Americans], the first that attracts attention, and the first in enlightenment, power, and happiness, is the white man, the European, man par excellence; below him come the Negro and the Indian.

These two unlucky races have neither birth, physique, language, nor mores in common; only their misfortunes are alike. Both occupy an equally inferior position in the land where they dwell; both suffer the effects of tyranny, and though their afflictions are different, they have the same people to blame for them.

Seeing what happens in the world, might one not say that the European is to men of other races what man is to the animals? He makes them serve his convenience, and when he cannot bend them to his will he destroys them.

In one blow oppression has deprived the descendants of the Africans of almost all the privileges of humanity. The United States Negro has lost even the memory of his homeland; he no longer understands the language his fathers spoke; he has abjured their religion and forgotten their mores. Ceasing to belong to Africa, he has acquired no right to the blessings of Europe; he is left in suspense between two societies and isolated between two peoples, sold by one and repudiated by the other; in the whole world there is nothing but his master's hearth to provide him with some semblance of a homeland. . . .

Those same abuses of power which now maintain slavery would then become the sources of the greatest dangers facing the southern whites. Nowadays only descendants of Europeans own the land and are absolute masters of the whole labor force; they alone are rich, educated, and armed. The black man has none of these advantages, but being a slave, he can manage without them. When he has become free and responsible for his own fate, can he be deprived of all these things and not die? What gave the white man his strength in times of slavery would expose him to a thousand dangers once slavery is abolished. . . .

Once one admits that white and emancipated Negroes face each other like two foreign peoples on the same soil, it can easily be understood that there are only two possibilities for the future: the Negroes and the whites must either mingle completely or they must part.

I have already expressed my conviction concerning the first possibility. I do not think that the white and black races will ever be brought anywhere to live on a footing of equality.

But I think that the matter will be still harder in the United States than anywhere else. It can happen that a man will rise above prejudices of religion, country and race, and if that man is a king, he can bring about astonishing transformations in society; but it is not possible for a whole people to rise, as it were, above itself.

Some despot subjecting the Americans and their former slaves beneath the same yoke might perhaps force the races to mingle; while American democracy remains at the head of affairs, no one would dare attempt any such thing, and it is possible to foresee that the freer the whites in America are, the more they will seek to isolate themselves.

ALEXIS DE TOCQUEVILLE, 1848
DEMOCRACY IN AMERICA

CONTENTS

Preface

The social sciences are unique among the sciences in their dependence upon the whims of their subject matter: unlike molecules, cells, and falling objects, human beings act upon interests and desires, leaving the social scientist to follow in their wake. This is particularly true in the area of racial and ethnic relations, in which people's feelings are a central part of the subject. But beyond this difficulty, social scientists face an additional problem posed by the somewhat artificial boundaries between their disciplines. The individuals we study cross those boundaries at will, as, for instance, when the social aspects of their daily lives come to be expressed in political terms. Then the sociologist hits a brick wall while the political scientist is at a loss to know where this new political creature came from.

In this book we have tried to give a *complete* picture of minorities in the United States. To do so we had to ignore the boundaries between sociology and political science. Particularly, we found that ethnic and racial relations were more likely than other social phenomena to inhabit the terrain between sociology and political science. Ethnic and racial groups are clearly social phenomena, yet so many of their actions, as well as actions taken against them, are political. By combining social and political science approaches, we can present a more complete picture of how these groups form, the conditions that motivate them, and their political responses to these conditions.

The first two chapters of the book, which give an overview of the social and political experiences of minorities in the United States during the past two centuries, will make the reader sensitive to the background and context of racial and ethnic communities. The chapters are not meant to be exhaustive, for a full account would take many volumes. Instead they are a primer of the major historical threads of such experiences, as well as a foundation upon which to build through other research.

The third and fourth chapters examine the concept of social stratification in relation to the circumstances of minorities in the contemporary United States. Economic relationships are necessarily emphasized, but not in "harsh," concrete economic perspective. Instead they are presented in terms of the "soft," subtle political and social interrelationships often characterized as political economy. Chapters 3 and 4 also introduce the fundamental problems that stratified societies confront, while illuminating through specific examples (group formation, legal interpretation, and the international context) how ethnic and racial minorities fit into society socially and politically.

Chapters 5 and 6 discuss the minority reaction to majority pressures. Chapter 5 emphasizes the social pressures of organization and identity, while Chapter 6 deals with the reasons minorities become politically active and develops a typology of minority political action. Chapters 7 and 8 give the other half of this picture: how majorities respond to minority demands and pressures. These chapters emphasize formal and informal responses of the dominant elements of society. Specifically, social organizations, voting, ideology, and even the use of social science are highlighted as mechanisms of majority response. Chapter 9 views the impact of pluralism on minorities and gives some insights into the future of minority relations in the United States.

In addition to providing a broad perspective on minority relations, we have integrated rather than segregated theory and substance. Each chapter is an additional link in our broad theoretical view of social stratification. As a result, there is no discrete "theory" section or "descriptive" section, as is found in many other texts (which tend to forget about theory after the first few chapters). Theory and description accompany each other throughout this book. Our purpose in doing this is twofold: first, we wanted the link between theory and substance to be obvious and interesting. Second, we wanted to draw attention to the similarities of the various dominant–minority relationships that overshadow many of the unique characteristics of individual ethnic and racial groups. Many of the situations encountered by blacks in the United States today, for example, were encountered by the Catholic Irish over 100 years ago. Linking theory with substance points up just such comparisons while adding coherence to an otherwise unwieldy collection of social artifacts.

Because the book has an original perspective and offers explanations of minority behavior and politics that have not appeared in this form anywhere else, we believe that it contributes to the professional literature on ethnic and racial groups. We think that sociologists, political scientists, and other social scientists will find in it much that will interest them. But this is not an esoteric tome addressed only to our colleagues. Rather it is intended for use in sociology and political science courses in social organization, minority sociology, minority politics, political behavior, and American institutions, as well as in courses in economics, anthropology, and American, black, or ethnic studies programs. With this goal in mind we have touched on several topics that, although well known to most academics in this field, must be included to introduce the subject matter to the student. All the principal theoretical perspectives are treated, and all of the major ethnic and racial groups in the United States are included as instances of particular social and political phenomena. Consistent applications of a single theoretical perspective—social stratification—ties the topics together, but each chapter can be understood on its own. Instructors will find in this book all of the material normally covered in minority textbooks, but it is covered here in an interesting and provocative way.

Our intent has been to write a stimulating and readable book. We have minimized the jargon of social science without oversimplifying or talking down to the student. Important special terms are defined clearly and realistically. Theoretical and empirical research results are presented within the flow of the text for purposes of clarity and comparison. In short, we have attempted to combine the basics of a social scientific approach to ethnic and racial relations in such a manner that the student will be attracted to further study in either sociology or political science and will have the background necessary to carry it out.

The text is in every sense a collaborative effort. The order of our names on its cover is not meant to reflect a major, or minor, contribution by either author. Without each other's insights, criticisms, and encouragement neither of us could have managed the full scope of the subject.

As in any project of this nature, a multitude of persons ought to be thanked for their help or encouragement. None of this work could have been done without the intellectual foundation provided by William R. Campbell and Cynthia Enloe. Additionally, our colleagues at Eastern Kentucky University and the University of Richmond helped through discussion and assistance. A special note of thanks is due to Thomas R. Morris, who helped make Chapter 4 clear, well-defined, and readable. Invaluable information for other sections was provided by Keith Algier, Steve Savage, John Denton, Doug Burnham, John Curra, and Mark Goldstein. The editorial assistance of Steve Rutter and Sheryl Fullerton was greatly appreciated, as was the help of our student assistants, Lee Farnum and Colleen Murphy. We owe special appreciation to the University of Richmond for a Faculty Research Grant and to the Center for Advanced Study in the Behavioral Sciences for a Summer Fellowship. This period, and the interaction with other colleagues that it provided, made possible the writing of Chapters 6 and 8. Charlene Tipton, Beverly Futrell, and Hildegard Howell also made an invaluable contribution through their typing and retyping of the manuscript.

Finally, two groups of people especially deserve our thanks: first, the students at Eastern Kentucky University and the University of Richmond who acted as guinea pigs for our ideas and who, upon reflection, probably provided more of the thinking involved in this book than we would like to admit. Second, we thank our wives. Our great debt to them is obvious, but more importantly, only Connie and Sue fully appreciate the love that went into this book and all the evenings and "lost" weekends involved in making this project a reality.

Chapter

Ethnic Groups in the United States: A Short History

ONE

INTRODUCTION: SOCIAL GROUPS
AND CULTURE

Imagine a scene somewhere in the country. A farmer is standing on a country road looking fondly at his most prized possession—several hundred acres of good farm land. A stranger comes walking down that road and strikes up a conversation.

"That's a mighty nice piece of land there," says the stranger.

"Yup," replies the farmer.

"Belongs to you?" asks the stranger.

"Yup," replies the farmer.

"How did you come by it?" asks the stranger.

"Well," replies the farmer, "I got it from my father, who worked it all his life and left it to me."

"Well, how did he get it?"

"From my grandfather."

"But how did he get it?"

"From his father before him."

"But how did he get it?"

"Well," replies the farmer, "he fought for it."

"That's fine," counters the stranger, "I'll fight you for it."

If you were imagining this scene somewhere in the peaceful Midwest of the United States, it no doubt seemed a bit absurd. Such a fight would involve far more than just the two men in the conversation. The farmer, in particular, would call upon the police and judicial powers of his state for support, and the stranger would discover that he had taken on a foe of considerable might. Even though the land was originally taken by force, the farmer is not willing to leave that option open to future comers. More important, the farmer's state agrees with him: by giving him a legal deed of ownership, it has committed itself to backing the farmer with its might. It is unfortunate for the previous owner of the land (in this case, probably an American Indian) that no such powerful ally was available when the farmer's great-grandfather came on the scene with the same desire as the stranger of our story. However, it is very probable that even the previous owner (or his ancestors) acquired the land in much the same way that it was acquired from him. Finding the "true" owner of a piece of land is usually impossible; how any one owner controls that land is, however, much more easily discovered. It is a matter of power.

Understanding how power works in societies can be extremely complicated, although it is basically an easy concept to define. *Power* is defined by its results. If you have power you can control the behavior of others, either by making them do what you want them to or by preventing them from doing what you don't want them to. The outcome could be decided by who has the bigger club, but the case of the farmer suggests that power can easily become a complicated concept. The farmer's power rests not in *his* weapons but in his social group and *their collective* weapons. To understand power, therefore, we must understand something of how people form social groups.

Studies of social groups make up much of the subject matter of the social sciences. Of that mass of information, a few basic observations will help us in this discussion. First, social groups are human creations; they represent a creative response to the problem of survival on earth. People are supposedly the most intelligent animal on earth, but that intelligence does not insure survival against faster and stronger predators unless it is put to work creatively. It is easy to see the fruits of human intelligence in the making of weapons, for instance, but the core secret of human survival is our ability to work cooperatively in groups. While we are not the only species to stumble onto this secret, we are able to do more with it because we can build on it over time as new problems arise. We can organize and reorganize our ways of relating to each other, and we can invent and construct physical aids, such as tools and shelter, as we organize ourselves. Over time, this process of organization can be called culture.

The concept of *culture,* a second basic observation about social groups, is perhaps the most general concept employed in the social sciences. It includes practically everything that makes a social group work. A culture is a group's beliefs, ideas, and patterns of relating to each other, and the physical creations or artifacts that group members use as they live. In short, everything that makes up a way of life is part of culture. Not surprisingly, people within a particular culture become attached to their way of doing things. This attachment is more than a mental exercise, however, since the culture lives in individuals as much as they live in the culture.

Third, and finally, while all humans form social groups to survive, the kinds of groups they form vary considerably. All groups, for instance, need to develop some way to care for their younger members until they are grown, but beyond that bare necessity, anything goes. No universal law states that there must be a family with a mother and a father, as is common in the United

States. The kinds of cultures to which people become attached can be very different, and since those cultures live within individuals, it follows that individuals from different cultures are very different. That observation is not earth-shaking in this day and age, but it is nevertheless worth repeating here because cultural differences among groups of people form the starting point for the study of minority and majority group relations. We shall refer to these cultural groups as *ethnic groups.*

This chapter examines the variety of ethnic groups that make up American society today. In particular, it examines the historical circumstances under which these groups came to (or were brought to) the United States, paying special attention to the social circumstances under which they entered the new society and how they coped with their new situation. The chapter also introduces a few of the concepts basic to the study of ethnic relations — beginning tools for understanding why these situations occurred as they did.

RACE AND ETHNICITY

Before we begin talking about ethnic groups in terms of minority and majority status, let us follow a conceptual tangent that haunts the study of ethnic relations. That tangent is race. We do not seek to exhaust that topic in this brief section, but rather to provide an introduction so that the ghost will not seem unfamiliar when encountered later on.

As we stated above, an ethnic group is a group of people who share a common culture. Another way of stating that is to say that they share common ethnicity. Ethnicity is not a complicated concept to apply, since culture is observable and that observation can be agreed upon by both the observer and the observed. The concept of a racial group, however, is not so easily defined.

Since an ethnic group is a group of people who share a common cultural heritage, we might suggest that a racial group is a group of people who share a common genetic heritage. Genetic heritage could be roughly defined as a cluster of genetic information that, *as a cluster,* differs from other clusters of genetic information. Thus, a given individual in one racial group might have the same shape of nose or the same blood type as an individual from another racial group but, on the whole and as groups, they would have different characteristics. This seemingly simple definition appears to make sense in everyday observation; most people think they can distinguish between white people and black people, for instance, by looking for a cluster of physical characteristics that are supposed to separate the races. White people are supposed to have lighter skin, finer hair, thinner noses, and so on. If a particular individual happens to have somewhat darker skin, he or she might still be classified as white due to the presence of other "white race" characteristics. The problem, however, is that parents who are generally classified as black could have children who might be generally classified as white (as long as the children do not challenge the new classification). Conversely, "white" parents might have children classified as black purely on the basis of appearance. We are often not the efficient biologists we think we are.

The real problem with the concept of race is that although we think it is a biological term, its meaning derives from the social interactions of non-biologists. When people become convinced that two or more races exist, then those races do, in fact, exist in the everyday lives of the people who are labeled accordingly. We thus have at least two possible definitions of race: a scientific definition and a social definition. With regard to the scientific definition, biologists do not unanimously agree on the meaning or even the existence of race. As interesting as that dispute is, it does not directly affect us, for our concern forces us to the second, or social, definition of race. We must be concerned with what nonbiologists think of race, for it is their decisions that affect individual lives in society.

A brief look at history suggests that nonbiologists are more confused by the concept of race than are biologists. For example, some Americans of northwest European ancestry suggested in the early part of this century that they belonged to a different (and, of course, superior) race from Poles, Italians, Greeks, and other southeast Europeans. The latter group they thought to be, at best, feebleminded. This idea, which seems ridiculous today, is little more than 50 years old; one wonders how our ideas of race will stack up 50 years from now.

Let us offer a tentative solution to this confusion. Returning to our original concept of ethnic group, we find that groups of people who are said to differ racially invariably also differ ethnically from whoever is doing the labeling. Thus, racial groups are also ethnic groups. This is true for a remarkably simple reason. The term *race* is usually used to justify doing something unpleasant to someone else. It becomes less upsetting to do that unpleasant thing if the victim can first be defined as unworthy or in some way unequal. It is much easier, for instance, to enslave someone who is defined as ignorant by reason of belonging to an inferior race. This makes it easier to give human beings the status of farm animals; like the black slave, farm animals are not thought capable of handling a more independent situation. In a strange twist of logic, the slave owner can even conjure up the belief that he is doing the slave a favor. People do not face discriminatory treatment because they are racially different; rather they are defined as racially different to justify discriminatory treatment. The long and short of this is that these kinds of social situations keep people separate from each other. If they did not enter such a situation already ethnically different, a relatively short stay in a racist social situation would create that difference. As we suggest, racial groups are also ethnic groups.

Our tentative solution, then, is simple: we shall employ the term *ethnic group* in a general sense to cover those groups now defined as *racial groups*. When ethnic groups are defined as racial groups by other ethnic groups, we shall then want to know who those other ethnic groups are and why they want to use the term *race*. *Race* will become an *object* of our study rather than a tool of our study.

MINORITY AND MAJORITY STATUS: A QUESTION OF DOMINANCE AND SUBORDINATION

The terms *minority group* and *majority group* are used for reasons more of tradition than of science.[1] Traditionally, a minority group was a relatively small ethnic group living within the country of a much larger ethnic group. In addition, the minority often found itself getting the short end of the stick, because the larger majority group would help itself to whatever was valued in the society before giving the minority group a chance. The majority group's ability to dominate the minority appeared at first glance to be the result of its larger size; hence the names *minority* and *majority*. The problem, however, is that smaller groups can dominate larger groups if they are more powerful. Power can come with larger group size (which fits the terms), but it can be achieved in other ways as well. That power is more important than group size leads to the following definitions. A *majority group* is a social group of common culture that controls the organization and distribution of rewards in a society. A *minority group* is a social group of common culture that is subject to the decisions of the majority group. The general term *rewards* here refers to the wide range of possessions and activities within a society that its members might value, such as jobs, prestige, and power. Access to rewards in any society is always a matter of utmost concern, and control over that access is perhaps the ultimate measure of power. A majority group, by definition, is the ethnic group that has that power. A minority group, by definition, is one that does not. More accurately, then, we should perhaps call a majority group a dominant group and a minority group a subordinate group. These terms will be used interchangeably throughout the remainder of this book.

An additional advantage of the terms *dominant* and *subordinate* is that by emphasizing power relations between groups, they encourage us to look beyond common culture or ethnicity as a basis for group formation. Recently the term *minority group* has been applied to *any* group that lacks power, whether or not it is also an ethnic group. Thus, we could (and later shall) refer to women, homosexuals, and the physically handicapped as minority groups because of the subordinate position in which members of those categories are often placed. As will be clear later, however, there is a major difference between ethnic- and non–ethnic-based groups in how they respond to differences of power in society. The primary concern of this book is *ethnic* minority and majority groups. To understand them, we shall examine non-ethnic

1. See William Newman, American Pluralism: A Study of Minority Groups and Social Theory (New York: Harper & Row, 1973), for a discussion of the history of these terms. Most such discussions start with the definitions provided by Louis Wirth in "The problem of minority groups," in Ralph Linton (ed.), The Science of Man in the World Crisis (New York: Columbia University Press, 1945).

minority and majority groups. But whether or not the groups under discussion are ethnic, the critical factor is power in society.

The question of control over the organization of and rewards in a society is a political question, and the limits of that control make up the political boundaries (or national borders) of that society. This raises a question of the relationship between political power and culture, since there cannot be minority and majority groups unless at least two ethnic groups exist within the same political boundaries. If every ethnic group had its own nation state under its political control, this book would not exist. That is not the case, of course, and we must therefore pay some attention to how different ethnic groups come to share common political boundaries (Mack, 1963: 227–28).

How Ethnic Groups Come Together: The Beginnings of Dominance and Subordination

Cultures vary among social groups because those groups develop in varying degrees of isolation. How is it then that we encounter more than one culture within one set of political boundaries? There are only two possibilities: either the boundaries move (which is politely termed invasion, purchase, annexation, or the like), or the people move (which is called migration and may be either voluntary or involuntary). When political boundaries move to include new ethnic groups, those new ethnic groups usually acquire minority status; their culture is usually both different and less powerful. In the case of migration, the situation is somewhat more complicated. Involuntary migration (such as made possible slavery in America) immediately suggests minority status, and we shall come to see that it probably results in the most oppressive minority situation of all. But voluntary migration can be caused by and result in a number of situations. At one extreme, for instance, an ethnic group might face mass starvation in its own land and therefore "voluntarily" move into an inferior status in another society simply to stay alive. That was the case with many Irish immigrants to the United States, who fled the massive potato famine in Ireland in the late 1840s. At the other extreme, an ethnic group that had a skill of great value to another culture might be invited to migrate. Americans have migrated along with their skills around the world to answer such invitations. The former situation would result in a minority status for the migrating group, while the latter case would very probably result in a highly favored position for the migrating group.

In short, any understanding of minority–majority group relations must begin with an understanding of the circumstances under which those ethnic groups initially came to share the same political boundaries. This is a question of history, and sometimes a very difficult history to locate; minority group members are seldom historians and their activities rarely interest those dominant group members who are. When that interest does occur, it often results in biased conclusions. Imagine a white slave owner writing a history of the African people in the United States; it would provide a less than complete picture of anything except the historian's perspective. Nevertheless, this question of history must be answered if we are to understand current minority–majority relations.

The United States has existed as a nation state for just over two centuries. During that time, two processes have been occurring that are important in terms of the previous discussion. First, the political boundaries of that nation have been changing continually, expanding from the original 13 colonies to the current size through a series of assorted wars and purchases. Second, that nation state has come to be populated by peoples of many cultures from all over the world. Some of these ethnic groups immigrated voluntarily and some, notably Africans, arrived here very much against their will. Because of migration and the expanding political boundaries that also added new ethnic groups, the United States has witnessed all three possible situations for minority group formation: voluntary migration, involuntary migration, and changing boundaries. Each situation results in two or more ethnic groups sharing the same political boundaries. More often than not, one of those groups manages to work its way into a position of dominance. How a group works its way into that position, and the reasons other groups cannot stop it, often stem from the way in which those groups initially came together. As we have said, that is a question of history; for our purposes it will be a history of the United States.

THE VOLUNTARY IMMIGRANTS

Let us begin at the end of our history of the United States so that we may better understand the beginning. The United States today might more properly be called England-West. It has been politically independent for two centuries, yet its culture is still more clearly English than any other. Other cultures have influenced this country to about the extent that your great-grandmother influenced your genetic makeup; in other words, we are not entirely English in anything we do but primarily English in everything we do.

Lest you think that we have announced the guilt of the butler in chapter 1 of the mystery story, we emphasize that it is no great insight into American life that our culture is primarily English. The butler in this case is the English immigrant, and to anyone who has grown up in American society, the English immigrant can do no wrong from the first Thanksgiving in the fourth grade history book to the Hollywood heroics of the white Indian fighter who wins the affections of his lady friend at the expense of a few thousand Indians. (The Indians, of course, never received top billing.) So we have a butler to whom attention is called on every page of the story. It is no surprise to discover at the conclusion (the present day) that the central figure of the story is still the most important. The irony of this analogy, however, is that the English immigrant is never (or at least, seldom) viewed as guilty. This is not surprising, since the butler himself wrote the fourth grade history book and influenced the Hollywood movie. Our purpose here is not, however, to point a finger. Our history cannot be told if we face heroes and villains at every step of the way. We shall be looking at groups of people who are often in conflict, and we have no sure way of knowing whether the vanquished would have handled the situation any differently had they won.

The Colonial Days

Returning now to the beginning of the story, we find what is today called North and South America in the hands of a great many people living within many different cultures and political boundaries. By today's standards of population density there were not many of them, but there were enough to occupy most of the land fit to live in; there were also enough to fight over control of that land from time to time. Today we call these people Indians (because of Columbus's misconceptions about where he was) and we often think of them as a group despite the variety in their cultures. Remember, however, that the degree of difference between one culture and another is a matter of perspective. From the perspective of the first European explorers, all of these people were so far from European culture that they looked much the same. This perspective, however open to dispute from a social scientist, is nevertheless very important, since those Europeans came to have the power in the area and their perspective led them to treat the native peoples accordingly in much the same way. Whatever the conceptions of those native people as to their own uniqueness, their lives came to be circumscribed along the lines of their common situation at the hands of the Europeans. They became involuntary members of a new society through invasion.

The Europeans themselves, of course, represented several different European countries, and conflict arose among them independent of the Native American population. The Spanish were first, but they held dominance just long enough to destroy the few really strong native cultures in the New World before Spain itself fell on hard times at home and withdrew its support from the early Spanish colonists. Various arrangements of coexistence developed from Mexico south as the Spanish colonists and the Indians worked together to survive.

Although the first, Spain was by no means the only European nation interested in the New World. Practically every western European nation entered the fight for land and resources. Narrowing our view to the colonization of North America, we find the dominant competitors to be Spain (headed into a tailspin), England (definitely on the rise), France (England's traditional adversary), and the Netherlands (founder of the city of New York). Unfortunately, this long and interesting story must be limited here to the observation that Spain lost its interests (although it found a cultural stand-in much later in Mexico), the Dutch were eased out of the New York area completely (as the change in name from the Dutch New Amsterdam suggests), and the French were cornered into the Canadian province of Quebec and the American "province" of Louisiana, in both of which areas the French language and variations of its culture are alive today. England was finding the same success in the New World that it was then experiencing in most of its enterprises around the world, and it expanded rapidly in what was to become the United States.

By the time of the American Revolution in 1776, the 13 colonies were definitely English in their cultural outlook as well as their cultural background. Thus, the Revolutionary War had more of the characteristics of a family feud across an ocean than of a revolution. This is of course supported by the fact that the majority of the revolutionary leaders were of English background and the resulting American Constitution had a distinctly English flavor in both form and content. Even considering all this, America had already begun to take on the cultural diversity that would later earn it the label, "nation of immigrants."

The Scotch-Irish

By the time of the revolution there were several groups of people in the colonies who, while they had come from the British Isles, saw themselves as distinctly non-English. Most numerous of these were the Scotch-Irish, a group of people who originated in Scotland but developed culturally in the north of Ireland before coming to America. The Scotch-Irish were culturally different from the southern Irish, most notably in religion. The latter group (who would come to the United States later in great numbers) were Catholic, while the Scotch-Irish were Protestant (and were responsible for bringing the Presbyterian denomination to America). Nevertheless, simply being Protestant was not sufficient from the point of view of the English Puritans who had arrived here first, and the Scotch-Irish often found a less than hearty welcome. In addition, many of them immigrated as indentured servants, a status of temporary slavery (usually six to eight years) in return for payment of passage to America. While it is difficult to know now how well or poorly those indentured servants were treated, none were happy with the arrangement, and their future was colored by the inferior status in which they entered the new society. It is also difficult to know now how many Scotch-Irish came to America, as no official statistics of immigration were kept before 1820, but their numbers have been estimated at 250,000 by the time of the revolution (Jones, 1960: 22). They continued to come for several decades after independence and became a fixture on the American scene.

The Germans

A sizable number of Germans had also come to and settled in the colonies before the Revolutionary War. The majority settled in the Quaker colony of Pennsylvania, founded by William Penn. By 1776 the German population of that colony was between 100,000 and 150,000 (Jones, 1960: 29). Like the Scotch-Irish, the Germans began to realize that their adopted country was heading toward domination by English culture. Like many non-English groups before and after them, the Germans sought to maintain their way of life, at least on the local level, through living in ethnic communities and supporting distinctive cultural elements such as churches and German-language newspapers. While many non-English religious denominations have survived in America (such as the German Lutheran Church), few non-English cultures have. Few ethnic groups have had such a continual stream of new immigrants to this country as the Germans, yet most of the cultural distinctiveness of the early German communities has long since disappeared.

The Huguenots and the Jews

We shall deal with two additional ethnic groups together because of their common need of finding religious tolerance: the Huguenots and the Jews. In every other way they are unlikely bedfellows. The Huguenots were French Protestants who found life less than easy in a predominantly Catholic country. They first came to the colonies at the end of the seventeenth century, and some continued to come during the eighteenth century. Because they were literally people without a country, they willingly faded into the dominant English culture of the colonies.

The early Jewish immigrants, on the other hand, arrived under Dutch protection in the then Dutch colony of New Amsterdam. By 1776 there were around 2,000 Jews in the colonies, many of them Sephardic Jews from Spain and Portugal (Wirth, 1928: 136). Like the Indians whose cultural differences were ignored by Europeans, Jews from many different areas would come to be perceived in America as the same because they shared a belief in Judaism. Discrimination directed primarily at later Jewish immigrants came to be felt by the descendants of the original Jewish settlers, who had found remarkable religious tolerance in the early days. Perhaps not surprisingly, descendants of earlier Jewish arrivals felt less than congenial with the new arrivals, who shared a religion with them but who were otherwise culturally quite different.

The Africans: An Early Note

Finally, we note an incredibly important day in 1619. On that day a ship docked in Jamestown, Virginia, and unloaded a cargo that included 20 African servants. They were not yet slaves, for slavery did not yet exist in the colonies, but the status of the indentured servant was a familiar one and seemed to fit the new arrivals. They were not white like the other servants; even more important, their culture was far more different from the dominant English culture than was that of the indentured Scotch-Irish. Perhaps most importantly, the new African arrivals were not Christian.[2] It is hard to imagine the early English colonists permanently enslaving the Scotch-Irish, but they felt no such inhibitions regarding Africans. In 1661 Virginia became the first

---

2. See Donald L. Noel, "A theory of the origin of ethnic stratification," Social Problems 16: 157–172 (1968), for a discussion of this issue.

colony to legalize permanent slavery, and by the time of the Revolutionary War, the institution of slavery had become a basic part of the new nation. It would be many years before these people would take a direct part in the minority–majority group conflicts of American society; meanwhile, their numbers grew. By the outbreak of the Civil War there were four and a half million people of African descent, 90 percent of whom were slaves (Pinkney, 1975: 16). Never before had such a large group of people had the task of suddenly creating a new position for itself in American society—and the results were to be unique in American history.

The Post-Revolutionary Years: A Period of Consolidation and Adjustment

The ethnic groups noted above were not, of course, the only non-English groups in the colonies at the outbreak of the Revolutionary War. They were probably the largest, but more important to our discussion is their very presence in the colonies; even though the United States was to become a basically English country, at its birth it contained considerable cultural diversity. During the next 200 years the United States would gain far more cultural diversity than it had at the revolution, yet those same two centuries would see increasing dominance by English culture.

The early days of the new nation appear to have been fairly peaceful in comparison to what was to come later. During the first 30 years of its existence, the United States became the new home of only 250,000 more voluntary immigrants. The vast majority belonged to ethnic groups already here (Jones, 1960: 65). Hence, there were few new problems of cultural adjustment during the period. The majority of the Africans entering the country involuntarily at this time were slaves and therefore not seen as a group whose cultural concerns should be considered. Native American Indians, of course, would inhibit European expansion, but that expansion had yet even to come close to exhausting available land. By 1820 the territory of the United States occupied by European culture extended westward only to the Mississippi, and whatever Indians were not killed in their original homes were forcibly moved west of the Mississippi. President Andrew Jackson was convinced that Europeans would never need this land, which was given to Indians without much worry. It would later be taken back with the same amount of consideration. Waiting in the wings was yet another ethnic group, the Mexicans, residents of what was then northern Mexico and is now the southwest United States. They would enter the United States several decades later as the spoils of a war with Mexico and would add yet another ethnic group to the ever expanding political boundaries. However, it would be many years before their voice would be heard in minority–majority politics. The 1800s were a time of primarily European domination, as voluntary immigration steadily increased and the new arrivals moved directly into the growing American society.

The 20 years between 1820 and 1840 brought about 750,000 voluntary immigrants to the United States (Jones, 1960: 93). Once again, this new group contained much the same cultural groups that were already represented here. Nevertheless, this period in American history is significant because it saw the first immigration of a new ethnic group that would make a profound impact on American society both in numbers and in culture: the Catholic Irish.

The Catholic Irish

All but the northernmost tip of Ireland is predominantly Catholic and, incidentally, traditionally anti-English. Before 1815 very few Catholic Irish immigrated to the United States. The Scotch-Irish, who had been coming, were of a different religion and generaly different culture. For 30 years after 1815, the Catholic Irish constituted an ever increasing although as yet relatively small segment of the overall European immigration. The importance of this immigration is that the United States was becoming established as an acceptable route of escape from Ireland. Such an escape became necessary during the massive potato famine between 1846 and 1850.

The potato is perhaps an odd historical figure. Its importance in modern European history has been exceeded, however, by only a very few people. The potato had become the food of the peasant. An abundant crop could be grown on a relatively small parcel of land (which was all any peasant had to work with). Because of the potato's efficiency, the population of Ireland increased 172 percent between 1780 and 1840, as Ireland became the most densely populated country in Europe (Duff, 1971: 8). The average Irish peasant consumed potatoes at every meal, every day of the year. Four years of potato crop failure in Ireland began in 1845; the first year half the crop was lost, followed by two years of almost complete crop loss (Duff, 1971: 10; Jones, 1960: 101). Eight million people were without food. Between 1846 and 1850, 870,000 Catholic Irish came to the United States, and by 1860 there were 1,600,000 Irish in the United States (Duff, 1971: 10).

If the Irish potato famine staggers the imagination, so did the influx of new immigrants stagger the imaginations of those already in the United States. The newcomers were universally poor and without skills; there were so many of them; their sentiments were anti-English; and finally, they were not Protestants. Problems of cultural adjustment faced earlier in American history shrank in importance in the face of this new onslaught. To the people already here, the Irish appeared to be fundamentally different, and their religious difference came to be a convenient symbol and a basis for prejudice. Those Irish who found work were uniformly relegated to unskilled jobs. Although most of the new immigrants had come from rural areas, they became city dwellers in the United States, like many other, later ethnic groups. The skirmishes between ethnic groups that had been common in the United States now escalated to a kind of trench warfare, as the competitors became so much more concentrated. Many forms of discrimination that American blacks would face after emancipation were faced first by the Irish: they were banned from many neighborhoods, public facilities, and places of employment. "No Irish need apply" began a trend: only the name of the ethnic group need be changed as other groups followed. Ironically, ethnic groups in America that previously had not gotten along with each other now found that they had a mutual dislike of the Irish, another pattern that would repeat many times over. Every new group that imported increasing cultural diversity into American society also brought closer together the groups already here.[3]

As time passed, the condition of the Irish in American society improved. They proved their loyalty during the Civil War; almost 200,000 Irish fought for the Union. They also had unusual success in city politics (Duff, 1971: 21, 53). The Irish controlled Tammany Hall, the New York City Democratic party machine, for 50 years; any politician who lost the support of Tammany lost the large Irish vote (Duff, 1971: 53; Jones, 1960: 143). In retrospect, an ethnic group's discovery of the political power inherent in group unity is still another repeating pattern begun with the Irish.

The Catholic Irish are now viewed as the end of the first of two chapters of European immigration to the United States. Despite the turmoil that surrounded their entry into American society, they were eventually viewed as culturally very similar to groups already here, in comparison with new immigrants who arrived later. Until the 1880s all Europeans in the United States had come from countries in northwest Europe. It was as if a boundary had been drawn diagonally through Europe, extending from the southwestern end to the northeastern end. Those northwest of the boundary had been coming steadily, while those southeast of it had yet to begin coming. After 1880 the number of northwestern European immigrants dropped; the number of southeastern European immigrants rose until World War I. The northwestern Europeans are often referred to as the old immigrants, the southeastern Europeans as the new immigrants. Those new immigrants came in such numbers and brought such different cultures as to dwarf the earlier impact of the Irish. They also brought a whole new dimension to the relations between dominant and subordinate groups.

The End of the Nineteenth Century:
A Time of Transition

By 1900 it was clear that a new era in immigration was well under way. The shift in the source of European immigrants was obvious. (See figure 1.) In 1882 there were 788,000 immigrants, of whom 87 percent were from countries in northwest Europe. In 1907 there were 1,285,000 immigrants, 80 percent of whom were from countries in southeast Europe (Jones, 1960:

---

3. See Georg Simmel, Conflict and the Web of Group Affiliations (New York: Free Press, 1955), for a discussion of this phenomenon. In particular see pp. 34–35, 92–96.

FIGURE 1.   European Immigration to the United States, 1820–1930

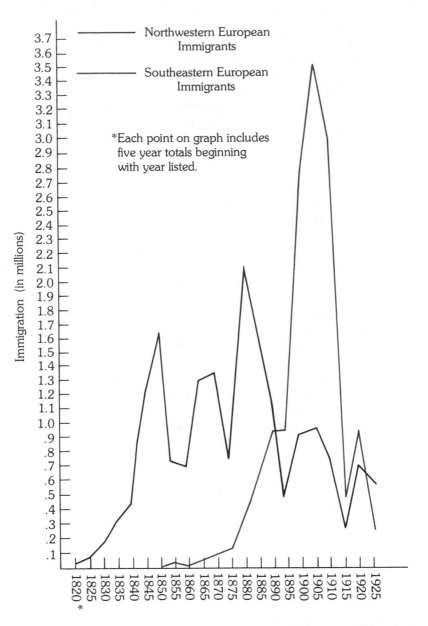

SOURCE: United States Bureau of the Census, International Migration and Naturalization (Washington, D.C., 1970).

179). While these two regions of Europe might not seem very different to us today, Americans around the turn of the century had an altogether different view. To them, the culture of southeast Europe was wholly alien, and people from that region were seen as a grave threat. Ideas of racism developed, later to be dusted off by Adolf Hitler, that placed northwestern Europeans in one race (the Aryan race) and southeastern Europeans in an inferior race.[4] The growth of these ideas, the occurrence of World War I, and a postwar depression led to the passage in 1924 of the Johnson-Reed Act (commonly called the National Origins Act), which selectively cut off immigration by means of a quota system. The impact of the quota was to allow further immigration from northwestern Europe but to curtail severely or eliminate immigration from southeastern Europe. The law went fully into effect in 1929 and effectively ended the great age of immigration to the United States. Antiforeign feeling had erupted regularly in the history of the United States, but never before had it so completely dominated the federal government.

We shall next look at two groups that illustrate the situations common to the "new immigrants": the Italians, from the far south, and the Jews, from the far east.

The Italians

By 1880 only 75,000 Italians had made their way to the United States. In the next five years, over 100,000 more would arrive as immigration from Italy rose steadily. Between 1906 and 1910 over a million Italians immigrated, followed by almost an additional million between 1911 and 1915 (United States Bureau of the Census, 1970: 105–6). But sheer numbers are only part of the story. The vast majority of the Italians who came were from southern Italy, a poverty-stricken, largely rural region (Rolle, 1972: 2–3; Jones, 1960: 200). They were poor, unskilled, and Catholic, as the Irish had been when they first arrived, but in addition they did not speak English and were basically unfamiliar with English culture. Like the Irish, the majority of the new Italians clustered in the cities, becoming a highly visible new cultural group. By this time the Irish, firmly entrenched in big-city politics, were moving steadily into civil service occupations and other skilled work (Duff, 1971: 38). They were more than happy to leave the unskilled work to the incoming Italians and other immigrant groups from southeast Europe. A pattern was repeating itself: the Irish became culturally more acceptable to other, more established cultural groups, whose opprobrium was now directed at newer immigrants. Similarly, the Italians would begin to be accepted several decades later when American blacks began to move in large numbers to the cities of the North.

The Eastern European Jews

Jews from eastern Europe were, of course, culturally very different from the Italians. They came to the United States for largely different reasons, but their reception was similar for similar reasons. Between 1881 and 1926,

---

4. See Madison Grant, The Passing of a Great Race (New York: Charles Scribner's Sons, 1916), for one of the more famous examples of this perspective.

2,300,000 Jews entered the United States, most of them natives of what is now Poland and the Soviet Union (Wirth, 1928: 150). Jews had always been persecuted, but the level of that persecution had risen sharply around the turn of the century. The Russian pogroms, in which the czar's troops systematically murdered Jews, resulted in massive emigration from Russia. The United States had become the most available escape route, as it had earlier for the Irish. These Jews entered a society that already contained members of their religion, but the earlier Jews had come almost exclusively from northwestern European countries. Beyond their religious differences, the earlier Jews were far more similar to the dominant English culture of the United States and had enjoyed considerable toleration and a fair degree of acceptance. The new Jewish immigrants, however, were rural peasants whose culture differed from both English and northwestern European Jewish culture. These new immigrants came in large numbers, concentrated in large northern cities, and began to compete in the unskilled labor market (Wirth, 1928: 148). Their arrival unleashed anti-Semitism in the United States that ultimately affected the earlier Jewish immigrants as well.

Asian Immigration

Just as the northeastern United States was becoming home to waves of European immigrants, the west coast was becoming the focal point of Asian immigration. The largest group was the Chinese, who began to enter the United States in 1850. The vast majority of the Chinese immigrants were men from southern China who perceived the move more as a temporary expedition than as permanent immigration. Their goal was to accumulate wealth and then return to their native land. As unskilled laborers, they were immediately useful to the railroad companies in building the transcontinental railroad. However, they soon became the object of racist attacks from non-Asian Westerners who, among other things, did not appreciate the competition for jobs. In an 1871 Los Angeles riot 22 Chinese were hanged, and the 1885 Rock Springs, Wyoming, massacre claimed 29 Chinese (Kitano, 1976: 15). Less physical attacks took the form of attempts to end Chinese immigration, which bore fruit in 1882 when the door from China was closed (Jones, 1960: 204). In the meantime the "Chinatown" pattern in western cities had begun, as Chinese male immigrants banded together for mutual support, protection, and pleasure. The pleasure of camaraderie took on particular significance after Chinese immigration was ended, because very few Chinese women had immigrated by then and almost all states had miscegenation laws that prohibited Chinese from marrying non-Chinese. The lack of families greatly hindered the establishment of an ongoing Chinese community.[5]

The second largest Asian immigrant group, the Japanese, began to arrive soon after Chinese immigration ended. They found anti-Asian sentiment

---

5. See Stanford M. Lyman, Chinese Americans (New York: Random House, 1974), for a discussion of early Chinese communities in the United States.

already established and readily adaptable to them. The Japanese emperor had not permitted emigration until 1885, when increasing population density on the islands plus favorable earlier Western contacts made the idea more appealing. Between 1885 and 1898, Japanese immigrated to Hawaii; in 1898, when Hawaii was annexed to the United States, Japanese began coming to the west coast states (Kitano, 1976: 8). California, the most popular destination, had little over 1,000 Japanese in 1890, but their numbers increased to over 10,000 by 1900 and over 40,000 by 1910 (Kitano, 1976: 210–11). Unlike the Chinese, many Japanese immigrated as families; in other cases families selected wives in Japan and sent them over to join waiting grooms. In either case, the early Japanese communities were family-centered and industrious. Industriousness, though American as apple pie, incited racist attacks on the Japanese from those sectors of the non-Asian population that feared competition. As the Japanese became successful at truck farming, such fears led to the passage of the California Alien Land Law of 1913, which prohibited aliens (which is to say, Japanese) from owning land (Kitano, 1976: 18–19). Although this law could be circumvented by Japanese fathers, who could transfer ownership to their American-born children, it indicates the building resentment and racism that would erupt at the outbreak of World War II.

The entrance of the United States into World War II, and in particular the Japanese attack on Pearl Harbor in Hawaii, resulted in widespread fear and distrust of the Japanese-American communities in the western United States. Ironically, there was no such fear in Hawaii itself (which then and now has the largest Japanese-American population of any state), because there had been so much cross-cultural contact. Nevertheless, the western states convinced the federal government to "relocate" the Japanese-American population through the auspices of the United States Army. Beginning in early 1942, all persons of Japanese descent (which of course included a great many American citizens) were sent for the duration of the war to what can only be called concentration camps. An important exception to this rule was the case of young men in the camps who volunteered for military service. They were combined with Hawaiian Japanese-Americans to form an all–Japanese-American army unit. Sent to Europe, this unit, the 442nd, compiled one of the finest records in the history of the American military (Kitano, 1976: 82). After the war these men, along with relocation camp inmates, returned to their former communities, where they faced much of the same racism they had left four years before. Nevertheless, a now very changed Japanese-American population went to work to overcome the setback of lost property and time.

Conclusions

We have examined several groups of people, very different culturally yet similar in two ways: all immigrated voluntarily to the United States and all had to cope with varying degrees of domination by a foreign culture. The domination—which often took the form of labor exploitation, discrimination of various kinds, and even racism—was not, however, as severe as that faced by cultural groups that entered the United States involuntarily. Perhaps part of the explanation for this difference lies in the voluntary or involuntary entrance; for instance, voluntary immigrants probably perceived their experience, however bad, in a more positive way since it was their own choice. They could also go back where they came from, if they had to. American blacks were not permitted to do this until it was too late, and Indians and Mexican-Americans already were where they had come from. But for Indians and Mexican-Americans home just wasn't the same, and there was nowhere else to go.

Perhaps the psychological advantages of voluntary entrance are not as important as some of the more practical advantages. Voluntary immigrants not only decided to come in the first place, but they could also decide, to some extent, how and where they would live after they arrived in America. For many of them that choice was the city and industrial employment on the wage system. Their choice proved wise: the United States became increasingly industrial and urban, and many voluntary immigrants were in the right place at the right time. As their area of employment expanded in a growing economy, they were there to grow with it.[6]

One other important difference cannot be ignored. If you enter a society involuntarily, you are by definition powerless. The temptation for a strong cultural group to exploit and manipulate a weaker one is perhaps too great to be resisted, and history is seldom the story of resisted temptation. Turning now to the cultural groups that entered the United States involuntarily, we find just such a story of exploitation and manipulation.

THE INVOLUNTARY IMMIGRANTS

As we said earlier, there are two ways in which an ethnic group becomes an involuntary part of different political boundaries: either the group is brought to a new location within the boundaries, or the boundaries are brought to the group. The history of the United States includes both occurrences. An example of the first method, the slave trade resulted in the involuntary entry of Africans into the United States. An example of the second method, the Mexican War during the late 1840s resulted in the expansion of United States boundaries to include what is now the American Southwest. This boundary expansion made American citizens of the Mexican citizens who were living in the area. Finally, most American Indians are an example of both forms of involuntary entry. A great many tribes first saw their land invaded by European expansion and later were forcibly moved to less desirable parts of

---

6.   See Robert Blauner, "Colonized and immigrant minorities," in N. Yetman and H. Steele (eds.), Majority and Minority, for a more extensive discussion of the differing situations of voluntary and involuntary immigrants.

the country as their original land became more in demand. Although each of these three groups is culturally unique, and although each entered the United States in a different manner, all nevertheless entered involuntarily. That one similarity gives these three groups another unenviable similarity today: of the major ethnic groups in the United States, blacks, Mexican-Americans, and American Indians are the most disadvantaged.

Blacks

The institution of slavery began inconspicuously in 1619 and grew steadily larger and more oppressive before its demise during the Civil War. Slavery in the United States was unusually cruel because the captured Africans were systematically separated from members of their families or tribes when they were sold in the United States. The slave owners' purpose was to break down native cultures more quickly and to replace them with a tailor-made slave culture more suitable for the work and lifestyle demanded by the system. All children born to slaves were automatically slaves, and families thus formed could be broken up if the owner had economic or punitive reasons for doing so. In short, slaves were not legal persons in the United States except for the strange way they were counted (one slave equaled 3/5 of a man) to facilitate helping the slave owners increase their numbers in the House of Representatives. Beyond that, slaves could not own property, they could not enter into a contract of any kind, and they had no legal recourse whatsoever. They were pieces of property and could be used and disposed of as their owners saw fit. The one small advantage the slave did have was that he or she was relatively expensive property, which provided protection from some grosser abuses.[7]

Beyond the legal restrictions, blacks were also limited socially. The most notable restriction concerned education; it was generally against the law to teach a slave either reading or writing. Once again, the rationale behind the law was that slaves could thus be more easily controlled. While the law certainly served this purpose, it also placed blacks at an extreme disadvantage; upon emancipation they had few skills to use to improve their situation. The inferior education most blacks have received since emancipation has not made their task any easier.

The end of slavery did little to improve the situation of blacks in the United States. While it was a necessary condition for improvement, many other obstacles stood in the way. The vast majority of blacks had been slaves;

---

7. For further information regarding slavery in the United States, see Basil Davison, The African Slave Trade (Boston: Little, Brown, 1961); Stanley Elkins, Slavery (New York: Grosset & Dunlap, 1963); E. Franklin Frazier, Race and Culture Contacts in the Modern World (Boston: Beacon Press, 1957); Thomas F. Pettigrew, A Profile of the Negro American (Princeton, N.J.: D. Van Nostrand, 1964); Kenneth M. Stampp, The Peculiar Institution: Slavery in the Ante-Bellum South (New York: Vintage Books, 1956); and Frank Tannenbaum, Slave and Citizen (New York: Vintage Books, 1946).

therefore the vast majority of free blacks after the Civil War found themselves unskilled and living in the rural South. The relatively short period of Reconstruction was of temporary benefit to those blacks, but the end of Reconstruction and the return of political control to the white Southerner placed the black once again in a situation of powerlessness. With options severely limited, the only viable alternative to starvation appeared to be sharecropping. As practiced in the South at the end of the nineteenth century, the system of sharecropping kept blacks with almost as little power as had slavery. Typically, a sharecropper farmed land belonging to someone else and shared the profits from the crop with the owner. The sharecropper took the risks, however, and was responsible for buying such necessities as seed and farm tools. Since former slaves had no available capital, they purchased on credit with the understanding that they would pay debts out of profits from the expected crop. Food and clothing were purchased the same way. More often than not, all these purchases were made from the land owner himself, who arranged prices so that the sharecropper's profit would never be enough to pay back the debt. When the crop came in, the sharecropper's remaining debt was listed against the next year's crop. In the process of producing the next year's crop, however, more debt was incurred. In short, to sharecrop was to be forever and increasingly in debt. In addition, it was against the law to attempt to leave the area while in debt. Sharecroppers were almost as effectively tied to the land as slaves, but now no one cared whether they starved to death in the process.[8] As immigrants from southeastern Europe moved into the northern cities and gained footholds in the industrial economy, 90 percent of the black Americans were still living in the South, many locked into the sharecropping system (Pinkney, 1975: 29).

The same period of American history that witnessed the legal slavery of sharecropping also saw the final institutionalization of racial segregation through what have come to be called the Jim Crow laws. These laws, as a group, forced racial separation in practically all aspects of life, from separate drinking fountains and washrooms to separate schools and neighborhoods. Perhaps ironically, such laws originated in the North before the Civil War, in response to growing numbers of free blacks (Woodward, 1966: 17). Free blacks, though free from the bonds of slavery, nevertheless faced severe restrictions on their activities in almost every northern state. Such laws were, of course, unnecessary in the South until the Civil War, since slavery provided a far more complete form of domination. With the emancipation of the southern black population, southern whites began looking for alternative means of domination. They found those means in the Jim Crow laws. During the later years of the nineteenth century the southern states enacted the vast collection of Jim Crow laws. By the turn of the century American blacks found

---

8. See Pete Daniel, The Shadow of Slavery: Peonage in the South 1901–1969 (New York: Oxford University Press, 1972), for a history of the American black and the institution of sharecropping in the South.

themselves once again firmly and legally placed in a situation of subordination. In the legal sense, this subordination lasted until 1965.

World War I was a major turning point for blacks in the United States. War is often a time of combined labor shortage and industrial expansion, and blacks living in the South looked appealing to northern industrialists who needed workers. Between 1914 and 1920, an estimated 400,000 to 1,000,000 blacks left the South for work in northern industry and for the cities, where that industry was located (Pinkney, 1975: 30). Jobs were available for the duration of the war, but the return of soldiers after Armistice began the pattern of black employment in the North: last hired, first fired. The end of the war was also the beginning of large-scale antiblack racism in the North, much of this racism coming from relatively recent European immigrants who now found themselves competing with blacks for jobs. There had always been some blacks in the northern cities before the mass exodus of World War I. As early as the first census of 1790, almost 60,000 free blacks lived in the North. By 1860 there were close to 500,000 (Pinkney, 1975: 36). These free blacks often played the role of strikebreaker because they were often more desperate for jobs than the incoming Europeans who were trying to form labor unions. This made blacks understandably unpopular with many European groups, particularly the Irish. Thus the influx of blacks into the North during World War I did not produce racism overnight, but rather awakened a racism that had been long in development.

Not surprisingly, the depression of the 1930s affected blacks more severely than most other groups, and it was not until World War II that the next major turning point occurred. Briefly, everything that happened during World War I happened again, for exactly the same reasons, with the addition this time that many blacks moved to industrial jobs in cities on the west coast. The end of World War II once again produced massive black unemployment, as white soldiers returned to work in a slowing peacetime economy, but by this time the major urbanization of American blacks had occurred. Blacks, still a definitely disadvantaged group, were no longer scattered throughout the rural South and locked into a semifeudal economic system. They were now concentrated, far more aware of their situation and of their options. One of these options was the civil rights movement of the 1960s. Even though that movement began in the South, it probably would never have occurred without the awareness and unification that came from mass migration to northern cities. It is not surprising, therefore, that those cities are today the major target of black political activity.

Mexican-Americans

Mexican-Americans (or Chicanos) originally entered the United States under the terms of the peace treaty that followed the United States' war with Mexico in the 1840s. Before that war, the area that is now the entire southwestern United States was controlled by Mexico, and before that by

Spain. Spanish settlement of the area began around 1600. As happened with other Spanish settlements, the original settlers soon found themselves in varying degrees of isolation. When Spanish control passed to Mexico the isolation continued; few Mexicans could be convinced to move north and strengthen the Mexican hold over the land. As the Mexican government watched European settlers pour into what is now the state of Texas, it became obvious that Mexico would soon lose control over the northern provinces. Heroics of the Alamo aside, the result of the war with Mexico was a largely foregone conclusion at its outset.

At the end of the war there were about 60,000 Mexicans in New Mexico, 5,000 in Texas, 7,500 in California, 1,000 in Arizona, and a few settlements in what is now Colorado (Moore, 1976: 12). Each of these areas entered the United states somewhat differently. In New Mexico, for example, the basic activities of the people and the power relationships among them remained stable. Texas, on the other hand, was the scene of much of the conflict of the war. Even though many Texas Mexicans had favored the formation of the Texas Republic, they were soon very far from the seats of power and commerce as Texas entered the Union. California, of course, became engulfed in the gold rush. The old Mexican ranchos could not survive the rush of the Forty-Niners to the gold fields and the rush of merchants to the Forty-Niners. However different the various situations, there was one important point in common: in no territory did the Mexican population really maintain political control. It did for a while in New Mexico, but even there the Spanish language passed out of use in the legislature and control over land and power slowly slipped from Mexican hands. The same transfer occurred more quickly and more completely in each of the other territories. Only recently has any political power whatsoever been in the hands of Mexican-Americans.[9]

There is an important second chapter in the history of Mexican-Americans in the United States, the story of immigration from Mexico after the treaty of 1848. This immigration of primarily poor and rural northern Mexican peasants did not occur on a large scale until the early 1900s. In the half-century between the end of the war with Mexico and the beginning of large-scale migration from Mexico, European dominance was established throughout the Southwest. Only New Mexico still had a numerical majority of Mexicans, but even that advantage was no match for incoming settlers or, more importantly, for the power of the United States government, which had firm ideas of how the territory should operate. By the time new Mexican immigrants began arriving, the minority status of Mexican-Americans was well established in the area. The newcomers, almost entirely unskilled, found work, when it was available, primarily on railroads and in agriculture. When work was less available, such as during the Great Depression, the familiar pattern of ethnic

---

9. See Stan Steiner, La Raza: The Mexican Americans (New York: Harper & Row, 1969), for a colorful history of the Mexican-Americans' struggle.

group competition over employment repeated itself, and Mexicans joined the ranks of so many other ethnic groups pronounced racially different from Europeans. Such clashes followed the ups and downs of the economy, major flare-ups occurring in the 1930s and again in the 1950s. In both periods, many Mexicans were deported to Mexico under the charge of being illegal aliens. Many no doubt were, but welfare and immigration officials were not overly concerned with absolute accuracy on that point. In times of prosperity, on the other hand, Mexicans were more than welcome as industrial and agricultural workers. In short, Mexican-Americans fell into the familiar pattern of the involuntary immigrant. Even though many of them were technically voluntary, their low status had already been established in the course of conquest, and their lives were very much at the mercy of the dominant Europeans who alternately used them and discarded them as the situation required.

Native Americans (American Indians)

It is perhaps ironic that a social scientific history of cultural groups in the United States would come last to the very first group to occupy the territory. History encounters them first, but the focus on power and domination that directs us finds them last. A complete history of Native American Indians would have to be long and complex to capture the uniqueness of each tribe. However, because this uniqueness was not apparent to the incoming Europeans, the manner in which they exercised their domination was highly standardized for all tribes. As a result, our social scientific history of these peoples will be relatively short. Despite their uniqueness, they have seldom been in a position to express it in the face of the overwhelming power of the Europeans. That power was used to place almost all American Indians in a common situation, and it is that common situation that concerns us.

From the point of view of Europeans, Native American Indians have always had two grave drawbacks. First, they could never be successfully exploited as a labor force. Attempts in the early days failed because tribal cultures proved to be too strong an obstacle and returning to the tribe was too easy. The latter problem was not, of course, a factor in the control of Africans, which made them far more desirable as laborers (Noel, 1968). Second, Indians were constantly physically in the way as European settlement expanded westward. In light of these two drawbacks, Europeans had the choice of either killing Indians or moving them to undesirable land. Both solutions were adequate from the European point of view. The magnitude of their domination is perhaps best expressed by statistics. There are today approximately 1,000,000 Native American Indians living in the United States. From all estimates, there were at least that many here when Columbus arrived, and there may well have been several million more than that (Josephy, 1975: 585–86). Even using the lesser figure, zero population growth during centuries in which European populations were increasing astronomically in America indicates something of the level of European interference and indifference. As Californians in the 1930s would find it easier to move Mexicans than to feed them, the earlier Europeans often found it easier to kill Indians than to move them.

The Indians who were moved (and many tribes were moved more than once) found themselves in the curious limbo of the United States government–created reservation. The reservation was and is a no-man's-land between two cultures. It is organized along the lines of tribal autonomy and group activity that made up so many Indian tribes. However, the tribe has no real political control; the government has taken up the position of legal guardian, supposedly acting in the interests of the tribe. More often than not, government actions were and are designed to make the Indian as European as possible, imposing European forms of education and political processes from without. The result was that many Indians became non-Indians but very few became Europeans.

Since 1924 Native American Indians have been legal citizens of the United States, yet they are still caught between two worlds. On the reservation all control is in the hands of the Bureau of Indian Affairs, part of the executive branch of the federal government. There is no legislative recourse to actions by the Bureau. Off the reservation, American Indians have the rights of a United States citizen—yet legal freedom is only part of the battle. The non-Indian, non-European culture of the reservation, coupled with the lack of political control by Indians, gives the contemporary Indian little future on or off the reservation. Indians have no power in either place and cannot compete economically in the modern industrial world. The use of political pressure as a group, with which other cultural groups have achieved so much is, for Indians, nonexistent. Their group has been defused by the powerless institution of the reservation. Off the reservation, they are largely on their own.

CONCLUSION AND SUMMARY

The contemporary United States is a complex society. On one hand, it is a remarkably cohesive country in which state laws are coordinated with federal laws and representative power changes hands smoothly. It also appears to be united culturally; one can speak English and purchase Coca-Cola anywhere one goes. But below the surface (and outside the offices of the mighty who enforce the use of English and distribute the Coca-Cola), it is a country of group cultural and political differences, often of conflicting lifestyles and interests. The source of those conflicts lies in the country's history. As we look more closely at those conflicts and at their sociological and political bases, this history can be a clue as to why the great "nation of immigrants" is not always the harmonious melting pot that some desire it to be.

The short history of the United States given in this chapter differs in two ways from that in most standard history books. First, it is organized around some of the concerns and concepts of social science. We examined the growing American population in terms of the many ethnic groups that accounted for that growth, focusing on the patterns of dominance and subordination that arose among them. Second, our interest in those subordinate ethnic groups led us to examine the social and historical circumstances of many poor and powerless people who are often passed over in standard histories in favor of more powerful and seemingly more important historical figures. In the course of examining those subordinate ethnic groups, we noted the fundamental importance of voluntary versus involuntary entry into American society: voluntary entry carried with it a freedom of adaptation and opportunities for advancement that were denied those groups that became American citizens against their will.

Chapter

Minority Politics: A Look at Its Foundation

TWO

THE POLITICAL REALM OF
ETHNIC DIFFERENCES

We have concentrated so far on the character of individual groups as they arrived, voluntarily or involuntarily, in the United States. All such immigrants settled in cultural clusters in the big cities, as well as in small towns, with unique problems and political attitudes. Some of these clusters, such as the German settlement in Sheboygan, Wisconsin, and the Cajuns of Houma, Louisiana, remain intact today. How did this multitude of immigrants affect the political character of the United States? And how much do these initial political roots continue to affect American politics? Certainly, the immigrants loved and married, had children, earned wages, voted, amused themselves, and, eventually, died. But these settlers also organized various groups and organizations to affect, change, or maintain their social environment—that is, they entered the arena of politics.

The term *politics* is not easily defined, especially in the case of ethnic and minority groups, because it seldom refers to the formal structures of government. Ethnic groups did—and still do—field candidates and vote. However, formal participation is merely the tip of the iceberg. Ethnic groups were involved in influencing their members' political values and specific views on law and justice, as well as in forming quasi-official organizations to represent them or their interests. At a more informal level these groups might throw political party picnics or provide liquor for wakes. The United States has a distorted vision of itself as a country that would rather do without politics. However, as Alexis de Tocqueville pointed out well over a century ago, we are a nation of joiners. The various contending minority and ethnic groups of our nation are, in fact, the seedbed of modern politics. Issues such as unemployment, the environment, and civil rights often have their political roots in minority politics.

The United States, is also, as we saw in Chapter 1, a nation of immigrants. With the exception of Native Americans, no United States citizen has roots in America before the mid-sixteenth century—and the average citizen's American roots lie in the mid-nineteenth century. Most of our social and political institutions have had to be created in an environment of coexistence among many peoples of diverse cultures and conflicting interests. Any fundamental analysis of American politics falls back on some type of groups. We shall argue throughout this book that such groups are usually some form of ethnic or minority group.

This book uses ethnic and minority groups to explain problems in the American environment that were either largely ignored or never adequately dealt with in most of the political science and sociological literature before 1960. Of course, many social scientists have argued that the United States can be best understood as a melting pot, or as a society in which older groups (those that had been here longer) competed with new arrivals. The limitation of such theories, briefly, is that they do not allow us to understand fully some of the historical paradoxes involving American minorities. For example, even though most black Americans' ancestors were in the United States before most white Americans' ancestors, there are still barriers against blacks' full participation in politics and society. Also, although the majority of Chinese and Swedes arrived in America in the same era, no laws restricting civil rights and forbidding new immigrants were passed against the Swedes, as they were against the Chinese. Finally, a plantation owner building a bridge in pre–Civil War New Orleans responded to an inquiry from his engineer as to whether he should hire Irish workers or use black slaves: "Damn it, man! Slaves cost money; who cares if an Irishman falls off the bridge and breaks his neck?" These few examples illustrate the difficulty of making clear-cut distinctions between the situations of and reactions to minorities. That is, it is often impossible to isolate the social or political circumstances of a minority and the majority reaction to them. Social scientists often discuss excessive divorce rates or low voter turnout without ever linking those social or political phenomena to the broader context of majority attitudes. Additionally, we often fail to recognize that our view of what is a minority changes, sometimes over hundreds of years and other times within a single decade. It is the interplay between the majority and the minority that creates the energy for minority politics.

This chapter examines the social and political pressures that create prejudice and discrimination. The discussion will lead us to the question of why immigrants to the United States supported institutions like the political machine, as well as suggesting the reasons why such machines were not so useful to involuntary immigrants and people of color. As an alternative, people identified as members of racial groups used many quasi-political institutions, such as mutual aid societies and fraternal lodges, to try to affect the policies of the various levels of American government. We shall also see that many less democratic, more corrupt, and violent groups had a significant impact on minority politics. But the central theme of this chapter is the vast difference between the political experience of groups identified as *racial* types and the political experience of groups considered only *ethnic* minorities.

THE POLITICAL SIDE OF SOCIAL DEFINITION

In-Groups and Out-Groups

To understand the politics of in- and out-groups, which exist at all levels of social relationships, we must first understand what they are. An in-group is a clique or group which feels that some sort of bond distinguishes it from outsiders. The distinction can be social—such as class, or fraternity or sorority membership; political—such as membership in the Democratic, Socialist, or Republican party; physical—such as race, height, or left-handedness; or any other distinction. Out-groups are usually not outside by choice, but rather have been forced out through being defined as such by those in the in-group. Differences between groups are, of course, totally artificial. The in-groups decide arbitrarily what characteristics are acceptable—and thus who is able to take part in the advantages the in-group has attained through its status, power, or influence. College campuses abound with in- and out-groups: fraternities, sororities, honoraries, and even dorm cliques distinguish artificially among people. To say that a Fiji is better than a Lambda Chi, and that both are better than a Teke, is as absurd as it would be to suggest that all students in the political science honorary are better than students not admitted to such exalted honorary societies. Such distinctions are relatively harmless; however, similarly artificial and arbitrary distinctions are often used to discriminate against people for their entire lifetime (and their children's lifetime as well), with far-reaching effects.

Distinctions between in- and out-groups are selected characteristics that *society* chooses to emphasize. Whether a renowned anthropologist, a bigoted bus driver, or an entire society asserts the existence of such differences, all rest on the fallacious assumption that *groups* of people differ substantively from each other. As we said in chapter 1, the seemingly scientific term *race* (any of the major biological divisions of humankind), for example, is no more than an idiosyncratic and very selective interpretation of incidental human characteristics.[1] Eye color, hair color, or a recessed or protruding navel could just as well be the criterion for race as skin pigmentation. In fact, skin color is not an absolutely reliable indicator of race. Creoles in southern Louisiana are often much darker than their black neighbors, yet these neighbors are considered black and the Creoles white. Distinctions among classes of human beings

---

1. See Michael Banton and Jonathan Harwood, The Race Concept (New York: Praeger, 1975), chapters I and II, *passim*. Concepts such as culture have also come under attack for their biases; see Roy Wagner, The Invention of Culture (Englewood Cliffs, N.J.: Prentice-Hall, 1975).

often arise from a psychological determination by the in-group of what is important, rather than from any biological basis, such as phylum or biological class.

We do not suggest that there are *no* differences among people or races. Physical characteristics like consistency of earwax, greater or lesser ability to digest milk, and blood types do predominate among certain racial groups— but there is tremendous variance within these racial groups. For example, a higher proportion of Caucasians have Rh negative blood (an average of 35 percent of the white population); the negative Rh factor occurs in only an average of 17 percent of the black population. (Goldsby, 1977: ch. 4). Although there *are* differences among groups of people, none of these differences comes close to being absolute. It is *even* more important to emphasize that because human beings share almost 99 percent of their genes with apes, any difference *between* human beings, in terms of their characteristics or their potential, is insignificant. Even if there were significant differences, they would not justify unequal treatment (Allport, 1954: 85–87). The root cause of discrimination is the political morality of a society and the values of its citizens. How much the citizens value and *practice* equality and justice determines how much or how little discrimination there is in that society.

Stereotypes

In most societies the bases for discrimination are *stereotypes*. Stereotypes are generic—that is, general, all-encompassing—statements about a group of people with no allowance for individual variation, such as "all blacks are lazy" or "all Jews are cheap." Stereotypes are broad psychological perceptions applied to all segments of a community. Ethnic and racial stereotypes are learned at a very early age (some psychologists say by the time a child is three or four years old) and have little if anything to do with direct contact with the stereotyped group. Stereotypes are actually most easily formed when there is no contact with the ethnic or minority group in question. Fred Uhlman describes the intrusion of stereotyping on the friendship of two boys in the dawn of Nazi Germany:

> *My mother comes of a distinguished —once royal —Polish family, and she hates Jews. For hundreds of years Jews didn't exist for her people, they were lower than the serfs, the scum of the earth, untouchables. She detests Jews. She's afraid of them though she has never met one. . . . She believes you have undermined the religious faith, and that you are in the service of world Jewry, which is only another word for Bolshevism, and that I'll be a victim of your devilish machinations (Uhlman, 1977: 86–87).*

Stereotypes have a structure and meaning of their own within cultures. Denigrating names (or *ethnophaulisms*) in the American language such as *wop, kike, chink,* and *nigger* have a complete grammar and very specific rules for social usage (Ehrlich, 1973: 21–23). For example, it is generally considered crude to call a black person a nigger to his face, yet "nigger" jokes are considered acceptable in some of the most liberal social circles. Anyone who objects to such derision is labeled humorless or defensive. Of course, geography affects both the terminology and the social role of the stereotype. Degrading terms for Cajuns in Louisiana, Bohemians in Iowa, or Chinese in California might seem totally out of place in other areas of the country.

The practice of viewing individuals in terms of group stereotypes has played a crucial role in American politics since the nation's founding. Stereotyping can lead to divisions *among* ethnic groups. Fred Barbaro points out that there is currently significant resentment against blacks among the Puerto Rican, Jewish, and Mexican-American communities, who feel that blacks have received preferential treatment (Barbaro, 1974). Yet stereotypes have also encouraged effective political action through coalitions of several minority groups. There are a number of examples of such coalitions, but few have had as profound an impact on American society as the coalition of ethnic groups under a political boss. Often the boss and the machine were the only ways for minority groups to have any effect on the American political system.

VOLUNTARY IMMIGRANTS: THE GROWTH OF THE POLITICAL MACHINE

When most voluntary immigrants arrived in the United States, they encountered hostility and resentment. Even their compatriots who had been in America for just a few years were only too willing to label and stereotype them. From the moment they set foot in immigration facilities like Ellis Island, the immigrants faced at best apathy toward their needs and at worst abuse and hatred. Expecting streets paved with gold, plenty of jobs, and relief from the miseries they had faced in their homelands, they were disillusioned by the reality of their first contact with their adopted country. Immigration officials were often impatient, arbitrary, and hardened; they would refuse entry into the United States for any type of illness and sometimes on a whim—and the immigrants had no recourse. Their names were often changed, especially if the immigration office had a hard time with foreign spellings: Steinbraunner became Stein; Marconni became Mason; Hilomovitz became Gilman.

After they were admitted, immigrants found disappointing and miserable conditions in the cities where most of them lived. Jobs were few. Most immigrants had to live in ghettos, both because of lack of money and because they sought out people from their homelands who spoke their language, would help them find jobs, and might even support them while they got settled. In some cases immigrants found it impossible to get jobs outside their community because of the resentment of those citizens who were now part of the in-group. Especially in the beginning, minority communities were not aberrations, as we tend to think today, but natural outgrowths of the needs of their new citizens.

The Political Machine

The nineteenth century, then, with its flood of new immigrants, rapid population growth, industrial giants, and governing elites, was an ideal spawning ground for the political machine and the bosses who ran it. The hundreds of immigrants settling in the big cities provided the machine with more and more reason for its existence. Poverty was rampant; state and local governments increasingly limited the work immigrants and minorities could do. Bossism developed out of the difficult situation many minorities found themselves in. Machines served their constituencies through a quasi-political system that coped with problems more effectively than the formal political system ever could. Bosses could cut through red tape to obtain licenses for pushcarts or other businesses. They could influence the immigration service to allow a wife, a mother, or an uncle into the United States when the official procedure might take years. The bosses won these favors through influence, political pressure, or bribes. Although corrupt, the machine served a vital social and historical purpose. It greased the wheels of government and played ombudsman for a multitude who otherwise would have had little or no power.

There is no single profile of the political machine. In New York the machine was Democratic; the Irish of Tammany Hall dominated city politics there for almost 100 years. In Philadelphia the machine was Republican. Bosses ran states, such as Huey Long of Louisiana; entire cities, such as Richard J. Daley of Chicago; and local districts, such as George Washington Plunkitt of one ward in Tammany's New York.

The Boss

The machine itself, of course, could not have existed without the boss. The boss used either the largest minority or a coalition of minorities to lift himself into office. Most often the boss was a member of one of the largest minority groups, which he used as a base for political activity. He maintained his hold on his constituency by using patronage (giving public jobs to loyal followers) and by providing services when they were needed. By doing the right thing at the right time—from helping someone fill out citizenship papers to aiding the victims of a fire in his district—the boss stayed in power.

If a family is burned out I don't ask whether they are Republicans or Democrats and I don't refer them to the Charity Organization Society, which would investigate their case in a month or two and decide they were worthy of help about the time they are dead from starvation. I just get quarters for them, buy clothes for them if their clothes were burned up, and fix them up until they get things runnin' again. It's philanthropy, but it's politics, too—mighty good politics. Who can tell how many votes one of these fires brings me? The poor are the most grateful people in the world, and, let me tell you, they have more friends in their neighborhoods than the rich have (Riordan, 1963: 28).

The machine was not without its faults. Contemporary scholars may have become a bit too enamored of the romance of the all-caring machine and its swashbuckling corruption. More often than not the machine made money, at the expense of the rich *and* the poor. Most bosses felt that illegal financial rewards were part of the job. George Washington Plunkitt, the great Tammany sage, often pointed out that there was a drastic difference between honest and dishonest graft. (The former meant taking advantage of your position to make investments; the latter was outright bribery.) Somehow in the post-Watergate era the distinction no longer makes sense. And although the machine understood survival, it had no social vision. It could not make changes, nor could it deal with cities in decay or with growing urban problems. It could cope only by covering up, denying, or lying about the problem.[2]

The Spread of the Political Machine

Political machines flourished from New York City to San Francisco; in the heartland cities such as Omaha, Cincinnati, Kansas City, and Minneapolis; and in the South in New Orleans and Atlanta. Machines came in different forms and with different spheres of influence and represented a wide range of interests, but their most profound impact was that they introduced generations of immigrants and their offspring to American politics. Machines gave these people a sense of the worth of the vote and of the process of democracy. The machine had a symbiotic relationship with the immigrants: each helped the other to survive. In its best sense, it was a type of apprentice democracy for ethnic minorities. It made them a permanent focus of American politics because they were invaluable allies, and dangerous opponents, at almost every electoral level from the city council to the presidency of the United States. For example, in the presidential election of 1976 against Gerald Ford, Jimmy Carter won only 48 percent of the white vote; the heavy black vote in his favor gave him the victory.

The election of 1976, however, is not typical of the political experience of blacks and other people of color. The political process, which worked so well for the voluntary immigrants, particularly those from Europe, had a mixed result for involuntary immigrants such as blacks. The notion of race, as it was *culturally* interpreted in the United States, was an important factor in the difference.

INVOLUNTARY IMMIGRANTS: EARLY POLITICAL SITUATIONS

Although most of the involuntary immigrants were people of color, not all people of color were involuntary immigrants. The Chinese and Japanese, for example, came voluntarily. But all people of color faced similar difficulties that

---

2.   See Mike Royko, Boss (New York: E. P. Dutton, 1971), for a demonstration of this shortcoming of the Daley machine in Chicago.

stemmed from the idea of *race,* which became popular in the nineteenth century. Although social and natural scientists have posited many "racial features"—such as cranial capacity (at this writing Cornell University still has a brain collection), foot structure, and arch of the backbone—the most prominent, and probably the only, real difference is skin tone. (And even skin tone is an unsafe criterion.) Using skin color to define supposed physical differences is a new concept. The use of race as a basis for distinguishing the development of peoples began with the publication of Edward Long's *History of Jamaica* in 1774. Long, a plantation owner, asserted that blacks and whites were two different species, and that blacks were doomed to their inferior status. His argument that "race mixing" was poisonous and dangerous to civilization created what purported to be a scientific justification for slavery (Banton and Harwood, 1975: 18–19). (It was scientific because Long owned a large number of black slaves and thus was able to observe them directly!)

Interestingly, Long's treatise set the stage for one of the major intellectual currents of the nineteenth century, racism, and the subsequent use of race to explain sociological differences. The idea of racism hardly seems intellectual. Yet the justification of racial differences by some of the greatest minds of America, including both Thomas Jefferson and Abraham Lincoln, became almost a national passion. This is not to say that discrimination was necessarily justified, but that differences according to color were legitimized. (This intellectual current is so strong in modern everyday thinking that it has almost become accepted as an unquestionable fact.) Long's treatise, and the fountain of sociological and political work that flowed from it, laid the basis for the nightmarish racial politics of the twentieth century, from Adolph Hitler to South African apartheid.

In the racist perspective race is a crucial political factor in the efforts of both minority groups and the majority to affect the governing of society. Imagined unchangeable characteristics of certain humans control individuals' reactions to each other. Sociology becomes a type of politics through which folklore and myth are elevated into science. Because of cultural stereotypes, bosses tended to use people of color, of whom the largest number in the United States are blacks.

Blacks

Though the boss system provided benefits for many ethnic groups, most involuntary immigrants found themselves without any such system. Even where such a system did exist, they did not benefit as much from it as did voluntary immigrants. Certainly, under bosses such as Huey Long of Louisiana in the 1920s, blacks did experience some lessening of terrorism and improvement in education and health facilities. But Long was still a racist— just not as rabid as others, like Senator Theodore Bilbo of Mississippi. Long refused to give blacks the essential ingredient that appeared to make bossism palatable to the voluntary immigrant: the ballot. Thus, for people of color the system was not even an apprentice democracy. Blacks in Louisiana were powerless against the whims of the Kingfish and his machine. Even under the modern-day machine of Richard Daley, blacks and Puerto Ricans found themselves powerless victims of corruption.[3] Of course, Daley victimized others, but these groups suffered most of all. For example, blacks in Chicago were often escorted into the voting booths to vote for the machine, but they received little of the federal antipoverty funding and had only token positions in the police and fire departments. Daley felt that he could take the black vote for granted, because Republican nominees were bound to be even more conservative on the race issue than Democrats. (Given politics in the state of Illinois, where the Republican Party is dominated by the antiminority groups of southern Illinois, Daley's assumption was less than prophetic.)

To Daley's apparent credit, blacks did accrue more benefits in Chicago than in other metropolitan areas. However, in this case the benefits are relative. Under Daley blacks had more than the little given them in other areas, but in all cases they were denied the boost in status and money that other minorities enjoyed under machines. Generally, American blacks were victims, rather than beneficiaries, of the machine system. The distinguishing features of race insured that involuntary immigrants and people of color would not "make it," as had Anglo-Saxons and ethnic minorities before them. Given racial prejudice, the machine, as well as the democratic process of majority rule, insured their isolation from broad political participation in the community, as well as in society at large. For instance, for a number of years the closed primary was voted in by a majority in the southern states, functionally eliminating black political participation. A closed primary excludes certain groups from having a voice in nominating candidates. In the South, where the Democrats dominated the nomination process for over 100 years, the closed primary was tantamount to disenfranchisement. The majority's justification was that political parties were closed clubs and could exclude whomever they wanted from membership.

American Indians

Although blacks are the most visible victims of exclusion from American politics, the group that probably lost the most because of their lack of political power is the American Indian, or Native American. Any hope they had of political influence was shredded by the guardianship of the federal government and the institutionalization of the Indian on *federal* reservations. We emphasize *federal* because that is how reservations were administered: Indians had no internal or external control of their communities. Rather, much as in federal penitentiaries (also called reservations), Indians were "protected" by the Bureau of Indian Affairs, which decided what they would eat, where they would live, and ultimately what style of living they would adopt. In

---

3. See Royko, Boss, chapter 7.

addition to being deprived of their culture, Indians were also stripped of their political rights. As long as they identified themselves as Indians, they were subject to the federal government through the Bureau of Indian Affairs. The BIA has a long history of insensitivity to the Indians' needs, and even of outright corruption. Lands promised to the Indians in treaties were taken away and sold cheaply, to land exploiters in Arizona and oil developers in Texas and Oklahoma. Although Native Americans were technically enfranchised in 1924, states (including New York and North Carolina) disputed their right to vote even into the 1970s.

Today, states including Maine and Washington are fighting strong legal challenges from Native Americans. Technically, the Indians own one third of the state of Maine through treaty provisions written in the nineteenth century. However, the Congress is actually considering a bill to nullify all treaties between Native Americans and the United States. The arbitrary nature of such an act is obvious, yet it is questionable whether such a small minority can harness effective political clout against it.

Indians also experienced a number of other de facto liabilities that led to political inequality. Social problems are prevalant on Indian reservations, such as a high alcoholism rate, high infant mortality rates, a life expectancy almost 30 years less than that of the average white, poor educational facilities, and lack of an economic base. Few industries are located near reservations; unemployment is "ten times the national average, that is, it ranged from 40 to 60 percent, depending on the general economic conditions. It was estimated that 50 percent of the housing available to the Navajo was unfit for human habitation and that as much as 90 percent of all Navajo housing was below minimum standards for health and safety" (Makielski, 1973: 58–59). Given the host of difficulties confronting them, the innate prejudice, and the physical segregation of the American Indian, there simply was no opportunity for the growth of an institution like the political machine. In a sense the Indians are the only minority in the United States which can legitimately claim to have been colonized. That is, their land was taken over by outsiders who subsequently captured complete social and political control over their lives. Usually, the Indians were the victims of patronage appointees or bureaucrats in the federal government, and they had no political power to change their condition. The psychological perception of racial "differences" has determined the Indians' treatment in American society.

Asians

The political machine likewise did not take root in the Oriental communities throughout the United States. Again, as a "colored" community—even though very few of them were involuntary immigrants—the Chinese were effectively segregated from political power, sometimes by law and more often by physical violence. The western states passed segregation laws and laws authorizing special—and unfair—taxation of the Chinese, such as the Foreign Miner's License Tax, the Cubic Air Ordinance, and the Chinese Police Tax. The Chinese Police Tax was used to support police, because the Chinese were said to bring trouble wherever they went—usually because whites attacked them. Laws were passed to limit Chinese immigration far earlier than to limit immigration of other groups.[4] Chinese immigration was effectively curtailed from 1882 to 1943, when some restrictions were lifted in deference to our Chinese allies during World War II.

Most of the riots and other violence against Orientals occurred in the West, although anti-Chinese violence has been noted from Boston to New York to Mississippi. Riots were commonplace in California. A particularly gory incident occurred late in the nineteenth century in a mining town in Wyoming. Over 30 Chinese were burned alive, as the white citizens of the town—men, women, and children—celebrated this orgy of racism and blood.

Discrimination against Orientals was just as widespread as violence. In 1928 an Oriental boy won highest honors in the school in Ruleville, Mississippi. The whites of the community were so "disgraced" that they banned all Orientals from their school system. After the Oriental parents sued the school board, a justice of the Mississippi Supreme Court found that "the term white race is limited to the Caucasian race, and the term colored race includes all other races." Thereafter, Orientals were subject to most of the same segregationist southern laws as blacks (Wu, 1972: 145–49).

Because the right of the Chinese to vote was so severely limited, their only effective political organizations were internal and usually factional, that is, divided into competing groups. Secret societies, often called *tongs,* had little impact outside the Chinese community but often used violence to keep its members in line. The tongs did not attempt to organize community members for fear that such organization might destroy their control.

The only restraint on anti-Chinese activity in the United States was the influence of the Chinese government. China had most-favored-nation status with the United States, which guaranteed just treatment of each other's citizens. Even so, although the federal government continually promised to intervene in cases involving discrimination against Chinese-Americans, it took little or no action.

Most of the anti-Chinese discrimination was also inflicted on other Orientals who settled in the United States, particularly the Japanese. Few instances of government-sponsored discrimination are more repugnant to the spirit of the American Constitution than the internment of Japanese-Americans during World War II. Earl Warren, then governor of California (and later to be chief

---

4.   Laws to limit the number of southern European immigrants were not passed until the early twentieth century. By this time European immigrants of all kinds were firmly entrenched in American society. Nonetheless, attempts were made to prove the genetic inferiority of these groups. In fact, the first use of IQ in the United States was to demonstrate the mental inferiority of Jews, Italians, and Poles. See William Ryan, Blaming the Victim (New York: Random House, 1976), appendix.

justice of the United States Supreme Court), was instrumental in having the federal government confiscate all property owned by either *issei* (Japanese who had immigrated to the United States after 1907 and therefore could not become American citizens, by law) or *nisei* (native Americans born of Japanese immigrant parents). Additionally, all persons of Japanese descent were imprisoned in camps in some of the most isolated and inhospitable areas of the country. Ironically, not one of these Japanese-Americans was ever convicted of disloyalty to the United States.

Involuntary Immigrants and Racism

Involuntary immigrants and immigrants of color experienced similar mistreatment, mainly because of racism. Racism, an idea that had originated only in the late eighteenth century, had flowered by the nineteenth century with strong impact on the political makeup of the United States. There are many other explanations for discrimination against these groups—different culture, lack of economic resources, the experience of slavery—but each pales in the face of the impact of racism. Racism set the tone for the treatment and the political role of racial minorities in the United States in the nineteenth and twentieth centuries.

It would be wrong to suggest that minority groups passively accepted the abuse of the majority. Rather, many fought back—politically if they could, but more often legally or with physical violence. These groups' activities within the context of the political system, against great odds, are one of their most profound contributions to American politics.

EARLY DIRECTIONS IN ETHNIC POLITICS: ACCOMMODATION OR REBELLION?

The machine was not the only course of political action for ethnic and minority groups. Difficult as the racial situation was for the involuntary immigrants, they also made a concerted effort toward effective political action. In times of crisis they formed viable groups or coalitions to affect politics in any way they could, from lobbying groups to underground newspapers to financial contributions to "less racist" candidates. Most such action was distributed randomly throughout the country and accomplished largely by a few distinctive leaders. But in almost all cases these individuals, and the organizations they led, have left a lasting imprint on both their groups and the rest of society.

Many social organizations provided necessary services for both voluntary and involuntary immigrants, such as the Knights of Columbus, the Hebrew Aid Society, and the Knights of Pythias. They provided not only social aid, such as children's camps and low-cost insurance, but also a gathering place and a training ground for leaders to engage in political action. Many small meeting houses or fraternal lodges developed leaders for the moment or for generations to represent the interests or ideas of a minority group. By no means complete, the following brief history of some major black leaders and groups will convey the fervor and commitment of minorities and their political impact.

Inevitably, most minority and ethnic groups, like the rest of society, had no single direction or leader at any given time. The danger of a discussion like this is that it might seem to imply that all members of a minority or ethnic group were united behind a single movement or a single leader. More accurately, a number of competing groups and leaders within a minority were usually divided over issues and tactics. Such clashes often pitted moderates, who wanted to work within the system, against radicals. The moderates advocated obeying the law and trying to use the political system to minority advantage; the radicals espoused actions beyond the legal system, from boycotts to violence. Sometimes, in the midst of turmoil such as the black civil rights movement in the 1960s, there were several distinct positions, each with a different leader (for example, Martin Luther King, Jr., Malcolm X, Eldridge Cleaver, Whitney Young, Stokely Carmichael, and Huey Newton).

The Beginnings of Black Politics:
Booker T. Washington and W.E.B. Du Bois

The classic political dialogue on the position of a minority in society occurred between Booker T. Washington and W.E.B. Du Bois in the late nineteenth and early twentieth centuries. Indeed, this dialogue between the two black "giants" of the era set the stage for most of the civil rights movement in the last half of the twentieth century. Washington argued in his famous Atlanta Exposition Speech in 1896 that blacks must "cast down their buckets where they are." That is, Washington felt that blacks should not necessarily aspire to an education, but should become the best at what they were doing, whether it was carpentry, farming, or blacksmithing. He also felt that blacks had to live with the system of segregation of that day. When they had developed their full potential, whites would recognize it and end segregation. With this aim Washington lobbied southern legislators to set up trade schools to train young blacks in manual labor. Whites viewed him as *the* spokesman of the black community, and President Theodore Roosevelt invited him to the White House.

Du Bois vehemently denounced Washington's position as selling black people back into slavery. He disagreed with Washington's contention that blacks should aspire only to trade school, demanding an educated "talented tenth" who could lead the black community. Du Bois initially advocated legal resistance to segregation and any other roadblocks to black achievement. In 1909 he helped found the Niagara Movement and later the National Association for the Advancement of Colored People (NAACP). He became editor of the NAACP newspaper, *The Crisis*, a post he held for almost 40 years. From this position Du Bois became more and more strident in opposing racism and segregation in the United States. Additionally, as a respected sociologist (trained under such notables as Max Weber, William James, and George Santayana), he published many treatises on the plight of black Americans, including *Black Reconstruction, The Philadelphia Negro,* and *The Souls of Black Folks.* For Du Bois the essential issue of the twentieth century was the color line, the issue that forced him to renounce the United States and move to Africa a few years before his death in 1963 (see Gilman, 1972).

In hindsight it is easy to judge Du Bois right and Washington wrong. However, many historians feel that Washington saw his path as the only feasible one for the survival of the black community, given the racism then present in the United States. Washington did succeed in convincing whites, who had previously disdained even trade schools for blacks, to support black schools such as his own Tuskegee Institute. His methods gained political power for blacks, in the sense that all of the apparently social issues had political motives. If blacks became an indispensable, trained work force, in Washington's mind, their power would eventually spring forth as political strength. There is a basic tension between the pragmatism of Washington and the idealism of Du Bois. However, the pragmatism was not without an idealistic side; the period of the 1950s and 1960s demonstrated quite the contrary. And even Du Bois's idealism was tempered somewhat with the pragmatism of the era; he counseled future generations against condemning Booker T. Washington outright. Du Bois understood that Washington must be analyzed in a historical context: he "had felt the lash" (that is, he had been a slave), and his perspective was very different from that of Massachusetts-born and Harvard-educated Du Bois.

An Example from Early Indian Politics:
Tecumseh and Pushmataha

Most minority groups appear to face a dilemma similar to that embodied by Washington and Du Bois: whether to try to live with prejudice and segregation or to rebel against them. The American Indians were no exception, as is obvious from the following documents involved in an 1812 attempt to unite the Shawnee, Choctaw, and Chickasaw against the whites. First, Tecumseh's argument for resistance:

Sleep no longer, o Choctaws and Chicasaws, in false security and delusive hopes. Our broad domains are fast escaping from our grasp. Every year our white intruders become more greedy, exacting, oppressive, and overbearing. Every year contentions spring up between them and our people and when blood is shed we have to make atonement whether right or wrong, at the cost of the lives of our greatest chiefs, and yielding up large tracts of our lands. Before the pale-faces came among us, we enjoyed the happiness of unbounded freedom, and were acquainted with neither riches, wants, nor oppression. . . . Are we not being stripped day by day of the little that remains of our ancient liberty?

*Do they not even now kick and strike us as they do their black-faces?
How long will it be before they will tie us to a post and whip us, and
make us work for them in cornfields as they do them? Shall we wait for
that moment or die fighting before submitting to such ignominy?
(Jacobs and Landau, 1971: 54)*

Now Pushmataha's plea for reason:

*The war, which you are now contemplating against the Americans, is
a flagrant breach of justice. . . . It is a war against a people whose
territories are now far greater than our own, and who are far better
provided with all necessary implements of war, with men, guns, horses,
wealth, far beyond that of all our race combined, and where is the
necessity or wisdom to make war upon such a people? Let us not be
deluded with the foolish hope that this war, if begun, will soon be over,
even if we destroy all the whites within our territories, and lay waste their
homes and fields. Far from it. It will be but the beginning of the end that
terminates in the total destruction of our race . . . yet I am not so
insensible and inconsistent as to advise you to cowardly yield to the
outrages of the whites, or willfully to connive at their unjust encroach-
ments; but only not yet to have recourse to war, but to send ambas-
sadors to our Great Father at Washington, and lay before him our
grievances . . . (Jacobs and Landau, 1971: 58–59).*

Both leaders made legitimate arguments for dealing with the white majority in
different ways. Their political strategies, common to voluntary and involuntary immigrants, help us understand such groups' political positions.

Nationalism: From Mormons and Marcus Garvey to Black Muslims

All the positions we have discussed so far have emphasized action within
the political system of the United States. There are several other alternatives.
One, alternately called nationalism or self-segregation, advocates a group's
leaving or totally isolating itself from the American political structure. The
Native American today is forced to choose between the meager cultural
heritage offered by the reservation and the even more meager economic and
social advantages available in the white world. In the American Jewish
community today, the question is whether to espouse Zionism or assimilation.
In the mid-nineteenth century the Mormons were so persecuted that they left
the East for the desolation of Utah and its isolation from the federal government of the United States. In the 1920s many blacks were so frustrated by
racial discrimination in the United States that they joined Marcus Garvey's
back-to-Africa movement, which would have provided transportation for
blacks to return to their "native" lands. In the 1950s the Black Muslims also

espoused nationalism, promoting a united black social, cultural, and political group separate from white society.[5]

Minority Gangs: The Sicilian Mafia and Chinese Tongs

There were other solutions to the problem of developing political power. The most "conservative" — that is, authoritarian — solutions were those of the Italian mafia or cosa nostra and the Chinese tongs. We consider these groups authoritarian because they did not ask the community's participation in their takeover of power and they were not generally thought to be part of the ethnic community. For example, few Italians considered the mafia Italian. They associated it with Sicily, and it seemed totally unfair that they should be deemed identical with a group that largely repulsed them. However, in certain situations strong individuals or groups effectively used illegitimate means to govern their communities. In other words, contrary to the widespread belief, the greatest victims of minority gangs were the minorities themselves. For example, Italian shopkeepers found themselves victimized by the mafia; black gangs seldom roam into the suburbs, instead victimizing other blacks. (One of the ironies of crime statistics is that crimes are segregated in our society: if you are white, the odds are significant that any rapist, robber, or murderer confronting you will also be white.) But such organizations or gangs were a potent, albeit corrupt, way of gaining benefits and — in a rather perverse way — justice from city hall or the police.

Vigilante Politics: The Molly Maguires and Early Race Riots

Violence in the form of vigilantism and anarchism has also been used by minorities, especially in the nineteenth century. The most famous group of the period was the Molly Maguires. Although often characterized as apolitical and mafia-like,[6] in many ways the Maguires represented the only viable competition to the large railroad and coal mining interests in southern Pennsylvania. Using the Ancient Order of Hibernians as a front, the Mollies successfully intimidated mine owners into accepting unions. The group also succeeded in intimidating most of the miners. It is a sad commentary on democratic values — in the sense of the competing interests of society — that when the Pinkerton agents hired by the railroad finally destroyed the Maguires, they also destroyed any chance the union had had to deal with the giant corporations of the time. Unionism did not have the economic or political power

---

5. For insight into Black Muslin arguments, see Malcolm X, The Autobiography of Malcolm X (as told to Alex Haley) (New York: Ballantine Books, 1965).

6. See Sir Arthur Conan Doyle, The Valley of Fear (New York: Berkley Medallion Books, 1964) for an anti-Irish story about Pinkerton infiltration of a group similar to the Molly Maguires.

needed to compete, and the Mollies had at least effected some changes in the mining camps. In fact, the stranglehold of large companies over many mines and miners is still a pervasive problem in many parts of Appalachia.[7]

Unfortunately, most vigilantism struck against minorities. Examples are the vicious attack on Spanish-speaking people in San Francisco in the 1850s by the Committee of Vigilance, and the mass expulsion within 24 hours of all Orientals from Seattle. The most well-known vigilante group, the Ku Klux Klan, controlled whole regions of the South with its white supremacy doctrine for almost 100 years. Most riots were directed against minorities—Jews, blacks, and Orientals—rather than created by them against the majority. Riots were also bloody. The riots in Atlanta and New Orleans in the early part of the twentieth century took hundreds of black lives, as did the antiblack riots in Detroit in 1943. Unlike the black riots of the 1960s, earlier riots involved large groups of whites who invaded a minority community, usually because of an exaggerated rumor, burning buildings and killing innocent people. Men, women, and children participated with equal vigor. Knowledge of such acts of terror, and of the broad participation of the majority community, is crucial to understanding the difficulties of minorities in the United States in achieving political power.

Early Minority Coalitions

The battle waged by minorities was not always entered into alone, nor was it always unsuccessful. Many groups banded together to overcome discrimination and prejudice, or in some cases for mutual political benefit. Certainly, some hostility and direct confrontation *between* minorities did occur, but there have also been many instances of mutual cooperation. Blacks and Jews had a consistent sympathy for each other's plight throughout the first half of this century (see Weisbord and Stein, 1970), as did Italians and Slavs, Irish and Italians, and Greeks and Spaniards in various parts of the country. Divisions occurred, as between Jews and blacks, when society forced them into competition for the same goods.

Groups, or coalitions of groups, were by no means passive in the face of discrimination. In several cases they directly confronted majority groups that they judged to be weak and unable to defend themselves, gaining significant power. For example, in the late 1950s a group of Lumbee Indians was being harassed by the Ku Klux Klan. (Indians in North Carolina were treated as a

---

7. Appalachia stretches from Alabama to New York; many immigrants became coal miners in this area. Many of these towns retain their very Slavic, German, or Italian names, if not a semblance of their culture. There are reported instances of trainloads of immigrants leaving New York City for the promise of high wages in the coal fields of Pennsylvania, Kentucky, and West Virginia. These unfortunates found only squalor because of the company store, company houses, and company law. All of these groups were subject to exploitation by the vast holdings of the Mellons, Carnegies, and Vanderbilts, who time and again successfully destroyed any attempt at unionization. For a discussion of one attempt, see Stuart C. Gilman, "A review essay on social terrorism: Dreiser's Harlan Miners Speak Revisited," Mountain Review (Fall 1975).

race separate from black and white; establishments around Lumberton were required to have six bathrooms, to accommodate both sexes and three races.) The Klan had burned crosses in front of the homes of two Indians who had moved into a white neighborhood, and planned to culminate its protest with a cross burning just outside Maxton, North Carolina. Armed with rifles, 500 Indians surrounded the gathering of 100 Klansmen and began shouting for the Klan leader and shooting their rifles. Although no one was injured seriously, it was the last Klan rally in that county of North Carolina (*Newsweek*, 1958: 27).

SUMMARY

This chapter has emphasized the importance of the concept of race in the development of minority politics in the United States. Minority political activity has ranged from the political boss to the minority group leader, from nationalism to violence, and from passive acceptance of discrimination to direct confrontation. The political history of minorities in the United States was sketched out in this chapter, but a comprehensive history was not its primary purpose. Rather, we hoped to give you a sense, a feeling, for the historical development of minority politics. In this sense the history of the Molly Maguires is also the story of Appalachian coal miners, Polish steelworkers, and the Black Panthers. The tragedies of the Chinese- and Japanese-Americans allows us to envision the difficulties our newest immigrants, the Vietnamese, might confront.

This brief history should have explained the importance of stereotyping as a psychological and political phenomenon as well as the political impact of in-groups and out-groups. We have also investigated how all of these factors became intertwined with the new concept of race as it developed in the western hemisphere. The next chapter will relate race and social class as social foundations and it will quickly become clear why some groups were destined to do well in American society and other groups were elected for failure. It will not be apparent until Chapter 4 how these pressures tended to form specific political alignments within minority communities. The number of major threads from this chapter can be fully understood only as we weave them into a whole cloth in the following chapters. We must examine the social and political history of minorities, as we have done in these first two chapters, before we can understand their contemporary situation in the United States.

Chapter

Social and Ethnic Stratification

THREE

ETHNIC DIVERSITY: WHEN DIFFERENCE MAKES A DIFFERENCE

So far much of our discussion has focused on hatred and conflict between dominant and subordinate ethnic groups. Appreciating the intensity of response to ethnic differences does not, however, explain why people think such differences important. We must not confuse the *causes* of conflict with the *fruits* of conflict. Cultural differences may in fact be only a convenient justification for hatred and conflict, rather than the cause of them. The different lifestyle of another ethnic group from your own may simply be a convenient excuse for your dislike for members of that group. In some circumstances, cultural differences form a basis for attraction between people.

The "Foreign Visitor"

For example, take the case of the "foreign visitor."[1] By "foreign" we mean simply that the visitor represents a culture different from that of the hosts; by "visitor" we mean the normal use of the word, emphasizing that visitors, by definition, ultimately leave. Such visitors may receive a hearty welcome and lavish attention from the host community *because* of cultural differences, not in spite of them. Not all such visitors enjoy their stay, since other variables besides welcome are certainly important. But the point is that cultural differences, *in themselves,* do not naturally lead to hatred and conflict; in fact, they

---

1. See Georg Simmel, The Sociology of Georg Simmel (Kurt Wolff, ed. and trans.) (New York: Free Press, 1950), for additional discussion of this topic.

often lead to the opposite. Harmony between cultures can occur under a range of circumstances; a warm welcome can be found by a foreign exchange student in the United States or by an American Peace Corps volunteer in the field. How, then, does the foreign visitor situation differ from meetings of cultures that lead to conflict?

By far the most important aspect of the foreign visitor situation is its temporary nature for all concerned. A great deal of discomfort can be tolerated as long as the end is in sight. Of almost equal importance is the fact that the foreign visitor is singular, not plural. One representative from a foreign culture is much less obtrusive than a boatload of them. Combining these two simple observations leads to a tentative conclusion: the foreign visitor is welcome because his or her short stay prohibits social, economic, or political ties to the host community; and by virtue of being just one person, the visitor promises not to be underfoot during his or her stay. In short, the foreign visitor is no threat to any of the continuing concerns of the host community. The visitor will not make laws affecting the hosts, will not compete economically with them, and will not marry their children. If that same visitor should decide to return along with family and friends for a permanent stay, however, *all* of these activities may occur. And whether or not the foreign visitor (now an immigrant) tries to engage in such threatening activities, the hosts imagine that he will, which makes the threat a reality to them.

This chapter will examine the social circumstances under which people come to be threatened. As we shall see, many of these social circumstances are beyond the control of the individuals involved. For example, the violence of football is best explained not by the personalities of the players, but by the scarcity and necessity of scoring touchdowns—a goal imposed on the players by the rules of the game. In society, the "rules of the game" are contained within a system of *social stratification*. Social stratification ranks the importance of activities within a society and creates scarcity (as of football touchdowns) by making the more important and highly rewarded activities hard to occupy. It is easier, for example, to occupy the activity of janitor in the United States than it is to occupy the activity of corporation president. By imposing such "rules of the game," social stratification is the source of many of the threats people feel as they interact individually and in groups. Many of the groups are ethnic groups, but the competition and conflict caused by social stratification can occur between and among other kinds of groups, too. Social stratification also helps to form groups: people band together to compete more effectively against an outside threat.

First we shall look at the general nature of social stratification, to learn how its rules lead people into groups and encourage the formation of stereotypes, prejudice, and discrimination. Then we shall investigate specific kinds of groups, looking for similarities and differences between nonethnic minorities (such as women and homosexuals) and ethnic minorities. The primary goal of this chapter is to explain how social stratification forms ethnic groups and leads to conflict between them.

THE NATURE OF SOCIAL STRATIFICATION: RULES OF THE GAME

In turning to the topic of social stratification, we are no longer looking at individual people. A social stratification system is a particular way of organizing human *activities* within a society; it organizes the humans themselves only insofar as they engage in the various activities. Social stratification is a method that many, in fact most, societies have stumbled onto for organizing their members. It is not, however, the only method.

Humans, like other animals, have to work for their living. In a human society that work is done in coordinated groups, but the method of coordination can vary. In the first, and most simple, method, individuals band together for protection while each pursues the end of survival. For example, if a group of people survive by gathering edibles from their environment, each person is responsible for gathering his or her food. Each is also responsible for making containers for transporting food once it is collected, for preparing food once it is transported, and so on. In short, each individual is more or less on his or her own, and each person engages in identical activities. In the most basic sense of the word, this is a society of equality. Under most environmental circumstances, however, it is not very efficient.

A second method of coordinating human activities is called division of labor. A division of labor does not necessarily change the activities in a society, but rather reorganizes through specialization the people who engage in them. Dividing the labor in our example above, some people would specialize in making containers for transporting food, others would specialize in gathering that food, and still others would prepare the food. Other activities, such as building shelters, would be similarly specialized. Division of labor increases the efficiency of the society because each person presumably becomes more adept at his or her task through repetition and experience. In its pure form, the division of labor need not have any effect on the equality of the societal members; each recognizes his or her dependence on the others and therefore their importance. In actuality, however, this is rare. It is much more common for a social division of labor to be accompanied by social stratification.

Social stratification is a ranking of human activities into a hierarchy, ranging from those activities considered *most* important or valuable to those activities considered *least* important or valuable.[2] In practice in any given society, the

---

2. We are emphasizing the aspects of social stratification that will help us understand ethnic relations. For additional general material on social stratification, see Mark Abrahamson, Ephraim Mizruchi, and C. Hornung, Stratification and Mobility (New York: Macmillan, 1976); John F. Cuber and William Kenkel, Social Stratification in the United States (New York: Appleton, 1954); Kingsley Davis and Wilbert E. Moore, "Some principles of stratification," American Sociological Review, 10:242–49; S. N. Eisenstadt, Social Differentiation and Stratification (Glenview, Ill.: Scott, Foresman, 1971); Irving Krauss, Stratification, Class and Conflict (New York: Free Press, 1976); Gerhard E. Lenski, Power and Privilege: A Theory of Social Stratification (New York: McGraw-Hill, 1966); and Daniel W. Rossides, The American Class System: An Introduction to Social Stratification (Boston: Houghton Mifflin, 1976).

highly valued activities bring wealth, prestige, and power to the lucky individuals who are permitted to engage in them. Conversely, the little- or non-valued activities bring few rewards; in some cases they even bring torment and shame to the unlucky individuals who must engage in them. Other activities, ranked at various positions in the hierarchy, bring greater or lesser rewards to their participants, depending upon their rank.

The term *activity* is used here in its most general sense. While in most cases an activity is labor or work (or, for most of us, jobs), it can also be any group of behaviors that is ongoing in a society. In the United States today, for instance, the term includes the collection of interest on investments, criminal activities, retirement on social security, and unemployment, among other activities. Although unemployment might seem the ultimate of *in*activity, the economy of the United States is structured so that a certain percentage (usually at least 5 percent) of the work force will be unemployed when all available jobs are occupied. The "job" of being unemployed is therefore to wait for work, hopefully with some kind of economic assistance while waiting. The point is that unemployment is an activity that someone has to fill; for many, it is a lifelong career at which, through experience, they become adept. It is also one of the lowest-ranked of the "professions."

Later in this chapter our understanding of social stratification will help us to understand the competition and conflict that arise between and among groups of people. Three features of social stratification bear directly on that competition and conflict.

Social Stratification Ranks Activities, Not People

Social stratification is a ranking of activities, not people. People become ranked only insofar as they fit into the various activities. People can alter their ranking by changing activities. An individual who begins life in a poorly ranked activity can gain personal power, wealth, and prestige by gaining entry to a more highly ranked activity. But that individual will hold those rewards only as long as he or she holds the activity. Considering the advantages of the top-ranked activities and the unpleasantness of the lowest-ranked activities, a good deal of competition is understandably involved, and the better activities are hard to come by.

Social Stratification Is Formed and Maintained by Power

Highly ranked activities are not necessarily any better or more important than activities ranked at the bottom of the hierarchy.[3] Just as English-speaking people can agree that the word *chair* represents the object on which you are probably sitting right now, so they can decide that people who attempt to heal the sick are more important than those who pick up the garbage. It is a matter

---

3. With this assumption we are taking one side of an ongoing social scientific dispute. The opposing point of view is best expressed in Davis and Moore, "Some principles of stratification."

of social agreement. If ranking becomes a matter of social *disagreement* (for example, when garbage collectors go on strike), it then becomes a matter of social power. Activities that reward their occupants highly provide those occupants with power, among other rewards, and that power can be used to maintain the highly ranked position of that activity in the stratification system. More simply, people who find themselves in highly ranked activities are in an excellent position both to keep themselves in those activities *and* to keep those activities in good standing. Hence, social stratification is the result of, and is maintained by, power.

Social Stratification Is Also a Political System

Because social stratification is produced and supported by power, it is therefore a political as well as a social system. While the system may appear fairly rigid in comparison to the lifetimes of the individuals who act within it, it nevertheless *can* be changed through political action. When individuals conflict politically over the ranking of the stratification system (for instance, in a labor union strike), they are conflicting not as individuals but rather as representatives of their activities. Any gains won will benefit the individual only as long as he or she remains in the victorious activity. This point is fundamental to understanding change in conflict, a topic that will concern us later.

In sum, a system of social stratification provides the rules and the playing field of a social "game" into which inequality is structured through the ranking system. If the stratification system is structured so that people can change activities, the inequality of the system then leads to competition as individuals struggle to improve themselves within a limited number of opportunities. As in all games, the players are subject to the structure and the rules; all their actions and subsequent emotions are produced by, and understandable only in terms of, the game. The social stratification game is structured so that some may win and some must lose. That is the basis for much of the bad feeling, competition, and conflict that will concern us later.

THE EXPERIENCE OF SOCIAL STRATIFICATION: THE PERSPECTIVE OF THE PLAYERS

Now let us turn to the people involved in the social stratification system. How does a system of social stratification shape the human experience? The answer to this question has been in dispute for some time, and it will not be settled here. Nevertheless, it is a necessary beginning: we must understand how the game of social stratification is viewed by the players, both winners and losers, and how their views direct their actions. This section focuses on how individuals form groups based on their common experiences within stratification, how changing experiences in stratification lead individuals to change the groups they belong to, and how individuals respond to the competition of stratification with stereotypes, prejudice, and discrimination.

The Category and the Group

A *category* is a collection of individuals who have something in common. Technically, that something could be anything that an outside observer, such as a social scientist, might emphasize—for example, being left-handed and blue-eyed. The point of categories, however, is to call attention to some similarity among individuals that is useful in understanding other things about those individuals, and the category of being left-handed and blue-eyed does not appear to do that. If the category instead included all black women in the United States, its usefulness would be more apparent. Being black and being female in the United States are both factors to which our society calls attention; they shape the experience of the individuals who are so defined. In fact, we could say that individuals in the category of black females encounter certain situations and experiences that no one outside the category could ever share. In short, the idea of the category helps us understand how collections of individuals both share experiences with each other and differ in their experiences from other collections (or categories) of individuals. Perhaps most importantly, the idea of the category emphasizes that individuals share common experiences not because they go out of their way to share them, but because society, by its structure, "sees to it" that they share them. The category calls attention to the ways that society shapes our experiences.

Individuals who share a category may have much in common; however, there are two things they do not share. First, they do not usually know each other or even necessarily care to know each other. Second, they may not share the observer's enthusiasm for the category itself. They may, in fact, think that they share *nothing* with the other individuals with whom the observer has placed them. This disagreement does not matter because the concept of the category belongs to the observer, not to the observed. If the disagreement continues, however, the concept of group cannot be applied, for that concept belongs to the people.

A *group*, in the usage of social science, is a collection of people who (1) know each other (or know of each other), (2) agree that they share something (at least their groupness) and (3) have continuing interactions with each other. The group exists in the hearts and minds of the people involved; if it does not exist there, it does not exist. When groups do exist, their actions can change the course of human societies—a result that a lone individual can never hope to attain. It is not surprising, therefore, that one of the primary questions in social science is how the idea of groupness develops simultaneously in a collection of individual minds.

Members of a group feel that they have much in common. Members of a category also have at least one very important thing in common. If the category is a significant one in a given society, the individuals' common membership in that category will lead them to a number of common experiences in their everyday life. It is just such common experiences that can form the basis of a group. All that is needed is for the individuals in the category (or some of them, at any rate) to recognize their shared situation. In a circular way, the nature of a society itself (which forms the categories) can lead to the formation of social groups, which, through their actions, can change the nature of their society.

Lest it appear that members of categories automatically recognize their shared situation, we should point out that a great many categories in most complex societies work at cross-purposes. For instance, one important category in the United States consists of all people who are poor—obviously a significant shared feature of their lives. But within the category of poverty, there exist other, conflicting categories. Some poor people are white and others are black, for instance. A poor white person may not want to form a group with all other white people since many of them do not share the common experience of poverty; nor will he or she want to form a group with all other poor people since many of them do not share the common experience of being white. That example only begins to explore the contradictions and conflicts between and among categories. Forming a group on the basis of a category is not so much a matter of recognizing *a* shared experience, but rather of deciding *which body* of shared experiences (or categories) is the most important. Changes in the overall society can direct an individual's decision, as, of course, can other people with vested interests. For example, the Great Depression of the 1930s swelled the ranks of the unemployed, placing the same category many people who had never before had much in common. The American Communist Party also grew during this period, successfully calling attention to the common category membership. The social scientist's problem is to learn more about the individual decision making process, beginning with the important categories that are the basis for that process.

Social Class

One of the most important social qualities that leads to group formation is activity. Your activity (or job) becomes separated from those of others through the division of labor, and your attention is drawn to all others who share your activity. If this group is highly organized, we call it a labor union or association. But social stratification is the *ranking* of various activities into levels of greater or lesser importance. For example, you might note that you share experiences with others outside your activity but within the same general level of stratification. This more general category, formed by those who share a common level within the stratification system, is called a social class.

A *social class* is a collection of activities that share approximately the same position on the hierarchy of social stratification.[4] A banker and a corporate executive, for example, engage in very different activities in their jobs, but

---

4. For additional general material on social classes, see footnote 2.

both activities occupy more or less the same level of stratification in terms of the power, prestige, and wealth they bring their occupants. At the other extreme, a janitor and a farm worker engage in very different activities, yet they too share a position on the stratification hierarchy. The extremes are much easier to classify than the activities that fall between them. The major source of confusion is finding appropriate places on the hierarchy to divide each class from the others. The president of an automobile company, the owner of the local dealership, and the car salesperson engage in three activities that clearly vary in the power, wealth, and prestige they bring their occupants. But are the occupants in three different classes? We could argue that the company president and the dealer share a class because they are both in business for themselves, while the salesperson works on salary or commission. We could also argue that the dealer and the salesperson share a class because, in terms of wealth and power, they are more like each other than either is like the corporation president.

How many classes are there in a society such as that of the United States? Some people, like Karl Marx, would argue that there are only two: one class owns all the business and manufacturing interests, and the other class works for them (Marx, 1956: 178–202; Marx and Engels, 1947: 68, 22–23). At the other extreme, others would suggest that the stratification hierarchy can be compared to the thermometer with an infinite number of gradations from top to bottom (Cuber and Kenkel, 1954). While Marx's perspective might seem oversimplified, the other extreme creates so many categories that the concept of the class category as a basis of group formation becomes almost worthless. Either way, one fact cannot be ignored. *Every* mature adult in a stratified society such as that of the United States is aware, to some extent, of the stratification hierarchy and his or her relative position on it. Because this information is not taken lightly by the vast majority of people, we must learn how social classes shape an individual's experiences and, specifically, how those experiences lead people to form groups based on their class categories.

Social Class and Individual Experience

It is perhaps ironic that a society such as that of the United States, which emphasizes equality and democracy, has such a separation between and among classes and that classes provide their members such different experiences.[5] Nevertheless, social interaction across class lines tends to be either sporadic or superficial, or both. The reason is partly the financial differences

---

5. The term *experience* as employed here is intentionally general. Anything that you perceive, either consciously or unconsciously, falls under the heading of experience. Your waking life and your dreaming life are all part of your experience. We are suggesting that the impact of class membership on an individual is broad, to say the least. Practically every imaginable belief and behavior tends to vary by class. Classes specialize in the music they listen to, the churches they attend, the candidates they vote for, the sports they play, the way they raise their children, and so on. It seems only reasonable that such a variety of behavior must reflect a corresponding variety of experiences.

from one class to the next. Large, expensive homes are effectively prohibited to the lower classes. This means that lower- and upper-class neighborhoods will be separated, which in turn means that children of different classes will not meet and play with each other. To the extent that schools serve neighborhoods or that wealthier children attend private schools, children will continue to be separated during their school years. Should they meet through a device such as busing, they will still not necessarily socialize beyond the superficial level required by attending the same school. Their parents will by definition be engaged in different kinds of work, so they will not likely meet, either. And while all of these people are separated, they will be living, working, and playing with very little input from other classes. In short, all aspects of their lives, from the most important to the most trivial, will develop in relative isolation and, therefore, in different directions. And whatever that development is, it will be passed from one generation to the next. A growing child learns to shoot craps, go bowling, or play polo not by choice but rather by doing whatever activity is prevalent in his or her social environment. The same is true of modes of speaking, ways of worshiping, attitudes toward education, and so on. As differences develop through isolation, so they persist through isolation.

When individuals do meet across classes, they usually become uncomfortable in the face of their differences and they retreat. The classes into which they retreat are ready-made environments for group formation. When class membership is permanent (that is, determined for life), groups formed from the common experience of that class will also be permanent. But that, of course, is not the case in the United States. It is very easy to drop down in class in the United States (unless you are already on the bottom), and it is possible (although often difficult) to move up. In a society where individuals change classes, their groups will also change as their new classes give them new interests and experiences. A longshoreman who becomes a published author or a chorus girl who becomes the star of the show will probably find old friends drifting away with old interests, to be replaced by new friends who fit in better with present concerns. Let us next look at the circumstances under which people change class, that is, at social mobility.

Social Mobility

Social mobility is the movement of an individual from an activity at one class level to an activity at another class level, either upward or downward.[6] In everyday terms this usually means either getting a much better job or being

---

6. Social mobility may also be horizontal, referring to movement among activities within the same class; and geographical, referring to physical movement within the same society. While these concepts are not of primary concern to us, they are both employed in the area of ethnic relations. For more information on horizontal social mobility, see Abrahamson et al., Stratification and Mobility, p. 204; for more information on geographical social mobility, see "Population distribution, internal migration and urbanization," in The Determinants and Consequences of Population Trends, vol. 1 (New York: United Nations, 1973).

fired or demoted. But mobility means more than that to the individual concerned. As we said above, an individual's class has a far greater influence on him or her than the opportunities or limitations associated with money. Class becomes a way of life or a culture; individuals who change class, then, experience a new way of life: new people, new ideas, new expectations, and new behaviors. The socially mobile individual is not unlike the immigrant who pulls up stakes and tries to succeed in a new culture. And like the immigrant, the socially mobile individual may always remain a greenhorn in the new class culture. Despite its drawbacks, however, upward social mobility is one of the most popular social goals in the United States; money may not buy happiness, but most people seem to want to find that out for themselves. If upward social mobility is a popular goal, preventing downward social mobility is an essential goal. From this perspective it is obvious why the overall amount of social mobility in a stratified society directly concerns each individual.

Caste and class societies.   The concept of social mobility can apply to an entire society just as it can to one individual. Stratified societies range from permitting no social mobility to allowing a considerable amount. A pure *caste* (or closed) *society* is characterized by total rigidity: individuals do not move up or down in level during their lifetimes and, as a rule, their children inherit their caste (see Abrahamson et al., 1976: 13–17; Krauss, 1976: 18–19; Kolenda, 1978). Not surprisingly, people in caste-like societies become very aware of their castes. At the other extreme, a pure *class* (or open) *society* is wide open: individuals have the opportunity of moving up (and the danger of moving down) throughout their lifetimes, and any gains or losses they achieve will not affect their children, who must make their own way.

It is almost impossible to find a real society that is entirely a caste or a class society. The society of the United States, for example, falls somewhere between the extremes; it is possible here for individuals to move up or down, or for children to be at different levels from their parents. On the other hand, it is very difficult to achieve upward mobility in the United States; and in fact, most people do not change levels during their lifetimes, and most children remain at their parents' level. Later we shall discuss the social processes that both allow and prevent social mobility in the United States. For the present, however, we can make three basic observations about social mobility.

Social mobility changes expectations.   Social stratification creates structured inequality, changeable only through social mobility. In a caste society change is impossible, by definition. Individuals in such a society are never exposed to the possibility of improving their situations; they see their caste as an unalterable part of themselves. The presence of any social mobility in a society, however, introduces the idea, if not the reality, of change. Individuals in the lower classes may now become dissatisfied with their lot and seek to change it.

Social mobility introduces competition.   Social mobility introduces competition into a stratified society. A caste society is rigid and therefore secure. Everyone knows his or her place and need not fear or hope for change. The presence of social mobility eliminates that security, at least potentially, by placing all activities in a competitive arena. Your neighbor may now become either an object of envy or a threat to your position, depending upon whether the neighbor is above or below you in the hierarchy. Everyday life is potentially a war with two fronts in which the individual must attempt to advance while at the same time protecting against attack from the rear. Competition becomes more intense when people realize that there are a finite number of positions in stratified systems; there is room for only a given number of people at any level. When some individuals are upwardly mobile, some others must be downwardly mobile to make room for them. Remember the 5 percent who are unemployed even in the best of times in the United States? It does not matter who the individuals are in that category, but *somebody* has to be there. It is a position in the game and the unluckiest players will find themselves there. It is not surprising, therefore, that the competition introduced by social mobility sometimes results in conflict.

Social mobility can vary in degree: caste versus class.   Finally, the *degree* of social mobility affects the formation of social groups. We can make this point with the example of the conflict that often occurs between labor and management. Remember that labor unions and corporation executives are both groups formed from categories. The nature of social stratification places the two categories of individuals into situations of conflicting interests. Each category of individuals realizes there is much in common *within* its category—much of that commonness coming from its opposition to the other category. (It is in the interests of management to increase profits, and it is in the interests of labor to increase wages and other benefits.) Therefore, the categories form groups and compete.

But how strong would the groups be if there were a good chance that any given worker might next month become part of the management, or that any given executive might next month become one of the workers? If the executive achieved gains for management one month, those same gains would work against his or her interests the following month. And if the worker achieved gains for the union one month, those gains would go against his or her interests the next month in the position of management. In short, a large amount of social mobility in a society prevents groups based on class categories from forming. People may still be in competition and conflict, but they will attempt to improve their situation *individually* rather than to improve the overall situation of a class they may soon leave behind.

In summary, in the absence of social mobility (in a caste society) groups form but there is no competition or conflict between or among those groups. With a very large amount of social mobility (in a class society) competition and conflict occur but not groups based on class. Finally, a moderate amount of social mobility both forms groups based on class categories *and* encourages competition and conflict between and among those groups. The society of the United States, where there is a moderate amount of social mobility, is characterized by *group* competition and *group* conflict. Individuals recognize the possibility of improvement, but they also recognize that the best means for achieving improvement is to work through the group of which they are a part to improve its overall status. Returning to the labor–management example, most workers realize that a group strike for higher wages has a better chance of success than individuals' attempts to gain a place on the board of directors.

As we have seen, a system of social stratification with a moderate amount of social mobility tends to produce interest groups from the categories of class within it. These groups form because individuals in those categories see groups as their best response to threats from other classes and as their best hope for achieving some improvement in their lives. To understand how individuals in those groups strive to improve and defend themselves, we need to know more about (1) how individuals view other groups and/or categories in relation to their own, and (2) how they fight back when threatened. The first question deals with ideas, beliefs, stereotypes, and prejudice; the second question deals with behavior and discrimination.

STEREOTYPES, PREJUDICE, AND DISCRIMINATION: RESPONSES TO SOCIAL STRATIFICATION

Stereotypes

A stereotype is a piece of knowledge (an idea or belief) about a piece of the social world. By "piece of the social world" we mean the way in which we subdivide an otherwise overwhelming confusion of human beings into manageable pieces, such as black or white, men or women, rich or poor. A stereotype begins with just such a piece. It is important to step back momentarily from the concept of stereotype in order to realize that we think of objects in the world in the same way that we think of human beings. The term *chair*, for instance, refers to many different objects that are commonly used for sitting. The term *chair* ignores all differences in substance, construction, and appearance, instead calling attention to the one thing all the objects have in common—their use. We want a place to sit down; we are not interested in the differences among the things we sit on. Similarly, a term such as *black people* refers to many different human beings who share one trait that is important to the user of the term. Like the term *chair*, *black people* ignores differences in favor of calling attention to similarities that are thought important. In this sense, any descriptive term does damage to the thing it describes by doing only a partial job of description, but this kind of mental organization is necessary so that the vast variety of experience can be made manageable (Levin, 1975: 14–18; Schutz, 1970: 116–20).

Now we can return to the first part of our definition of stereotype: a stereotype is a "piece of knowledge." A piece of knowledge is simply an idea or belief that the holder of that piece of knowledge finds convincing. The "knowledge" is usually nothing more than a collection of adjectives that the user of the stereotype believes is an accurate description of some group of people. Most stereotypes can in fact be reduced to the following simple form: "(*insert name of human group here*) are (*insert adjective here*)." For example, blacks are lazy, women are illogical, Poles are dumb, Jews are cheap. Enough of these statements will tell you all you think you need to know about some group of people. If their group is in the way of your group or threatens your group, you can make sure that all of the adjectives are negative, as in the examples.

Stereotypes in some form will be with us as long as people encounter strangers. One of the advantages of small communities or societies is that every individual can know every other individual personally; there is no need for generalized types. But when everyday experience includes coping with strangers, stereotypes must enter the picture. Strangers are by definition people about whom you know nothing personal. But when you have to deal with strangers, you want to know as much about them as possible so that you know what to expect. A stereotype provides a generalized description based on very little information—that is, a guess. If you can group the stranger on the basis of appearance or some other clue, you can organize your behavior to be consistent with what you think you know about that group. Stereotypes are a response to such a need. While they may change over time, both in content (their "piece of knowledge") and in the way in which they divide human beings into groups (their "piece of the social world"), they will nevertheless always be with us. So long as you expect to meet strange chairs or strange black people or strange anything, you will need your stereotypes.[7]

The Psychology of Prejudice

Prejudice is simply a negative attitude toward a group of people (Levin, 1975: 12; Rose, 1974: 97–129; Simpson and Yinger, 1972: 24–27). It is built upon stereotypes, which specify the boundaries between groups of people (enabling you to find the people you dislike), and which provide a handy set of reasons for your negative attitudes. A dislike of black people can be rationalized with the stereotype, "They are lazy and stupid"; a dislike of Asian people can be justified with the stereotype, "They are ambitious, clever, and inscrutable." Almost any adjective can fuel a negative stereotype if it is thought of and said in just the right manner. As Gordon Allport pointed out, Abraham Lincoln is admired for being thrifty, hard-working, ambitious, and devoted to the rights of the average person. Jews, on the other hand, are hated for being tight-fisted, overambitious, pushy, and radical (Allport, 1954: 189).

The prejudiced personality.   Since prejudice is an attitude or belief, it

---

7.   For further discussion of stereotypes and their use in classifying unknowns in social situations, see Abrahamson et al., Stratification and Mobility, pp. 7–9, 17–18; and Alfred Schutz, On Phenomenology and Social Relations (Chicago: University of Chicago Press, 1970), pp. 120–21.

seems to fall at least as much within the province of psychology as of sociology. Not surprisingly, therefore, there has been much research into the psychology of prejudice, attempting to determine the nature of prejudice and its psychological roots. One direction this research has taken has been a search for what might be called the prejudiced personality. The assumption behind this research is that prejudice is a general orientation toward the world, rather than a specific set of ideas or beliefs regarding particular groups of people. An additional assumption is that prejudice is somehow pathological in nature and indicates an emotional disturbance in the prejudiced individual. The most famous research on the prejudiced personality was done by T. W. Adorno and his associates, who studied the authoritarian personality.

The years immediately following World War II saw considerable reflection on the fascism and anti-Semitism that had characterized Nazi Germany. Adorno and his colleagues concluded that there existed a set of personality characteristics that, as a set, might be described as "potentially fascistic," and that this set of characteristics might further be linked to prejudice (Adorno et al., 1950: 1–3). They came to label this potentially fascistic personality as the authoritarian personality; they explained it as the result of particularly harsh and restricted childhood socialization. They described the authoritarian personality as follows (Adorno et al., 1950: 228):

a. Conventionalism. *Rigid adherence to conventional, middle-class values.*
b. Authoritarian submission. *Submissive, uncritical attitude toward idealized moral authorities of the in-group.*
c. Authoritarian aggression. *Tendency to be on the lookout for, and to condemn, reject, and punish, people who violate conventional values.*
d. Anti-intraception. *Closed to the subjective, the imaginative, the tender-minded.*
e. Superstition and stereotypy. *The belief in mystical determinants of the individual's fate; the disposition to think in rigid categories.*
f. Power and "toughness." *Preoccupation with the dominance–submission, strong–weak, leader–follower dimension; identification with power figures; overemphasis upon the conventionalized attributes of the ego; exaggerated assertion of strength and toughness.*
g. Destructiveness and cynicism. *Generalized hostility, vilification of the human.*
h. Projectivity. *The disposition to believe that wild and dangerous things go on in the world; the projection outward of unconscious emotional impulses.*
i. Sex. *Exaggerated concern with sexual "goings-on."*

This set of personality characteristics would, among other things, automatically orient an individual toward prejudice. The "problem" of prejudice, therefore, is a "problem" of overall personality; according to Adorno and his colleagues, as long as indiviuduals have authoritarian personalities, prejudice will exist.

An additional and supporting piece of research within this tradition is E. L. Hartley's (1946) study of prejudiced attitudes. Hartley found that individuals prejudiced against ethnic or racial groups showed the same prejudices when confronted with questions about fictional ethnic groups such as Wallonians, Pirenians, and Danerians. The implication is that an individual who displays prejudice against even a nonexistent group (which precludes having rational reasons for his or her dislike) must be described as having a prejudiced orientation toward the world.

In opposition to this line of research, Walter Kaufman (1957) found that the authoritarian personality correlated with prejudice only in individuals who were also highly concerned with social status. Individuals without such concerns might have authoritarian personalities without prejudice or might be prejudiced without having authoritarian personalities. Kaufman's implication is that perhaps it is the concern with social status that encourages ideas of prejudice. Additionally, Bruno Bettelheim and M. Janowitz (1950) found that downwardly mobile individuals were much more likely to exhibit prejudice than were socially stable or upwardly mobile individuals. Research such as this suggests that the prejudiced personality might be highly dependent on its social situation; an individual's orientation toward the world is not enough, by itself, to explain the presence of prejudice.

Maintaining self-esteem.   Self-esteem is an individual's subjective evaluation of his or her self-worth. That worth can be measured against some objective standard (such as success in following the Ten Commandments), or it can be measured against the performance of others in the individual's immediate environment. In the first case, the individual's self-esteem can rise only through personal achievements; in the second case, self-esteem can rise *either* through personal achievements *or* through the failure of others. When others fail, one's own performance looks superior. Individuals whose self-worth is measured relative to others therefore may choose between expending their energy on their success and helping others fail. For those who choose to help others fail, prejudice is an excellent tool; it downgrades others, making the prejudiced individual feel superior by comparison. The important question is therefore not so much the maintenance of self-esteem (since everyone must do that) but the extent to which individuals measure it through comparison with others.

In a study of career aspirations among college students, James A. Davis (1966) found an interesting connection between the prestige of the occupation aspired to and the grades of the student. An A student from a low-prestige college was more likely to aspire to a high-level occupation than a B student from a high-prestige college, even though the B student had probably worked harder for his or her grades against stiffer competition. Assuming that aspiring to a high-level occupation reflects high self-esteem, it appears that students are likely to rank themselves in comparison with those around them, even if they know they are at a second-rate school. Conversely, students at a first-rate school do not consider the caliber of their competition when they are surpassed by others in the immediate environment. As the title of Davis's article suggests, the campus is indeed a frog pond in which the size of the frog tends to be measured by the size of the pond.

Stanley Morse and Kenneth J. Gergen (1970) continued Davis's line of research, setting up a bogus job application situation in which applicants confronted actors posing as their competitors for the job. Some of the "competitors" acted highly competent; the others portrayed total incompetence. After their contact with the actors, the real job applicants were given tests designed to measure their self-esteem. As expected, the applicants who had confronted the stiff competition showed a definite drop in self-esteem, while those who had faced low competition showed a rise in self-esteem. Morse and Gergen's study seems to confirm that most people measure their self-esteem in comparison with others they encounter rather than against a fixed standard.

Jack Levin related this line of research directly to questions of prejudice. He first separated his subjects into "self-evaluators" and "relative evaluators"; the self-evaluators tended to evaluate themselves against fixed standards, while the relative evaluators relied more on the immediate competition (Levin, 1975: 50). Levin exposed the subjects to situations in which their performances and abilities were questioned, and then tested their prejudice against Puerto Ricans. He found that the individuals labeled as relative evaluators responded to attacks on their abilities with increased prejudice, but the self-evaluators showed no such increase. Thus, it appears that prejudice can be a way to increase self-esteem *if* the individual involved measures that self-esteem against the performances and abilities of others rather than against a fixed standard. But even relative evaluators must first feel a threat to their self-esteem before they will defend themselves with prejudice. We must therefore examine what things people perceive as threats and how they generally respond. In psychological studies of prejudice, this question is usually framed within the more general "frustration-aggression hypothesis."

The frustration-aggression hypothesis.   The frustration-aggression hypothesis was introduced by John Dollard and his associates. Their basic postulate was that "aggression is always a consequence of frustration" (Dollard et al., 1939: 1); that is, any experience of frustration must somehow result in aggression. That aggression, however, need bear no direct connection to the actual source of frustration. For example, it could be displaced (the individual who loses a job comes home and kicks the dog), or it could be turned against the self (the individual who loses a job develops an ulcer) (Dollard et al., 1939: 2). The connection between the frustration-aggression hypothesis and studies of prejudice is that prejudice is seen as an example of displaced aggression; frustrated individuals take out their frustrations by aggressive acts of prejudice against a weak minority group that cannot fight back (not unlike kicking the family dog).

The idea of displaced aggression generated vast quantities of research in the psychology of prejudice. Two examples will indicate both the range of research and the common findings. Neal E. Miller and Richard Begelski (1948) found that a relatively trivial frustration (preventing a group of people from attending a movie they wished to see) increased their scores on tests designed to measure prejudice. At a much different level, Carl I. Hovland and Robert Sears (1940) found that lower prices for cotton in the American South correlated with higher rates of lynching of blacks. Aggressive attitudes (as measured by testing) as well as overt aggressive behavior (such as lynching) both appear related to frustration. Is this aggression truly displaced, or do the frustrated individuals who act aggressively toward a minority group actually feel that minority to be the source of their frustration?

Leonard Berkowitz points out that frustrated individuals prefer to be aggressive directly against the source of their frustration. If that source is absent or too strong to be attacked, frustrated individuals will direct their aggression not toward the weakest opponent handy, but rather toward whoever they feel is closest to the actual source of their frustration (Berkowitz, 1962: 138–39). In short, kicking the family dog may be safe and convenient, but the dog is usually so far removed from the source of the frustration that the kick is a useless gesture. In the case of actual instances of prejudice or aggression against a minority group, we must ask whether the minority group in question is actually seen to have some relation to the frustration felt by the prejudiced or aggressive individuals. For example, relative to the Hovland and Sears research on the relation of cotton prices and lynching, we might ask whether whites saw blacks as economic competitors who posed a real threat during times of economic instability.

Such questions apply not only to the frustration-aggression hypothesis, but also to the prejudiced personality and the need to maintain self-esteem. In each case, the psychological responses of prejudice can be best understood in their social contexts. Prejudiced personalities are expressed in some social circumstances more than in others, and frustration occurs as a normal part of our everyday social experiences. The psychological process known as prejudice can perhaps be best understood by widening our focus to include a sociological perspective.

The Sociology of Prejudice

Prejudice can be used as a weapon. Prejudice, and the stereotypes that accompany it, discredit whole groups of people who might otherwise be a social threat. If you are a white person and a black person is competing for your job, you may be able to save your job by convincing others (especially your employer) that blacks are lazy and irresponsible. Losing your job (or even the threat of losing it) can lower self-esteem and create frustration. If your employer is too strong to be the object of your aggression, prejudice becomes all the more useful as a weapon in fighting the secondary source of the frustration. In more general terms, prejudice is the natural outcome of the competition inherent in social stratification; prejudice helps maintain a social position when the potential social mobility of others threatens that position.

Prejudice produced by social competition becomes most noticeable when the individuals or groups involved are of similar rank. This puts those individuals or groups into competition for the same jobs, housing, education, and any other rewards that people get more or less of, depending upon their class level. It is therefore not surprising that most anti-black prejudice in the United States is found among working-class whites, for they are in direct competition with blacks (who are similarly ranked, for the most part) and feel threatened by them (Levin, 1975: 72–73).

Prejudice can also become part of the culture of a group, passed from parents to children along with the rest of their culture. The world view, as transmitted, takes a "we versus they" form, making each individual feel even further from the opposing group and, at the same time, more firmly rooted in his or her own group. Just as a social stratification system can make people create groups from the categories provided by the system, so too can that same stratification system strengthen those groups, once formed.

Discrimination

Attempts by groups either to improve their class position or to defend it from another group usually extend well beyond the realm of ideas. We combine these group actions under the heading of *discrimination:* any actions taken vis-à-vis another group designed to hinder the competitive abilities of individuals in that group. The purpose of discrimination is to give the group doing the discriminating a competitive advantage within some arena (or arenas) of the stratification system. The appeal of discrimination stems from an interesting fact: competition *can encourage* excellence but it only *requires* being "better than."[8] One can be better either through excellence or through hindering the opponent. Discrimination, of course, does the latter. It can operate directly, as in refusing employment to members of certain groups, or indirectly, as in constructing biased employment tests that require information not present in the culture of certain groups. We shall see specific examples of discrimination in Chapters 7 and 8. Our concern here is the role of discrimination in forming and maintaining competitive groups in a society. That role is summarized by two important observations.

First, discrimination is basically an attempt to control unrestricted social mobility, by introducing elements of a caste society into a class society. Rather than allowing individuals to compete for mobility *as individuals,* it forces them

---

8.   This observation is often expressed as the "zero-sum" aspect of competition. See Jack Levin, The Functions of Prejudice (New York: Harper & Row, 1975), pp. 107–9.

to compete *as groups*. Discrimination separates those groups so that members of higher-ranked groups can achieve and hold their position against intruders. Those who discriminate give in to the temptation to load the dice. The higher a group is ranked, the more power it has, and therefore its ability to enforce its brand of discrimination is increased. The lower-ranked groups are forced to play with the dice provided for them.

Second, just as prejudice and stereotypes can become part of a group's culture, thereby keeping that group apart from others, so discrimination can maintain group separation and lead to further conflict. At the outset, discrimination maintains groups on separate ranks in the stratification system, which tends to keep groups separate. But in addition, discrimination rubs salt into the wound. The we–they orientation that is begun by prejudice is nourished by the continued experience of discrimination. Recognizing that another group has loaded the dice to ensure your loss tends to solidify your group; discrimination convinces the affected group that the only hope for improvement is group action, rather than individual effort.

THE IMPACT OF DISCRIMINATION ON FORMING SOCIAL GROUPS

We have seen that social stratification creates competition and that competition encourages individuals and groups to use discrimination as a weapon. As discrimination closes the routes of upward social mobility, individuals look to their groups for advancement. Therefore, discrimination is a major factor in the formation of social groups within a stratification system. Highly ranked groups, which are in a position to discriminate, use that weapon for a variety of reasons against a variety of people. When a highly ranked group designates an attribute as undesirable (ethnicity, sex, appearance, occupation, or the like) and discriminates against that attribute, that category becomes significant for individual experience, and conditions are ripe for a group to form around that attribute. This section will examine three basic types of social groups that can be formed by discrimination.

The Ideological Subordinate Group

Members of an ideological subordinate group have some characteristic that upsets the dominant group enough to make it discriminate against them. We use the term *ideological* to emphasize that the disliked characteristic of the subordinate group violates the beliefs of the dominant group without necessarily posing any direct economic threat. For example, homosexuals could be considered an ideological subordinate group. They face numerous forms of discrimination, particularly in employment. But that discrimination occurs primarily because their lifestyle violates the majority's belief in heterosexuality in the United States. Similarly, women can be considered an ideological subordinate group; their attempts to gain positions of power and responsibility are often met by discrimination imposed by men who prefer that women "stay in their place." Finally, the physically handicapped might be considered an ideological subordinate group. The dominant ideology that disapproves of them is less clear than in the two earlier examples, because no one wants to admit disliking the handicapped. Nevertheless, the physically handicapped in the United States face much unwarranted discrimination because they somehow don't fit in with the dominant idea of how things (and people) should be.

The important similarity in the three examples above is that individuals in each group may vary considerably except for the one characteristic that binds them. They may be rich or poor, of any religion, and of any ethnic group. In fact, the dominant group discriminator may find one or more of these ideological subordinates in his or her own family. Most importantly, none of these people can be considered more of a direct economic threat to a member of the dominant group than another member of the dominant group would be.

The Subordinate Class Group

The second type of group formation from discrimination involves members of already existing class categories. This type directly involves the competition inherent in social stratification: the discrimination is a response by the members of one class to the upward mobility of members of a lower class. As the discrimination continues, the two classes become increasingly separated. This separation is a product both of the normal separation between classes (as discrimination decreases mobility), and of the anger and frustration that often accompany discrimination. The best example of this type of group formation is probably the distinction between management and labor. Unlike the first type of group formation—the ideological subordinate—this type is a practical product of competition. Even though the groups may conflict bitterly, they can still understand each other's perspective. There may very likely be cultural and ideological differences between the groups, but those differences are not fundamental to the conflict. In short, this type of group formation appears to be the exact opposite of the first type. The first type is based almost entirely in the cultural world of ideas and beliefs; the second almost entirely in the practical realm of economic give and take.

The Subordinate Ethnic Group

The third type of discrimination-based group formation is a combination of the first two. Consider a potential subordinate group that, first, is already culturally different from all other groups in the society and, second, is concentrated in one of the lower classes. More powerful groups might be expected to have a double motivation for discrimination. On the one hand, they might fear or at least dislike the *culture* of the potential subordinate group, and on the other hand, they might fear the *mobility* of that group into their own class level. The more powerful group might therefore be expected to unite even more strongly to protect itself from this two-sided threat. The potential subordinate group becomes subordinate in reality, and its members are strongly pulled together because of (1) their common cultural heritage, (2) their common class position, and (3) their common experience of discrimination. All the actions and emotions that characterize the first two types of discrimination-based group formation become intensified in this third type.

The Three Types of Discrimination-Based Group Formation: Their Use in Understanding Ethnic Relations

Of the three types of group formation discussed above, only the third type describes the situation of ethnic groups within social stratification. One of the main problems in understanding ethnic relations is that so many social phenomena occur simultaneously; ethnic groups are often disliked because they are culturally different *and* because they pose an economic threat as a group. Much research in this area is confused because researchers often focus on one source of conflict while ignoring the other. Studying black–white relations in the United States today, for example, we confront many millions of people in each group who live culturally isolated from each other *and* compete for jobs. The researcher whose concerns are prejudice and stereotypes learns something about the cultural isolation between the groups but little of the practical reasons why the groups distrust each other. The researcher concerned only with the competition built into social stratification risks overlooking the cultural isolation between the groups. A combined approach seems necessary for full understanding.

To call attention to the dual nature of ethnic relations, we have separated the two sides of the issue into two types of group formation. Each of the first two types reflects one side of the dual nature of ethnic relations. This separation enables us to look at groups that face discrimination because of their violation of cultural norms and values (the ideological subordinate groups) without having our understanding clouded by the impact of economic differences. We can then appreciate the importance of being culturally different from the dominant group when no other threats are present. For example, that homosexuals can generate such intense discrimination because of their alternative lifestyle suggests the degree to which the dominant group will defend its beliefs when only those beliefs are threatened. Similarly, we can look at groups such as labor unions, which differ only by class (the subordinate class groups), to see the degree to which the dominant group will defend its power and economic position through discrimination when only that economic threat is present. If we then come back to ethnic groups (which pose both kinds of threats), we should better understand the part each kind of threat plays in generating discrimination from the dominant group. In this sense, our looking at groups helps us understand the social dynamics of threatening the dominant group.

The following section will focus on ideological subordinate and subordinate class discrimination-based social groups; specifically, we shall look at women, homosexuals, the handicapped, and labor unions. The final section in this chapter will return to ethnic groups, examining the peculiar situation of discrimination against ethnic groups known as ethnic stratification.

HOW DISCRIMINATION CAN CREATE NONETHNIC GROUPS: EXAMPLES OF IDEOLOGICAL SUBORDINATE AND SUBORDINATE CLASS GROUPS

Women

Women as a subordinate group are perhaps the best example of the force of long-standing historical stereotypes. In the Old Testament, coveting your neighbor's wife is the same as (or perhaps even less serious than) coveting his other possessions, such as his ox, his ass, and his house. (Notice the lack of direction to women about coveting others' husbands; God seems to see only men as worthy of this advice.) The years between the Old Testament and the present day have witnessed numerous restatements of and elaborations on the basic male view of the inferiority of women. The following quotation, from German philosopher Arthur Schopenhauer, was written in 1851, but it could as easily have been written last year or 1,000 years ago—the stereotype has changed so little.

> *You need only look at the way in which she is formed to see that woman is not meant to undergo great labour, whether of the mind or of the body. She pays the debt of life not by what she does but by what she suffers; by the pains of childbearing and care for the child, and by submission to her husband, to whom she should be a patient and cheering companion. The keenest sorrows and joys are not for her, nor is she called upon to display a great deal of strength. The current of her life should be more gentle, peaceful and trivial than man's, without being essentially happier or unhappier. (Schopenhauer, 1928: 434)*

According to the stereotype, women are to stay in their subordinate place, are genetically incapable of rational or logical thought, and are naturally suited to be "cheering companions" to men and to do the work men would rather not, such as cleaning the house and raising the children. If women are genetically incapable of competing with men in the realm of rational or logical thought, one might well ask why men need to discriminate against them to deny them the chance to compete.

The low status of women is a fact of stratification as well as an element in our cultural beliefs. The sexual division of labor may well have been one of the first such divisions historically; it has always been an important criterion in the ranks of social stratification. The results of this history are obvious: in the United States today, men hold the vast majority of powerful positions; the occupations in which women predominate almost invariably are poorly paid, low-prestige, powerless positions. Many of the traditionally female occupations are extensions of the roles of wife and mother. Protecting and nurturing roles, such as grade school teacher or nurse, pose little threat to male dominance of society. But if discrimination against women is so closely tied to the stratification system, why do we not treat them as a class group? The answer lies in the institution of marriage.

What makes women unique relative to discrimination is marriage. Women cannot, as a rule, achieve upper-class positions as individual workers, and that is where they face discrimination. They can, however, achieve those positions as wives. The institution of marriage is not properly a romantic matter but rather a legal matter through which, traditionally at least, women become attached to men and thereby indirectly attain whatever their husbands attain. Even the husband's prestige is passed on to the wife. It is important to note the word *indirect*. An *individual* woman has no direct access to wealth and power; as a wife, she has such access only through her husband. Thus, he never gives up ultimate control—he maintains his dominance.

The attachment of the wife to the husband's position, however indirect, was and is a very real social phenomenon. That women are a part of their husbands' class level is important to our discussion, because so long as women identify with their husbands' class level, they will *not* identify with women married to men at other class levels. Even though societal discrimination may affect all women, marriage is a way to avoid that discrimination—and to avoid the common experience necessary for group formation. Women have long been a subordinate *category*, but marriage has largely prevented them from becoming a subordinate *group*.

A number of changes have recently occurred in the roles of women in the United States. For our purposes the most important are the increasing number of working women and the rising divorce rate. Both of these changes have confronted women with sex discrimination, a factor that has played no small part in the growth of the women's movement. Yet, even though women have become more aware of sex discrimination, the differences among them in terms of class, religion, ethnicity, and so on have remained important, which has inhibited group formation. In particular, women who hold dual subordinate category membership (black women, for example) must decide which category deserves their primary allegiance: does the discrimination faced by a black woman give her more in common with a black man or with a white woman? The decision is not easy; she has experiences in common with each category, along with a number of experiences unique to her dual category.

It is not surprising, therefore, that in many areas of subordinate group formation, there are changing group boundaries and fluctuating group alliances. Of special interest in the case of women as a subordinate group, however, is the long-standing cultural definition of women's role, which brings the weight of tradition to the support of sex discrimination. While it can be argued that men and women are in competition for scarce resources in a stratified society, it is difficult to isolate the importance of that competition in the face of traditional cultural beliefs.

Homosexuals

Like women, homosexuals come in all shapes, sizes, religions, classes, ages, and cultures. Unlike women, they come in both sexes; more importantly, they are defined by behavior rather than by an accident of birth. That many heterosexuals consider homosexual behavior immoral and therefore discriminate against individuals who engage in it has led to another subordinate group formed from a discrimination-based category. But once again, as with women, we are hard pressed to write off this discrimination as purely a response to competition. Perhaps even more clearly than with women, we have here an example of cultural beliefs and stereotypes demanding discrimination as the only logical response. Discrimination against homosexuals proceeds with a vehemence that society saves for labeled deviants. We must know something about deviance, then, to understand this subordinate group.

Deviance is behavior that is outside (or deviates from) the normal, expected range of behavior within a society (see Bell, 1976). Deviance is always relative to other, normal behavior at a given time and place; no behavior is inherently deviant. Deviance is also a *label*. Someone must call attention to abnormal, or deviant, behavior and label it as such before we can speak of it as being deviant (see Schur, 1971; Becker, 1963). In particular, the label giver must be in a powerful position for the label to influence and convince others. In a modern society such as that of the United States, such powerful positions are clearly delineated: psychiatrists can label behavior as mentally ill, judges can label behavior as criminal, and so on. Once behavior has been officially labeled as deviant, we can speak of individuals who engage in it as deviants.

We must make one further distinction: even if people agree that certain behavior is deviant, the label does not automatically apply to individuals who engage in it—*unless* their behavior is known to the label givers. A burglar who has never been caught is not officially a criminal even though he knows that he would be so labeled if detected. To the burglar, stealing may not seem like deviance, because he is not treated by others as a deviant.

Deviance thus has two parts: the labeling of the behavior and the labeling of the individual who engages in that behavior. If the behavior results in sanctions (like discrimination) when detected, we have a curious case of the potential of group formation based on discrimination. Deviant subordinate groups cannot necessarily draw upon the entire deviant category for members, but only upon those individuals within the category whose deviance is known and who have therefore faced the discrimination necessary for group formation. Deviants who have not been detected may be well aware of their deviance and may be in personal sympathy with the more public group activities of the labeled deviants. But at the same time, hidden deviants may feel they have more to lose than to gain by publicizing their deviance. In the case of homosexuality, such secretive deviants are referred to as passing or closet homosexuals. Like women who successfully follow the traditional female role, closet homosexuals can avoid a major portion of the discrimination that affects the category and creates the group.

The concept of deviance as applied to homosexuals leads to a dispute over definitions between homosexual groups and the heterosexual world.[9] The concept of deviance and its labeling are beyond the control of the homosexual community. Homosexuals argue that they should be defined not by what they do but by who they are. They insist that homosexuals do not choose to engage in homosexual behavior, but rather follow a natural (perhaps inborn) inclination over which they have no control. They argue that like women, blacks, and members of other subordinate groups, homosexuals have no control over the characteristics that dominant groups use to define them. The importance of this counterperspective is clear: a group that *cannot* conform has a more legitimate basis from which to fight for acceptance.

While discrimination against homosexuals is similar to discrimination faced by other categories of people, it becomes unique in practice because of the homosexual's potential invisibility. For instance, in the United States military draft, homosexuality was both grounds for exemption and grounds for dishonorable discharge. To apply for the exemption, the homosexual had to go on record as a homosexual; that record would, of course, follow him in the future. For a homosexual who desired to pass as a heterosexual, this was no solution. The alternative was to be drafted, but one then had to conceal homosexual activity to avoid a dishonorable discharge—which, like the draft exemption, would also haunt one's future. Thus, the unwilling soldier faced discrimination, but so did the homosexual who desired a military career; the grounds for rejection remained the same.

Such discrimination is not unique to homosexuals. It affects homosexual individuals approximately as anti-Semitism in Nazi Germany affected Jews. A Jew would find himself discredited and jailed if it was discovered that he was of Jewish background. The affected individual can avoid the discrimination by remaining invisible. However, the discrimination can not only prevent advancement but can also come crashing down like a sledge hammer at any moment after advancement has occurred. The more the passing homosexual achieves, the farther he or she can fall if discovered.

Discrimination against homosexuals in the United States military is but one

---

9. The organized fight for acceptance from the heterosexual community has a relatively short history. In the United States, as in most of the Western world, viable political organizations representing homosexual rights did not appear until after World War II. In the United States, such early homosexual organizations as ONE, Inc. and the Mattachine Foundation began both quietly and peacefully as efforts to aid the homosexual community and educate the heterosexual community (see Laud Humphreys, Out of the Closets: The Sociology of Homosexual Liberation [Englewood Cliffs, N.J.: Prentice Hall, 1972], pp. 51–58; and Donn Teal, The Gay Militants [New York: Stein and Day, 1971], pp. 38–60). These "reformist" tactics continued throughout most of the 1950s and into the 1960s when, perhaps with the character of the decade, homosexual political organizations became more radical, more visible, and at times, violent. By the early 1970s, the idea of gay liberation had become firmly established as one front in the battle for group rights in the United States. Homosexuals, like other minority groups, demanded the right to compete.

example of the broad social, economic, and political discrimination that homosexuals face in this country. While the forms of discrimination themselves are not unique to homosexuals, the stereotypical justifications behind them are. And even more clearly than in the case of women, those stereotypes appear to be a direct cause of the discrimination.[10] The common belief that a male homosexual cannot be trusted with young boys stems not from homosexuality per se but from the belief that homosexuals, by definition, are animals at worst and immoral at best. It is not surprising, in view of such attitudes, that the more powerful, heterosexual community responded to homosexuals with its arsenal of social weapons, declaring homosexuality illegal and institutionalizing discrimination against homosexuals.

The competition imposed by a stratification system does not provide an adequate explanation for the strength of discrimination against homosexuals. Like women, homosexuals enter their category from all walks of life. They never exist as a group to threaten the economic interests of another group. Also like women, they can avoid much direct discrimination by conforming to acceptable social roles; a woman can marry a wealthy and powerful man, and a homosexual can achieve success by passing as a heterosexual. On the other hand, like a woman who enters the economic marketplace *as a single woman*, the homosexual who enters that marketplace *as a homosexual* experiences the force of direct discrimination, which, of course, creates a category. The category is formed only *after* discrimination occurs; it is not pre-existing, unlike a social class. Unlike a social class (or an ethnic group that occupies a social class), the existence of the category does not cause (or encourage) discrimination; rather, the category is caused (or encouraged) by the discrimination.

The Handicapped

Handicapped individuals are those who, either by birth or through accident, are physically different from the norm. This category includes a wide variety of physical differences, from blindness, deafness, and paralysis to mental retardation to long-term debilitating diseases. Medically these cases are very different from each other, but socially they are very similar (Sagarin,

---

10. Stereotypes regarding homosexuals do not have quite the historical Western tradition of stereotypes regarding women. While the subjugation of women can be easily traced at least to the Old Testament, homosexuality has during some periods enjoyed a certain fashionability. Homosexuality was popular among the ancient Greeks and Romans, for instance, particularly among the upper classes. Socrates, Michelangelo, and Leonardo da Vinci, creatures of their time in this respect, illustrate the wholly different societal approach to sexuality that existed during their lives (Bell, 1976: 265). Not until the Middle Ages and the growth of the Catholic Church did homosexuality come to be generally regarded both as unnatural and as sinful. While much of the "knowledge" of the Middle Ages has been rejected by modern science, this particular perspective was embraced by modern psychiatry, which came to view homosexuality as a sickness. This "scientific" orientation actually differs little from the common modern stereotype, which defines homosexuals as perverted and unnatural.

1971). Any of a wide range of physical differences can confront the affected individual with (1) situations in which physical differences are not allowed for (such as steps impeding an individual in a wheel chair); (2) social and economic discrimination not directly warranted by the limitations imposed by the affliction (such as a refusal to hire a wheelchair-bound individual for a sedentary job); and (3) uncomfortable social responses from more "normal" people who are either embarrassed or disgusted by physical differences. Except for the first situation above, which is unconscious and, at worst, inconsiderate, the other common social experiences faced by the physically handicapped stem from a set of ideas and feelings that the physically normal hold about them. In short, and for a variety of reasons, most physically normal people want as little as possible to do with the physically handicapped. The irony and uniqueness of the handicapped as a minority group lie in the covert way those ideas and feelings are held. Very few people will admit disliking the physically handicapped; most people, in fact, express admiration and sympathy for the handicapped and enjoy nothing more than a stirring novel or movie depicting a handicapped individual's fight to overcome that handicap. But the same physically normal people actually want to come no closer than that to a handicapped person. Very few other minority groups are loved and avoided with the same intensity.

What is the source of negative feelings toward the handicapped? One possible explanation is that the handicapped are a constant reminder of human mortality. Human beings are, after all, animals that are born and die and suffer a variety of animal infirmities in between. Human beings also have relatively highly developed brains, which they can use to create the illusion of immortality day to day; few people are constantly aware that the vividness of their lives will have an end. But the ability of the brain to maintain that illusion depends upon health. Bad health reminds us that we are animals, which in turn reminds us that we are mortal. An obviously physically handicapped person is a reminder of how fragile is our existence, dependent upon the proper functioning of our bodies to allow us to pursue the uniquely human activities we find so rewarding.

The handicapped have much in common with women and homosexuals. A handicap can happen to anyone, regardless of class, religion, age, sex, or culture. Thus, the handicapped are another group whose category is caused by discrimination. The many social and medical differences among the handicapped would normally keep such individuals from grouping together. It is their common experience of discrimination that encourages group formation. Since the handicapped are not a pre-existing category in terms of social stratification, we cannot argue that discrimination against them results from their posing an economic threat to another class. Discrimination against them must have other sources. As is the case with women and homosexuals, those sources must lie in the ideas and feelings of the physically normal who are motivated to discriminate. As we said, those ideas and feelings are not so much hate as fear. Fear, and the selfishness of the physically normal in not wanting to put themselves out a little, lead to perhaps the least vindictive discrimination there is. The handicapped face employment discrimination not because they are hated, but because the employer would simply rather not have them around.

Labor Unions

We grouped women, homosexuals, and the handicapped together because the discrimination they face is due almost entirely to a lack of cultural acceptance. None of the three groups is part of a class category that would explain the discrimination in terms of economic competition between them and other social groups. Now we would like to examine a group in the opposite situation: a group formed from a class category within a system of social stratification, but not subject to the lack of cultural acceptance that characterizes women, homosexuals, and the handicapped. In short, we need a group that faces discrimination as the practical result of competition but that is neither feared nor hated for its cultural or behavioral differences. Finding such a group is difficult; we can come close, however, with labor unions.

Labor unions are groups of workers who share a common class category and usually an occupational category. If they share the latter, they also share the former, for sharing an occupation not only puts individuals in the same class but also gives them the same day-to-day activities. Thus, although a labor union does not contain all the members of a class category, it nevertheless is based on that class in that it groups together a subset of it. If the common class membership as well as the common occupation seems important to union members, labor unions can form alliances or federations that more clearly approximate a class group. The American Federation of Labor in the United States is an example of such an alliance. That members of one union will honor the strike of another union indicates the importance of these ties that are rooted in common class membership.

The natural adversary of the labor union is management, either the owners of the enterprise that employs the workers or representatives of those owners. In either case, management clearly represents a different class (with greater power, prestige, and wealth) and naturally has opposite interests from the workers. In a capitalist economy, profit is directly related to expenses, and wages paid to employees are a large part of expenses. Thus, workers have a natural interest in higher wages and management has a natural interest in lower wages. (We use the term *natural* in this context to indicate interests directly created by the stratification system.) Competition is inherent in the system. It is therefore not surprising that both labor and management recognize the categories with opposite interests into which they have been placed and that both form groups to improve the relative situation of their category.

We might expect that management, having more power, would employ various forms of discrimination to maintain or enhance its power. This was particularly true in the early days of labor unionism in the United States.

Management could fire and blacklist any employee who engaged in labor union activity; it also used its influence with government to pass laws designed to inhibit union activity (Higham, 1955: 45–52; Cohen, 1970). Only since the 1930s have American labor unions had the legal power to protect their members and to demand collective bargaining. Perhaps most importantly, unions have the right to strike—their only direct power over management.

Today the leaders of some successful unions may seem to be practically on the same side as management. However, various forms of discrimination were once applied to all unions and are still applied to newer ones such as the United Farm Workers. Perhaps ironically, older, established unions sometimes form alliances with management to discriminate against newer unions. For example, in the 1970s California agricultural growers and the Teamsters Union formed a coalition against the United Farm Workers (*U.S. News and World Report*, 1975: 82–83). Of particular interest to us, however, is the practical approach to discrimination found in union–management conflict.

Though hostility can and does arise in the course of union–management conflicts, all involved are also capable of viewing the situation in practical terms. Unions understand the goals of management, and management understands the goals of workers. Each realizes that they would have opposite interests, were they on the other side of the fence. Discrimination in labor–management conflict takes on the characteristics of business: adversaries attempt to maximize their gains and minimize their losses. The differences between labor and management rarely lead to the extremes of prejudice and stereotypes that accompany homosexual–heterosexual conflict or black–white conflict. When a union achieves gains, management refigures its expected expenses for the coming year and reorganizes its prices accordingly, and everybody goes back to work. Costs are figured economically more than emotionally.

The importance of labor unions and union–management conflict to our discussion is twofold. First, they are an example of class categories within a system of social stratification and of the way in which those class categories encourage group formation. The categories themselves provide certain kinds of interests and perspectives for their members. Though union–management conflict is a special and (now) highly organized example of conflict between two class-based groups, our observations of that conflict can still help us understand other, perhaps less well organized or clear-cut, instances of class conflict, where members of the two classes differ ethnically as well as by class.

Second, a comparison of union–management conflict with the earlier examples of women, homosexuals, and the handicapped leads us to a conclusion about discrimination. Discrimination can be encouraged purely by class differences as one class attempts to limit the competitive ability of the other; in this instance, discrimination can also operate *relatively* free of intense hatred or fear between the two groups. On the other hand, discrimination can also be encouraged by negative cultural ideas and feelings toward a certain group, independent of class differences. Carried to extremes, such discrimination will create class differences where none existed before. However, in any case the groups formed through the acts of discrimination can magnify those negative ideas and feelings so much that seemingly permanent barriers arise between groups. Under such conditions, any attempt by the subordinate group to improve its situation by fighting discrimination will create intense emotions on both sides.

We can use our information about how discrimination forms social groups to examine ethnic relations. As we shall see, many ethnic groups in the United States are largely concentrated in certain classes. Since those ethnic groups are also, by definition, culturally different from each other, all of the elements in ideological subordinate and subordinate class groups come into play. Ethnic groups can be discrminated against because they are culturally different *and* because they occupy a lower class that may become a threat. Groups can then form based on ethnicity because people share class, culture, and a common experience of facing (or administering) discrimination. We have examined each of these elements separately; now we shall look at the composite picture that emerges when a system of social stratification becomes a system of ethnic stratification.

ETHNIC STRATIFICATION: THE FORMATION OF ETHNIC GROUPS

As we have seen, people often employ acts of discrimination when they are threatened, whether by the economic demands of another (lower) class or by the behavioral "demands" of a group they define as culturally different. We have also seen that a class, in the absence of social mobility, tends to isolate its members over time; the vast majority of an individual's meaningful everyday life takes place within his or her class. As a result of class separation, different lifestyles develop that correspond to certain classes. To a certain extent these lifestyles exist independent of other differences within classes, such as religion. A lower-class Catholic and a lower-class Protestant who work together and are economically limited in their choices of residence or entertainment will come to share much despite some cultural differences. We could say that different classes create different cultures for their members and that these different cultures can be a basis for group conflict.

Two kinds of cultural differences can exist between groups: they can differ culturally by tradition, and they can differ culturally by class separation. The traditional cultural differences are the more important of the two, but differences in cultural tradition may be forgotten over time unless social circumstances call attention to them through acts such as discrimination. Since the goal of discrimination is to prevent social mobility for the groups at whom it is directed, discrimination faced by an ethnic group can keep its members from rising out of a lower class. And since class separation is sufficient to *create* cultural (or, at least, lifestyle) differences between groups, that separation should have a tremendous impact on *maintaining* cultural differences that already exist. Thus, an ethnic group that faces discrimination will (1) have already existing traditional cultural differences, (2) have its attention called to that ethnicity by discrimination, (3) develop hostility toward the discriminating group(s) based on ethnic differences, and (4) have its ethnicity maintained by the effects of class separation brought about by discrimination.

If, for example, we consider black–white relations in the United States, we find that (1) blacks entered the United States with a culture very different from the dominant European culture already established here; (2) blacks were placed into the situation of slavery, which called attention to their differences from the white population; (3) blacks developed hostility toward whites, who clearly were responsible for their subordinate situation; and (4) blacks still occupy the lower classes in the United States, out of proportion to their numbers. Class separation has been largely responsible for maintaining the differences between black and white lifestyles. Such circumstances create groups with a stronger bond than that usually found among members of nonethnic groups, and hostility between groups reaches correspondingly higher levels in the course of the conflict.

Ethnic groups in the United States occupy different class levels within the stratification system, and someone's ethnicity is often a very accurate indicator of his or her class. This special type of social stratification is called ethnic stratification. As ethnic groups come to be clustered at various levels of stratification (that is, as discrimination cuts off upward social mobility), the members of those groups respond with a variety of emotions, thoughts, and actions. This section will investigate the relationship between the responses of ethnic group members and the structure of ethnic stratification within which they live. It will also discuss the impact of ethnic stratification on ethnic group formation and ethnic group political conflict.

The Structure of Ethnic Stratification

Like social stratification in general, the special case of ethnic stratification should be viewed as a form of social organization that is imposed upon the members of a society.[11] This is not to suggest that people do not create their societies; rather, forms of social organization last longer than individuals. To one individual or even several generations, the social organization within which they live may appear as almost unchanging. Social organization becomes a "given" to be dealt with in everyday life. Stratification takes on the characteristics of a game in which individuals are assigned positions of greater or lesser advantage and are then required to compete according to the rules. In

---

11. For further information on ethnic stratification, see Tamotsu Shibutani and Kian Kwan, "Reference groups and social control," in Arnold Rose (ed.), Human Behavior and Social Processes (Boston: Houghton Mifflin, 1962); Richard Schermerhorn, Comparative Ethnic Relations: A Framework for Theory and Research (New York: Random House, 1970); and James A. Geschwender, Class, Race, and Worker Insurgency (New York: Cambridge University Press, 1977).

this sense, ethnic stratification is identical to social stratification, except that a few extra rules affect the play of the game.

Let us examine possible arrangements of social stratification within some imaginary societies. Consider a society of 16 people who must fit into 16 positions within a stratified hierarchy. If we construct that hierarchy with four classes, we have the stratification structure shown in figure 2a. Imagine that

FIGURE 2a

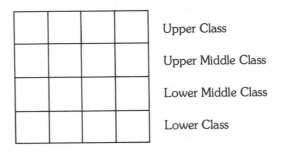

the 16 individuals have come together to form this society from four different societies, bringing with them four different cultures that we shall call ▲, ◆, ●, and ■. If each culture contributes 4 individuals to the new society, we can then refer to the 16 individuals as ▲1, ▲2, ▲3, ▲4, ◆1, ◆2, ◆3, ◆4, ●1, ●2, ●3, ●4, ■1, ■2, ■3, and ■4. Our task now is to distribute these 16 individuals into the 16 stratified positions that, for purposes of this discussion, are waiting for them.

Social Stratification without Ethnic Stratification

One of the ways to distribute the 16 individuals is shown in figure 2b. In this case, each class has one representative from each of the four cultures, and each culture is distributed equally among the four classes. Defining our

FIGURE 2b

▲1	◆1	●1	■1	Upper Class
▲2	◆2	●2	■2	Upper Middle Class
▲3	◆3	●3	■3	Lower Middle Class
▲4	◆4	●4	■4	Lower Class

concept by its opposite, the distribution illustrated in figure 2b describes a total *lack* of ethnic stratification within a system of social stratification. We began with this example to show that *ethnic* stratification is a special case of *social* stratification — or, more accurately, that ethnic stratification refers to a particular arrangement of ethnic groups within social stratification. In figure 2b, there is no relationship between ethnicity and class membership; hence, it would not be to an individual's economic advantage or disadvantage to be a member of a particular ethnic group. With that in mind, let us speculate about the futures of various cultures in this society.

Consider the situation of ▲1. At the beginning of this society, ▲1 will be drawn in two directions in the course of everyday life. Engaging in economic activities, ▲1 will be working with ◆1, ●1, and ■1. Although ▲1 shares no cultural ties with any of these people, they will have very definite economic interests in common. In particular, they will have to worry about maintaining their membership in the upper class. As with all other stratification systems, the best positions in this system are on top, and others will want them and take them if they are not defended. ▲1 *might* not have to worry about ▲2, as their shared culture might prevent a power struggle, but ▲1 has no such assurances regarding the behavior of ◆2, ●2, and ■2. All of them would prefer membership in the upper class and would not think twice about displacing a stranger. Since fear of being displaced is shared by all of ▲1's compatriots in the upper class, it would not be surprising if they banded together on a business basis to protect their mutual interests. Since they would have access to upper-class resources (such as power and money), they would no doubt make a formidable group.

But ▲1 wants more from life than power. Business associations with other members of the upper class cannot displace the warm glow of friendship and experiences shared with members of one's culture. ▲1 will thus be drawn to ▲2, ▲3, and ▲4 — but here is where problems might start. ▲1's economic activities in the upper class will result in discrimination against members of lower classes as the ladder of social mobility is removed. As ▲2, ▲3, and ▲4 realize that ▲1 is responsible for many of their economic problems, they may cease to feel so warm toward their previous friend. ▲1 may, in turn, resent their accusations; at the same time, ▲1 may begin to feel closer to other upper-class members with whom a shared upper-class lifestyle is already growing through their increasing interactions. In short, ▲1 must decide between a culture that is becoming hostile and a class that is becoming friendly. Beyond that, shared everyday experiences in the upper class will create a common lifestyle, whereas the *lack* of those shared everyday experiences with other members of culture ▲ will make those cultural ties seem less strong. If this arrangement continues, all four original cultures would most likely disappear, to re-form within each of the four classes. Elements of old cultures might well continue to exist here and there, but the dominant cultural differences would most likely exist between classes, independent of the ethnic ancestry of the individuals involved.

Ethnic Pluralism within Social Stratification: A Possible Outcome

The stratification system in figure 2b might have an alternative result. Instead of groups forming by class boundaries, under certain circumstances the ethnic groups might survive even though their members occupied different class positions. The overall picture would resemble four separate societies bound together in one; individuals within each ethnic group would have to interact primarily with each other to keep the cultures alive. Each ethnic group might occupy a separate region of the country, or specialize in a particular area of the economy. Whatever the arrangement, some mechanism for ethnic group separation would have to exist to prevent group formation based on class, which occurred in our earlier example. Some class grouping would be expected, particularly at the upper-class level in each ethnic group; it might even tend to support the overall ethnic divisions, as upper-class members of each group would benefit from the system. Such an organization of ethnic groups within a system of social stratification is generally referred to as cultural pluralism, structural pluralism, or horizontal ethnic differentiation.[12]

Complete Ethnic Stratification: A Pure Case

Figure 2c illustrates a second way of distributing the same 16 individuals within the same social stratification hierarchy.

FIGURE 2c

▲1	▲2	▲3	▲4	Upper Class
◆1	◆2	◆3	◆4	Upper Middle Class
●1	●2	●3	●4	Lower Middle Class
■1	■2	■3	■4	Lower Class

It is the exact opposite of the distribution in figure 2b. Figure 2b illustrated a complete *lack* of ethnic stratification; Figure 2c illustrates a *pure case* (or ideal type) of ethnic stratification. As you can see, there is a perfect one-to-one relationship between class and ethnicity: each ethnic group clusters at a

---

12. For further discussion of the concepts of cultural and structural pluralism, see Horace M. Kallen, Culture and Democracy in the United States (New York: Liveright, 1924), and Milton Gordon, Assimilation in American Life (New York: Oxford University Press, 1964). For further discussion of horizontal ethnic differentiation, see Cynthia H. Enloe, Ethnic Conflict and Political Development (Boston: Houghton Mifflin, 1973).

certain level of the stratification hierarchy. Within this society, to know an individual's ethnicity is to know that individual's class, and vice versa. Such examples of ethnic stratification are generally referred to as caste societies, because a complete absence of social mobility is usually needed to keep ethnic groups so separate within a social stratification system. The closest the United States has come to such a system was the institution of slavery, in which to be a slave was to be black and, at least for most blacks in the South, to be black was to be a slave. American slavery, like any other ethnic stratification system, facilitates the ultimate separation of groups: they become ranked both by class and by ethnicity. As figure 2c shows, an individual such as ●1, has everything in common with other members of culture ● and practically nothing in common with members of the other three cultures. Beyond that, all members of culture ● would likely share a fear of culture ■, which might someday replace them, and an envy of culture ♦, which they would like to replace. If social mobility is not possible, such feelings might exist only below the surface, but they would definitely exist and would be very evident, should social mobility ever begin.

Ethnic Stratification: A More Realistic Picture

We have seen the two extreme (and unlikely) distributions of the 16 imaginary individuals. A third distribution of the same individuals, shown in figure 2d, provides a more realistic picture of actual ethnic stratification.

FIGURE 2d

▲1	▲2	▲3	♦1	Upper Class
▲4	♦2	♦3	●1	Upper Middle Class
♦4	●2	●3	■1	Lower Middle Class
●4	■2	■3	■4	Lower Class

Figure 2d illustrates a less pronounced example of ethnic stratification than figure 2c. It incorporates some of the characteristics of figure 2b, in which ethnic groups were scattered among the classes. In figure 2d, the four ethnic groups are still clustered in various classes, but the relationship is no longer perfect. Culture ●, for example, still seems clustered at the lower middle class, but two of its members now occupy different classes and two individuals from different cultures now occupy its class. In short, the overall ranking of ethnic groups evident in figure 2c is still present, but that ranking is no longer quite so clear-cut; some individuals find themselves ranked apart from the majority of the members of their culture.

An individual will share experiences with other individuals if he or she shares with them either a class position *or* ethnicity. It is these common experiences, you recall, that provide the basis for group formation. A pure case of ethnic stratification such as the one illustrated in figure 2c combines all of these common experiences through the overlap of class and ethnicity, and from the individual's standpoint, it is impossible to separate the common experiences brought about by class from the common experiences brought about by ethnicity; class and ethnicity are one and the same. At the other extreme, when ethnic groups are randomly scattered around the stratification hierarchy (as in figure 2b), the individual can clearly separate the common experiences of class from the common experiences of ethnicity and must choose which set of common experiences deserves loyalty. In figure 2d, however, no such easy generalizations can be made. The ethnic groups are clustered in various classes sufficiently for us to label this situation ethnic stratification, but at the same time, there is enough scattering of individuals across class lines to create the problem of conflicting loyalties illustrated in figure 2b. To clarify this confusion, let us take the perspectives of a few of the individuals involved in figure 2d.

Consider the perspective of ●2. It seems fairly safe to guess that ●2 would have a great many common experiences with ●3. Both ●2 and ●3 occupy the lower middle class, *and* they share the cultural traditions of culture ●. They probably see themselves as being in somewhat the same boat. But we can only speculate on further group affiliations of ●2 because of the conflicting loyalties present in this society. For example, would ●2 feel a kinship with ◆4? On the one hand, ◆4 occupies the same class level, which means they might work together and perhaps live near each other. But on the other hand, ◆4 lives in the style of culture ◆, and it is possible that culture ◆ and culture ● have been traditional enemies or, less drastically, that they simply have habits that grate on each other. But even if culture ◆ and culture ● are relatively compatible, it takes two (at least) to form a group, and we would have to ask something about the previous group affiliations of ◆4. ◆4 might not, in fact, be interested in joining ●2 for a variety of practical reasons or previous commitments. If all of these problems are surmounted and ◆4 does join with ●2 and ●3, largely because of common class position, we would not be surprised then to discover changes in cultures ◆ and ● as they exist in the lower middle class of this society.

●2 might also feel something in common with ●1. Both have the common experiences of culture ● to unite them—but will the class differences intrude? ●2 might look up to ●1, feel envy toward ●1, or, more probably, both. In any case, ●2 will be aware of the class differences. ●1, on the other hand, is in an unusual position. ●1 is the most successful member of culture ● in the society and is the lone (and probably a recent) representative of that culture in the upper class. As a result, ●1 may feel somewhat insecure in dealing with the more established members of cultures ▲ and ◆, who traditionally have occupied the upper class. This insecurity could lead ●₁ toward ●₂ and ●₃; on the other hand, it could lead ●₁ to avoid both ●₂ and ●₃ in an effort to leave the low-status culture ● behind. ●₁ may, in fact, be busily buying new clothes, trying on new speech patterns, and attending a new church. The point is that all of these outcomes become very possible responses to the conflicting loyalties built into ethnic stratification.

Finally, how will ●₂ feel toward ●₄? Once again, a variety of feelings is possible. ●₄ may very likely be cultivating ●₂ in an effort at least to return to the lower middle class and to escape the social outcasts of culture ■. ●₂ may be tempted to respond out of a sense of loyalty to culture ●, but at the same time, ●₂ may realize that there is more to be lost than to be gained through associating with ●₄. If ●₂ is pursuing ◆₄, as we suggested above, any association with ●₄ would probably hinder ●₂. ◆₄ might be expected to accept a different culture, providing the class remains the same, but it is unlikely that an individual who differed in both respects would be appealing to ◆₄. If, on the other hand, ◆₄ has already rejected ●₂, ●₂ might be expected to show a little more interest in ●₄. This interest would also be heightened if all the members of culture ● began to organize politically to improve their overall situation.

American blacks in the 1950s somewhat resembled culture ● in figure 2d: although they were clearly stratified as a group, black individuals could be found in a variety of classes. Nevertheless, discrimination against blacks affected *all* members of the group to some degree. Such a situation could lead an individual (such as Martin Luther King, Jr.) to set aside his interest in personal advancement in favor of improving the status of his group as a whole. Our perspective on ethnic stratification is very useful in analyses of the birth and growth of such political organizations.

Social Mobility and Ethnic Stratification

So far we have discussed the tendencies of various individuals to group together without considering their possible reasons (beyond companionship) for doing so. One such reason, inherent in the stratification system, is to achieve upward social mobility. Let us return to ●₂'s perspective, assuming now that ●₂ is angry over a perceived discrimination against culture ● and wants to do something about it.

●₂ would turn first to ●₃. If ●₂ finds no agreement there, then there is probably no hope for organizing culture ● to improve their situation. Assuming, then, that ●₃ is interested, where would they turn next? No doubt to ●₄, as they would want to present a united front and, in addition, all political organizations, especially new ones, need workers. ●₄, having little to fear besides the threat of imprisonment (if the movement should lead in that direction), would probably be interested in joining. The member of culture ● most important to this organization, however, is ●₁. ●₁ is the wealthiest and most powerful member of culture ● and is in a position to bring the organization money, information, organizing skills, access to other powerful people, and assorted other advantages that come with a higher class position. ●1 also has the most to lose by joining the organization; unlike ●4, who cannot be threatened with a loss of wealth or social position, ●1 has no doubt struggled to attain some of both and may not want to gamble. In short, ●1 must decide whether to risk a relatively high economic position to raise the prestige of a relatively low-status ethnicity.

A political movement needs an enemy. For that role, the new culture ● organization will probably select culture ♦. The choice is almost inescapable. Members of culture ♦ are in the next higher positions from culture ● in almost every respect. Culture ♦ lives in the next better neighborhood, attends the next better schools, and holds the next better occupations. Whatever discrimination exists that affects culture ● is probably administered, if not created, by culture ♦, because culture ♦ has a built-in fear of culture ● advancing at its expense. Culture ▲ would make the most appropriate enemy. As the society's most powerful group, culture ▲ is probably most responsible for the overall arrangement of the other groups within the stratification system. But the actual members of culture ▲ are not visible to members of culture ●; their everyday lives do not bring them into direct contact with each other. (Members of culture ▲ will, of course, be visible to members of culture ♦, should *they* ever decide to organize for mobility.) We can summarize this process by observing that ethnic stratification encourages ethnic groups to conflict with other ethnic groups ranked near them in the stratification hierarchy.

Meanwhile, culture ♦ should not be expected to take the attack lying down. The now organized threat directly below them in the stratification hierarchy will encourage an organized response. Taking the members of culture ♦ separately, ♦4 will in some ways be the most threatened by the political movement of culture ●, since ♦4's strongest point—membership in a high-status ethnic group—is now being threatened. The possibility of dropping still further in class is also present. ♦2 and ♦3 will also be severely threatened by the new political organization. The possible loss of economic dominance (vividly illustrated for them by ♦4) will be uppermost in their minds. As ●2 and ●3 turned to ●1 for help, so might ♦2 and ♦3 be expected to turn to the most powerful member of their ethnic group for help. Should ♦1 decide to join the culture ♦ organization, they would make a formidable foe for culture ●.

With the two sides chosen, the game is ready to begin. Although in this example the two sides are the same size, they are far from evenly matched; culture ♦ has far more options at its disposal because of the initial advantage of occupying a higher class. The main forces of any stratified society, whether economic, political, or physical, are largely at the disposal of the higher classes. Culture ●, on the other hand, is likely to employ a narrower range of actions, such as strikes, boycotts, demonstrations, or, in extreme cases, armed revolt. Should they catch culture ♦ disorganized, still milder forms of political action, such as bloc voting, might be effective. Whatever the situation, however, culture ● begins the struggle at a definite disadvantage.

Co-optation

Of the many strategies that culture ♦ might employ, co-optation clearly illuminates the conflicts between class and ethnic loyalty that characterize ethnic stratification. In the case of ethnic group conflict, *co-optation* refers to raising the class position (real or imagined) of the subordinate group's leader, in hopes that that leader will come to identify with the opposition and forsake the former followers. The force of this method can be seen in the initial dilemma of ●₁ as culture ● began organizing. Although sharing a culture with members of the new organization, ●₁ occupied a higher class than the rest of the members. This higher class would give ●₁ a variety of interests different from other members of the group. Those different interests might, in fact, have led ●₁ at the outset to join with culture ♦ to put down the rebellion by the rest of culture ●. Since in our example those class interests were apparently not strong enough to lead ●₁ in that direction, culture ♦ might add to those interests by raising still further the class position of ●₁. Should ●₁ then decide to alter loyalties in favor of culture ♦, ●₁ will have been effectively co-opted. The importance of a leader such as ●₁ to a budding political movement makes this tactic particularly appealing to the more dominant group. It is hard to imagine, for example, the success of the civil rights movement without the presence of an *effective leader* such as Martin Luther King, Jr.

Ethnic Stratification: A Direction for Study

The purpose of our hypothetical examples has not been to provide a systematic analysis of ethnic group conflict, but rather to introduce a perspective and illustrate its use. The perspective of ethnic stratification does not provide a set of ready-made predictions for all occasions, but it does point up some of the concerns faced by individuals involved in ethnic group conflict. A focus purely on cultural differences between ethnic groups cannot explain the co-opted leader; a focus purely on class differences between ethnic groups cannot explain the dedicated leader who cannot be co-opted.

A word of caution is in order. Though it calls attention to the interrelations between class and ethnicity, the perspective of ethnic stratification provides only the basic framework within which to conduct individual analyses of particular ethnic group conflicts. The perspective of ethnic stratification does not explain ethnic conflict; it only points us in the right direction to find explanations.

SUMMARY

The goal of this chapter has been to explain how ethnic groups form and why they come into conflict with each other in a multi-ethnic society. We began by looking at social stratification systems, to better understand the general social situation within which ethnic conflict occurs. Social stratification creates categories of classes in a society, as activities are ranked by the rewards they receive. Individuals who occupy the same class category often notice that similarity, grouping together for purposes of mutual defense and advancement. One of the main factors that affects this group formation is social mobility; there must be enough movement from one class level to another to introduce the idea of change, but if too much mobility occurs, individuals will not occupy class categories long enough to identify with their class.

As individuals compete for the scarce rewards within a stratification system, they may attempt to hinder the competitive abilities of others who are striving for the same rewards. Such attempts to hinder others are acts of discrimination, which are often accompanied and justified by stereotypes and notions of prejudice directed against the group subject to discrimination. As discrimination closes routes of upward mobility for certain individuals, they often form groups in defense. We specified three types of such groups: (1) the ideological subordinate group (which faces discrimination for threatening the values of the dominant group); (2) the subordinate class group (which faces discrimination for threatening the economic position of the dominant group); and (3) the subordinate ethnic group (which faces discrimination for both reasons).

Because of discrimination, the subordinate ethnic group is unable to advance in the stratification hierarchy. It becomes clustered, as a group, in the lower class levels of the stratification system. This clustering, known as ethnic stratification, provides the specific social setting within which ethnic conflict occurs. We examined various arrangements of ethnic groups, within ethnic stratification systems of varying degrees of social mobility, to understand how such social settings affect (1) how ethnic individuals see the world and their place in it, and (2) how those individuals group together to defend their interests and advance their group's position within the stratification system.

Chapter

The Politics of Stratification

fOUR

HOW STRATIFICATION BECOMES A POLITICAL QUESTION

By now the concepts of social stratification, ethnic stratification, class, and caste should be fairly clear to you. The question we confront in this chapter is, how do all of these apparently sociological issues become political? That is, how does government deal with ethnic groups, and what is the impact of these groups on government activity? In American society there is tension between minority rights and the role of social class. We will discuss the impact of minorities on cities and government in the United States, and present a perspective to view it in by examining how these same issues are handled in other countries. The reasons for the conflict between the demand for minority rights and the structures of social class will be explained through the tension made evident by the Supreme Court cases involving minorities. This chapter gives a brief overview of the legal history of minorities before America's highest court. The chapter also evaluates the significance of ethnic and minority politics in American politics as a whole.

The Political Side of Discrimination

The first issue we shall deal with is the use of social class and caste as social concepts and as political ideas. As we said in Chapter 3, a pure caste system exists only in theory. Though the ante-bellum South and Nazi Germany came close to replicating the theory, there simply has never been a society in which *every* social position was fixed according to ethnic group. The thing that makes a caste system a political reality is not its absolute character, but the translation of social perceptions into informal rules or laws. That is, any type of social agreement sanctioned by society that hinders the competitive ability of a minority group is by definition political. Such a social agreement is discrimination, and discrimination is a political issue.

In defining discrimination as political, are we not flagrantly violating the sociologist's turf? If all societal discrimination is political, why bother looking at the sociological aspect? Discrimination *is* a political issue, not only because the government has passed laws designed to limit it, but also because our society has broad philosophical commitments to justice and equality. Both justice and equality require nonarbitrary decisions. The Fourteenth Amendment to the United States Constitution made it illegal to discriminate on the basis of race and ethnic background. Thus, our society confronts a paradox: how to reconcile a commitment to nonarbitrary treatment of its members with the reality of discrimination. For this reason all sociological, anthropological, and economic elements of a minority's situation are at least potentially, if not in reality, political.

In the last chapter we distinguished between class and caste. Indeed, the real distinction between ethnic stratification (where each ethnic group belongs to a different class) and social stratification is how people perceive the importance of class in their daily social interaction. These distinctions become political whenever individuals attempt to have the society at large lend credence to the distinctions through laws, rules, or informal agreements. For example, if my neighbors and I enter into an agreement not to sell any of our homes to blond-haired people (for we all know how inferior they are!), our act is ultimately political. It is political because property rights, contracts, and business transactions are guaranteed by the government. Refusing to sell our property to blond-haired people, an agreement called a *restrictive covenant,*[1] is illegal; but unless the blond-haired person was willing to sue, or to ask the

---

1. Restrictive covenants were outlawed by the Supreme Court in the case of *Shelley* v. *Kraemer*, 331 U.S. 1 (1948). However, as late as 1968 there was a significant question whether a private owner could restrict the sale of property without prior agreement. In *Jones* v. *Mayer*, 392 U.S. 409 (1968), the Court said a private owner could not. Alfred H. Mayer Co. had refused to sell Joseph Lee Jones a home in the Paddock Woods community of St. Louis County for the sole reason that he was black. The Court wrote:

> For this court recognized long ago that, whatever else they may have encompassed, the badges and incidents of slavery —its "burdens and disabilities" —included restraints upon "those fundamental rights which are the essence of civil freedom, namely the same right . . . to inherit, purchase, lease, sell and convey property, as is enjoyed by white citizens," Civil Rights Cases. Just as the Black Codes, enacted after the Civil War to restrict the free exercise of those rights, were the substitutes for the slave system, so the exclusion of Negroes from white communities became a substitute for the Black Codes. And when racial discrimination herds men into ghettos and makes their ability to buy property turn on the color of their skin, then it too is a relic of slavery.

There is a vast difference between the Court's position and reality in the United States. Is more than one race represented in your neighborhood? This political problem will be explored later in this book. For an excellent legal history of the problem, see Clement E. Vose, Caucasians Only: The Supreme Court, The NAACP, and the Restrictive Covenant Cases (Berkeley: University of California Press, 1969).

government to sue, nothing would be done to prevent us. In this situation the blond-haired person is not merely socially stratified. His financial ability to buy a house is not in question, only an arbitrary identification by the color of his hair. Yet a single case is not sufficient evidence of perfect ethnic stratification; even 100,000 cases would not be enough.

In the social sciences there are no absolutes. Class and caste are not fixed notions; rather, they enable us to understand tendencies. The example of the blond-haired home-buyer is merely one indicator, or piece of information, with which to begin to make judgments about the nature of social stratification in society. Specifically, are decisions about class—and subsequent social or political limitations—arbitrary, or are they in line with society's notion of fairness? You might feel that class is, by definition, arbitrary. We shall deal with this issue shortly, when we discuss Karl Marx.

The Political Side of Stereotypes and Prejudice

The use of stereotypes, or pre-definitions, to make decisions is commonplace. As a child you learned very quickly that you could not walk through walls. You did not need to test your hypothesis about the structure of walls each time you decided to leave a room. Certainly, stereotypes about walls are very useful. However, especially when they concern ethnic minorities, stereotypes become highly political in American society. Unlike the stereotype about walls, the stereotype of miserliness often applied to Jews is impossible to verify; a single personality type is not common across an entire ethnic group. Yet there is no scientific method to dispute the stereotypes, because there is no way to test miserliness as you can the density of a wall. In addition, there are always other stereotypes to account for any exceptions to the first stereotype. For example, read the following fictional dialogue, created by Gordon Allport (1954: 13–14):

Mr. X: *The trouble with the Jews is that they only take care of their own group.*

Mr. Y: *But the record of the Community Chest campaign shows that they give more generously, in proportion to their numbers, to the general charities of the community, than do non-Jews.*

Mr. X: *That shows they are always trying to buy favor and intrude into Christian affairs. They think of nothing but money; that is why there are so many Jewish bankers.*

Mr. Y: *But a recent study shows that the percentage of Jews in the banking business is negligible, far smaller than the percentage of non-Jews.*

Mr. X: *That's just it; they don't go in for respectable business; they are only in the movie business or run night clubs.*

Stereotypes that become accepted in our minds are not easily changed, even by contradictory evidence.

Stereotypes become political when they cross the often subtle line between personal opinion and community action. By community action we mean something as simple as a group of friends meeting to decide to discriminate. We prejudice—that is, *pre-judge*—our actions against a person because of what we perceive as that person's unchangeable characteristics. For example, as a rather precocious first grader, one of the authors of this book joined a "woman-haters" club. (He has since resigned.) Club activities—pulling girls' hair, chasing them, and doing other dreadful things—had a socializing impact. You might argue that such activities are hardly political. However, in the long run they are the roots of societal discrimination, such as resenting a woman's competing equally with a man. If we do not begin to understand the origins of political prejudice in our early social experiences, we never fully appreciate why political prejudices exist. (The woman-haters club formed some of the author's early attitudes toward women, and as inane as these prejudices are, they still tend to haunt him.) Prejudices against women are supported not only by early socialization, but also by religion and law. Indeed, some very intelligent people have made a strong case for prejudice against women (see Christenson, 1973: 35–40). It is not the prejudice itself that makes this a political issue, but the use of prejudicial information to make political decisions.

Few prejudiced people see themselves as engaging in a political act. For example, if I do not want my children to go to school with children whose parents are members of the Georgia Democratic Party, why should they be forced to? This is none of the government's business; it is a private decision I make on behalf of my children. Unfortunately, nothing is quite so simple. If I do not want my children to attend school with Georgians, and the school I want to send them to is better funded and better staffed, then I am using government to protect my prejudices. The political nature of prejudice is much more apparent to those who are objects of prejudice. No member of an ethnic or minority community considers himself cheap, dumb, or inferior. Indeed, individuals often try to overcompensate to dispel stereotypes, or at least the applicability of stereotypes to them. For example, recent studies have shown that Jews in America, who are considered by some to be clannish and miserly, often overcompensate by being very friendly and extremely generous. They feel that if they turn down a request for money, someone might think of them as being "Jewish."

The political aspects of prejudice against individuals are obvious. An individual who is the object of prejudice often feels humiliated, yet powerless to do anything about it. A group of students recently did a series of clandestine interviews with Ku Klux Klan members in Virginia. One Klan member, who heads the personnel department of a large corporation, said that he accepted applications from blacks, but took them home and burned them to avoid complying with affirmative action laws. Employment agencies often print secret codes on their interview forms that distinguish not only race, but also class. One employment agency insured the segregation of faculties in a county and city school system by sending whites to the predominantly white county system and by telling blacks that no jobs were available.

If you have never experienced prejudice against your ethnic or minority background, you might have difficulty recognizing it. However, there are telltale signs. Job openings are advertised, yet they are all filled on the afternoon you go job hunting. Homes are for sale in a particular area, but when you ask about them the real estate agent suddenly finds that someone has already put a down payment on each one. All of these are instances of political acts because they involve government guarantees of rights, such as to own private property, or the refusal to enforce such civil rights.

ETHNIC MINORITIES AND POLITICAL OFFICE IN THE UNITED STATES

A Brief Look at National Politics

One of the keys to group political and social power in the United States is to elect group members to political office or to have them hired into the political bureaucracy. This is especially true for minority groups. As we saw in Chapter 2, ethnic groups found that political machines could benefit them.

Over time, a particular group's social class (and thus its "inferiority" or "superiority" to others) can change. One of the most pronounced attitude changes toward a minority has been in the attitude toward the Irish, and toward Catholics in general. In seventeenth and eighteenth century British society the Irish were considered the lowest possible class. There were laws forbidding Irish immigration to Great Britain. Prejudice was so vehement that satirist Jonathan Swift published his essay *A Modest Proposal,* lampooning the British attitudes. Swift proposed solving the Irish potato famine and overpopulation simultaneously by providing recipes for preparing and cooking Irish children. Anti-Irish and anti-Catholic sentiment also existed in the United States. Al Smith's attempt to defeat Herbert Hoover for the presidency in 1928 was short-circuited by anti-Catholic feeling. By 1960 American attitudes toward the Irish and toward Catholics had shifted enough for John F. Kennedy to be elected president. Yet Kennedy barely won the election even though his party, the Democrats, appeared to be at the apogee of its strength. Some observers suggest that lines of division in voting have been redrawn, from Catholic against Protestant to black against white (Ladd, Hadley, and King, 1971). Such a change in voter attitudes could have far-reaching effects on minority politics in the next several decades.

Whatever the new voting alignments may be, ethnic and minority representation among officeholders has changed little. The average member of Congress in the United States is not only late-middle-aged, native-born, and middle-class, but also male, white and of northwest or central European ancestry — and his father was a professional or a manager (Lowi, 1977: 238). As tables 1, 2, and 3 demonstrate, there has been little change in the makeup of Congress in the last 20 years.

Table 1.   Blacks in Congress, 1959–1978

Congress	Senate		House	
	Blacks	Whites	Blacks	Whites
95th (1977–78)	1	99	15	420
94th (1975–76)	1	99	15	420
93rd (1973–74)	1	99	15	420
92nd (1971–72)	1	99	12	423
91st (1969–70)	1	99	9	426
90th (1967–68)	1	99	5	430
89th (1965–66)	0	100	6	429
88th (1963–64)	0	100	5	430
87th (1961–62)	0	100	4	431
86th (1959–60)	0	100	4	431

Data from Congressional Quarterly Almanac, various years.

Table 2.   Women in Congress, 1959–1978

Congress	Senate		House	
	Women	Men	Women	Men
95th (1977–78)	1	99	16	419
94th (1975–76)	0	100	19	416
93rd (1973–74)	0	100	14	421
92nd (1971–72)	2	98	13	422
91st (1969–70)	1	99	10	425
90th (1967–68)	1	99	11	424
89th (1965–66)	2	98	10	425
88th (1963–64)	2	98	11	424
87th (1961–62)	2	98	17	418
86th (1959–60)	1	99	16	419

Data from Congressional Quarterly Almanac, various years.

At the state and local levels there are also relatively few minority politicians and a small number of women. Thus, notwithstanding the major social changes that have occurred in the United States during the past 30 years, there is still a large gap between actual political representation of groups and what their relative numbers would justify.

Table 3. Religious Affiliation of the 93rd, 94th, and 95th Congresses

Religion	93rd Congress (73–74) House	Senate	94th Congress (75–76) House	Senate	95th Congress (77–78) House	Senate
Protestant	295	74	294	76	273	76
Catholic	100	14	109	15	117	14
Jewish	12	2	20	3	22	5
Other[1]	20	10	2	6	19	5
None	5	0	10	0	4	0
Total	432	100	435	100	435	100

Data from Congressional Quarterly Weekly Report, 6 Jan. 1973, 18 Jan. 1975; and Congressional Quarterly Almanac, 1977.

1. Includes Mormon, Greek Orthodox, Eastern Orthodox, and Adventist.

The Changing Racial Composition of American Cities: Rise of the Black Politician

The only geographical area where minority groups have had significant representation has been the core areas of large cities. Carl Stokes, elected mayor of Cleveland in the 1960s, was the first of many minority mayors (most of them black) across the country. Cities as diverse as Los Angeles, Cincinnati, New Orleans, Detroit, and Richmond have had or continue to have black mayors. However, this increase has more to do with the changing racial composition of large cities than with an *absolute* increase in minority voting or a change to egalitarian values. Because of federal pressure for integration, busing, and open housing over the last several decades, most major cities are now comprised of two separate populations: those who make up the inner city, and those who live in the suburbs. Suburbs tend to be predominantly white, and core city areas black. In a number of cities, business has deserted core city shops and stores for the more attractive suburban shopping centers. Orlando, Florida, has had such a radical shift of population that it can be described as a "doughnut community"; that is, all major business and cultural activities occur in the suburbs, while the inner city has a high percentage of deserted buildings, a veritable ghost town.

Although there is an increasing number of black mayors, many govern depressed areas. The most affluent members of society move out, eroding property values, which in turn decreases the city's tax base. They take with them businesses and corporations. The phenomenon is encouraged by archaic laws that limit the cities' ability to annex suburbs that are living off the cities' resources, yet cannot be taxed to bolster the inner-city economy. For example, Richmond, Virginia, has been so hampered in annexing that its suburbs are now larger in both population and area than the central city.

Some black-led cities are making a slow comeback with the help of federal funds.[2] Detroit is one example.

In 1956, 83 percent of all money issued in paychecks in the three-county Detroit area was issued in Wayne County, which is mostly Detroit. By last year the figure had dropped to 65 percent. In 1963, metropolitan consumers spent 41 cents of every dollar in Detroit proper. In 1976 they spent 26 cents.

Last year, the value of Detroit real estate slipped below $10 billion for the first time in years. With the tax base steadily shrinking, the city has become dependent on the state and federal governments for the revenues it needs to provide basic services within a balanced budget. Few analysts think that is going to change soon.

The city has embarked on a program of tax relief for industries that stay in Detroit and expand, and there is some evidence this has stanched the flow. (Stevens, 1978: A–15)

Can black politicians garner resources to benefit people in the inner cities, thereby giving credibility to the black politician in the minds of the voters? That is the important question, and it remains to be answered.

It would be inaccurate to suggest that minority political power has been derived only from those members of minorities who have won public office. Given our faith in democracy, it is difficult to admit that a number of the political and social advances made by ethnic and minority groups in this country have come through illegal or violent actions. As we saw in Chapter 2, unions were one very important vehicle for gains by immigrants. Yet, during most of the nineteenth and early twentieth centuries, unions were illegal. So were the nonviolent movements of suffragettes in the early 1900s and of blacks led by Martin Luther King, Jr. Violence used to cure social evils—from the Sons of Liberty to the Tobacco Night Riders[3] to the Black Panthers—has

---

2. New York City, though not now led by a black mayor, fits this pattern. Many Americans objected to the federal "dole" to New York during its monetary crisis in the mid-1970s. Certainly, some of its problems had been caused by waste, but the largest share of economic difficulties was due to the most affluent people's moving to Long Island or to other suburban communities sheltered from New York City taxes.

3. *"On December 1, 1906, 250 masked and armed men swarmed into Princeton, Kentucky, and took control. They disarmed the police, shut off the water supply, and captured the courthouse and telephone offices. They patrolled the streets, ordered citizens to keep out of sight and shot at those who disobeyed. Then they dynamited and burned two large tobacco factories and rode off singing 'the fire shines bright in my old Kentucky home.'*

"A year later, they struck again, at Hopkinsville, Kentucky. They occupied strategic posts and dragged a buyer from the Imperial Tobacco Company from his home to pistol-whip him. As usual, they marched out singing, but this time the sheriff organized a posse to pursue the raiders and attacked their rear. The pursuers killed one man and wounded another before the raiders drove the posse back into Hopkinsville.

"Violence, we are told, doesn't pay, but the Night Riders enjoyed a considerable measure of success. By 1908, the Planters Protective Association was handling nine-tenths of the crop

played an important role. Violent activity forces passive citizens to confront issues; gives credence to more moderate members of the minority, who want to work within the system; and—as after the ghetto riots—produces government monies and resources.

ETHNIC POLITICS AND THE INTERNATIONAL SCENE

By now we should have convinced you of the importance of minority groups in the United States. After all, the purpose of this book is to examine minorities in America. But although we are concentrating on only one society, you should be aware of the broader context of minority politics. Many students believe that ethnic and racial groups, and the problems associated with these groups, are inherently American problems. History courses teach that the United States is a nation of immigrants; if you assume that only immigrants create minority conflicts, you may wrongly conclude that minorities are an issue only in the United States. There is no nation in the world today which is not confronted by some sort of major political challenge by minorities—from Canada to India, from Malaysia to Chile. For this reason, we should adjust our focus momentarily to minority politics in several countries besides the United States. These other examples will provide some perspective and prevent you from making the easy, but totally wrong, assumption that minority politics is only an American problem. Ethnic politics also plays a major role in such diverse countries as Great Britain, South Africa, and China.

Great Britain: Long-standing Ethnic Differences and Recent Immigration

One major political issue in Great Britain is limiting the immigration of "coloureds," generally people of Indian or Pakistani origin although some Africans are included in this group. These people came to England from former British colonies; some have been there for generations. Their right to immigrate was granted them by virtue of their membership in the British Commonwealth. Margaret Thatcher, Conservative Party leader, used the racial issue in her successful campaign to become prime minister in 1979. The issue, which cuts across class lines, will continue to be a major problem in the United Kingdom (*Newsweek*, 1977a). Proposals for "curing" the coloured problem have ranged from limiting immigration and civil rights to outright expatriation of immigrants to their countries of origin. (Anyone familiar with

---

produced in its area. *The power of the big tobacco companies was broken and they were buying their tobacco through the Association at substantially increased prices. From the depressed conditions of a few years earlier, the black patch area of Kentucky and Tennessee prospered. Mortgages were paid off and new homes, new buggies, and new barns appeared everywhere"* (William A. Gamson, "Violence and political power: The meek don't make it," *Psychology Today* [July 1974], 35–36).

FIGURE 3.   UNITED KINGDOM of Great Britain and N. Ireland

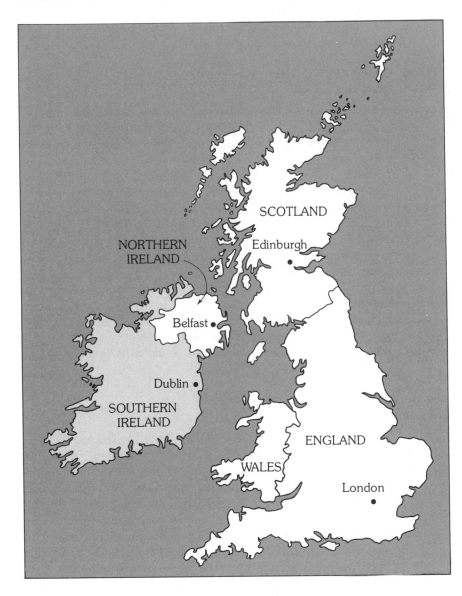

American history will recognize these proposals.) And, of course, the issues have spawned extreme ideologies on both sides: followers of Oswald Mosley have donned the cloak of neo-Nazism to cure their country's problems; members of the coloured community, lodged mostly in ghettos, have also turned to extreme ideologies.

The British problem is complicated by the situation in Northern Ireland and by the secessionist Welsh and Celtic elements within England itself. The Irish question in England is centuries old. The first coloureds for the British, the Irish have always been looked down upon as a lower class, incapable of civilization except in very rare cases. The situation in Northern Ireland involves a series of political issues based on ethnic perceptions. From the British point of view, people in Northern Ireland are as much a part of Britain as are the Scots or the Welsh. The population of Northern Ireland is primarily Protestant and has significant cultural ties with England. Additionally, there is great fear that if the British allow Ireland to absorb this territory (Northern Ireland), the new Catholic majority will discriminate overtly against the Protestants. The Irish, especially the Catholics in Northern Ireland, see themselves as artificially separated and prevented from unifying the entire Irish island (see figure 3). They see England as the villain who has economically and politically dominated the Irish because of inbred racism.

Both the Celts and the Welsh have also advocated separating from Great Britain, emphasizing their different ethnic origins. Indeed, because it comprised so many varied peoples, the British Empire induced a great deal of ethnic tension—and gave birth to minority politics—throughout the world. The closest example is Canada, like the United States a former British colony. French separatists, with a strong foothold in the Canadian province of Quebec, advocate making it a separate, French-speaking nation. Indeed, even without national separation, French Canadians have attempted to assert themselves in every facet of life, from bilingual signs and education to establishing French as the language for conducting business. Canada faces other ethnic challenges as well, from Oriental, Jewish, and eastern European ethnics. Even the Eskimos in northwestern Canada have been active as a minority group.

South Africa and Rhodesia: The Politics of Race

Some former British colonies, such as Australia, have simplified their problems by severely restricting immigration by people of minority races. Rhodesia and South Africa have based the entire legal and moral structure of their societies on the issue of race. In Rhodesia and South Africa what we have been calling minority politics is actually majority politics, for whites in both countries comprise a small minority. However, it does not make sense to talk of blacks, who make up 85 percent of the population of South Africa, as a majority, because given the pseudocolonialism of *apartheid* (the legal segregation of the races), blacks have no power at all. We must redefine minority politics on an international level to distinguish people who are systematically excuded from political power (that is, who have a minority share of power) solely on the basis of their group identification or classification. (This definition will be useful later, when we further explore other aspects of the American minority problem, most notably women.) In South Africa the various African tribes have no power within the social and political system. They cannot vote; they have only limited education and are restricted to certain occupations;

black and white communities are totally segregated; and travel is tightly controlled by the central government.

It would be simplistic to damn South Africans or Rhodesians as manifestly evil. Seeing apartheid as the work of madmen distorts our understanding of the circumstances. Even the Nazis were very careful to lay the foundation of their destruction of the Jews in well-developed "scientific" and ideological studies (Mosse, 1968: 57–92). Most white South Africans believe that apartheid is right and moral. Like segregationists in the South 20 years ago, they use the Bible, scientific studies, and moral persuasion to defend their segregated social system. They start from the "indisputable fact that the whites of South Africa have not merely a doubtful right to the land which they have settled and brought to the highest prosperity, but, rather, they are completely justified in owning and controlling it."[4] In other words, the South Africans, like any other national group, feel that they are in the right. Again using the most extreme case, the Nazis in Germany also had broad support from many of the German people, who felt their actions were both moral and justified (see Mayer, 1955).

In South Africa race dominates politics. Ethnicity defines social class almost completely in one of the most rigid class systems in the world today. The exceptions are sometimes bizarre. Sandra Laing, a South African girl whose parents were both white, was born with dark skin and African features. Her attendance at the all-white school elicited cruelties from the white children and an outcry from their parents. The South African solution was to redefine her as black and expel her from the school.

South Africans pay a heavy price for their racism. Not only is there the constant threat (some feel the inevitability) of a bloodbath, but South Africa is also plagued by economic stagnation. As Cynthia Enloe points out,

> If pressures for modernization are blocked too long by ethnic barriers, a society ultimately confronts two unpleasant alternatives: either it will have to sacrifice economic growth and social development for the sake of maintaining the communal status quo, or it will have to alter ethnic relations radically. Whatever the decision, the country will undergo a profound transformation. If authorized policy-makers refuse to face their choices, they court revolution. The Republic of South Africa currently has this problem. (Enloe, 1973: 29)

Thus, any concerted effort to use rigid ethnic or racial distinctions to make political decisions in society appears to lead to violence, rebellion, or revolution.

---

4.   Wilhelm Röpke, "South Africa: An attempt at a positive appraisal," reprinted from Schweizer Monatshefte, 44th Year, No. 2, May 1964, and distributed by the South African embassy to the United States. The South African embassy and consulates across the United States distribute hundreds of pamphlets such as "Why Apartheid," "In Defense of Apartheid," and "Crisis in World Conscience." They should be appreciated for what they are: propaganda.

The People's Republic of China

The Chinese People's Republic—communist China—is not a country that most Americans consider to have major ethnic diversity. Yet one study suggests that China has approximately 45 million ethnic people who have a significant political impact (Dreyer, 1976). Although the Chinese government initially encouraged the dominant ethnic group, the Han, gradually to merge with the other nationalities, the cultural revolution during the 1960s persecuted ethnic enclaves as remnants of the decadent past. June Dreyer suggests that the government has recently taken a more lenient approach toward minorities.

Summary

Ethnic politics in China, the Soviet Union, Belgium, and a number of other countries give us insight into general political problems throughout the world that are not often thought to relate to minorities.[5] An international perspective also fosters our understanding of the problems of minority and ethnic politics in the United States. First, knowing the international context helps us put our own minority problems into perspective. Second, it gives us a firmer grasp on the various issues involved. Finally, we can better understand the impact of social class upon groups not only in the United States but throughout the world.

THEORIES OF ETHNIC POLITICS: THE PLURALISTS AND THE ELITISTS

Political scientists take many views of the issue of minority politics. Although it is a bit simplistic, we shall lump the major schools into two categories: the pluralists and the elitists. Pluralists believe that society is composed of groups who compete for power on a relatively equal footing. Elitists believe that society is constructed in such a way as to protect persons in power and to insure that persons or groups out of power are continually prevented from sharing any meaningful social benefits. Unlike sociologists, political scientists have only rarely analyzed race and racism as determining factors in politics; only a few studies examine the interrelationship between race and class.[6]

---

5. For an excellent discussion of various issues of ethnic conflict throughout the world, see Martin O. Heisler (ed.), Ethnic Conflict in the World Today, an issue of The Annals of the American Academy of Political and Social Science (vol. 433, Sept. 1977).

6. For a simple but insightful overview of the four models used in sociology, see James A. Geschwender, Class, Race, and Worker Insurgency (New York: Cambridge University Press, 1977), pp. 1–16.

The Pluralist Model

The dominant interpretation of minority politics is the pluralist model, of which Robert Dahl is by far the most important advocate. His classic study, *Who Governs?*, argues that a multiplicity of groups or other institutions operates in society. From this perspective Dahl observes the historical development of politics in New Haven, Connecticut. The first period of his history is dominated by the "patricians," descendants of the Puritans. They based their power on their social and religious dominance of the area, and on the Anglo-Saxon founders of New England. In the mid-nineteenth century the patricians lost power to the "entrepreneurs," who used the massive industrialization of the Northeast to engineer their claim to power. By the early twentieth century the new European immigrants, labeled the "ex-plebes," began wresting power from the entrepreneurs. Dahl characterizes the first two periods as elitist, and the last as the beginning of pluralist politics in the United States. This view has been used to suggest that minority politics has much to do with the shifting of power, and that there are no fixed or caste relationships in modern American society.

The Elitist Model

The elitist model suggests that there is a continuing elite in the United States who control politics at the local, state, and national levels. Racial minorities are excluded from the elite. By *elite,* the social scientists do not necessarily mean those who hold elective office. Rather, the elite includes people who actually wield power in the business, social, or political community. As we said earlier in this chapter, there are today many black mayors. However, from the elitist perspective, few of them have significant power, since the economic and social forces of their areas have moved to the suburbs. Although many political scientists have written in this vein, Peter Bachrach is probably the most well-known.

Pluralism and Elitism: A Comparison

Many pluralists do not argue with the suggestion that there are elites. "The crucial point, which they are quick to underscore, is that multiple political elites in a democracy—as distinguished from a system ruled by a single and unified elite—compete vigorously among themselves on issues of public policy and for public office and thereby generate a basic restraint against the violation of democratic norms and rules by any one elite (Bachrach, 1971: 10–11)." Bachrach disagrees with this characterization:

> *This position is unconvincing to theorists who believe that a pluralistic elite system does not provide sufficient cohesiveness to guard against a take-over by a demagogue; to theorists who are not satisfied with a theory which explicitly emphasizes the importance of the stability of the political system and ignores its ability to provide the necessary political*

*condition to advance the self-development of ordinary men and women.
. . . (Bachrach, 1971: 10–11)*

A dichotomy is apparent; which side is more right?

Unfortunately, neither proposition gives a very satisfactory explanation of minority politics in the United States. The pluralists seem to suggest that minorities are identified with cultural perceptions; as soon as these perceptions change, they will gain power in society. Yet we know that minorities tend to fall into certain social classes, and that these classes tend to prevent them from overcoming prejudice. For example, blacks (among the oldest immigrants) and American Indians (the only natives of this continent) neither have nor appear to be developing any significant power. The elitist model seems a more satisfactory explanation of minorities than the pluralist perspective, yet it does not take into account ethnicity and minority status. That is, the elitists see everyone outside the elite as equally subjugated. However, poor whites still have significant advantages over nonwhites. Social scientists have demonstrated that "majority" status confers advantages in getting jobs, education, and a host of other rewards in society. And you can have significant difficulties if you are of the wrong minority type: a black in Richmond, Virginia; an American Indian in El Paso, Texas; or a Jew in parts of upstate New York. The "view from the bottom" of society is not necessarily the same everywhere.

Most of our discussion in this chapter has centered around the theoretical problems of minority politics and how to distinguish a minority. The broader question of how minorities fit into the larger society has yet to be answered. As we pointed out in Chapter 3, social stratification does not necessarily mean ethnic stratification. That is, the simple existence of social classes does not mean that a person's class is determined by his race. However, it is important to note that political decisions are made on the basis of class distinctions. Without even considering the issue of ethnicity, it is easy to observe the impact of class on politics.

How little we question class distinctions becomes clear in any discussion of inheritance. In America we accept without question the right of individuals to inherit large sums of money, no matter what their moral character or their ability, and regardless of the impact of such laws on our commitment to equality. William Buckley once commented that "everyone should have the right to be born with 10 million dollars in the bank." Yet many of the political theorists who laid the foundation for American society thought inheritance was dangerous. John Locke argued that a son has no right to his father's estate because he has not earned it.

Today, class is so ingrained that we hardly notice it. For example, imagine two students who have the same good academic qualifications for college, but who have not won scholarships. If one of them is upper-class, he can attend Yale University for $9,000 a year, which probably guarantees his continuing upper-class existence. We hardly think twice when the second student, a truck driver's son, is doomed by lack of funds to a college without the prestige and job-attracting power of Yale. Certainly this example is oversimplified, but it does demonstrate how seldom class is used to criticize society or politics. If we are to examine the politics of class in detail, the most powerful microscope available is the writing of Karl Marx.

KARL MARX AND ETHNIC STRATIFICATION

What follows is *not* a pure Marxist analysis of class and ethnicity. Rather, we shall use Marx to illuminate and emphasize the interplay between politics and class. In so doing, we shall oversimplify Marx and make the issue of class appear to be his only focus.

Social Class

Marx argued that the fundamental relationship between people is class. There are fundamentally two classes of people: the proletariat, or working class, and the bourgeoisie, those who control the means of production. "The history of all hitherto existing society is the history of class struggles," asserts *The Communist Manifesto*:

Freeman and slave, patrician and plebeian, lord and serf, guildmaster and journeyman, in a word, oppressor and oppressed, stood in constant opposition to one another, carried on an uninterrupted, now hidden, now open fight, a fight that each time ended, either in a revolutionary reconstitution of society at large, or in the common ruin of the contending classes.

Most modern writers, such as Frantz Fanon, see a natural similarity between the working-class struggle that Marx described and the situation of contemporary minority groups. From Marx's perspective, classes put an arbitrary and unchangeable limit on what individuals can achieve. Contrary to the American dream, in which those who work hard can change their social class for the better, Marx saw a large and growing working class. Most American students would object that there are increasing numbers of white-collar workers and that, therefore, Marx must have been wrong. However, Marx defined workers as those who did not own the means of production. For the vast majority of Americans the only appreciable property they own (or in most cases owe on) is their home. Even in income there has been little narrowing of the gaps between classes during the past 30 years of remarkable prosperity. As table 4 shows, shares of income earned by the bottom and the top halves of society have remained almost stagnant since World War II.

Class and Ethnicity: The Foundation of Ethnic Stratification

In the vast majority of cases, minorities are not only treated arbitrarily by the political forces of society, but they are also found in the lowest income groups.

Table 4.   *Aggregate Family Income*[1] *in the United States for Selected Years since World War II*

	1947	1955	1960	1966	1972	1977
	%	%	%	%	%	%
Lowest Fifth	5.0	4.8	4.8	5.6	5.4	5.2
Second Fifth	11.9	12.3	12.2	12.4	11.9	11.6
Third Fifth	17.0	17.8	17.8	17.8	17.5	17.5
Fourth Fifth	23.1	23.7	24.0	23.8	23.9	24.2
Highest Fifth	43.0	41.3	41.3	40.5	41.4	41.5
Top 5 Percent	17.5	16.4	15.9	15.6	15.9	15.7

SOURCE: U.S. Bureau of the Census, *Current Population Reports,* P–60, No. 118, March 1979, p. 45.

1.   The after tax distribution is even more skewed by class than this table suggests. The lower three fifths of the population actually receive less because of the regressive effect of local, state, and federal taxes. See Edward S. Herman, "The income 'counter-revolution,'" *Commonweal* (3 January, 1975).

Marx felt that economic oppression of minorities was necessary in capitalism. He extended his analysis to the American Civil War, the Irish question in the nineteenth century, and the English treatment of India. In all of these cases Marx saw the need for the bourgeoisie to exploit individuals because of their "race," to avoid the inevitable working-class rebellion against capitalism. That there were supposedly inferior races allowed the capitalist to convince the workers that their situation was not as desperate as it seemed. After all, the worker could have been black, Irish, or Indian. Additionally, minority group workers could be hired cheaply, providing a great margin of profit. There are many contemporary examples of this practice, but few so tragic as the use of illegal Mexican immigrants as fruit and vegetable pickers in Arizona and California. Marx felt that in such situations the minority would be blamed for being so inferior; because they are easily victimized, the capitalist would not be criticized.

Commenting in *Capital* on the American Civil War, Marx pointed out that the slave is a mere commodity. This is not because of his slavery as such, but because of how the political and economic systems treat him. That is, a minority is a thing to be used, like cotton, wood, or paper. Slavery is only a double curse upon his already servile relationship to those who own him. Marx reminded his readers: "*Mutato nomine de te fabula narratur*" (This could be thy story under a different name). For "slave trade," read "labor market; for Kentucky and Virginia, Ireland and agricultural districts of Scotland and Wales; for Africa, Germany" (Marx, 1973: 199).

Marx assumed that slavery and minority groups were vestiges of feudalism and would totally disappear under the yoke of capitalism. He stated this most profoundly in his essay "On the Jewish Question." Although the essay has been misunderstood as anti-Semitic, it is rather one of Marx's best discussions of the problems of minority status in capitalist society. For Marx, the various minorities evaporate in the sea of the proletariat, because all workers view themselves as victims of the economy. Therefore, no minority can be free in the context of the capitalistic, stratified society.

Political Responses by Ethnic Minorities

We can begin to understand the circumstance of minority groups in the political arena if we realize that they are victims of both class and race. This is the essential feature of ethnic stratification, and Marx makes us fully appreciate its dual nature. Because minorities usually have to live with both ethnic stereotypes and lower-class status, we would expect, given Marx's theory, that they would have a class orientation and a left-of-center political ideology. Albert Szymanski, using Gallup Polls for support, points out:

> *Non-whites are considerably more likely to oppose the death penalty (50 percent versus 34 percent), support amnesty for Vietnam War resisters (54 percent versus 39 percent), oppose reductions in federal social spending to create jobs (58 percent versus 44 percent). Sixty-eight percent of non-whites compared with 56 percent of whites opposed bombing Laos in 1973, 54 percent (versus 41 percent of whites) favored cutting off aid to Vietnam in 1973, and 44 percent (versus 36 percent of whites) thought that less money ought to be spent on defense. . . . In 1976, 60 percent of non-whites compared with 56 percent of whites favored ERA, while 81 percent of non-whites (versus 72 percent of whites) said they would vote for a qualified woman candidate for president of the United States. (Szymanski, 1978: 109)*

At least on the surface, there appears to be a significant difference in attitudes between whites and nonwhites in the United States. Studies of ethnic minorities such as Jews, Poles, and Italians have found a tendency to vote along class lines.

Even when individual members of a minority succeed economically, they are often still excluded from socializing with their class peers because of their minority status. In Richmond, Virginia, an all-white country club refused admission to former Kansas City Chiefs all-pro linebacker Willie Lanier. Lanier could easily have paid the club membership fee, but he was rejected. He is black. In other words, just because an individual breaks class barriers by earning a high income, there is no guarantee that racial barriers will fall at the same time.

Minority groups are by no means teeming masses of left-wing radicals. The poll results reported above show that nonwhites tend to lean more to the left than whites. But such tendencies are not unanimous among minority groups, and in a number of instances the differences between white and nonwhite attitudes are almost infinitesimal. For example, the other side of the poll is that 50 percent of nonwhites favor the death penalty, 46 percent oppose amnesty for Vietnam War resisters, 42 percent favor reduced federal social spending, and so forth. Additionally, nonwhites have more confidence than whites in big business (Szymanski, 1978: 109). So, although it is safe to *suggest* that nonwhites and (logically, from Marx's perspective) other minorities would be more left-oriented as groups, it would be a gross generalization automatically to make such an assumption about all the members of a minority group. It would also be wrong to assume that political involvement of minorities, especially in the protests of the 1960s, linked them with the left-wing movements primarily led by white college students. Indeed, while white protesters demonstrated over national issues, notably the Vietnam War, with New Left ideology, blacks overwhelmingly focused on local government issues. Additionally, most of the people involved in the protests of the 1960s "cannot be called 'poor.' They rank higher on every measure of social status than do their non-protesting fellows in their racial communities" (Eisinger, 1974: 603). The protests of the 1960s often involved the issue of minority politics, but did not necessarily signal a leftward orientation among minorities nor a broad class representation among those minorities involved.

The combination of race and ethnicity with class does have a political impact, but social scientists are still not fully certain of its dimensions. Our Marxist combination of race and class is very important to our analysis; the discussion above should not be construed as weakening the usefulness of this framework. Although it might appear that demonstrations composed of middle- and upper-class minority individuals do not fit our theory, we point out that just because poor minority group members tended not to participate does not mean that they did not support those who marched. After all, political silence[7] does not always indicate satisfaction with the status quo.

Political decisions concerning minorities often marry class and ethnicity; for example, American blacks tend to be poor and Episcopalians tend to be upper middle class. The combination of race and ethnicity with class, which Marx emphasized, is emphasized throughout this book as the key to understanding minority politics. In Marx's view, a society might try to redress blatant offenses against minorities, such as legal segregation, lynching, or the denial of voting rights. However, so long as society believed that class is a *natural* development, separate from political decision, there would be no essential change in minority status. No matter how educated, cultured, or wealthy a member of a minority is, society will react to him or her as a black, a Jew, a Chicano, and so on. Class is a hidden yet important part of American cultural values. Nowhere have the issues of social class and minority status been more ambivalent than in the area of constitutional interpretation by the Supreme

---

7. For a discussion of political silence, see Lewis Lipsitz, "On political belief: the grievances of the poor," in Phillip Green and Sanford Levinson (eds.), Power and Community: Dissenting Essays in Political Science (New York: Random House, 1970).

Court. The Court has consistently failed to confront the importance of class in changing racial attitudes. We shall now delve into some of this judicial history.

PREJUDICE AND THE LEGAL STRUCTURE: A HISTORICAL VIEW

It is an especially bitter irony that prejudice (literally, pre-judgment) is the exact opposite of what the American legal system purports to be. Yet throughout American history many cases involving minorities have been prejudiced because of the cultural biases of the times. In recent years there appears to have been a radical change away from this trend, toward a more egalitarian society. However, many Americans feel that Supreme Court rulings on desegregation of schools and housing and on the explosive issue of busing have *made* law rather than interpreted it. This section will discuss the implications of Supreme Court decisions on minority civil rights, and will relate them to our political view of social stratification.

The Role of the Court

The Supreme Court cannot originate cases; that is, it does not have the power to reach into society and right wrongs or select issues at its pleasure. To be heard by the Supreme Court, a case must be brought by a complaining party; the case must not be moot (that is, it must be relevant at that time); and at least four justices must agree to hear it.[8] The justices usually grant a *writ of appeal* or a *writ of certiorari* —that is, they agree to hear the case—in fewer than 5 percent of the cases appealed to them. The decision to hear a case rests on its importance to constitutional issues and its subsequent impact on other cases. Though it may appear that the Court decides a large number of questions, actually it substantially limits itself.

Pre–Civil War Law: The Subordination of Indians and Blacks

There were minority grievances against the United States at the time of the nation's founding. Most of these disputes involved blatant prejudice against American Indians or black slaves, and therefore revolved around the question of whether they were people in the eyes of the law. Although the question of class standing for minorities did not develop until the abolition of slavery, commentators as early as Alexis de Tocqueville saw in North America "naturally distinct, one might say hostile, races. Education, law, origin, and external features too have raised almost insurmountable barriers between them" (de Tocqueville, 1969: 42). This hostility led to total oppression of blacks and near extermination of Indians. Thus, the issue of class was not unimportant;

---

8. The Court refused to find in *DeFunis* vs. *Odegaard,* 416 U.S. 312 (1974), a case involving reverse discrimination, because DeFunis had already been admitted to law school and therefore there was no substantive question.

rather, the most important problem was the legal sanction of prejudice against minorities.

As early as April 1773, slaves petitioned legislators for the same rights that the colonies were fighting Britain for:

> SIR, THE EFFORTS made by the legislative of this province in their last sessions to free themselves from slavery, gave us, who are in that deplorable state, a high degree of satisfaction. We expect great things from men who have made such a noble stand against the designs of their fellow-men to enslave them. We cannot but wish and hope Sir, that you will have the same grand object, we mean civil and religious liberty, in view our next session. The divine spirit of freedom, seems to fire every human breast on this continent, except such as are bribed to assist in executing the execrable plan. . . . (Grant, 1968: 28)

In *Commonwealth of Massachusetts v. Jennison* (the Quock Walker case) in 1783, the chief justice of the Massachusetts Supreme Court decided that the Massachusetts Constitution declared "all men to be free," which is "totally repugnant to the idea of being born slaves," thereby nullifying the right to hold slaves in that state (Blaustein and Zangrando, 1968: 44–46). The concern over slaves' rights remained a national issue for the next 80 years, culminating in the Civil War. It is important to note that the issue of slaves' rights was not merely a conflict of North against South; it also led to controversies *within* each area of the country. For example, John Brown, who led the raid on Harper's Ferry, Virginia, was a Southerner; William Lloyd Garrison, the famous abolitionist, barely escaped lynching in Boston by jumping from a second-story window. These intrasectional conflicts would play a major role in civil rights interpretation after the Civil War.

During the same period the American Indian was losing both military and legal battles. The Cherokee tribes of Georgia, among the most sophisticated of all American Indians, had their own government and educational systems. They tried to resist a federally ordered removal through legal actions designed to force the state of Georgia to recognize their autonomy. Chief Justice John Marshall and the Supreme Court sided with the Indians, arguing that Georgia had no jurisdiction over their lands. However, President Andrew Jackson is purported to have said, "Justice Marshall has made his decision, now let him enforce it." Jackson ignored the Court and removed the Cherokees along the infamous "trail of tears"; during the march, one third of the tribe perished. Jackson considered the Indian relocation the most important accomplishment of his administration.

In the late 1850s Dred Scot, a black, sued his owner for keeping him in slavery after he had been brought into Illinois, a designated free area under the Missouri Compromise. This suit was one of the most important cases involving minorities in the nineteenth century. Scott's attorneys argued that as soon as he had been brought into a free territory, he became a free man. The

Supreme Court not only disagreed but also questioned whether any *freed* slaves had rights or could be considered citizens. "We think they are not," wrote Chief Justice Roger Taney for the court,

> *and that they are not included, and were not intended to be included, under the word "citizens" in the Constitution, and can therefore claim none of the rights and privileges which that instrument provides for and secures to citizens of the United States. On the contrary, they were at that time considered as a subordinate and inferior class of beings, who had been subjugated by the dominant race, and, whether emancipated or not, yet remained subject to their authority, and had no rights or privileges but such as those who held the power and the Government might choose to grant them. . . . (60 U.S. 393 [1857])*

Thus was citizenship redefined until the situation was rectified by the Civil War and the Thirteenth, Fourteenth, and Fifteenth Amendments. These amendments created a legal structure for minority rights, and the Fourteenth Amendment apparently addressed the question of class by guaranteeing "due process of law."

Reconstruction in the South

Most 1950s history texts end the story of the American civil rights struggle with the Civil War. However, this was only the beginning of a broad struggle by *all* minorities to win basic civil rights. The period after the Civil War was unsettled for all Americans, both politically and socially. Southerners were not sure what rights blacks had, and they spent a great deal of the decade after the war recovering from the devastation it had wrought. The Supreme Court whittled away at the Fourteenth Amendment protections for minorities in the so-called Slaughter House Case, 83 U.S. 36 (1873). It is especially ironic that this case so limited the Fourteenth Amendment, since it involved neither blacks nor discrimination. Instead, it was a suit by a group of New Orleans butchers against a syndicate that had an exclusive monopoly on butchering livestock in that city. They argued that such a monopoly violated the due process clause of the Fourteenth Amendment. The Supreme Court interpreted the amendment as protective only of *national* law; in other words, it held the states exempt from having to obey many of the provisions of the Constitution.

Building on this foundation, the cases of *United States* v. *Reese* and *United States* v. *Cruikshank* all but destroyed the impact of the Fourteenth and Fifteenth Amendments. *Reese* involved a black man who had sought to register to vote in Lexington, Kentucky. When he attempted to pay the required poll tax, it was refused. When he tried to vote on election day, he was again turned away. The federal government indicted the white election officials, but Chief Justice Morrison Waite, in his decision for the Supreme Court, refused to uphold the indictment. He argued that the Fifteenth

Amendment did not intend for states to accept all voters, but only that they could not discriminate on the grounds of race. In other words, blacks turned away from the polls had to prove that they had been prevented from voting *only* on the grounds of their race. *Cruikshank* involved a mob of whites who broke up a meeting of black voters and lynched two of the blacks. The Court failed to uphold the conviction of those responsible for the violence because the federal government had not demonstrated that the only reason the meeting was broken up was because of race. Additionally, the Court found that although the states are obligated not to deny equal protection of the laws, a mob attacking a black voters' meeting is not the same as a state.

> *It was a group of private individuals, and what they did was not "state action." And only state action—that is, action by the state itself in the form of a law or in the person of a public official—was covered by the Fourteenth Amendment. In short, it was not the federal government's business if a state failed to prevent a mob from interfering with a Negro group's right to assemble peaceably. (Kluger, 1975: 61)*

Thus, less than ten years after the Civil War—a war fought in large part to provide all Americans with equal rights—the Court was ready to destroy these protections completely.

One of the most important events of the era leading to this destruction of rights was the Hayes–Tilden election of 1876. Samuel Tilden actually beat Rutherford B. Hayes, but agreed to a questionable re-evaluation of the *electoral* vote if Hayes, the Republican, would end Reconstruction in the South. On its face, this agreement appears unimportant, for only parts of Virginia and the city of New Orleans were under federal rule. However, the Hayes-Tilden compromise was really an agreement to end federal enforcement of black rights in the South.

The period of eroding civil rights culminated in the Civil Rights Cases of 1883, 109 U.S. 3 (1883). The five suits involved the denial to "people of color" of accommodations in hotels and theaters. The Court decided that such a denial was no "badge of slavery," nor was it a state action. (The former would have been outlawed by the Thirteenth Amendment and the latter by the Fourteenth.) Thus, due process, which outlawed the use of race to determine class, was effectively nullified. In addition, the Civil Rights Act of 1875, which was in question in these cases, was found unconstitutional. This ruling effectively ended the period of Reconstruction and began an era of discrimination against black Americans and other minorities.

The End of Reconstruction: The Rise of Jim Crow Segregation

What happened in the 20 years following the Civil Rights Cases of 1883 cannot be understood absent from the historical context. This was the era in which the Bourbon South, the Populist movement, and Jim Crow laws were born. The Populists were trying to unify poor blacks and poor whites to outvote the Bourbons. The Bourbons, the ruling class in the South at the time, used the race issue to divide and ultimately destroy the Populists. Jim Crow laws, or segregation laws, were not new to the South, but they had never until this period been uniformly instituted. In fact, in some sections of the South certain types of segregation had not even been heard of.[9] All of the segregation laws were legitimized by *Plessy* v. *Ferguson,* 163 U.S. 537 (1896), which ignored the protection against state interference in the civil rights proffered in *Cruikshank* and found that separate but equal facilities were within the legitimate interpretation of the Constitution. In effect, *Plessy* made the political issues of race and class rigid and incapable of change.

Such court rulings not only led to a denial of civil rights to blacks in the South, but also served to legitimize violence against a people the Court saw as better "protected" in a segregated environment. During the 25-year period after *Plessy*, an estimated 100,000 blacks were killed in riots and lynchings. It should not be assumed that the black population was passive in the face of this violence. With the founding of the National Association for the Advancement of Colored People in 1909, blacks set in motion a series of cases for the protection of blacks' rights. Simultaneously, other groups brought legal actions trying to protect the civil rights of Orientals, Jews, Italians, and many other minorities. American society had interpreted *Plessy* as a license for wholesale discrimination against minorities.

The Supreme Court had begun to take the role of protector of minority groups by the time of *Moore* v. *Dempsey* in 1923 (261 U.S. 86 [1923]). In a race riot in Arkansas, more than 200 men, women, and children, both blacks and whites, had been killed. Seventy-nine blacks were accused of murder. Other blacks were whipped until they agreed to testify, and blacks were excluded from the jury. The trial took less than an hour; the court-appointed defense attorney called no witnesses and did not even put the defendants on the witness stand. Within five minutes a dozen blacks were found guilty of murder. The trial court sentenced them to death and gave 67 others extended prison terms. Justice Oliver Wendell Holmes, writing for the Supreme Court, reversed the convictions on the grounds that the trial had been a farce. But his decision strictly limited itself to the issue of discrimination because of race, and ignored any case that would open the question of class.

The Court continued to erode the implications of *Plessy* in *Powell* v. *Alabama,* 287 U.S. 45 (1932), and *Norris* v. *Alabama,* 294 U.S. 587 (1935). Both of these Supreme Court decisions involved the famous Scottsboro Case, the most sensational trial of the 1930s. Nine black teenagers, two of them 13 and 14, were accused of raping two white girls on a freight train on which all of them had been riding. One of the girls was a

---

9.   For insight into this period, see C. Van Woodward, Origins of the New South (Baton Rouge: Louisiana State University Press, 1972), and The Strange Career of Jim Crow (New York: Oxford University Press, 1966).

known prostitute, and most historians agree that the only crime the Scottsboro boys were truly guilty of was being black. The state refused to provide them an attorney and excluded all blacks from the jury. The *Powell* case guaranteed the right to an attorney in cases involving crimes punishable by death.[10] The *Norris* case did not uphold the guilty verdict, because blacks had been unfairly excluded from the jury. Even with these protections, the Scottsboro boys were imprisoned; the last one was released in the late 1960s.

Between the World Wars: The Legal Response to Southeast Europeans

The period between the two world wars was rife with discriminatory judicial actions against other minorities. These actions were legitimized by the "Red scare" of the early 1920s and by Attorney General Alexander Mitchell Palmer's anti-bolshevik attack. Palmer saw aliens and radicals as one and the same 30 years before the heyday of Senator Joseph McCarthy. Palmer arrested over 6,000 suspected radicals; over 600 of them were deported. This era resurrected not only anti-black and anti-minority sentiment, but also the Ku Klux Klan, and it gave birth to such figures as the anti-Semitic Father Charles Coughlin and Gerald L. K. Smith.

The Supreme Court, in *Whitney* v. *California* and *Gitlow* v. *New York,* gave an air of legitimacy to anti-foreign actions. Additionally, psychologists such as Lewis Terman, Robert Yerkes, and Henry Goddard added a social-scientific air of certainty to prejudice. They took Alfred Binet's IQ test, disregarding his anti-genetic and humanitarian views, and applied it to the immigration problem. "Goddard, in fact, took Binet's test out to Ellis Island and rushed back with the startling news that the majority of immigrants from Southern and Eastern Europe were actually feeble-minded, including 87 percent of Polish immigrants, 83 percent of Jews, and 79 percent of Italians" (Ryan, 1976: 305). William Ryan charges that these IQ tests, in combination with the isolationist environment of the 1920s, led to restrictive immigration laws that were blatantly racist. These laws effectively eliminated all nonwhite immigration to the United States. Fifteen years later they also led to the death of thousands of European Jews who, refused sanctuary in the United States, were sent to their deaths in Nazi concentration camps.

The most famous anti-foreign case of this era was the 1921 trial of Nicola Sacco and Bartolomeo Vanzetti, professed anarchists who were accused of murdering two guards during a payroll robbery. There was no compelling evidence against them; they are believed to have been convicted because their ideas were so repugnant to Boston society. The trial judge referred to

---

10.   Most Americans do not realize that the provision of an attorney, apparently guaranteed in the Constitution, had been under question for many years. In fact, the issue was not finally settled until the landmark case of *Gideon* v. *Wainwright* in 1963.

them privately as "those anarchist bastards," and the Supreme Court turned a deaf ear to the outcry against their conviction in the United States and around the world. In 1927 Sacco and Vanzetti were both electrocuted. Discrimination against immigrants became legitimate (Higham, 1968).

World War II: The Internment of Japanese-Americans

The most controversial event in modern American history involving an entire minority group was the internment of Japanese-Americans in concentration camps during World War II. One of the staunchest advocates of the internment was Earl Warren, then governor of California and later to be chief justice of the Supreme Court. In *Korematsu* v. *United States*, 23 U.S. 214 (1944), the Supreme Court found Japanese detention a reasonable legal device. Justice Hugo Black, speaking for the majority, was well aware of the racial implications of the case.

It should be noted, to begin with, that all legal restrictions which curtail the civil rights of a single racial group are immediately suspect. That is not to say that all such restrictions are unconstitutional. It is to say that courts must subject them to the most rigid scrutiny. Pressing public necessity may sometimes justify the existence of such restrictions; racial antagonism never can.

Certainly, this case could present major difficulties if the Court in the future sees it as a precedent. For in any case of racial subjugation it is obvious, given the intensity of racism, that it is impossible to distinguish "public necessity" from "racial antagonism."

Brown v. Topeka Board of Education: Separate Is Not Equal

After the war the Court returned to the issue of defining civil rights, further limiting the *Plessy* decision and relieving the outright prejudice against minorities. In 1950 the Justices found that separate but equal law schools in Texas were inherently unequal (339 U.S. 629 [1950]), as were segregated facilities within professional schools (339 U.S. 337 [1939]). In the latter case, a minority student had been segregated in class by being seated in an anteroom, and had even been assigned separate tables in the library and the cafeteria. Thus, it is important to recognize that the landmark case of *Brown* v. *Board of Education*, 347 U.S. 483 (1954), 349 U.S. 294 (1955), was the culmination of a trend in judicial decision making, rather than a radical departure. In *Brown* the Court found that "separate but equal" was "inherently unequal." It appeared that the court was willing to recognize the inherent tie between minority status and class. Many activists, such as Martin Luther King, Jr., were convinced that it had. This period saw a multitude of desegregation suits, initially in the South and ultimately throughout the United

States.[11] The Court also overturned decisions involving overt discrimination by police in the South (*Screws v. United States,* 325 U.S. 91 [1945]) and the use of restrictive covenants, agreements not to sell property to people of a certain race or religion (*Shelley v. Kraemer,* 334 U.S. 1 [1948]).

The 1960s and 1970s: The Growth of Civil Rights

Certainly, the era of the 1960s must be considered the peak of civil rights advocacy in the United States. Laws and cases proliferated, outlawing discrimination in housing, hiring, and education against racial and ethnic minorities, women, homosexuals, and the handicapped. However, during the 1970s, what has been called the Nixon court (Simon, 1973) somewhat altered the Court's direction. In one case, involving a desegregation order in Charlotte, North Carolina (*Swann v. Charlotte-Mecklenburg Board of Education*), the Court found that segregation in the city was due to previous segregation laws and, therefore, that busing was legal. However, in *Richmond v. State Board of Education,* 412 U.S. 92 (1973), two adjoining, predominantly white counties refused to join the city of Richmond in developing a joint integration plan. Richmond was and still is one of the most segregated communities in the South. Yet an equally divided Court upheld a lower court ruling that independent political entities (counties) could not be tampered with. In effect, this reinforced the white flight to the suburbs, by suggesting that if you are wealthy enough the laws enforcing integration do not have to affect you. You can either move or send your child to a private school. This case shows both the ambivalence of the Court in confronting racial discrimination and its unwillingness to deal with class issues.

In *Rodriguez,* 411 U.S. 1 (1973), the Court again refused to do anything to change economic inequities. Like the *Richmond* suit, *Rodriguez* challenged the "class" right to determine government boundaries. This case questioned the Texas system of financing public education through local taxes. Mexican-American parents in San Antonio argued that their children were unfairly penalized because they resided in a district with a low property tax base. In effect, this is the situation across the United States, which is one of the few nations in the world that decentralizes its school systems to this degree. The Court refused to deal with the question of minority prejudice and class. Justice Louis Powell, a native of Richmond and a former member of the Richmond board of education, delivered the opinion of the Court, which held that the Fourteenth Amendment did not concern issues of class.

The promises of school desegregation and equal education were quickly slipping away. However, this should not be seen as a change from the more liberal Warren court. As Frank I. Michelman points out, this is exactly where the Warren court drew the frontiers of equal protection. Michelman argues

---

11. See *Cooper v. Aaron* (the desegregation of Little Rock), *Goss v. Board of Education* (Nashville), *Griffin v. Prince Edward County School Board* (Virginia).

that if prices can be used to discriminate, there is no difference between discrimination against minorities and class discrimination:

> *It is no justification for deprivation of a fundamental right . . . that the deprivation results from a general practice of requiring persons to pay for what they get. Such a construction forces the inquiry on the crucial variable—the nature and quality of the deprivation—and thereby avoids the distractions, false stirring of hopes, and tunneling of vision which result from a rhetorical emphasis on acts of discrimination that consist in nothing more than charging a price. (Michelman, 1969: 58)*

In other words, as we noted in discussing Marx, relieving discrimination without resolving the issues of class gives minorities promises but little real change.

It should be obvious by now that it is impossible to separate discrimination based on race from discrimination based on wealth. If you can afford a better home, better education, better recreation, and a generally better environment for your children, then they have an advantage over others. The question is whether it is fair that this advantage is distributed largely along racial or ethnic lines. For the most part the Supreme Court of the United States has said that it cannot interfere in this area.[12] How minimal can protection of the rights of those at the bottom of society be? A crisis may be lurking for a "system that separates liberty from equality, and separates both from fraternity. And the problem has a final, disturbing dimension: So long as poverty and race remain so closely linked, the reminder that a nation cannot permanently endure half slave and half free will echo with haunting relevance" (Tribe, 1978: 1136).

Bakke: The Future of Affirmative Action

One additional example should suffice to demonstrate other legal ambivalence in this area. In *Griggs* v. *Duke Power Company* the Court argued that Duke Power had not intentionally discriminated against blacks but had discriminated in effect by the use of a device—diplomas and intelligence tests—that had nothing to do with job qualifications. The Court also expanded civil rights for women in the area of abortion and job protection. However, the justices found that companies are not required to give certain types of compensation to women on leave for childbirth, and they made a number of other limiting rulings. *Bakke* v. *University of California at Davis* also presents a significant threat to affirmative action legislation protecting minorities. Justice Powell again delivered the opinion of the Court. However, because the Court was so badly split (five to four), in all likelihood the *Bakke* case will resolve nothing. Rather, because of the close decision, and because

---

12.   For example, see *Harper* v. *Virginia Board of Elections* (1966), *Edwards* v. *California* (1942), and *Griffin* v. *Illinois* (1956). These cases appear to provide minimal protection for those at the bottom of American society.

FIGURE 4.   Median Income of Families, 1950–1974

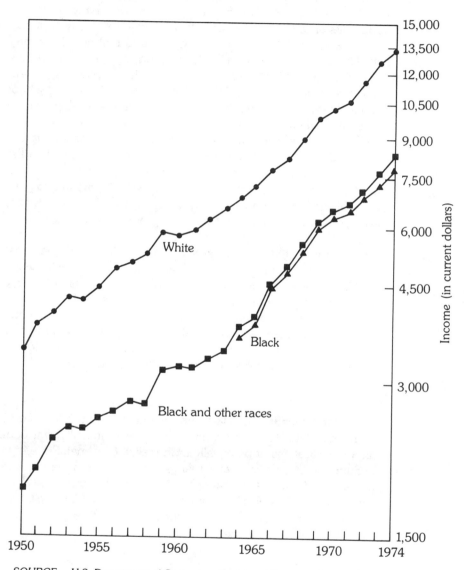

SOURCE: U.S. Department of Commerce, Social and Economic Statistics Adminsitration, Bureau of the Census.

Justice Powell's opinion appears to represent neither the liberal nor the conservative faction of the Court, *Bakke* will merely lead to a plethora of additional cases. And it is likely that even these will be contradictory, as the recent case of *U.S. Steel Workers* v. *Brian Weber* suggests. The legal impact of affirmative action will be discussed more fully in Chapter 8.

    In summary, it is important to understand that the Court has shown an ambivalent attitude toward minority groups. During certain historical periods it has been willing to challenge prejudice against minorities; however, the Court has demonstrated continuing reluctance to tamper with the issue of social class. The Court's decisions have tended to vary with public attitudes. Additionally, the Court has increasingly found that its rulings may have no actual impact. For example, the Court found segregation of schools in Prince Edward County, Virginia, unfair. Yet the school system is presently just as segregated as it was in the 1950s. (Now, however, the public school is almost entirely black, for the whites have set up a so-called private academy.) Indeed, the ambivalence of the Supreme Court, the "benign neglect" of the Nixon and Ford administrations, and the lack of a commitment to equality in the United States have led to a backlash that could place minorities, notably but not only blacks, further behind the white majority than ever before. Even after *Griggs* it is still harder for a black high school graduate to get a job than for a white dropout to do so (Newman et al., 1978: 39–43). And as figure 4 illustrates, there has been little narrowing of the income gap between 1950 and 1974.

The history of the legal struggle of minorities has amply demonstrated the importance of class in the politics of civil rights. For minorities who are easily identified because of their color or other characteristics, it has been almost impossible to change their status. The law is presently blind in terms of legal status, but it refuses to confront the issue of class. Even though private white institutions have made a mockery of the *Brown* case in a number of areas in the United States, the Court has argued that it is impossible to interpret the Constitution in a manner that prevents class discrimination.

SUMMARY

The interpenetration of class and race plays a vital role in contemporary American politics. This chapter has demonstrated that all forms of discrimination are political, either potentially or in reality. Our brief, 200-year history of the Supreme Court's civil rights rulings shows how important it is to view the political manifestations of civil rights in light of the economic advantages of majority status. This problem confronts not only the United States, but most other countries as well. *The* issue of the twentieth century, as W.E.B. Du Bois commented, is the color line.

Chapter

A Clash of Cultures: Varieties of Interethnic Group Contact

five

Chapters 3 and 4 focused on the importance of stratification to the social and political relations between ethnic groups. We have called attention to *class* membership as a determining factor in how members of ethnic groups organize their thoughts and actions. That emphasis is necessary, since the highly visible *cultural* differences between ethnic groups tend to overshadow the class differences that may accompany them. Nevertheless, we do not intend to belittle the importance of those more observable cultural differences. As we have tried to show throughout Chapters 3 and 4, the culture of an ethnic group is one determinant of how that group responds to its place in the stratification hierarchy. The culture of a group can influence its tendency to hold racist attitudes, its susceptibility to co-optation, and the militancy with which it pursues its political interests, among other behaviors. These behaviors may be initially encouraged by stratification, but they come to be expressed through already established cultural patterns.

Understanding the cultural patterns of ethnic groups appears at first to be a question of history. Tracing the sources of various cultural traditions would help us understand the nature and strength of those traditions and might, in fact, allow us to predict how a particular ethnic group might respond to a new situation. Historical analysis is essential, but it cannot by itself predict how ethnic groups are likely to act in a particular minority–dominant group situation. The reason is that minority–dominant group situations involve a wide variety of social and political pressures, which in turn greatly affect the cultures of the groups involved. The culture of an ethnic minority group entering a particular confrontation with a majority group will likely be different from the culture with which the minority entered previous confrontations. Each confrontation has an impact on the cultures of the groups involved, and the cultural changes so produced can be understood only in terms of those confrontations. For example, the culture of the descendants of the first Italian immigrants to the United States is very different from the culture of the descendants of those who stayed in Italy. A separation for close to a century explains part of this difference, but much more important is the social and political environment to which the first Italians immigrated. The use of the hyphen in ethnic group names (Italian-American, for instance) suggests more than dual nationality; the culture of an Italian-American in the 1970s has at least as much to do with America as it has to do with Italy (see Rolle, 1972; Jones, 1960: 200).

While a historical analysis could certainly find its way through the maze and confusion of immigration, some additional perspectives from the social sciences can simplify the process. In particular, the social sciences focus on the types of cultural interactions that occur when ethnic groups meet. This chapter will explore some of those types of interactions.

THE MYTH OF THE MELTING POT

The first type of cultural interaction soars through the imagination but seldom makes it off the ground in the real world. It is generally referred to as the melting pot (or amalgamation), and its lack of substance leads us to present it as a myth. It is dreamed of and fought for but seldom, if ever, achieved. Those who desire to see a melting pot occur in cultural interaction allow themselves to be convinced that it is occurring when, in fact, it is not. But for all its elusiveness, the melting pot is a basically simple idea that, in the world of cooking, if not of cultures, occurs daily.

The vast variety of our foods results from the transformation of ingredients during the different cooking processes. Ingredients melt or blend with each other as they are heated, so that the result is not just the sum of the ingredients but something new. In fact, it may be difficult when tasting a finished dish to determine exactly what ingredients went into it. In cooking, at least, the melting pot refers to the manner in which very different ingredients combine and become transformed through cooking in the pot. The result is (we hope) a tasty blend that reflects the contributions of the various ingredients.

By substituting the terms *culture* for *ingredient* and *society* for *pot*, we can move the idea from the kitchen into the world of cultures in contact. However, keep in mind the role of the cook. After all, the cook is responsible for holding back on the garlic so that it will not dominate the dish; when ethnic groups meet and their cultures come into contact, there is never a "cook" with an unbiased interest in the outcome of the cultural blend.

Applied to the world of cultural contact, *melting pot* refers to the mixing and blending of cultures through intermarriage (see Gordon, 1964a: 115–31; Newman, 1973: 63–67). While the melting pot depends on intermarriage to mix people from different ethnic groups, intermarriage by itself does not result in a melting pot. The cultural elements (ingredients), when blended, must produce a new culture. For example, two languages could combine vocabulary and grammar to form a new language; two religions could combine their beliefs and rituals to form a new religion; two styles of dress could merge into one new style; and two styles of cooking could combine to form one. Though they do not begin to catalog the many facets of culture, these examples provide some idea of the give and take involved in blending different cultures into one. The result would be a totally new culture, composed of equal parts of the individual cultures that blended to form it. The key words are *equal* and *give and take*. As we shall see, the problem with the melting pot is that the meeting of ethnic groups usually results in more taking than giving, and whatever cultural mixing occurs is usually anything but equal. If your culture happens to be the garlic, you will be more than happy to have it dominate the soup, regardless of how distasteful it is to the other diners.

The Melting Pot as Description

St. John de Crèvecoeur: Letters from an American Farmer.   The term *melting pot* has often been used by observers when two or more cultures appear to be mixing more or less equally. The early history of the United States prompted such descriptions, the first of them written in 1782 by J. Hector St. John de Crèvecoeur, a naturalized American citizen. In *Letters from an American Farmer*, Crèvecoeur describes the "mixture of English, Scotch, Irish, French, Dutch, Germans, and Swedes" in the United States:

> Can a wretch who wanders about, who works and starves, whose life is a continual scene of sore affliction or pinching penury; can that man call England or any other kingdom his country? A country that had no bread for him, whose fields procured him no harvest, who met with nothing but the frowns of the rich, the severity of the laws, with jails and punishments; who owned not a single foot of the extensive surface of this planet? No! Urged by a variety of motives, here they came. Everything has tended to regenerate them; new laws, a new mode of living, a new social system; here they are become men: In Europe they were as so many useless plants, wanting vegetative mold, and refreshing showers; they withered, and were mowed down by want, hunger, and war; but now by the power of transplantation, like all other plants they have taken root and flourished! . . . What then is the American, this new man? He is either an European, or the descendant of an European, hence that strange mixture of blood, which you will find in no other country. I could point out to you a family whose grandfather was an Englishman, whose wife was Dutch, whose son married a French woman, and whose present four sons have now four wives of different nations. He is an American, who, leaving behind him all his ancient prejudices and manners, receives new ones from the new rank he holds. He becomes an American by being received in the broad lap of our great Alma Mater. Here individuals of all nations are melted into a new

race of men, whose labors and posterity will one day cause great changes in the world. (Crèvecoeur, 1974: 5–6)

Crèvecoeur notes a degree of ethnic intermarriage in the early days of the American nation. While intermarriage may not have been as pervasive as he suggests, its presence at all is noteworthy, as it suggests a breaking of ties to Europe, where such intermarriage would never have occurred. But was intermarriage accompanied by a corresponding intermarriage of cultures, as Crèvecoeur suggests? Though American culture then and now is certainly unique, it is difficult to identify in it *major* contributions from any of the nationalities Crèvecoeur mentions, except for the English. Customs, and notably religions, from non-English ethnic groups survive in the United States, but for the most part, intermarriage resulted more in an "Englishification" of the population than in a melting pot of cultures. Indeed, most surviving non-English cultural elements in the United States today are those of ethnic groups that *did not* intermarry with the dominant English. While Crèvecoeur was certainly observing a new phenomenon, it is questionable that he was observing the melting pot in action.

Frederick Jackson Turner: The Frontier in American History.   In 1920 American historian Frederick Jackson Turner applied the melting pot label to the same group of northwest Europeans that Crèvecoeur had described, but Turner applied it to a later period of American history. In his influential book *The Frontier in American History,* Turner described the late eighteenth and early nineteenth centuries in America as a melting pot of European immigrants and attributed the phenomenon to the demands of frontier life. He suggested that the difficulties of settling the frontier made ethnic differences seem trivial by comparison.

> *The frontier is the line of most rapid and effective Americanization. The wilderness masters the colonist. It finds him a European in dress, industries, tools, modes of travel, and thought. It takes him from the railroad car and puts him in the birch canoe. It strips off the garments of civilization and arrays him in the hunting shirt and the moccasin. It puts him in the log cabin of the Cherokee and Iroquois and runs an Indian palisade around him. . . . Thus the advance of the frontier has meant a steady movement away from the influence of Europe, a steady growth of independence on American lines. . . . In the crucible of the frontier the immigrants were Americanized, liberated, and fused into a mixed race, English in neither nationality nor characteristics. (Turner, 1920: 3–4, 22–23)*

Once again, we ask whether American experience produced individuals who were "English in neither nationality nor characteristics." Turner does not stress the melting pot as strongly as did Crèvecoeur, but he does speak of the "creation of a new type" in describing the American pioneer, and he describes the northwest Europeans as "accepted," "intermingling," and "mixing." The "new type" formed from that "intermingling," however, seems highly English in characteristics if not in nationality. In the nineteenth century as well as in the eighteenth, the most pronounced non-English characteristics were found in those pockets of non-English ethnicity that maintained themselves apart. Rather than forcing groups together, the frontier could also be viewed as providing the space for non-English ethnic groups to isolate themselves to preserve their cultures. Elements of German and Scandinavian culture still exist in the rural areas of the Midwest where that isolation has prevailed; members of those cultures who were "accepted" and who "intermingled" in the cities have long since passed into cultural oblivion.

Turner did realize that the melting pot is not an everyday occurrence, but rather the product of a force of some magnitude, such as the frontier. Though that particular outside force was apparently not great enough to create a true melting pot, it nevertheless indicates that the give and take required for a melting pot is not entered into voluntarily by the ethnic groups involved. With that fact in mind, we shall explore a third and final example of the melting pot in hopes of finding a situation that more accurately fits the term. We shall turn to the history of Spanish America, and the mixing between early Spanish explorers and the native Indians. Although we shall argue that once again the melting pot is not fully operating, we shall find that Spanish America comes closer to the ideal and indicates some of the forces needed for the melting pot to occur.

The melting pot in Latin America: a case in point?   With the primary exception of Brazil, the area that is today Mexico and South America was initially conquered and "civilized" by Spanish explorers. The native peoples affected are commonly grouped together as "Indians," even though they represented a great many cultures. Between Columbus's landing in America in 1492 and the present, there has been considerable intermarriage between the Spanish and the Indians. Observers have commented on the new *raza* (race) so formed; even today, there is a Mexican-American political organization called *La Raza Unida* (the united race). Most Spanish-Americans today have either an Indian heritage or a mixed Spanish and Indian heritage; only a minority of the population can truthfully claim pure Spanish heritage. The situation has all the earmarks of a potential melting pot, but it is somewhat more complicated than that.

The most important difference between the Spanish control of South America and the English control of North America was probably the relative power of the two homelands in the sixteenth century. The power of England was on the rise; that of Spain was waning. The problems of Spain in Europe ultimately resulted in a forced isolation and independence for Spanish America. Early Spanish explorers had been content to ship American natural resources back to Europe, but the later Spanish colonists had to turn to the business of making their way on the new continent on a more permanent basis. Their adjustments involved intermarriage with Indians along with complex and shifting economic and political arrangements with the Indians.[1] In short, while their power was unequal, the Spanish and the Indians became increasingly dependent upon each other—a situation completely lacking between the English and Indians in the United States. The Spanish introduced a great many cultural elements to the Indian population (both through and independent of intermarriage) and picked up some cultural elements from the Indians. Once again, however, give and take was somewhat one-sided; the clear technological dominance of the Spanish allowed them to maintain a general cultural dominance throughout the area. Nevertheless, the dependence of the early Spanish on the Indians forced the groups to be relatively close. Whatever melting pot elements the situation had were caused by events beyond the control of the two ethnic groups involved. It was a matter of necessity rather than of choice.

In general, the melting pot depends on power. Whenever two or more ethnic groups come to share the same society, it is in the interests of each to maintain and promote its culture within that society. To the extent that your culture dominates a society, you and your offspring will have built-in advantages in all facets of life. If your culture does not dominate your society, you will have a built-in handicap. The giving required for the melting pot is never in the interest of any ethnic group, and therefore it is seldom if ever voluntary. It appears that the melting pot depends on two ethnic groups being equal in power so that neither can dominate the other. Historically, that almost never occurs; the closest approximation is through historical accidents, such as the case of Spanish America, where the more powerful group is forced to give a little to survive.

Although elements of the melting pot do occur, most situations to which the term is applied are misnamed. For that reason we recommend caution in using the term, and we suggest that it is more a myth than a reality. But lack of basis in reality has not hindered belief in a great many myths; that is the case of the melting pot, an idea too appealing to be dropped. As we have seen, ideas and beliefs about ethnic groups are often just as important to this discussion as are facts. We cannot ignore ideas about the melting pot.

The Melting Pot as Ideology

An *ideology* is an idea that reflects the interests of the person or group that promotes it. A rich person, for instance, would clearly have a vested interest in promoting the idea of private property. For that person, the idea of private property is an ideology. We want to know, of people to whom the idea of the melting pot appeals, which of their interests the idea promotes. Since a

---

1. For a more detailed history of Spanish America, see George M. Foster, Culture and Conquest: America's Spanish Heritage (Chicago: Quadrangle Books, 1960); and Magnus Morner, Race Mixture in the History of Latin America (Boston: Little, Brown, 1967).

powerful ethnic group has everything to lose in a melting pot, it is not surprising that the melting pot is an ideology of minority groups.

One of the earliest and certainly one of the most colorful presentations of the melting pot as ideology is offered by Jewish-American playwright Israel Zangwill. In his 1909 play, *The Melting Pot*, Zangwill creates the character of David, a Jewish immigrant from Russia, who presents the ideology.

> DAVID   *Not understand! You, the Spirit of the Settlement! Not understand that America is God's Crucible, the great Melting-Pot where all the races of Europe are melting and re-forming! Here you stand, good folk, think I, when I see them at Ellis Island, here you stand in your fifty groups, with your fifty languages and histories, and your fifty blood hatreds and rivalries. But you won't be long like that, brothers, for these are the fires of God you've come to —these are the fires of God. A fig for your feuds and vendettas! Germans and Frenchmen, Irishmen and Englishmen, Jews and Russians —into the Crucible with you all! God is making the American.*

> MENDEL   *I should have thought the American was made already— eighty millions of him.*

> DAVID   *Eighty millions! Eighty millions! Over a continent! Why, that cockleshell of a Britain has forty millions! No, uncle, the real American has not yet arrived. He is only in the Crucible, I tell you —he will be the fusion of all races, perhaps the coming superman. (Zangwill, 1909: 31–34)*

Zangwill provides a tentative addition to the idea of the melting pot. In describing the forming American as "perhaps the coming superman," he suggests that the melting pot may create not only a new culture but a naturally superior culture as well. This may be an extension of the social Darwinism prevailing when the play was written, which held that only the best elements of anything will survive competition—but note what it adds to the ideology: the melting pot is presented as necessary for cultural improvement. Ideologies tend to be ideas "for sale," and naturally they are packaged as attractively as possible.

Israel Zangwill was a Jewish immigrant from England. Jewish immigrants from northwest Europe faced relatively little discrimination when they first arrived in America, but they later experienced the anti-Semitism directed against Jews from eastern Europe, who began to arrive around 1900. It was during this period of American history that Zangwill wrote *The Melting Pot*. By 1909, Jews in the United States had much more to gain through a melting pot than did Americans of English or other northwest European stock.

In general, the idea of the melting pot would probably appeal to any minority group that is forced to give up much of its culture to survive in a society dominated by another culture. If put into practice, the melting pot would allow their culture some recognition, thereby benefiting their group. On one hand they would benefit from the economic and political equality that the melting pot would give them. On the other hand, the melting pot would allow them to maintain at least part of their culture by introducing elements of that culture into the national life. Because powerful ethnic groups tend to deny both of these benefits by their domination, it is not surprising that many minority groups find the idea of the melting pot appealing.

THE RESPONSE OF THE DOMINANT GROUP

We turn now to less mythical descriptions of cultures in contact; specifically, we turn to a variety of descriptions that are either promoted by or generally acceptable to the dominant ethnic group in the society. One could argue that *any* variety of cultural contact must be more or less acceptable to the dominant group; if it were not, they could probably alter the situation. That argument has a great deal of merit, but we prefer to emphasize *degrees* of acceptability. This section deals with situations either promoted by the dominant group or generating at least the tacit acceptance of the dominant group. The following section examines situations that usually achieve, at best, the grudging acceptance of the dominant group and that are never promoted by them.

Genocide and Expulsion

Genocide is actions by the dominant group that cause the deaths of most or all members of a given subordinate group. These actions might be systematic and intentional, as they were in Nazi extermination camps; or they might be largely unintentional, as was the spread of smallpox among American Indians after the arrival of the Europeans. (But even "unintentional" genocide can be noticed and encouraged. There is evidence that smallpox was intentionally spread by European colonists who sent blankets infected with smallpox into Indian villages [McNeill, 1976: 251].) We focus here only on intentional genocide.

Expulsion refers generally to the physical removal of most or all members of a subordinate group from within the boundaries of a nation state. Under this heading, we might include the removal of eastern United States Indian tribes to reservations west of the Mississippi before that land was part of the United States.

Genocide and expulsion are clearly different responses on the part of the dominant group, but we discuss them together for several reasons:

1. Both genocide and expulsion are extreme responses by the dominant group that have extreme consequences for the minority group. Their use indicates that the minority group in question has come to be viewed as an extreme "problem" by the dominant group: either the minority group cannot be exploited, or it stands in the way of important dominant group objectives, or both. Because American Indians committed both offenses, they were both killed and moved.

2. Genocide and expulsion often occur together. The dominant group's use of either usually indicates that its primary goal is to be rid of the minority group in question. Both killing and removing fulfill that goal. Depending on prevailing moral codes, the dominant group may fluctuate between the two tactics. An important exception was the Nazi response to Jews. The particular anti-Semitic ideology of the Nazis made expulsion too mild a gesture, since the Nazi goal was to eliminate Jews not only from Germany but from everywhere else as well. We should also note that while official moral codes may preclude the use of genocide, an unofficial policy of "careless" expulsion may result in a good many deaths.

3. Genocide and expulsion are difficult and/or expensive for the dominant group. When you consider that minority groups can usually be exploited and thereby make the dominant group wealthy, it is clear that both genocide and expulsion represent a flow of energy in the other direction. For purely economic reasons, both genocide and expulsion are tactics of the last resort.

4. Genocide and expulsion are both rare, at least in the modern industrial world. These tactics are usually not highly desirable from the standpoint of the dominant group—and certainly from the minority group's point of view. The dominant group will clearly prefer some form of exploitation; faced with the alternatives of murder or exile, most minority groups will accede to that preference.

5. Finally, both genocide and expulsion end the minority–dominant relationshp. Two ethnic groups must share the same political boundaries (or country) before they can be labeled minority and dominant. Genocide and expulsion represent the dominant group's inability to cope with that co-existence.

Perhaps because they are extreme, genocide and expulsion are clear and simple concepts. They may be employed for different reasons, but they are always a tactic of last resort. As we look next at the various continuing relationships that minority and majority groups work out, keep in mind the consequences when those relationships do not work out.

Segregation

Segregation is the dominant group's decision to separate itself, either socially or physically, from a given minority group. When that separation occurs, the minority group may be described as segregated. Remember that the term *segregation* refers only to group separation instigated by the *dominant* group; when separation is the *minority* group's choice, it is *separatism.* As we shall see, the two are very different.

Social segregation is a situation in which two ethnic groups live near each other and interact with each other regularly but only on a highly formalized basis. For example, in a master–slave relationship there is considerable interaction, but all interaction follows rigid cultural norms of formality.[2] Master

---

2. See Kenneth M. Stampp, The Peculiar Institution: Slavery in the Ante-Bellum South (New York: Vintage Books, 1956); and Stanley Elkins, Slavery (New York: Grosset & Dunlap, 1963).

and slave interact in terms of limited social roles and not as individuals who might aspire to a more well-rounded relationship. They are not and cannot be friends in any sense of the word. In such a situation, people can talk to each other every day without ever knowing each other.

Physical segregation is a situation in which two ethnic groups live spacially apart from each other within the same political boundaries. For example, the decision of the dominant group has placed American Indians in the reservation system. By its very nature, physical segregation includes social segregation; for this reason it is a more extreme measure on the part of the dominant group. In fact, there is only a very fine line between physical segregation and expulsion—but as we shall see, it is a very important line.

Social segregation.   As we said above, social segregation is characterized by regular but highly formalized interaction between the minority and the majority group. Interaction may be limited to the giving and receiving of orders, or it may encompass a wider range of human activities. In either case it is rigidly controlled. This control usually results in ritualized interaction patterns that allow people to function without becoming personally involved with each other. A ritual of everyday life, for example, is the standard greeting between acquaintances. To "Hello, how are you?" you may respond, "Fine, thank you, how are you?"—even if your doctor has given you only two weeks to live. The ritual allows you to interact with people with whom you are not close; it conveys an *image* of friendliness and closeness without the *reality*. A ritualized interaction pattern provides an excellent way to maintain social distance. Maintaining social distance is one goal of the dominant group that sets up a system of social segregation. It needs the minority group's physical presence but does not want too much social closeness. But why should the dominant group want the minority around, in the first place?

Social segregation almost always is accompanied by exploitation. The socially segregated minority has usually been maneuvered into activities that benefit the dominant group at minority expense. For example, slavery forced Africans into a variety of activities from field work to house work. Exploitation depends upon limiting the options of the exploited group so that they have no choice but to be exploited. The institution of slavery certainly accomplished that, but it also brings up one of the drawbacks of exploitation for the dominant group: if you exercise your power to force an individual to work against his or her will, you must stay nearby to make sure that your will is carried out. The more extreme the exploitation, the closer you need to stay.

High levels of exploitation not only require the presence of the dominant group but also provide fertile ground for that dominant group to develop feelings of prejudice or racism toward the exploited minority. There are two possible, related explanations for the growth of these negative attitudes. First, the dominant group very likely fears the exploited minority. Although they may be in no immediate danger, they can imagine how angry they would be in the minority's place. The fear of the potential expression of this anger can easily turn to hatred of anticipation directed against the minority; in a sense, the exploited minority is hated for acts committed only in the imagination of the dominant group. In such a situation, any expression of anger or revolt by the minority will be blown out of proportion by the dominant group, intensifying that hatred. The fear of American slave owners of a slave revolt is an example. The constant white fear of a black uprising was not supported by facts. The few uprisings that did occur were both small and largely unsuccessful from the slaves' point of view, only intensifying white fears of the future.[3]

A second reason for the growth of prejudice and racism in a situation of exploitation is the dominant group's need to justify the exploitation. The dominant group can live more comfortably with the gross and obvious inequality inherent in exploitation if they first define the exploited minority as inferior and deserving no better. The extreme form of prejudice called racism serves this purpose well by reducing the "other race" practically to the animal level in the minds of the dominant group. This makes it easier to treat them like animals. A similar process operates in wartime when the enemy is defined as something less than human; it is much easier to kill a Jap, a Kraut, or a Gook than a human being.[4]

Reasons for the rigid and formalized rules of interaction that occur within social segregation are now more apparent. The exploited minority must be kept close to the dominant group so that orders may be given and services rendered. However, it is a strained relationship because of exploitation, and considerable effort must be expended to find patterns of social interaction that permit the relationship to function. That relationship requires social distance; the formalized rituals that characterize social segregation permit that distance to be maintained. It is one of the marvels of human societies that people can live daily within touching distance, yet live social worlds apart through the rules of social interaction.[5]

Physical segregation.   Of all the ongoing relationships that minority and majority groups might establish, physical segregation is probably the most extreme. You recall that expulsion ends the minority–dominant relationship by moving the minority outside the political boundaries controlled by the dominant group. Physical segregation either moves the minority or isolates them where they are, but in either case, they remain within the political boundaries controlled by the dominant group. However isolated the minority group becomes through physical segregation, they nevertheless remain a

---

3. For more on white fear of slave revolts, see Stampp, The Peculiar Institution, pp. 134–40.

4. Language is usually a key to how the speaker defines the situation. For an elaboration on this theme, see Haig Bosmajian, The Language of Oppression (Washington, D.C.: Public Affairs Press, 1974).

5. See Peter Berger and Thomas Luckmann, The Social Construction of Reality (Garden City, N.Y.: Doubleday, 1966); and Erving Goffman, The Presentation of Self in Everyday Life (Garden City, N.Y.: Doubleday, 1959).

minority group, because their existence is ultimately under the control of a much more powerful group.

The best that a physically segregated minority can usually hope for is to be ignored. Although being ignored may not seem very undesirable, it is often the case that they are ignored only when things are not going well for them. For example, some tribes of American Indians have been moved to reservations; others have been permitted to remain on their lands, which have been declared a reservation. In either case, concern for the Indian usually comes last. Tribes that have been moved had the initial misfortune to be occupying land desired by Europeans. Tribes that have not been moved generally occupy land of little value. When reservation land comes to have value, or when resources on it (such as water or oil) become valuable, the European majority in the United States has a habit of noticing that value and exercising its dominance. When water is short and there is a choice between the Indians' animals and the white ranchers' cattle downstream, the political decision is usually made in favor of the white ranchers' cattle. However isolated a physically segregated minority may appear to be, the power of the state always lies in the background, to enter the picture when the interests of the dominant group become involved.[6]

Many American Indians prefer to have as little contact as possible with European culture. To them, the reservation system may not be the best of all possible worlds, but it is a step in the right direction—toward group separation. As we shall see later in this chapter, group separation can be a workable alternative, but to benefit from it the minority must have some control over the situation. Physical segregation, which by definition occurs on the dominant group's terms, can be one of the worst situations in which a minority might find itself. There are two major reasons for this: physical segregation imposes both isolation and a lack of power on the minority.

The lack of power that accompanies physical segregation prevents the minority from making their isolation a positive feature of their life. Many minorities, including some American Indian tribes, might prefer to remain separate to maintain their distinctive culture. But to maintain that culture, the minority must have at least enough group power to avoid dominant group cultural interference. For example, the Indian reservation was invaded by a school system organized by the Bureau of Indian Affairs along the lines of European culture; classes, of course, are taught in English (see Dumont and Wax, 1969). It is difficult for the older generation of any culture to "sell" its way of life to the younger generation when that culture is ignored or demeaned at every turn. Much of the force of any culture is its support by

---

6. See William H. Veeder, "Federal encroachment on Indian water rights and the impairment of reservation development," in Rudolph Gomez, Clement Cottingham, Russell Endo, and Kathleen Jackson (eds.), The Social Reality of Ethnic America (Lexington, Mass.: D. C. Heath, 1974); and Alvin M. Josephy, Jr., "Freedom for the American Indian," in N. Yetman and H. Steele (eds.), Majority and Minority: The Dynamics of Racial and Ethnic Relations (Boston: Allyn & Bacon, 1975).

sources of authority within the group. If part of the culture is transgressed, the force of the group will come down against the transgressor. In the case of physical segregation, where another culture stands in the wings, the minority "deviant" may earn rewards in the outside world by flaunting the rules of his or her immediate group. The physically segregated minority takes the line of exasperated parent: how can you raise children properly with all the bad influences out there?

If group power might turn isolation into a positive factor for the minority group, the *lack* of group power makes any amount of isolation a negative factor. The lack of power in the physically segregated minority prevents the group from rewarding its members for following the cultural ways; outside of emotional rewards, they simply have nothing material to give. Therefore the best route of individual advancement may well be conformity to the dominant culture (where the material wealth lies)—but group isolation makes that conformity difficult. To succeed in the dominant group's world usually requires a wide range of social and intellectual skills, particularly in the economic sector. The only way to acquire any kind of human skill is to have some kind of contact with another human who has that skill. Physical isolation prevents this. In the few social arenas where the dominant group's culture may be present (such as education), the contact is rarely sufficient to allow minority individuals to compete with dominant group individuals who live that culture 24 hours a day (even dreaming in it). The isolation of physical segregation keeps a minority group perpetually handicapped in its ability to compete in the dominant group's world.

Assimilation

As we approached the concept of the melting pot, we can best approach the concept of assimilation through a food analogy. Instead of focusing on the cook, however, we shall focus on the consumer. When you eat something, your body "attacks" it in an effort to break it down into substances that can be used to fuel your activities. Various proteins, fats, sugars, and so on are separated to be used or stored, while that which is undigestible is passed through. Several hours after a meal, the prepared dish you consumed has disappeared, but it is still present in its changed forms. Its impact can be measured in terms of the energy you expend (which it fuels). If you exercise too little and/or eat too much, its impact can be measured in a bigger you. In either case, you have assimilated the food. The food has not disappeared; it has simply had its form changed and been incorporated by a very powerful system—your body.

In the social world, *assimilation* is the incorporation of one ethnic group into the continuing culture of another ethnic group. There are several levels or forms of social assimilation, but its ultimate form is very similar to our food analogy. One ethnic group (usually a relatively weak one) intermarries with members of another ethnic group, simultaneously losing or giving up its cultural distinctiveness in favor of the culture provided by the stronger ethnic group. In a less extreme form, the weaker ethnic group might not intermarry with the stronger ethnic group, but after several generations takes on most of the culture of the stronger ethnic group. In either case, the assimilated ethnic group is not destroyed; it simply becomes part of the stronger ethnic group through the process of assimilation. Like the digested food, the original culture of the assimilated ethnic group is no longer recognizable or distinct. However, none of its component parts (its members) have been lost. They have simply become part of a very powerful social system through taking on its culture.[7]

Assimilation in one form or another is one of the most common outcomes when two cultures come into contact. This is particularly true in the history of the United States, in which a basically English culture has become the dominant way of life to which all newcomers must conform. As we said earlier, it is always in the interest of any ethnic group to promote its culture when it comes into contact with other ethnic groups. The more its culture comes to dominate a society, the more competitive advantage its members will have in that society. In the United States, people of English descent had the power to promote their culture as the dominant one in the early days of the nation. The English culture has not lost that domination since; over 200 years later, it is still people of basically English descent who hold a competitive advantage in the United States. Social assimilation, unlike the physiological version, is not accomplished in a matter of hours. It is a long process accomplished in a variety of stages.

Behavioral assimilation (acculturation).   The first level of assimilation is often referred to as acculturation. To emphasize the relationship of this level to the more general process of assimilation, we shall borrow an alternate term from Milton Gordon and refer to the level as behavioral assimilation (Gordon, 1964a: 67, 70–71). However labeled, the idea is the same. *Behavioral assimilation* refers only to that aspect of assimilation that involves the behavior of individuals in the minority group; when their behavior conforms to the general cultural patterns of the dominant group, they may be described as behaviorally assimilated. We use "behavior" in the broadest possible sense. Conforming to another culture involves changes in language behavior, religious behavior, dressing behavior, child raising behavior, play behavior, sexual behavior, eating behavior, and even thinking behavior. Although this list of cultural elements is not exhaustive, the idea is fairly simple: behavioral assimilation is an effort by members of the minority group to conform in every possible manner.

In introducing the term, Milton Gordon emphasizes its voluntariness for the minority. According to Gordon, behavioral assimilation is a conscious deci-

7. See Milton Gordon, Assimilation in American Life (New York: Oxford University Press, 1964); and William M. Newman, American Pluralism: A Study of Minority Groups and Social Theory (New York: Harper & Row, 1973) for a general discussion of assimilation.

sion made by members of the minority group; it may be the only element of assimilation over which the minority group does have control (Gordon, 1964b: 151). However, we suggest that control is ultimately somewhat limited by the dominant group. While the minority group must first decide to strive for conformity, they may have limited access to models of the behavior to which they want to conform. For example, the immigrant to the United States who wants to learn English must first find a speaker of English from whom he or she can learn. If the model happens to be another immigrant, who speaks English with a foreign accent, then the new immigrant will learn English with that same accent. The highest desire to conform will never allow that immigrant to speak like a member of the Harvard graduating class. If we generalize this example to all of the kinds of behavior that make up culture, the limits of behavioral assimilation become clear. The dominant group can allow or prevent access to the various arenas of cultural activities. The minority ethnic group member cannot learn without first coming into contact, whether the object of learning be language, physical or mental skills, or table manners. This observation will be very important later, when we examine the interplay between behavioral assimilation and other levels of assimilation that permit this contact.

To the extent that behavioral assimilation is voluntary for members of the minority ethnic group, the motives involved in the decision are fairly clear and basic in terms of survival. In the extreme, the dominant group may outlaw elements of the ethnic minority culture. In the United States, the institution of slavery included a variety of laws designed to break down African culture (Stampp, 1956: 362–63; Herskovits, 1941). Similar laws were passed relating to several American Indian religions, most notably the Native American Church (Blauner, 1975: 348). Thus, to avoid legal prosecution or other sanctions, members of a minority group may decide to conform.

A less extreme situation emphasizes the carrot more than the stick. Behavioral assimilation is often a requirement for employment. The ethnic minority is not required to conform, but rather encouraged to conform. Unless the individual can turn to an established minority ethnic community for employment, he may not have much choice but to conform, but his situation is certainly less oppressive than if nonconformity were outlawed. Since most sources of employment are controlled by the dominant group (by definition), the requirement of cultural conformity becomes a standard rule and thereby a common motive for behavioral assimilation.

Structural assimilation.   While behavioral assimilation is at least partly under the control of the minority group, structural assimilation is *completely* under the control of the *dominant* group. *Structural assimilation* refers to the dominant group's social acceptance of the minority group (Gordon, 1964a: 110–111). This acceptance may occur on two levels—the *secondary* and the *primary.*

Structural assimilation at the level of secondary relationships refers to the dominant group's acceptance of minority individuals only in institutional or public social settings. At this level the minority individual is permitted to work alongside dominant group members, to vote with them, to live near them, and to attend school with them. Any social setting that might be defined as public is included in this level of structural assimilation.

Structural assimilation at the level of primary relationships represents ultimate acceptance. When an ethnic minority group is accepted at this level, its members become welcome as private club members, personal friends, and finally, marriage partners. In such situations individual members of the dominant group have almost total discretion as to the people with whom they wish to associate. These are also situations for which most people maintain their highest standards. You can easily work with an individual whom you might object to inviting to a party. You might enjoy another individual's presence at a party whom you would hate to have as a son-in-law. While such feelings vary from individual to individual, they also occur in generalized form relating to the ethnicity of entire groups of people. When most members of the dominant group have no objections *based on ethnicity* to a certain minority group member as a potential spouse, then that minority group may be described as structurally assimilated at the primary level. More simply, the minority may be described as completely assimilated.

The three basic levels of assimilation tend to occur in the order in which we discussed them. That is, behavioral assimilation is almost always a prerequisite for structural assimilation at the secondary level. (This can be seen in the example above concerning cultural conformity and employment.) The same relationship holds between the two levels of structural assimilation. Minority groups rarely achieve total assimilation until they have first, as a group, achieved structural assimilation at the secondary level. Of the many reasons for this order, perhaps the most important is social class. Structural assimilation at the secondary level means, among other things, that the minority has achieved enough upward social mobility to have stepped out of rigid ethnic stratification and into a more random distribution throughout the stratification system. At this level of assimilation, they might better be described as a subculture than as a minority group. When this observation is coupled with the more general observation that people tend to party and marry within their class, it becomes clear that the minority must first occupy the same class with dominant group members before gaining ultimate acceptance from them.

Assimilation is neither an inevitable nor a one-way process. The assimilation of any particular ethnic minority may (a) never begin, (b) stabilize at any level, or (c) reverse direction, should either the minority group or the dominant group desire it. Of the three possibilities, the most common is the relative stabilization of a given ethnic minority at a particular level of assimilation, often between behavioral and structural assimilation. Since behavioral assimilation at least begins as a minority group decision, it is not uncommon for a minority group to embark on a course of assimilation when the dominant group has an altogether different arrangement in mind.

The major motive for behavioral assimilation is to achieve at least structural assimilation at the secondary level. That is the level at which the minority hopes to find decent jobs and decent living conditions. If those rewards are not forthcoming, behavioral assimilation becomes almost worse than no assimilation at all. By giving up their culture in hopes of achieving greater social acceptance, the minority group has burned a very important bridge. They can no longer either console themselves or take pride in themselves through their traditional cultural ways. This situation can lead to minority self-hatred. The minority group has accepted a culture that continues to degrade them. In a sense, then, their own (adopted) culture degrades their self-worth. For example, during certain periods in the United States lighter skin and straighter hair became valuable attributes within the black community. It is dangerous to accept anyone else's standards if those standards include a low opinion of you (see Poussaint, 1974).

Assimilation can also stabilize between the two levels of structural assimilation. This may be highly desirable from several standpoints. Since structural assimilation at the secondary level brings many practical benefits to the minority group, their main (or only) concerns may be satisfied. They may, in fact, have no interest whatsoever in becoming any closer to the dominant group. The dominant group may also be satisfied with this situation, for example, if the ethnic minority in question is useful economically but bothersome to have at parties or in the family.

Stabilization at any level of assimilation is relative. Societies do not stand still, even if they appear to do so over a generation or two or three. When two ethnic groups work out an arrangement that appears to be stable, that means only that the arrangement either is agreeable to both parties or cannot be altered by the party to whom it is disagreeable. Either situation might change over time. Much of this continuing process occurs within the political arena; it will be dealt with in Chapter 6.

Finally, we shall return to our earlier observation that behavioral assimilation depends on the dominant group. Behavioral assimilation requires that the minority group conform its behavior patterns to the culture of the dominant group. As we pointed out earlier, this level of assimilation begins as a decision of the minority group, but it continues only if the dominant group allows that minority contact with the behavior it hopes to learn. Some elements of culture are more dependent on this permission than others; style of dress, for instance, is relatively observable and can be copied. It is also a relatively important element of culture for the minority that hopes to assimilate behaviorally. Just as clothing is readily visible on the bodies of dominant group members, so the minority group member can be readily observed if he has not copied the style. But note the difficulties of behavioral assimilation, even in clothing. Clothing can be very expensive. Many people, in fact, wear expensive clothing simply to *limit* the ability of others to copy them. Because minority status carries no surplus of wealth, the expense of copying clothing styles can prohibit the copying. (A physically segregated minority could not even make use of the visibility of clothing.) Thus, even the most obvious elements of culture are not as easily assimilated as they might seem.

A more important and more complicated element of culture is language. A dominant group that demands cultural conformity will demand language conformity at the very least; the power that accompanies dominance allows them to force the minority to become bilingual. And a foreign language cannot be put on like a suit of clothes. Except for young children (to whom vocabulary and syntax may come more easily than zippers and buttons), the mastery of a second language takes many years. An adult who learns a second language may speak it with a "foreign" accent that persists indefinitely; the music of language comes easily only to children. The minority group member who wishes to assimilate behaviorally in terms of language is obviously fighting an uphill battle, which in many cases can never be totally won. Even for a child, the battle is difficult.

Although a child has the ability to reproduce language perfectly, he or she can reproduce only that language encountered in the social environment. The physically segregated minority has the greatest problems, but any degree of social separation from the dominant group is a hindrance. If the child goes to school with members of only his or her ethnic group and returns home at night to an ethnic family, the child will likely learn a dialect of the dominant group's language. In the United States, an ethnic child may encounter Standard American English (the official dialect of English approved by the dominant group) only from a teacher. And depending upon the child's school system, Standard American English may not be available even at school. Even if the child's teacher does speak "properly," the child's emotional attachment to the teacher can rarely compare with that felt for friends and family.[8] As a result, ethnic children in the United States usually learn an ethnic version of English that varies from Standard American English in any number of ways, from vocabulary and grammar to pronunciation and intonation. Even a slight variation in the child's speech will prompt most listeners to notice the difference—and thereby the ethnic difference. The more variation, of course, the more difficulty the child will have later if he or she should attempt to master the standard language; learning a different dialect of one language is not always much easier than learning an altogether different language.

Several social changes relating to language have had an impact on minority–dominant group relations. Television in the United States has made access to Standard American English much more available. The classroom teacher is now joined as a language model by the newscaster, the commercial, and the situation comedy. Because of the wide availability of television, it is difficult today to find children in the United States who have no facility with English. Segregation no longer provides total isolation.

---

8.   For more on the role of language in the public school classroom, see Courtney Cazden, Vera John, and Dell Hymes (eds.), The Functions of Language in the Classroom (New York: Teachers College Press, 1971).

In looking at behavioral assimilation in terms of dress and language, our intent has been to illustrate the relationship between behavioral assimilation and the forms of structural assimilation, which allow more thorough entry into the dominant group's culture. A minority group member may learn elements of the dominant group's culture when the dominant group permits it. Dress and language are only two elements of that complicated entity we call culture. The difficulty encountered by a minority group member in conforming language behavior is repeated many times over, in all the other arenas of behavior that make up culture.

THE RESPONSE OF THE MINORITY GROUP

We turn now to arrangements of minority–dominant relations that are generally promoted by the minority group instead of by the dominant group. As we said earlier, dominant groups must grant at least grudging acceptance to these arrangements; by virtue of their dominance, they could and would interfere, should their interests ever be seriously threatened. One of the dominant group's most important interests is to maintain the relatively smooth functioning of society, so that they can enjoy the fruits of dominance. Expressions of minority dissatisfaction with their status can seriously disrupt that smooth functioning; thus, a derived interest of the dominant group is to keep the minority either controlled enough and/or happy enough to prevent those expressions. With that interest in mind, the dominant group may accept arrangements not of their choice with a given minority group, in the more general interest of maintaining order in the society. Of the two general minority–dominant arrangements discussed in this section, both demand certain political and economic concessions but neither requires the social acceptance of the dominant group. That is the point, presumably, where the dominant group draws the line in the interest of order.

Examining minority group efforts to improve their overall status vis-à-vis the dominant group, we encounter many of the theoretical difficulties we faced in discussing the melting pot. Specifically, we must separate the reality of the minority group response from the rhetoric. Employing the terms we used earlier, we must not confuse *descriptions* of what really occurs with *ideologies,* which define what minorities hope will occur. This time the task is more difficult, for we are not uncovering a myth. Despite their rhetoric (or ideologies), minority groups can somewhat improve their overall status in the dominant group's society without sacrificing their ethnicity. We turn now to that balancing act.

As we have seen, all the advantages of assimilation for the minority group depend on the first level of assimilation (behavioral assimilation), in which the minority strives to conform to the dominant group's culture. We may therefore describe assimilation in terms of providing advantages to minority *individuals* but not to minority *groups*; by the time structural assimilation occurs, the ethnicity of the minority group has been effectively destroyed. (If the minority–dominant relationship temporarily stabilizes at the secondary level of structural assimilation, some degree of group separation may continue, but the impact of the minority group's culture will still have been lost.) However, there are alternatives to assimilation; through either conscious effort or historical accident, a minority group may find itself increasing its economic and political leverage, while at the same time staying separate from the dominant group. In this way, a minority group can improve its situation while remaining a group, maintaining the ethnicity that binds its members together.

We shall approach the minority group response with the aid of three concepts: horizontal ethnic differentiation, cultural pluralism, and separatism. All three are related (and the first two almost indistinguishable).

Horizontal ethnic differentiation is the existence of parallel ethnic communities and stratification hierarchies within a society.

> *One community may hold power disproportionate to that of others, but all have their class stratification hierarchies. At least a minority within each ethnic group enjoys prestige and perhaps wealth. Socio-economic tensions are not translated so immediately into communal tensions. Pluralism under such a stratification system appears more stable because of overlapping interests. Elites of several communities have a stake in preserving the social order. The danger lies less in interethnic conflict than in intraethnic unrest. (Enloe, 1973: 29)*

The value neutrality of the term *horizontal ethnic differentiation* (it is used only in academic circles) should help us limit this set of our observations to descriptions of minority–dominant relations that fit the definition above. Otherwise, those descriptions can very easily become confused with the ideological presentation of the same idea.

When we refer to the idea of parallel ethnic communities in an ideological sense, we use the term *cultural pluralism*. Cultural pluralism is the conscious political effort of a minority group to maintain its ethnicity (through promoting its culture), while simultaneously working to acquire political influence and economic advantages within a society (Gordon, 1964a: 132–59; Newman, 1973: 67–70). This political effort is designed to improve the overall situation of the minority group *as a group;* it is not necessarily designed to improve the economic and political situation of *individual members* of the minority group (although individual improvement may be a by-product of cultural pluralism and is invariably a stated purpose of it). In short, cultural pluralism is a specific type of political organization within a minority group. As such, it represents a certain ideological statement by the minority group.

Finally, *separatism* is the conscious political effort of a minority group to separate itself politically from the dominant group (Vander Zanden, 1972: 382; Shibutani and Kwan, 1965: 516). Either the members of the minority group may be physically removed from the political boundaries of the dominant group, or new political bundaries (to be governed by the minority group) may be set up within the old political boundaries of the dominant group. In either case, separatism is a minority group effort to establish political autonomy; if successful, it would end the minority–dominant relationship. The emigration of Jews to Israel and the efforts of some French Canadians to separate Quebec from Canada are both examples of separatism; the term is more frequently employed in the latter case. *Separatism* is sometimes also used in reference to horizontal ethnic differentiation in which group separation between minority and majority is extreme. In this sense, the Amish in the United States are sometimes referred to as separatists, even though they live within the political boundaries of the United States without having ultimate jurisdiction over their land (Smith, 1958). Like cultural pluralism, separatism clearly refers to a conscious political effort by the minority group; unlike cultural pluralism, separatism (if successful) ends the minority–dominant relationship.

Horizontal Ethnic Differentiation

The concept of horizontal ethnic differentiation provides an interesting insight into the more general concept of ethnic stratification. Using the symbolic representation of ethnic stratification that we used in Chapter 3, figure 5 describes a stratification system in which group ◆ might be described as horizontally ethnically differentiated.

FIGURE 5.

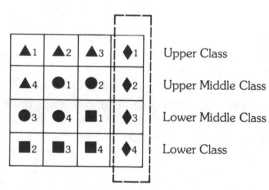

We emphasize that group ◆ *might* be described as horizontally ethnically differentiated—for we cannot tell for certain from the illustration. To fit the concept, group ◆ would not only have to occupy the variety of classes, but would also have to have retained its culture by maintaining ethnic ties across class boundaries. In figure 5 the dashed box indicates the separation of group ◆ members from other individuals in their classes. ◆3, for instance, would feel closer to ◆1 (despite the class difference) than to ●3 or ■1. Considering the importance of common class membership in a stratified society, this kind of group loyalty appears unlikely; it deserves a closer look.

Common ethnic traditions are important in binding the members of a minority group; they tend to produce group loyalty. As we suggested earlier, when ethnicity is combined with class membership (which is the situation of group ■ in figure 5), the ethnic ties are even stronger. But how can ethnic ties continue to have such force when the members of the minority group are scattered among the various classes? They often cease to have that force; but when they retain the binding force, it is because a very strong ethnic community exists. For that strong ethnic community to exist, the ethnicity of the group must be very much alive in the everyday actions of its members.

Generally, horizontal ethnic differentiation depends upon the social isolation of the minority group. We use the term *social* to refer not only to everyday social interactions among people, but also to other arenas of activity more generally described as economic and political. Thus, the members of a horizontally differentiated ethnic group would live together, worship together, play together, go to school together, and work for each other. The upper-class members of the ethnic group would have extensive business connections, like any other members of the upper class. They would use that dominance within their ethnic group, however, often in a somewhat paternalistic manner. If they owned apartment buildings, for instance, they might rent only to other members of their group. If they ran factories, they might employ only other members of their group. They would use their influence to help members of their group economically, at the same time keeping those members together within an ethnic community. In short, they would oversee a miniature ethnic society within a much larger society dominated by another culture. Because they had power, they could see to it that their minority ethnic culture stayed very much alive within the community by maintaining ethnic churches, newspapers, restaurants, theaters, schools, and so on. They would be responsible for lower-class members of their ethnic group, who would in turn be very dependent upon them.

While the dominant group would hardly be enthusiastic that so much power was in the hands of a minority ethnic group, they would have certain interests in common with the minority group. First of all, as Cynthia Enloe points out, the upper classes in both the dominant and minority groups would have a stake in preserving the status quo. Upper-class members of the dominant group could therefore depend on their counterparts in the ethnic community to help put down any ethnic dissatisfaction in the lower classes. Because of the economic separation along ethnic lines, there would be less job competition among the rank and file of both the dominant and minority groups. Beyond that, the general social separation of the groups would minimize intergroup hostilities arising from cultural differences; both the dominant and minority groups would look with equal disfavor on such goals as integration of housing or schools. In short, horizontal ethnic differentiation can provide the illusion of two separate societies, which eliminates much of the competition that sparks minority–dominant hostility.

Horizontal ethnic differentiation appears to foster exploitation *within the* minority ethnic group. One of the methods an upper-class member of the minority group can use to preserve the group is to limit options open to lower-class members of that group. The more time lower-class members of the group spend within the ethnic community, the less able they will be to compete outside that community. This is a phenomenon of behavioral assimilation; lower-class members of a horizontally differentiated ethnic group will be limited in their access to the dominant culture by the very structure of their ethnic community. They therefore have little choice but to work for the upper-class members of their group. The upper-class ethnic group members, however, have no such limitations, for to maintain their position they must be proficient with the dominant group's culture. They must understand the legal and business activities of the dominant group to provide that important link between the outside society and the ethnic community. It is clear that horizontal ethnic differentiation has the characteristics of paternalism: the upper-class members of the ethnic group take it upon themselves to make decisions "in the best interest" of lower-class members of their group. As Enloe points out, this situation can lead to differences of opinion and conflict within the minority ethnic group.

Cultural Pluralism

We turn now to the ideological side of horizontal ethnic differentiation: *cultural pluralism*. As we said earlier, cultural pluralism refers to the conscious political effort of a minority group to maintain its ethnicity (through promoting its culture), while simultaneously working to acquire political influence and economic advantages within a society. Cultural pluralism includes the political activities, goals, and beliefs that accompany a minority group's efforts to differentiate itself horizontally.

The origins of cultural pluralism: the American Jewish community. Unlike the term *horizontal ethnic differentiation, cultural pluralism* is used outside academia, often as a rallying cry for ethnic groups attempting to organize politically. In tracing the history of the term, we come upon Horace M. Kallen, an influential spokesman for the Jewish community in the United States around 1915. Kallen's now famous article "Democracy versus the Melting Pot" outlines a cultural and political alternative for minority groups that would later be labeled cultural pluralism.

> The outlines of a possibly great and truly democratic commonwealth become discernible. Its form would be that of the federal republic: its substance a democracy of nationalities, cooperating voluntarily and autonomously through common institutions in the enterprise of self-realization through the perfection of men according to their kind. The common language of the commonwealth, the language of its great tradition, would be English, but each nationality would have for its emotional and involuntary life its own peculiar dialect or speech, its own

individual and inevitable esthetic and intellectual forms. The political and economic life of the commonwealth is a single unit and serves as the foundation and background for the realization of the distinctive individuality of each nation that composes it and of the pooling of these in a harmony above them all. Thus "American civilization" may come to mean the perfection of the cooperative harmonies of "European civilization"—the waste, the squalor and the distress of Europe being eliminated—a multiplicity in a unity, an orchestration of mankind. (Kallen, 1915: 219–20)

Black power: cultural pluralism in the American black community. A more recent version of cultural pluralism is that of the black power movement in the late 1960s. Stokely Carmichael, a major spokesman for black power and leader of the Student Nonviolent Coordinating Committee (SNCC), combines group power with cultural pride (the two basic ingredients of cultural pluralism) in this 1966 statement of goals:

Black power can be clearly defined for those who do not attach the fears of white America to their questions about it. We should begin with the basic fact that black Americans have two problems: they are poor and they are black. All other problems arise from this two-sided reality: lack of education, the so-called apathy of black men. Any program to end racism must address itself to that double reality.

Almost from its beginning, SNCC sought to address itself to both conditions with a program aimed at winning political power for impoverished southern blacks. We had to begin with politics because black Americans are a propertyless people in a country where property is valued above all. We had to work for power, because this country does not function by morality, love, and nonviolence, but by power. Thus we determined to win political power, with the idea of moving on from there into activity that would have economic effects. With power, the masses could make or participate in making the decisions which govern their destinies, and thus create basic change in their day-to-day lives. . . . I remember that when I was a boy, I used to go to see Tarzan movies on Saturday. White Tarzan used to beat up the black natives. I would sit there yelling, "Kill the beasts, kill the savages, kill 'em!" It was as if a Jewish boy watched Nazis taking Jews off to concentration camps and cheered them on. Today, I want the chief to beat hell out of Tarzan and send him back to Europe. But it takes time to become free of the lies and their shaming effect on black minds. It takes time to reject the most important lie: that black people inherently can't do the same things white people can do, unless white people help them.

The need for psychological equality is the reason why SNCC today believes that blacks must organize in the black community. Only black people can convey the revolutionary idea that black people are able to do things themselves. Only they can help create in the community an aroused and continuing black consciousness that will provide the basis for political strength. In the past, white allies have furthered white supremacy without the whites involved realizing it—or wanting it, I think. Black people must do things for themselves; they must get poverty money they will control and spend themselves, they must conduct tutorial programs themselves so that black children can identify with black people. This is one reason Africa has such importance: the reality of black men ruling their own natives gives blacks elsewhere a sense of possibility, of power, which they do not now have. (Carmichael, 1971: 187, 191–92)

La Raza: cultural pluralism in the Mexican-American community. Cultural pluralism also found its way into the Mexican-American community in the late 1960s. As with the black power movement, there was a variety of Mexican-American ethnic organizations adhering to the philosophy of cultural pluralism. We quote here from the basic statement of purpose of one such organization, *La Raza Unida* (the united race). *La Raza* refers to the Mexican mixture of European and Indian ancestry, which, like all other forms of cultural pluralism, becomes a source of group pride.

PLAN DE LA RAZA UNIDA PREAMBLE

On this historic day, October 28, 1967, La Raza Unida organized in El Paso, Texas, proclaims the time of subjugation, exploitation and abuse of human rights of La Raza in the United States is hereby ended forever.

La Raza Unida affirms the magnificence of La Raza, the greatness of our heritage, our history, our language, our traditions, our contributions to humanity, and our culture. We have demonstrated and proven and again affirm our loyalty to the constitutional democracy of the United States of America and to the religious and cultural traditions we all share.

We accept the framework of constitutional democracy and freedom within which to establish our own independent organizations among our own people in pursuit of justice and equality and redress of grievances. La Raza Unida pledges to join with all our courageous people organizing in the fields and in the barrios. We commit ourselves to La Raza, at whatever cost.

With this commitment we pledge our support in:

1. *The right to organize community and labor groups in our own style.*
2. *The guarantee of training and placement in employment in all levels.*

3. *The guarantee of special emphasis on education at all levels geared to our people with strong financial grants to individuals.*
4. *The guarantee of decent, safe, and sanitary housing without relocation from one's community.*
5. *We demand equal representation at all levels of appointive boards and agencies, and the end to exploitative gerrymandering.*
6. *We demand the strong enforcement of all sections of the Treaty of Guadalupe Hidalgo particularly the sections dealing with land grants, and bilingual guarantees.*
7. *We are outraged by and demand an end to police harassment, discrimination and brutality inflicted on La Raza, and an end to the kangaroo court system known as juvenile hall. We demand constitutional protection and guarantees in all courts of the United States.*
8. *We reaffirm a dedication to our heritage, a bilingual culture and assert our right to be members of La Raza Unida anywhere, anytime and in any job. (Rendon, 1974: 331–32)*

Why cultural pluralism?   We could fill an entire book with more examples of cultural pluralism. Minority group status can make cultural pluralism very appealing. Variations on the theme are appearing on the American political scene with increasing frequency. Currently, ethnic consciousness is on the upswing in American life; individuals are unearthing the same ethnic background that their parents and grandparents had so carefully buried. Although it may be dangerous to give generalized reasons for the popularity of cultural pluralism, two such generalizations seem accurate. The ethnic groups that are most interested in cultural pluralism are those that (1) have very strong cultural traditions, and/or (2) have been denied structural assimilation. As we shall see, the second generalization is more often applicable.

At first glance, the strength of an ethnic group's cultural tradition appears to be a major determininant of their attraction to cultural pluralism. For example, the modern birth of this idea in the Jewish community of the United States supports this idea; few groups have been as adept as the Jews in maintaining a minority culture. Cultural pluralism offers a dream of continuing ethnic separation along with the "good life" of economic and political well-being. A group that has remained a separate ethnic minority for centuries should jump at such an opportunity. But in the case of Jews, as with other minorities, it is not easy to distinguish the importance of their desire to remain separate from the dominant group's desire for them to remain separate. Jews have remained separate for centuries, but they have also faced discrimination for centuries. That observation leads to the second generalization we made above—the denial of structural assimilation stimulates interest in cultural pluralism.

Like cultural pluralism, structural assimilation opens economic and political doors. Unlike cultural pluralism, it opens those doors to minority *individuals* but not to minority *groups*. In the case of Jews in the United States, the door of structural assimilation has been at least partly open several times. In particular, the middle 1800s were a time of relative opportunity for American Jews. At that time most American Jews were of northwest European background; religion aside, they were culturally very similar to members of the growing dominant culture in the United States (Wirth, 1928: 142–45). In addition, there were not large numbers of Jews in the population, nor were they especially concentrated geographically. In that situation of relative acceptance, structural assimilation was a real possibility. But all that changed with the arrival of Jews from eastern Europe around the turn of the century.

The new wave of Jewish immigrants came from rural areas instead of urban, in large numbers instead of small; and they concentrated in the major Eastern cities, which increased their visibility. Amid the generalized anti-foreign feeling that arose at the time grew a strong anti-Semitism, which ultimately came to affect all Jews, regardless of their background. In this context the two northwest European Jews noted earlier, Israel Zangwill and Horace Kallen, presented their political solutions for the increasing ethnic conflict in America. Zangwill's play *The Melting Pot* was produced in 1909, and Kallen introduced cultural pluralism in 1915. We can make at least two interesting observations. First, the compromise idea of the melting pot would certainly have eliminated the main strength of Jewish culture. Second, and more important to our discussion, Kallen introduced cultural pluralism into a social situation characterized by a growing lack of structural assimilation for Jews. Discrimination against any ethnic group is one of the strongest factors in creating group ethnic solidarity. Also, by definition it limits their options in the dominant society. The lack of structural assimilation (enforced by discrimination) provides very fertile ground for the growth of cultural pluralism. A strong ethnic tradition (like that of Jews) makes that ground even more fertile. The strength of ethnic tradition is hard to measure and still harder to explain. One thing, however, is clear: a strong ethnic "tradition" can be generated quickly if discrimination is intense.

The truth of that observation is supported by the popularity of cultural pluralism among American blacks. One of the goals of slavery in the United States was to strip away any African cultures held by the slaves. One means to this end was to mix individuals from different tribes on each plantation, so that the individual slave would have no support for his or her particular culture. Elements of numerous African cultures survived this treatment, but over-all, distinct African cultures were eliminated (Stampp, 1956: 362–63). The extent of present-day black cultural solidarity in America is not, therefore, a product of long-standing ethnic tradition, but a product of discriminatory treatment during their stay here. As discrimination continues, so solidarity continues. When all other doors are closed, the one that might open under pressure looks very promising.

Cultural pluralism as a political movement: the problems of powerlessness.   Once under way, cultural pluralism carries a special set of directives for the minority group's political organization. First, ethnic ties within the minority must be strengthened to produce a united front for bargaining. This necessity often creates considerable conflict within the minority group between those who favor the new movement and those who do not. Derisive terms such as *Uncle Tom, Tio Taco,* and *Oreo* have been used for members of the minority who reject the cultural pluralism movement. While the minority group is organizing, the dominant group may find itself strangely ignored as minority members fight among themselves. However, if the movement gains momentum, the dominant group may notice new and higher barriers between itself and the culturally pluralist minority.

Such barriers, a necessary part of cultural pluralism, are formed in two ways. First, the minority goes to great lengths to emphasize its attributes. Any element of cultural or physical distinctiveness can gain the stature of a group symbol. If distinctive elements are lacking, they can be created. Most cases of cultural pluralism involve a combination of pre-existing and created distinctions; for example, the Black Muslims combined the black experience in America with a new religion (Vander Zanden, 1972: 389–93). The distinctions are emphasized in a variety of public forums, such as schools and newspapers, to give them vitality within the ethnic community. The second means of forming barriers against the dominant group involves ignoring, criticizing, or attacking dominant group attributes. By simultaneously pulling the ethnic minority together and separating it from the dominant group, group solidarity is produced. The group's political organization is then ready to mobilize its group pride in hopes of achieving group power.

By their very nature, minority groups are not ideally suited for power plays in society. The old saying, "The poor stay poor," summarizes the obstacle: the minority group has little to work with. If its members are concentrated in a particular occupation, they can combine ethnic organization with labor organization: for example, the Chicano United Farm Workers, and the Irish Molly Maguires in the Pennsylvania coal fields in the 1800s (Nava, 1973: 109–10; Higham, 1955: 30, 47). The United Farm Workers have employed strikes and boycotts; the Molly Maguires depended generally upon violence. To be effective, boycotts must have support outside the minority organization (Nava, 1973: 146–48, 137–38). And violence, of course, can always be matched ten to one by the government (as the Molly Maguires discovered). The point is that most minority group tactics to increase power ultimately depend upon forces beyond the control of the group. Not surprisingly, therefore, most efforts at cultural pluralism encounter difficulty, since it is often in the interests of outside forces to prevent an increase in power within the minority group.

A less obvious, slower, but safer road to cultural pluralism is to work primarily for economic growth within the minority group while avoiding political confrontation as much as possible. Ideally, the minority group puts off political confrontation until it is in a position to hold its own, more or less. That political power can grow from economic power. Chinese control over

Chinatowns in some major cities and, more recently, the Black Muslims are examples of this general economic approach. A Chinatown looks less like a ghetto and more like an instance of cultural pluralism when property and business are owned and run by Chinese (Hsu, 1971: 2–3, 45–50), in contrast to the black sections of many American cities today, which are owned primarily by whites. The Black Muslims have been quietly attempting to build an economic base for their organization by buying land and business and by keeping all control in the hands of their members (Vander Zanden, 1972: 392–93). Community economic control, a goal of many efforts at cultural pluralism, is the basic ingredient of horizontal ethnic differentiation. When the political effort at cultural pluralism is successful, the overall result is the formation of parallel social and economic structures in which the minority can live separately and through which it gains power to represent its interests.

Separatism

Just as expulsion is an extreme response by the dominant group to the minority–dominant group situation, so separatism is an extreme response by the minority group to that situation. Both terms refer to the placement of the minority outside the dominant group's political boundaries, by moving either the minority or the boundaries. The difference between expulsion and separatism, of course, lies in the source of the decision to end the minority–dominant group relationship. As expulsion represents the dominant group's desire to be rid of the minority group, separatism represents the minority group's desire to be rid of the dominant group (and its attempt to do so through political organization).

Marcus Garvey.   In the history of the United States, one of the most notable and certainly most colorful separatist movements was Marcus Garvey's Universal Negro Improvement Association in the 1920s. Garvey preached black superiority and advocated that American blacks return to Africa. By 1924 Garvey had 100,000 dues-paying members and many more supporters within the black community (Vander Zanden, 1972: 388). His success within the black community provoked a hostile response from the dominant white community; Garvey was imprisoned in 1925, charged with using the mails to defraud, and deported in 1927 as an undesirable alien (he was a native West Indian). Without his leadership his movement lost impetus. However, it had planted some important ideas that would later be modified by the black power movement.

Quebec.   More recently, the French Canadian population in the Canadian province of Quebec launched a separatist movement. Unlike Garvey's movement, which advocated flight, the French Canadians hope to build a homeland in Quebec, free from current English Canadian rule. The dispute concerns the ethnic stratification within the province. Although the English-speaking population of Quebec is a numerical minority, they hold most positions of power. They maintain this dominance by virtue of their more general control over the rest of Canada (in which they are a numerical majority), which gives them control over the national government. It is the goal of the French separatists in Quebec to gain political and economic dominance over their province, through separatism if necessary. With the election to the provincial government of the separatist political party (the *Parti Quebecois*), a number of laws have been passed to further that goal. One of the most important and most disputed laws concerns the use of language.

The native language of French Canadians is, of course, French. For those who do not speak English, upward mobility into jobs that require English is out of the question. While Quebec is superficially a bilingual province, the positions of power have always been English-speaking. In 1977 the provincial government of Quebec passed a law requiring all business activities in Quebec to be conducted in French (*Newsweek,* 1977b: 63). Designed to open doors for French speakers, the law simultaneously closed doors for English-speaking business people, most of whom do not speak French. As a result of this law and the political sentiments it reflects, many Canadian businesses moved out of Quebec into other Canadian provinces and into the United States. A possible outcome of this movement could be the complete separation of Quebec into a self-governing country, with French as a national language and French speakers in all the major positions of power.

The future of separatism.   As we said earlier, separatism can result in the end of the minority–dominant relationship if it comes to fruition. Such an occurrence would be beyond the scope of our discussion, and in the arena of international relations instead. It is of interest to us, however, in that the roots of separatism lie in the basic situation of ethnic stratification, as do the roots of all the other arrangements between minority and dominant groups discussed in this chapter. Among these other arrangements, separatism stands out as an example of the durability of ethnicity when accompanied by class membership: that ethnicity can become a symbol for the exploited group, so that freedom from membership in the lower classes becomes synonymous with freedom for the ethnic group. If genocide and expulsion are the last weapons in the arsenal of the dominant group, separatism is surely the ultimate weapon of the minority.

SUMMARY

In addition to their varying power in society, one of the fundamental differences among ethnic groups is their ethnicity or culture. When different ethnic groups come to share one society, their cultures come into contact and often into conflict. This chapter examined the types of arrangements that ethnic groups evolve with regard to their cultural differences, as well as some arrangements they strive for but seldom achieve. In particular, we looked at the melting pot as an ideal of cultural harmony; at genocide, segregation, and separatism as examples of cultural rejection; at the variety of forms of assimilation through which minority ethnic groups attempt to conform to dominant cultural patterns; and at horizontal ethnic differentiation as an approach through which cultural differences survive in peaceful coexistence. In connection with horizontal ethnic differentiation, we examined the ideology of cultural pluralism as the minority group's political orientation for achieving that end.

Chapter

The Powerless: Minority Political Strategies

six

WHAT IS A POLITICAL MOVEMENT?

The most difficult problem for social scientists who study minority groups is probably the question of how and why such groups begin to act politically. Political activity is usually motivated by a feeling of relative deprivation. This chapter will discuss the interplay between relative deprivation, prejudice, and racism. Specifically, it will highlight the interdependence between class and race as a cause of tensions between minority groups and the dominant society. We shall seek to understand the presently changing face and intensity of minorities, for even among the best organized ethnic or racial groups, there are ebbs and flows of activity and what appear to be a number of strategies. The various "types" of political action are important, for they are linked with major social and political changes. This chapter provides a scheme for understanding apparently discrete forms of minority activity, and shows how they relate to the interplay between class and ethnic status. It will also discuss how each type of political movement tends to affect the society as a whole.

The term *political movement* has been used in so many different ways in the past decade that few scholars agree on its meaning. We shall use the term to denote any group that uses purposeful action in trying to change the political definition of itself or of society as a whole. Political movements try through a specific program of action to change the political institutions or processes that tend to define who we are or how we can act. Through laws, rules, or social mores, institutions define what is right and wrong in society. Minority political movements usually want to change either these institutional structures or the processes through which they express themselves (police, courts, department stores, and even the stock market). How does this theoretical concept work in practice?

Imagine that a women's group found that the university physical education department provided male golf team members with free showers, a sauna, laundry service, and unlimited golf balls. The women's golf team, meanwhile, had to change in the women's restroom and its members were issued one ball per person. If the women's group considered this discriminatory, they would try to convince the university that women golfers should be taken seriously. They would argue that the university's implied definition of women golfers as less important than men golfers is illegitimate. They might argue that men and women deserve equal treatment, or they could suggest that discrimination in a university is at odds with its role as a social institution. In either case the women's group would attempt to force the university to redefine its view of the golf teams, because discrimination implies that the women's team is inferior.

Social Class and Cultural Pluralism

Political movements tend to be class-differentiated; that is, most members of a movement belong to the same class. Because of the interrelationship between class and ethnicity, this is even more true of minorities. (Remember that class and income are not the same. Income is only one aspect of class, and in many cases wealth does not eliminate the onus of belonging to a minority group.) As we saw in Chapter 5, cultural pluralism is one possible reaction of a minority group to its situation, *if* it can choose its response. However, if the minority can choose without any social or political constraint by the majority, it would have no reason for political action. Minorities often attempt cultural pluralism while the majority continues to use institutional or procedural discrimination against them. For example, in the 1960s the Black Muslims attempted to isolate themselves from all white influences by purchasing stores, bakeries, newspapers, and radio and television stations. But no matter how independent members of the Muslim group were within their community, once they stepped outside it they were still at the mercy of majority social and political pressures.

The Vertical Society: Perfect Minority Stratification

Cultural pluralism is often used as a political tactic to reach a goal that the community perceives as useful. More often than not, it is used in reaction to restrictions imposed on the minority by the larger community. To understand why this occurs, we must review the idea of horizontal ethnic differentiation. In a society characterized by horizontal ethnic differentiation, if you know an individual's social class you do not automatically know his or her minority status, and vice versa; in other words, members of ethnic groups are totally dispersed throughout the various social classes (see figure 5). Obviously, there are no such perfect societies. However, understanding the ideal helps us understand its opposite. The negative image of horizontal ethnic differentiation is *vertical ethnic differentiation*. Vertical ethnic differentiation uses cultural pluralism to determine who will derive the most class benefits from society

(Enloe, 1973: 27–34). We shall refer to such societies as vertical societies. As figure 6a shows, in a perfectly vertical society if you know an individual's class, you have an excellent chance of guessing his or her minority group, and if you know an individual's minority affiliation, you can guess his or her class.

FIGURE 6a.

▲1	▲2	▲3	▲4	Upper Class
◆1	◆2	◆3	◆4	Upper Middle Class
●1	●2	●3	●4	Lower Middle Class
■1	■2	■3	■4	Lower Class

VERTICAL ETHNIC DIFFERENTIATION

An excellent example of vertical social and political construction is South Africa, where the policy of apartheid discriminates in every conceivable

FIGURE 6b.

▲1	▲2	▲3	◆1	Upper Class
◆2	◆3	◆4	▲4	Upper Middle Class
●1	●2	●3	■1	Lower Middle Class
●4	■2	■3	■4	Lower Class

FIGURE 6c.

▲1	▲2	◆1	●1	Upper Class
◆2	■1	●2	■2	Upper Middle Class
▲3	●3	◆3	■3	Lower Middle Class
▲4	◆4	●4	■4	Lower Class

FIGURE 6d.

▲1	▲2	▲3	■1	Upper Class
◆1	◆2	◆3	●1	Upper Middle Class
▲4	◆4	●2	●3	Lower Middle Class
●4	■2	■3	■4	Lower Class

fashion between blacks and whites. In figure 6a the Afrikaner minority would be represented by ▲ and the black minority by ■. Even South Africa, however, is not completely a vertical society. The importance of the distinction between horizontal and vertical ethnic differentiation is not in the absolute cases but rather the cases that fall on a continuum between perfectly vertical and perfectly horizontal. Figures 6b, 6c, and 6d illustrate several societal constructions. Which are horizontal and which are vertical?

It is fairly obvious that figure 6b is a vertical society in which culture ▲ and culture ◆ are the upper echelon and cultures ● and ■ are the lower. In that society, if you saw a ▲ walking down the street and guessed that he was upper-class, you would be right 75 percent of the time; if you guessed that he was upper- or upper-middle-class, you would be right 100 percent of the time. If you met a lower-class person in that society, you would be assured that he was a member of either ● or ■. Figure 6c shows a much more horizontal society, although it is not perfectly so. Figure 6d, which is closer to the reality of most societies, poses problems. Clearly the society in figure 6d still gives a tremendous advantage to cultures ▲ and ◆. However, ■1 and ●1 benefit from upper- and upper-middle-class status, respectively. If you guessed that cultures ▲ and ◆ made up all of the upper and upper middle classes, you would be right 75 percent of the time and wrong only 25 percent. It appears reasonable that if members of cultures ● and ■ consider themselves part of their ethnic groups, then they feel discriminated against.

Remember that this is a continuum; societies that fall midway between vertical and horizontal are difficult to classify. Luckily, *our* classification is not really important, for it is the members of an ethnic or minority group who decide the *political* importance of their position for us. If a minority objects to a society that institutes vertical ethnic differentiation to discriminate against them, and forms a political movement to fight discrimination, it is *their* definition of the situation that is of overriding importance in making this a political problem. Both the actual condition of a group in society, and its psychological attitude toward the political institutions and processes of that society, make vertical ethnic differentiation a crucial concept.

Although it is highly implausible, certain groups might not object to the vertical construction of society, even if they were in the lower class. More likely, such groups would experience cyclical political activity, often beginning with isolated events such as a police arrest or the closing of a business. Political uprisings, either in the voting booths or on the streets, tend to erode class privileges as the upper classes compromise as much as is necessary to maintain their position in society. Because the upper class has the most to gain from the status quo, they must try to make the lower classes appreciate the country and its benefits. If they do this successfully, socializing the lower classes through vehicles such as patriotism, then the vertical society can maintain a degree of stability. If they fail to inculcate such values, political violence is imminent.

The Psychological Dimensions of Class

In any vertical society, stability (or instability) relies on a balance of class discrimination and psychological perception. If the controlling group increases its class position at the cost of a minority, an offsetting psychological adjustment must be made. If such an adjustment is not made, the state will increasingly have to resort to police and repression. For example, early in their takeover of power in Germany, the Nazis carried out violence on the streets. Once Hitler was cloaked in legitimacy through election, however, it no longer seemed appropriate publicly to intimidate or kill large numbers of minority group members. The concentration camps then served both to police and to intimidate. Few modern vertical states have gone as far as the Nazis. For most, a combination of intimidation and propaganda has sufficed. Even in the more repressive regimes, such as Rhodesia and South Africa, a considerable amount of propaganda is used in addition to the tactics of fear and isolation in ghettos like Soweto. The issue of homelands—providing independent black states within South Africa—is absurd, because those states are totally dependent economically and politically on South Africa. Yet the governments of South Africa and Rhodesia both command considerable loyalty from the oppressed black majority; even their armies have sizable black contingents. The newly formed government in Zimbabwe-Rhodesia seems to hold promise for a peaceful settlement, but it is still unclear whether the whites are maintaining real political power.

Such phenomena demonstrate how important it is for vertical societies to maintain strong psychological justifications for their actions. The ruling class views itself as protecting minorities, not discriminating against them. Frantz Fanon argues that such colonial situations naturally produce people who depend on their oppressors. When they are asked to participate in some element of the society such as the military, it is a great honor, for they are being distinguished from the average lower-class member of that society (Fanon, 1967: 18–40). Lower-class soldiers are often some of the most loyal members of the social order, because they appear to have the most to lose if the state is overthrown. Psychological justifications of the vertical social order are a double-edged sword; they must be believed by members of both the majority and the minority. It is often falsely assumed that membership in the upper class in such a society makes it unimportant to justify one's social and political situation. On the contrary, such individuals must believe that their upper-class status benefits the entire society—but of course, they are much easier to convince of that than would be the lower class!

As we said in Chapter 2, the concept of race as a series of unchangeable social characteristics is relatively new. But it plays a vital role in the modern vertical state. Race is relative; in various regions and societies it is used to designate different groups. In Nazi Germany Jews were considered a race; today we seldom think of Jews as a racial type.[1] Most vertical societies use the notion of race or some derivative of it as a justification for their social construction. It seldom makes sense to construct a society vertically unless the ruling group believes that its status in that society is natural and permanent. In a sense social differences may be used as an *exclusionary principle* in deciding who gets goods, status, or political power; at this point ethnicity itself becomes a racial type.

THE AMERICAN EXPERIENCE

Social scientists often disagree on whether the United States is a vertical or a horizontal society. It is certainly clear that Rhodesia and the United States do not have the same social construction today, although that would not have been so clear in 1950. As we said earlier, vertical and horizontal are the extremes of a continuum, and the United States seems to exhibit characteristics of both. On the one hand there appears to be a broad commitment to equality in American life. This has been noted by observers of the American scene since Alexis de Tocqueville in the early nineteenth century. The civil rights movement and the massive political and social changes during the past 30 years attest to this commitment.

Yet Americans do discriminate. The President's Commission on Civil Disorders warned in 1968 that the United States was in danger of becoming two radically different societies, "one black and one white." Social psychologists have pointed out that Americans tend to feel the most social distance from people who are physically different from themselves. As table 5 shows, the determination of social distance has remained remarkably stable during this century. We emphasize that social distance does not necessarily translate into overt prejudice and class distinctions, but it is one element among the many that determine the situation of minorities in America.

Does social distance determine whether a society is described as vertical or horizontal? Certainly, one vital issue in the determination is the notion of economic status. As we saw earlier, the black–white income gap has not

---

1.   Although we do not necessarily agree with his overall thesis, Arthur Koestler gives an excellent overview of the literature on Jews as a racial type. See The Thirteenth Tribe (New York: Random House, 1976), chapter 8.

Table 5.　Social Distance Ranks of Americans, 1926–1966[1]

Target Group	1926	1946	1956	1966
English	1.0	3.0	3.0	2.0
Americans (white)	2.0	1.0	1.0	1.0
Canadians	3.5	2.0	2.0	3.0
Scots	3.5	5.0	7.0	9.0
Irish	5.0	4.0	5.0	5.0
French	6.0	6.0	4.0	4.0
Germans	7.0	10.0	8.0	10.5
Swedish	8.0	9.0	6.0	6.0
Hollanders	9.0	8.0	9.0	10.5
Norwegians	10.0	7.0	10.0	7.0
Spanish	11.0	15.0	14.0	14.0
Finns	12.0	11.0	11.0	12.0
Russians	13.0	13.0	22.0	22.0
Italians	14.0	16.0	12.0	8.0
Poles	15.0	14.0	13.0	16.0
Armenians	16.0	17.5	18.0	19.0
Czechs	17.0	12.0	17.0	17.0
Indians (American)	18.0	20.0	19.0	18.0
Jews	19.0	19.0	16.0	15.0
Greeks	20.0	17.5	15.0	13.0
Mexicans	21.0	23.5	26.0	26.5
Japanese	22.0	28.0	24.0	23.0
Filipinos	23.0	22.0	20.0	20.0
Blacks	24.0	27.0	25.0	26.5
Turks	25.0	23.5	21.0	24.0
Chinese	26.0	21.0	23.0	21.0
Koreans	27.0	25.0	28.0	25.0
Indians (from India)	28.0	26.0	27.0	28.0

1.　Social distance is the gap the "average" American feels between him- or herself and an ethnic group: the greater the number, the greater the felt distance.

SOURCE:　Howard J. Ehrlich, The Social Psychology of Prejudice (New York: John Wiley, 1973), p. 74. Reprinted by permission.

narrowed over the past 30 years. Additionally, Dorothy Newman and her associates point out that there has been little or no upgrading of blacks' job status (Newman et al., 1978: ch. 3). Even in the federal government, the nation's largest employer, blacks are still overrepresented in lower-status jobs and hold only a very few positions of high status (the so-called super grade jobs). Women in the United States also hold disproportionately many low-status, low-paying jobs, as do American Indians. For ethnic groups, lower-class status has varied geographically. Poles in the Northeast, Orientals in the West, and other groups in other regions of the United States experience discrimination in the areas of job status and salaries. Such discrimination varies within and between communities. For example, if we examine the relationship between race and job status in Michigan, we find a different situation in the state as a whole than in the city of Detroit or the city of Ann Arbor.

The Politics of Housing Discrimination

The most pervasive indicator of prejudice, and possibly of the vertical status of American society, is housing. Most Americans are willing to grant to minorities voting rights, equal job opportunities, and equal educational facilities, but only a minority of Americans appear to believe that in actual practice an individual should have the right to live wherever he or she chooses (Newman et al., 1978: ch. 5). There are many reasons for this apparent inconsistency in values. One is the myth that an integrated neighborhood will deteriorate because "unacceptable" minorities have poor hygiene and huge families, and generally make poor neighbors. The most telling argument is usually that integration lowers property values. All such reasons are over-generalizations, and the argument that integration lowers property values is out and out wrong. In fact, the opposite is more likely to occur (Newman et al., 1978: 144). Property values rise when racial groups integrate neighborhoods, because the selection of homes is usually so poor for such minorities. Values *do* drop when financial lending institutions *redline* an area—that is, designate it an unacceptable loan risk—because it is in transition. Redlining causes a decrease in values because it becomes impossible to finance a home in a redlined area. When a transitional neighborhood is not redlined, it usually holds its property values.

Other methods are used to insure that minority groups will not have access to property in designated areas, such as agreements between realtors, social constraints placed on property owners by their neighbors, and zoning. Exclusionary zoning has the effect of raising housing prices, thereby eliminating members of (generally poorer) minorities. However, we emphasize again that it is not merely class, and subsequent economic ability, that eliminates such people from the housing market. To "the degree that blacks have lower incomes, they are more affected by such policies, but again it is important to underline that economic differences between the races explain only a very small part of the observed racial segregation" (Newman et al., 1978: 161).

Neighborhoods: Political Organizations

Most of us cannot easily perceive that our own neighborhoods are segregated, even though they probably are. (National statistics show an increasing trend toward segregation [Sorenson et al., 1974: 7–9].) For example, a friend of ours had lived in a small midwestern town all her life. One day a group of us were discussing the social makeup of the community when one individual commented on the severely segregated housing patterns. Our friend, the native of the town, was outraged at the accusation and complained that she had seen no such discrimination. To convince her we all had to take an automobile tour through this small city whose streets she had traversed hundreds of times before. She was astonished, because suddenly the one small town of her childhood became three segregated minority communities. The white neighborhood was the preferred neighborhood, but interestingly the black neighborhood was the second most desirable area; in the bottom social—and if you will, racial—class were the so-called briars, or people from the Appalachian regions of Kentucky and West Virginia. All of the standard stereotypes were used to describe the briars: they were dirty, kept junk cars in their driveways, and "multiplied like rabbits." The point of the story is that housing segregation is not self-evident even to the people living in a neighborhood.

Most of the rules of housing segregation are informal; the few formal structures are enforced by a very small group of people, such as bankers and realtors. For that reason, if you ask most people how their neighborhoods evolved in the way they did, they would probably say through the natural choices of people.

Is American Society Vertically Structured?

An additional point that leads us to suggest the existence of a vertical society in the United States is the radically different perceptions of the black condition held by blacks and whites. Various sources suggest that the same is true of other minority groups in this country, notably American Indians and Chicanos. A Louis Harris survey conducted in the late 1970s detected a sharp difference of opinion between blacks and whites over the impact of the civil rights movement. Although 55 percent of the whites felt that blacks have tried to "move too fast" to gain racial equality, 48 percent of the blacks felt that their progress has been "too slow." Table 6 shows the stark difference in perceptions between blacks and whites in the United States, even though the survey reported in the table was taken at a time when most Americans interpreted the decline of political activity in the black communities as indicating satisfaction with their political, social, and economic gains.

Many other aspects of American society lead us to interpret it as a vertical structure: jobs, status, and medical care, for example. However, it would be wrong to imply that there are no arguments on the other side. Certainly, the United States has the highest material standard of living available today, and this includes most minority groups. It is also true that American government institutions are far more sensitive to minority rights than those of most other nations. There is in America more tolerance for dissent from majority beliefs, ideas, and policies than in the Soviet Union, Uganda, Uruguay, or South Korea. But, as we pointed out earlier, the actual or material component of discrimination is only half of the equation in describing vertical societies.

RELATIVE DEPRIVATION: THE RELATIONSHIP BETWEEN MINORITY STATUS AND PSYCHOLOGICAL PERCEPTION

The other half of the equation is minority individuals' psychological perception of their political situation. In some societies with extreme discrimination

Table 6.   Racial Perceptions of Discrimination against Blacks[1]

	Blacks		Whites	
	Yes	No	Yes	No
Are Blacks discriminated against in wages?	66%	29%	21%	72%
Are Blacks discriminated against in getting manual labor jobs?	54	40	10	86
Are Blacks discriminated against in getting white collar jobs?	76	18	34	59
Are Blacks discriminated against in getting skilled labor jobs?	73	23	26	68
Are Blacks discriminated against in getting decent housing?	74	23	34	61
Are Black teenagers discriminated against in getting jobs?	66	24	33	55
Are Blacks discriminated against in getting into labor unions?	57	34	18	65
Are Blacks getting a poor quality of public education?	61	35	19	76
Are Blacks being discriminated against by police?	71	23	28	60
Are Blacks getting less protection against crime than whites?	61	31	23	67
Are Blacks receiving unequal treatment if arrested for crime?	69	23	28	61
Are Blacks getting full equality?	19	75	59	33
Are Blacks being treated as human beings?	25	71	65	28

SOURCE: Louis Harris, The Harris Survey (New York: Chicago Tribune–New York News Syndicate, Inc., 12 Sept. 1977). Reprinted by permission.

1.   The actual Harris question was "Let me ask you about some specific areas of life in America. For each tell me if you think blacks are discriminated against in that area or not."

and prejudice, there is little minority action to redress these difficulties. It is absurd to assume that individuals so deprived believe that they deserve a lower status or lifestyle than other members of the society. More likely than not, their passivity is simply a reaction to their belief that they can do nothing about their situation. They feel powerless. This is often buttressed by the hope that things will improve.

The argument is often made that the poorest American is still better off than most people in India, China, or many other countries. This is a fallacious argument. We know that in American society there are tremendous pressures to consume. Because you are poor does not mean that you are isolated from advertisements on television, on radio, or in magazines. Wants and desires are remarkably similar across classes and minorities in the United States. The individual is deprived not in relation to a world economy, but within his or her particular political and economic system. Conversely, especially in some societies undergoing change, individuals argue that they are totally deprived, even though the material goods available to them are apparently equal. The point is that *state of mind* is usually far more important in evoking *political action* than is any of the empirical evidence of difference that we have discussed. This is not to say that the economic, social, and political disparities in society are unimportant, but rather that they become important as secondary, supporting reasoning, *after* individuals have become conscious of their social and political situation.

The realization that one is discriminated against is usually described as an awakening (Memmi, 1968: 3–39), a sudden realization or putting together of past events into a consistent pattern of discrimination. The awakening may suggest some sort of action as a way of relieving the situation; this is what we will call *coming to political consciousness*. Being politically conscious does not necessarily mean being radical. Rather, it is a complete change in the way an individual sees himself in the world, usually brought about by some event or series of events whose relevance the individual can explain only after becoming politically conscious.

The Davies J-Curve

One becomes politically conscious through the tension of material "goods" and the psychological perception that social scientists call *relative deprivation*. Interestingly, many social scientists believe, along with James C. Davies, that coming to political consciousness in revolutions occurs as situations in society are improving. The difficulty is that material "goods" — including possessions, status, and political power — do not increase at the rate people would like (see figure 7). Because of this, according to Davies, revolution occurs. Political consciousness for minorities follows the same basic pattern. That is, after their material goods and psychological satisfaction begin to rise, the two curves may diverge, with psychological needs rising at a much faster rate than material realities.

Political Action

At some point (X in figure 7), the diverging relationship between real goods and psychological needs forces a fundamental reevaluation of one's social and political position. This can result in a number of different forms of political activity. In Davies's scheme it is revolution. For our purposes, minorities begin to organize politically. It is at this point *for the member of the minority group* that the society *becomes* vertical. It is important to emphasize that this is a *human* process, not totally dependent on a series of external forces. Like most other human action, cognizance is required before social circumstances are "real."

The threshold in the J-curve of political consciousness, or the feeling of

FIGURE 7.   The J-Curve and the Formation of Minority
Political Movements

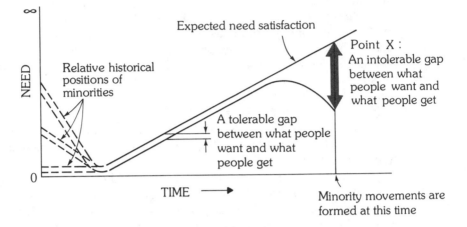

SOURCE: Adapted from James C. Davies, "The J-curve of rising and declining satisfactions as a cause of some great revolutions and contained rebellion," in Hugh Davis Graham and Ted Robert Gurr, Violence in America, vol. 2 (Washington, D.C.: National Commission on the Causes and Prevention of Violence, 1969), p. 548 and passim.

relative deprivation, results in five different types of actions in which minority groups can engage. The rest of this chapter will look at those forms of action.

A TYPOLOGY OF MINORITY POLITICAL ACTION

Although there appear to be only five forms of political action open to minorities, once they perceive that they live in a vertical society, an additional alternative exists: political inaction. A movement that consciously decides not to act will be termed *accommodationist;* accommodationists want to work within the current social and political circumstances. The five activity-oriented groups will be labeled *nonviolence, rebellion, identity* or *"power," radicalism,* and *nationalism* (see table 7). Historically, few such movements have been pure; that is, characteristics of several types often exist at the same time. Just as often, we find a changing balance among groups. The most concise example of these political phenomena occurred in the black political movement of the 1960s: during a mere decade, the black community experienced, at one time or another, the dominance of all of these types of groups.

The black political movements of the 1960s were not typical, for several reasons. First, that the black movement appeared to begin with nonviolence and then increased in intensity does not necessarily mean that other minority movements would pattern themselves similarly. There is nothing sacred about the order in which such movements evolve. In fact, later we shall give examples of movements that developed in the opposite order. Second, the

Table 7. Types of Minority Political Movements

	Accommodation	Nonviolence	Rebellion	"Power"	Radicalism	Nationalism
Political Emphasis	Present situation is tolerable and perceived as favorable to the individual	Majority attitude must be changed toward minority	Frustration and anomie; the need to do something	Majority has robbed culture or history; political power must come from minority's "roots"	Attacks the corrupt nature of capitalism; emphasizes the social class basis of discrimination	Need to remove their people from the majority; put pressure on national institutions for the "freedom" of their people
Tactics	Support of the present political system	Marches, breaking unjust laws, confronting majority with its "immorality"	Riots, violence, open confrontation with the government	Emphasize culture, potential destructiveness from majority community because of its dominant culture	Attempt to unite with other groups for successful change, or violent overthrow of institutions	Move people into separate territory or back to country of origin; use negotiation or violence, if necessary
Intensity	Low	Moderate	High	Moderate	High	High
Goals	Maintain status quo	Change laws or informal rules; basically supports political institutions	Release frustration; "make them notice us, know we are alive"	Identity of self and group; pride in belonging	Change the economic relationships; emphasize equality among all minorities	Create a separate cultural and political entity

black experience in the 1960s might suggest that it is always fairly clear which movement is dominant at which time. Martin Luther King and nonviolence were clearly dominant in 1960, while in 1969 Huey Newton and black radicalism seemed to hold sway. The apparent dominance of specific movements during various stages of the black experience might mislead us that other movements would also have clearly dominant political forms. On the contrary, such dominance is by and large media-created; even the apparent solidarity of blacks is deceptive. It is rare, when a minority is fully engaging a majority society, not to find all facets of political activity. That is, all six types of political movements usually exist simultaneously, and it is often difficult to tell which is the driving force behind a minority at a specific time.

The Interrelationship Between Class and Race

Political movements, no matter what type, are geared to address the interrelationship between class and race. For in a vertical society, a minority by definition is considered—or feels itself considered—a racial type.[2] Additionally, movements see race as inherently tied to class. Some people argue that a minority could come to political consciousness and find itself in the upper class. Although this is the contention of several theorists—including Karl Marx, who thought the vast majority of the bourgeoisie would experience such a change—it appears highly unlikely. Given human nature, few people in dominant positions in society would suddenly see themselves as exploiting others because of their social position. Rather, the tendency is to see oneself as deriving social position from individual merit and honest achievement. Thus, political consciousness among minorities tends to occur among the lower classes, and although the obverse cannot be discounted, it does not appear likely enough for further comment.

But how does each type of political movement perceive itself in society? The next sections will elaborate on what constitutes such political movements, what type of political values they extol, and what are some historical examples from the American experience. We shall begin with the least intense movement (from some perspectives a nonmovement with no intensity at all): the political accommodationists.

---

2.   This is far different from the biologists' notion of race. Most biologists argue that a race "is a breeding population with characteristic frequencies of inbred traits." Such traits are constantly changing, however, because of our genetic tendency for adaptation. For example, sickle cell anemia is supposedly a phenotypic characteristic of blacks; it is actually characteristic of people who live in areas of high malarial infection. Biologists believe that the sickle cell trait is one way the body has reacted to combat malaria, because carriers of the trait are much less likely to die from the disease. For an excellent introduction to this problem and to the general issue of a biological foundation of race, see Richard A. Goldsby, Race and Races, 2nd ed. (New York: Macmillan, 1977).

Political Accommodation

Most of the sociological literature published during this century has judged accommodation the most important political movement (nonmovement might be a better term) in most minority communities. In a sense that is true; after all, the majority of members of minority groups at most times are not involved in political activity. Minorities often emulate the rest of American society, in which relatively few people are politically active (Pomper, 1974: 1–11). Social scientists in the two decades after World War II emphasized accommodation in politics, along with the themes of acculturation and assimilation. However, this focus glossed over some interesting political movements that were then developing among minorities in the United States. Again, we do not suggest that accommodationists were unimportant. On the contrary, most minority group members do everything they can to nullify the differences society perceives, by emphasizing their individuality and their ability individually to overcome discrimination.

The political psychology of accommodation.   During periods of minority upheaval, accommodationists are in the most precarious of all positions. While they still may be scorned by the majority community, they also find themselves outcasts among their own minority group. It is incorrect to assume that all accommodationists are ashamed of their religion, or try to hide their race, or the like. Certainly, some do; but others simply find their ethnic or minority identity irrelevant. The accommodationist reaction to minority status involves complicated psychological mechanisms (Levin, 1975: ch. 1).

Rejection of one's minority status can result from a refusal to be categorized. Many people feel that such categorization types them, preventing them from acting as individuals. For example, an adolescent Jew may feel himself torn between being treated as an individual and being treated as a Jew. If someone suggests that he is too aggressive, or talks too much, or whatever other "Jewish" stereotype is relevant, he may wonder whether that person is addressing him or his Jewishness. The accommodationist does not want to live with that kind of tension; he attempts to eliminate such social-psychological anxiety by blending into the majority community.

Self-hate.   An extreme kind of accommodation can be found among individuals who hate themselves. This reaction is reflected in Eldridge Cleaver's *Soul on Ice*:

> *My interest in this area persisted undiminished and then in 1955, an event took place in Mississippi which turned me inside out: Emmett Till, a young Negro down from Chicago on a visit, was murdered, allegedly for flirting with a white woman. He had been shot, his head crushed from repeated blows with a blunt instrument, and his badly decomposed body was recovered from the river with a heavy weight on it. I was, of course, angry over the whole bit, but one day I saw in a*

magazine a picture of the white woman with whom Emmett Till was said to have flirted. While looking at the picture, I felt that little tension in the center of my chest I experience when a woman appeals to me. I was disgusted and angry with myself. Here was a woman who had caused the death of a black, possibly because, when he looked at her, he also felt the same tensions of lust and desire in his chest — and probably for the same general reasons that I felt them. It was all unacceptable to me. I looked at the picture again and again, and in spite of everything and against my will and the hate I felt for the woman and all that she represented, she appealed to me. I flew into a rage at myself, at America, at white women, at the history that had placed those tensions of lust and desire in my chest. (Cleaver, 1968: 10–11)

Hating oneself for a natural desire, or in some cases for one's very being, is one result of the extreme social and political pressures on some minorities.

Some form of self-hate is present among all minority groups. Denying one's minority and trying to emulate the majority are the most common form of self-hate. Takie Okamura, a Christian minister in Hawaii in the 1920s, preached that the Hawaiian Japanese should "forget the idea 'Japanese.'" He felt that if the Japanese simply did their jobs, they would eventually be accepted by Americans. "But above everything else remember that YOU ARE GUESTS OF THIS LAND, and be careful in everything you do" (Jacobs and Landau, 1971: 239–40). Among the Jews self-hate has been a constant problem; a German sociologist even coined a term for it: *jüdischen Selbsthass* —Jewish self-hate. Even in such perverse human inventions as the Nazi concentration camps, some Jews hated themselves for having to live with such misery. Self-hate is usually the product of severe political repression of a minority group. However, even the pressures of status will evoke self-hate, usually accompanied by a profound belief in, and disgust for, all the stereotypes applied to one's own group.[3]

A half-Hawaiian, half-Chinese Hawaiian Islander reflects this attitude:

I'm a Hawaiian myself and I hate to say this, but I don't care much for them . . . they are not ambitious people. Their only ambition is to play music. They don't care for anything else. Then you see a Hawaiian does not come to work after a pay-day. Pay-day today and the next day no work. I don't know what they do with their money, but I think they drink a lot.

I don't like their ways. They are funny. I think they are silly. They don't behave decently on the street. They misbehave. I know when I go out with them I feel funny when they don't behave decently.

I don't care to mingle with them because most of them are not

---

3.   The best analysis of such self-hate is still Frantz Fanon, *Black Skin, White Masks* (various editions).

educated. They don't do anything; most of them are loafers and I don't care to go with loafers.

They are so dirty. They eat just like pigs with their hands. Gee, there's one Hawaiian boy who sits right next to me . . . and his feet are full of dirt and mud. Gee! Dirty, can't stand it! And over here [pointing to his neck] full of dirt. When I see him like that I turn my back to him.

I hate Hawaiians, oh, I hate Hawaiians! If you treat 'em good they come back and treat you bad. . . . (Lam, 1936: 405)

Individuality.   It would be unfair to characterize all accommodationists as exhibiting self-hatred. On the contrary, most people who believe in accommodation believe in their individuality and self-worth. It is not that they do not want to be part of a group, but that they want the group to be treated like everyone else. They believe that because the government of the society cannot insure such treatment, the only way for any minority to improve itself is through hard work. They often see as paternalistic and insulting those who would differentiate them through special laws or special favors. Their attitude contains elements of the attitude held by Booker T. Washington, but it is common among many minorities today.

Accommodation is more likely to appeal to members of a minority who have a relatively high class status (Frazier, 1962). However, during periods of no major political or social crisis, accommodationists are in the vast majority across classes. Economic and political research suggests that the wealthier you are, the harder it is for you to forsake an accommodationist position. Obviously, the more material goods you possess, the less likely you will be to rock the boat. Although you may not be as comfortable as the average member of the majority in society, at least you are substantially ahead of the rest of your minority. Economic self-interest can be overcome, but it usually requires a political movement of profound intensity and a political environment of significant repression.

Political freedom and the market economy.   The underlying theme of accommodation is that the political system works: in a given situation, a group can rectify any wrongs done against it. In the United States this belief is accompanied by faith in the market economy and in the ability of economic gains to overcome racial and ethnic distinctions. Accommodationists believe strongly in the individual rather than in the group.

Thomas Sowell, a black economist and noted conservative, ridiculed the attempts of black militants (and their white liberal friends) to change the universities and make them more "relevant" in the 1960s. Sowell pointed to the sacrifices of those who had participated in civil rights marches:

They [former civil rights activists] are also veterans of an age in which they had to function as the only Negro or one of a handful of blacks confronted by many whites. People who have gotten used to standing up to a majority all of their lives are unlikely to go along with the group

> *psychology of today's black militants. Many who were willing to tell a white man to go to hell in the past are equally willing to tell a black man to go to hell now. (Sowell, 1972: 120)*

Sowell finds programs such as affirmative action insulting to blacks, because they suggest that black students cannot succeed in college, for example, without special help. Additionally, such programs actually destroy good black students by admitting ill-equipped students to "high-powered" universities where they have no chance for success. Even worse, charges Sowell, out of a sense of liberalism white doctors teaching in medical schools graduate unqualified minority doctors to whom they would not take their children for care (Sowell, 1972: 93). We shall explore the issue of affirmative action in depth in Chapter 8.

For many accommodationists, the issue of equality is usually moot, because they have such a fierce sense of individual freedom—the right to be different. As long as the accommodationist sees no apparent roadblocks in his way, he feels that there are no roadblocks for others in his group. The concept of social stratification as described by the vertical model is irrelevant to the accommodationists.

Limits of accommodation.   Although accommodation appears by definition to be opposed to minority political movements, there is a paradox. Anyone who feels that his participation in a political movement has been successful—no matter how extreme or intense his position—will usually become accommodationist. That is, as soon as he feels that his demands have been met, whether integrating a lunch counter or overthrowing a government, there is no logical reason for him to remain active in the political movement. Therefore, in the perfect horizontally differentiated society, everyone would be an accommodationist.

The accommodationist feels that society offers him the best that can be expected. Politically, institutions appear to be reasonably just, either because they *are* or because they give the minority group what he thinks it deserves. The majority of accommodationists (those without a conscious sense of self-hate) emphasize their individuality above all else. When they enter the political arena it is as individuals, who demand not to be labeled or categorized. In a sense this is nonminority political action, for in the accommodationist perspective society does, or will, treat them as individuals. Accommodation has no specific ideological flavor; in fact, conservatives, liberals, and (in a limited sense) radicals can be accommodationists.

Political Movements

When a significant gap develops between psychological expectations and material realities, and when the situation is seen as discriminatory against a specific group, political movements grow. They grow in several different forms, and political movements *within* each of these forms can have several levels of intensity. The first type of political movement which will be discussed is nonviolence.

Nonviolence as a political movement.   Dick Gregory, black comedian and pacifist, tells the following story:

> *About a year ago in Chicago I was walking down the street, downtown in the Loop, about ten o'clock in the evening. A white cat walking down the sidewalk, he see me coming, he jump all the way off the sidewalk and get in the gutter. Scared to death. He say, "Mister, you're not going to bother me, are you?"*
>
> *I said, "No, my man, I'm Dick Gregory, I'm dedicated and committed to nonviolence." "You mean you are the Dick Gregory? You don't carry no gun or no knife?" I said, "No." He said, "You don't do no shooting or cutting?" I said, "No." He said, "Well stick 'em up, nigger."*

It is important to understand that nonviolence has a crucial role in most attempts to end discrimination in this country and that it is an attempt to awaken the conscience of the majority.

Picketing, sit-ins, sit-down strikes and the like play a significant role in nonviolent activity. For most Americans, nonviolence is synonymous with Dr. Martin Luther King, Jr. and the black civil rights movement of the 1950s and 1960s. Dr. King was a dominant figure in this political movement. However, although Dr. King was important (some might argue dominant) in this area, he was not alone in employing this tactic. American Indians, Jews, Orientals, as well as many other ethnic groups—notably the Irish on the eastern seaboard—used this tactic with varying degrees of success.

A history of nonviolence.   Nonviolence as a political act was first noted in the West several thousand years ago. Aristophanes' *Lysistrata* not only describes the sexual desertion of the men by the women of Athens over the issue of war, but also their seizure of the Acropolis and the Treasury of Athens. Even the American Revolution began as a nonviolent enterprise with the Boston Tea Party. However, the father of modern notions of nonviolence was Henry David Thoreau, who coined the term *civil disobedience* in his essay of the same name. Objecting both to slavery and to the Mexican–American War (he viewed the two as interrelated), he counseled disobedience of government. To Thoreau, the place for a just person in an unjust society was jail. In fact, he refused to pay taxes as a form of civil disobedience, which led to his famous night of incarceration. He was furious that someone paid his taxes for him (many historians think that it was his close friend, Ralph Waldo Emerson). The idea of going to jail, of being punished for acting in a just manner, became an important political weapon.

In the United States blacks have used nonviolent action literally thousands of times, beginning in the early 1900s (Meier and Rudwick, 1976: 306–404). Such activities have been common in this country, not only among minority groups but also among other sorts of associations, including labor unions.

Sophisticated use of Thoreau's ideas initially occurred outside the United States. Mahatma Gandhi used civil disobedience as a weapon to free India from British colonialism. Gandhi developed the idea of nonviolence to a more advanced ethical stage: *satyagraha*, or truth force. Satyagraha presumes that once they are confronted with the truth, people cannot reject it. It also presumes that no human being is manifestly evil; rather evil is done because of ignorance or convenience. Thus, civil disobedience is not merely negative—disobeying—but positive in that it brings the truth forward for everyone to see. The British, confronted by 10,000 Indians lying across a railroad track so that trains could not pass, were unable to argue that these "ignorant" people cared little about their freedom and loved the rule of the British Empire.

Martin Luther King, Jr.   The standard of nonviolent activity and organization for some time in the future will be the black civil rights movement headed by Martin Luther King, Jr. Indeed, Americans' thinking about the 1950s and '60s is dominated by King and the civil rights protests. King developed the idea of civil disobedience into one of the most important political movements of this century. A Baptist minister, King combined his faith in Christianity (which included a profound belief in the ability of human beings to know good) with civil disobedience. King believed that something had to be done; otherwise, violence by blacks was inevitable, given the intolerable segregation in the South. "I began thinking," writes King,

> about the fact that I stand in the middle of two opposing forces in the Negro community. One is a force of complacency, made up in part of Negroes who, as a result of long years of oppression, are so drained of self respect and sense of "somebodiness" that they have adjusted to segregation. . . . The other force is one of bitterness and hatred, and it comes perilously close to advocating violence. (Storing, ed., 1970: 124)

It was clear to King, as well as to others involved in the civil disobedience movement, that nonviolence was the alternative to violence, the only chance for society to avoid bloodshed.

It would be wrong to assume that King was blinded to reality by his commitment to nonviolence. He believed in nonviolence and thought that violence was a waste of time, whether used for a purpose or merely for catharsis. However, he did support Ghandi's statement that "I prefer to see a man resist evil with violence than to fail to resist evil out of fear." King knew that some form of action must be taken. (In a sense, this emphasis on activity leading to a specific accomplishment led to frustration, and tended to drive individuals who were frustrated by the slow pace of nonviolence to turn elsewhere.) To King, nonviolence was preferable to violence not merely because of the moral force behind it, but also because it tended to organize "people into permanent groups to protect their own interests and produce change on their own behalf" (King, 1967: 37). Such organization would be crucial for maintaining political and social power, once the gross injustices of society were alleviated. Nonviolence had more than an immediate purpose.

King's major contribution to nonviolent activity, beyond the visibility he gained for civil disobedience as a political tool, was recognition of the need for massive organization. Participants in every civil rights demonstration King planned went through weeks of intensive training. Those who were to sit in at lunch counters had to learn to take intense abuse, so session leaders taunted them, spit on them, and physically abused them. Discipline and organization were the key elements of King's contribution. Those involved in the nonviolent movement believed profoundly that the actions of civil disobedience, in and of themselves, were liberating.

> *The television cameras are not able to portray the real truth. They cannot capture the strange truth that ten minutes after we are arrested and thrown into jail, we own that jail. When a man is jailed for doing right suddenly the jail becomes the prisoner. The people behind the bars are in control and the prison guards are the slaves of wrongdoing. (Gregory, 1968: 43)*

Television did have an impact, at least in the earliest days of the civil disobedience movement. The sight of brutal police and their dogs attacking peaceful protesters outraged most of the country. The political effect was to alienate the South, which had previously been considered merely peculiar. Segregation laws were seen as pernicious and evil. Pressure was even felt from abroad, because the United States had constantly touted itself as the model of democracy. The use of nonviolent protest to harness all these usually nonexistent or apolitical forces (united public sentiment, foreign pressure, and so on) led to major successes for King.

The use of civil disobedience by minorities.   The nonviolent movement is by no means the least intense kind of political organization. In some ways it takes far greater commitment, passively to face significant abuse, than to act in other ways. It is fair to say that nonviolence is the most conservative kind of movement, in the sense of respecting goverment institutions. Nonviolent activists must believe that (1) the institutions of society are fundamentally good and just; (2) the majority of society has the ability to understand and do something about injustice; and (3) as protesters they are willing, nay demand, to be punished for breaking unjust laws.

The third point above is often most confusing to observers of nonviolence. After all, if a law is unjust, why should one want to be punished for breaking it? For those who espouse nonviolence it is the direct confrontation between good and evil—such as the arrest of a six-year-old black girl for wanting to eat at Woolworth's—that forces society to review its attitudes toward its norms and institutions.

The emphasis of civil disobedience is on action. If one can overcome fear and act in a "moral" way, then justice, freedom, and the feeling of alienation from the rest of society will redress themselves. The initial action is the most difficult. When Rosa Parks, the black housekeeper, refused to give her seat in the back of the bus to a white man, she made an astonishing impact on American history. Her refusal became the symbolic catalyst for the highly successful Montgomery, Alabama, bus boycott and set the tone for civil rights activism in the next decade. As is true of most political movements, it is impossible to understand completely why that first action produced such a response. Let us inject the idea of relative deprivation. The year before Montgomery, the Supreme Court ruled in *Brown v. Board of Education* that segregation was invidious and illegal. This decision was greeted with great joy in the black community, some calling it the second freeing of the slaves. Yet as the months passed nothing changed. Expectations far outreached reality. Rosa Parks was the first to act on an idea whose time had come. A political epoch was begun when this one individual refused to obey the segregation laws.

Nonviolence was one among many types of political movement that might have arisen at the time. It is merely chance that a series of circumstances promoted King and nonviolence in the early 1960s. Other movements also existed, but with far fewer members and little or no visibility. It is important to note that when nonviolent action does not work, or is not perceived as viable, there are several other roads for a minority to take. The one with the least apparent organization is rebellion.

Rebellion: Violence as Political Action

What is rebellion? Why is it a political movement? Rebellion is usually defined as open or determined defiance of or resistance to any authority or controlling power. Rebellion movements are political because they defy constituted authority, but they differ from the other types of minority movements because their protest follows no overt program or plan. Rebellion movements act cathartically—that is, act to relieve pent-up energies and emotions—in the hope of solving a political issue. The issues vary, and rebellions are often sparked by isolated events having little or nothing to do with the issues. For example, a riot might result from a perfectly legitimate arrest by police officers. The incident itself is important only insofar as it becomes the last straw in a series of perceived abuses.

The activity of rebellion movements is violence. Although most social scientists are uncomfortable with the subject, violence does have a political use and is often a most effective weapon.[4] This statement is not made as a justification of violence or violent acts; the ethical question is different from the political one. American history has demonstrated that groups that engage in

---

4. We shall offer no definition of violence, for it is one of the most complicated of all social phenomena. On the definition and problem of violence, see H. L. Neiburg, Political Violence, or Weinstein and Grundy, The Ideology of Political Violence.

violence often have at least short-term success (Gamson, 1975). H. Rap Brown was probably right when he concluded that "violence is as American as apple pie."

Violence can and does take many forms. Riots, the most familiar, have been used not only by but also against minority groups. Other types of violence have involved street gangs and protective associations. An even more interesting form of violence used to defend minority political rights is often categorized in American history books as thievery, robbery, and murder. (Of course, this is not to say that all thieves, robbers, and murderers work in the interest of minority groups!)

Chicano violence.   The most effective use of illegal activities was made by Chicanos in the southwestern United States. From the Anglo (non-Spanish-speaking) point of view, these Chicanos were bloodthirsty bandits interested only in plunder and murder—a stereotype still prevalent in movies and on television. From the Chicano point of view they were rebels engaged in social protest. "Law enforcement" agencies such as the Texas Rangers often abused the Spanish-speaking population and withheld from them any constitutional forms of political participation, such as voting. The Chicanos saw themselves as conquered people. The United States had annexed California, Arizona, and New Mexico after the American victory in the Mexican–American War of the 1840s, and the revolt of Texas was more than a little encouraged by the United States government. Chicanos were colonized and trying to learn to live with the minority (Anglos) in control.

Most Anglos saw themselves as superior to the "lazy" Mexicans and were imbued with the idea of manifest destiny (Acuña, 1972: 35). The combination of pressures led to violence and fame for the great Chicano "bandits" of the period. They became Chicano folk heroes and symbols of brutality to the Anglo:

> In California such persons as Joaquin Murieta, Tiburcio Vásquez and Juan Flores engaged in the politics of insurrection. Joaquin Murieta became a legend in his lifetime. He terrorized much of the central valley, especially Calaveras County, until he was allegedly apprehended and killed in 1853. However, his reputation grew in leaps and bounds. Even after his death, victims of other guerrilleros credited Murieta with some of the deeds. Juan Flores was another guerrillero who became a thorn in the side of the Anglo authorities. He led a large group of Chicanos through the northern mining areas and through the cattle ranches of the central valley. Tiburcio Vásquez created much havoc for the Anglos. Vásquez's chief motive for the violence he created, according to Leonard Pitt, was to avenge Yankee injustice. (Navarro, 1974: 59–60)

Juan Cortina and Pancho Villa.   In the 1860s Juan Cortina led an open revolt in the lower Rio Grande Valley. Initially, reacting to violence against Chicanos by an Anglo sheriff in Brownsville, Texas, Cortina led a group of his ranch hands on a mission of revenge. Ultimately, Mexicans from both sides of the border flocked to him. Not until 1873 did the Mexican government, at the request of the United States, persuade Cortina to end his guerrilla activities against the United States.

In the early part of the twentieth century Pancho Villa plundered and murdered throughout New Mexico, becoming a symbol of resistance for Chicanos. President Theodore Roosevelt ordered General John Joseph "Black Jack" Pershing (so nicknamed because his first command was an all-black army company) to capture Villa. However, Villa's grasp of desert warfare was far superior, and Pershing had to retreat to the United States without success.

We do not mean to suggest that such folk heroes were motivated by pure political or ethical purposes. Some of these "bandits" *were* Robin Hoods, robbing the rich and giving to the Chicanos; others were concerned about their own gain and little else. No matter what their goals, they became revered by the mass of Chicanos and gave them a sense of self-worth. Chicanos were more willing to demand social, economic, or political rights after such examples had been set. The impact of the bandits on American politics and on their own people is undeniable.

The dimensions of rebellion.   Most rebellion movements are action-oriented; they seldom have a program, although many have had slogans such as "Burn, baby, burn." The underlying goal of all such action is social change. Most rebellion movements take place within an atmosphere of intensity that perceives violence as necessary for social change.

> You cannot have progress without friction and upheaval. For social change, two systems must clash, because it's a struggle for survival for one and a struggle for liberation for the other. And always the powers in command are ruthless and unmerciful in defending their positions and their privileges. (Schultz, 1962: 54)

The dichotomy of interests is crucially important, for backers of nonviolence assume that social justice is available for all. Those who espouse rebellion see a natural competition between groups in society.

History is full of people who believed that violence can gain individual freedom. Nat Turner, Denmark Vesey, and dozens of others instigated slave revolts during the early nineteenth century (Franklin, 1967: 145–241). There were the Molly Maguires in the coal fields of Pennsylvania; the American Indians, who fought a two-century-long war against the United States; people in Appalachia, who are often treated as a minority fighting the coal bosses and the East Coast tobacco companies—almost *every* minority group in this country has resorted to violence at some time in the last 200 years. Internationally, the *eta* of Japan[5] and the untouchables in India have participated in rebellion. (And other elements of society have also committed violence against them.)

In summary, although rebellion movements appear to produce only violence, they usually have a conscious or unconscious political theme. Additionally, rebellion movements play a vital role in making minorities aware of their circumstances. That is, such movements are often a catalyst in awakening political consciousness among groups, perhaps as the result of the successful use of violence, or of the use of severe repression, often accompanied by greater violence, by those in power. In any case, the use of violence can and often does have political ramifications for minority groups. Violence can succeed in gaining power, or it can lead to other political tactics.

"Power" Groups: The Use of Identity and Culture to Capture Political Power

Minority "power" groups attempt to recapture their cultural identity. Power movements (such as black power, red power, or Italian power) have a distinct program and political purpose. Although some condone violence, their major purpose is to recapture the essential values and styles inherent in their minority culture. They believe that their history has been distorted by the majority group, and that by recapturing it they can understand who they are. Finding their "roots" helps them understand the oppression of their ancestors, develop self-respect, and build political and social power on the cultural tradition.

To the external observer, recapturing one's group identity may seem romantic and unrelated to political power. However, one's history has much to do with success in gaining political power. First, we are confident that we can do something only insofar as we know others like us can do approximately the same thing. For example, if your friend John, who is just like you, does well on an algebra exam, you generally feel that you can do as well as John. However, if you are classed with the Johns in a society in which every John (and every ancestor of every John) is considered stupid, you may feel unable to succeed.

Second, people make gross generalizations about others, on the basis of very little information. The most vivid example of this is race or minority status. Another example of how small bits of information can change percep-

---

5. The *eta*, the outcast class in Japan, experienced all of the types of political movements described in this chapter. In Japan, as in India, caste was maintained through a vast network of social communication—even though the *eta* were not visually distinguishable to Westerners. Assumptions about the *eta* were also "biologically" based: they had no central digestive system and fewer vertebrae, and their necks did not cast shadows. See George A. DeVos and Hiroshi Wagatsuma, *Japan's Invisible Race: Caste in Culture and Personality* (Berkeley, Ca.: Center for Japanese and Korean Studies, 1966).

tion comes from a study done by psychologists who wanted to determine the impact of IQ scores on people's attitudes. In an experiment, the psychologists gave IQ exams to the students in several classrooms. Then they made a random sample of the students—including less intelligent, average, and smart students. They gave the students' teachers the random list, telling them that these students had made the highest IQ scores. When the psychologists returned after several months, they found that not only had the random sample of students significantly increased their grade point averages, but the teachers raved about the exceptional ability uncovered by the tests. Obviously, the beliefs others hold about us have a profound impact on our performance (Rosenthal and Jacobson, 1968).

Culture as a unit of political power. Most political power movements believe that a cultural identity adds to their power in several ways. Most importantly, it denies that the group wants to assimilate with the majority, that is, to become indistinguishable from it. Instead, such groups emphasize differences in clothing (for example, many blacks wear dashikis), cuisine, language (Yiddish is a very popular subject among Jewish college students), reading "lost" literature or group history, and the like. Power advocates feel (1) that they have an important cultural contribution to give to the rest of society; (2) they do not have to beg the rest of society to accept them; and (3) the differences they exhibit say nothing about equality or the goods they should receive, only that they are different and are proud of that difference.

The cultural redefinition suggests a strong, cohesive group with potential voting clout. The majority is put on notice that it is dealing with a group that is equal and deserving of the same benefits. It is one thing to deal with a group that is trying to become like you, and quite another to cope with a group that argues that it is both different and equal. Apparently minor victories, like the offering of black history or Chicano history courses at a university, are major concessions, because an institution of the majority has admitted that such areas are worth studying. Underlying this is the attitude that the minority group is merely different from, and not inferior to, the majority. The women's movement today emphasizes the contributions of women to society as *equals;* it holds that cultural contributions by women have been ignored, not because such contributions are unimportant, but because women accomplished them. (June Sochen [1974] argues that it is necessary to study "herstory" as well as history.)

Identity and minority pride. The major emphasis of the power movement is not on convincing those on the outside of the importance of one's culture, but on convincing the minority that they have a culture of which to be proud. The slogans "red power," "Italian power," and "black is beautiful" are advertisements by groups to themselves.

The emphasis on black pride today is an attempt to get black people to look at themselves as they are objectively. It is an effort to convince us that we are something, that we are somebody. And the evidence is all there; we have a proud history, we refuse to be kept in bondage, we will be free. Our determination is making history around the world. Our unbroken spirits are already the theme of folk songs. We just need to present the evidence to our people. (Tucker, 1969: 50)

Recovering history allows minorities to destroy stereotypes. Stereotypes have a profound impact on the individuals who are stereotyped. They may feel that if they do not behave according to the stereotype, they will be punished. For example, during the 1930s in Alabama, a black who bought a new car often wore a chauffeur's cap to make whites think that he was driving for a white person. If he was indiscreet he might be stopped and brutally assaulted by whites for trying to be "uppity."

Some groups began to review their self-evaluations as the result of power movements. American Indians often reflect with disgust that as children they cheered for the cavalry over the Indian. Power gave a new-found respect, as this review of the movie, *Stalking Moon*, demonstrates:

As the story goes, according to the blushing confession of the leading lady, she submitted to the "ferocious savage" Salvaje in order to save her life. She became his wife and bore his son. Now right away this confuses me. If he was such a ferocious savage, then why didn't he just have his way with the dear lady and then simply kill her? How come he made her his wife and allowed her to have his child? Well, anyhow — this pitiful little white woman went along for ten years, watching her son grow up, pretending not to hate. But suddenly, after ten years, she meets up with her own kind of people, that is to say, the civilized whites. She promptly seeks asylum for herself and her son, begging a good old army scout to take them along, which he does.

Meantime, Salvaje realizes his son has taken an unexplained trip with the little mother, and for some reason he sets out after them. Surely not because he loves them. Meanwhile we see that the good old scout and the little white lady have set up housekeeping and they're going to keep the little half-savage son also, presumably to teach him the niceties of life. There are a couple of fights along the way; in one, Salvaje emerges as a hateful fiend after wiping out several able-bodied white men at the stagecoach station; in the other fight, a weary, bedraggled but oh so heroic scout succeeds in killing that same ferocious fiend. After which the two pure lilywhites, all virtuously victorious, fade off into the sunset with Salvaje's son and the beautiful civilized prospect of the boy to be raised by his father's killer.

The way I see it, Salvaje risked his life and lost it, to try to regain his son, who was taken from him by an irresponsible, selfish woman. It seems quite natural for a man to get furious when his wife takes his child, deserts him, and goes off to play house with another man. (Horn, 1971: 83)

Pluralistic politics.   The accommodationist and nonviolence movements strongly support coalition politics, the joining with other groups to pressure or elect public officials. Power advocates generally feel that coalition politics takes advantage of their groups; they prefer a cohesive, pragmatic political organization open only to their group members. Clearly, this view accepts the notion that individuals can effectively use group organization; thus, it indirectly supports the viability of the government. Support for the system varies. Some power groups demand massive changes in the social system; others emphasize the use of segregated mechanisms within the social, economic, and political system. For example, black capitalists advocate that blacks massively buy small and large businesses, through which to gain economic and political power. They want federal government agencies to make loans and give advice to minority businesses because the Small Business Administration has a notorious history of discrimination.

Power movements stress the social and cultural unity of the minority: if unity can be maintained, political power will follow. Black power leaders demanded four things from black people:

(1) that they stop being ashamed of being black, (2) that they move into a position where they can define what freedom is, . . . (3) that they move to build a power base around the question of blackness, (4) that they move to build independent *political, social, economic, and cultural institutions that they can control and use as instruments of social change. (Bennett, 1966: 30)*

Black movements in the United States have always emphasized the group's culture and organization (Pease and Pease, 1968: 19). The Irish take-over of machine politics, the boss system, and St. Patrick's Day parades are elements of a form of cultural power movement. The history of Jewish self-pride and organization extends back into the nineteenth century. The use of unions; the Jewish theater (with its own plays, actors, recording stars, and theater buildings), producing nationally known figures like Paul Muni and Al Jolson; pride in Jews like Bernard Baruch and Albert Einstein; and formidable interest groups like B'nai B'rith and Hadassah were all elements of "Jewish power" long before the term was coined. In one form or another, such movements have arisen among most of the minority groups in the United States.

Recapturing culture.   Power or identity groups are vitally interested in recapturing their culture, which they believe has been "lost, stolen or strayed." They firmly believe that self-pride is the only key to success in the highly competitive social and political structure of American society. These groups tend to be socially conservative, in the sense that they believe that the rest of society will appreciate their own cultural identities. The power groups see ethnic clothing, food, literature, music, and the like as weapons to help them confront and compete in the pluralistic society outside their group. Power movements vary: some demand little change in society, and others demand great change. But all power movements believe that pride in one's roots leads to political and social rewards.

Radicalism: Economics Determines the Existence of Minorities

Radicalism among minority groups is largely a twentieth-century phenomenon. Radicals want fundamental change in the social, economic, and political institutions of the United States; they espouse using their minority group (in some cases, more than one group) to overthrow — violently or peacefully — the present society. Radicals believe that the economic system determines the position of minorities, and the resulting class differences inherent in society. They take an economically deterministic view of how minorities relate. Because of this economic emphasis, and for several other reasons we shall explore later, most radical groups use the language if not the ideas of Marxism. The difference between *language* and *ideas* is important; radical groups often use entirely different meanings for the rhetorical devices of Marxism, such as dialectical materialism, praxis, alienation, and exploitation. Also, while devout Marxists insist on using all of the Marxist themes as a whole (usually including at least Marx, Engels, and Lenin), most radical minority movements selectively emphasize only those parts of Marxism most relevant to them.

Radicalism has roots throughout American history, but minority movements were little involved until the 1890s. The most prominent groups to use rhetoric and planning dominated by economic concerns were the early labor unions. One might argue that labor unions are the equivalent of a minority group, for various reasons, but we shall not take that position. Rather we suggest that labor unions were an excellent model, along with socialism and Marxism later in the nineteenth century, for minority political movements. There were many other radical traditions in America. Orestes Brownson (1803–1876), considered one of the most radical men of his time, supported such radical organizations as the Workingmen's Union. During the same period, the locofocists, or Equal Rights party, advocated extreme social and political equality, with everyone leveled to one position. In a sense they were precursors of the Maoists, for they insisted that everyone dress alike to eliminate distinction by dress. The socialist communities sponsored by Robert Owen and others were another foundation for radical minority movements. Amana, Iowa; New Harmony, Indiana; Utopia, Ohio; and the all-black socialist community of Nashoba, Tennessee, became part of the intellectual and social tradition minorities would later use.

Who is oppressed?   Like power movements, radical movements emphasize recapturing minority cultural pride and self-awareness. Unlike power movements, they do not believe that self-awareness must come through the cultural isolation of the minority. The important issue for radical movements is oppression. From the radical viewpoint, *all* of society is oppressed, but only minority groups are consciously aware of it. This awareness exists because the economic system has pushed them "outside"; they are the only ones with an objective view of society.

The evil force against which radical groups expend the most effort is capitalism. The capitalist economic system victimizes society by upholding values such as competition, individualism, and racial distinction. In a capitalist society it is desirable to be more successful than others (that is, to have more money); therefore the majority use unfair tactics. Capitalism is a game of advantages. Since everything is legal in a society that values financial success alone, discrimination is a natural outcome.

Because the major purpose of radical movements is the end of capitalism, unity with other groups that have the same goal is legitimate.

> It isn't just a matter of trusting the goodwill of other slaves and other colonies and other peoples, it is a simple matter of common need. We need allies, we have a powerful enemy who cannot be defeated without an allied effort! The enemy at present is the capitalist system and its supporters. Our prime interest is to destroy them. Anyone else with this same interest must be embraced, we must work with, beside, through, over, under anyone, whose aim is the same as ours in this. Capitalism must be destroyed, and after it is destroyed, if we find that we still have problems, we'll work them out. (Jackson, 1970: 202)

The radical emphasis on unity with other groups tends to result in severe conflicts, not only with power movements, but with nationalists as well.

Radicals view biological differences, such as race, as products of the division of labor. That is, they feel that biological differences were used to justify the necessary class arrangements of capitalism.

> Blacks and whites being conceived as mutually exclusive types, those attributes imputed to the blacks could not also be imputed to the whites —at least not in equal degree —without blurring the line separating the races. These images were based upon the social function of the two races, the work they performed. (Cleaver, 1968: 78)

Such discrimination played two roles in capitalism. First, it provided a minority as a ready source of menial labor. Second, it convinced the vast numbers among the majority who were not terribly successful that at least they were better off —no matter how destitute —than the minority.

Forms of radicalism: minority unionism.   One of the first forms of minority radical activity was unionism, and most radical minority unions exemplified or actually joined the International Workers of the World (the Wobblies) in the early years. The Wobblies had a strong connection with international Communism, but they were surprisingly tolerant of varying degrees of Marxism. As early as 1903 Chicano and Japanese sugar beet workers went on strike in southern California. By 1915 unions of Chicano miners were striking at the Clifton, Morenci, and Metcalf mines in Arizona. During the same period Jews in the garment district of New York were attacking the industry management with strikes and sometimes with violence. In fact, it is hard to think of a minority group in the first 30 years of this century that did not use unionism to attack the capitalist system.

Minority groups felt that capitalism exploited them, further enriching members of the majority and impoverishing the minority groups. Great technical achievements, such as connecting the nation from east to west with railroads, were made at the price of mass sacrifices by minorities. The golden spike driven at Promontory Point, Utah, a contemporary commentator observed, was awash with the blood of thousands of Chinese, who had helped build the western section of the railroad from the Pacific. There is impressive historical evidence of the sacrifices minority groups have made to build the United States. For example:

> Chicanos . . . brought a newly-unified country the brawn and muscle needed for its development. They were poor and they lacked sophisticated skills. Yet they built the railroads, not only in the Southwest but in the North and East. Their sweat developed the vast agricultural lands. They plowed the land, planted the seed, and produced the harvest. Their labor constructed the houses and public buildings. They cut the timber and built the highways. And out of ground that had once been theirs, they created the West—for the use, profit and enjoyment of others. (Moore and Cuéllar, 1970: 23–24)

Minority groups initially used unions to gain access to the social and political goods of society, which was considered astonishingly radical. Unfortunately, especially as they grew large and achieved political power, unions were highly selective among minorities. Samuel Gompers, head of the American Federation of Labor, was profoundly affected by social Darwinism and particularly despised Asiatics. A pamphlet he coauthored demanded that the Chinese be excluded from the United States by law or "by force of arms," since the Chinese "found it natural to lie, cheat and murder" (Hill, 1967). When the Japanese and Mexican sugar beet workers asked the AFL for a charter, Gompers refused unless the Mexicans would desert the Japanese. This the Mexicans refused.

By the 1930s unions had grown in size, become an accepted part of the American economic system, and subsequently decreased in radicalism. Union struggles on behalf of minorities almost disappeared, with two important exceptions: A. Jennings Randolph and the Sleeping-Car Porters Union in the 1930s, and recently Cesar Chavez and the United Farm Workers.

There were other forms of radicalism during this era, notably Communist party membership. However, little of the Communist effort in the United States was directed toward alleviating the condition of minorities. Also, in the era of McCarthyism in the 1950s, any position that smacked of Communism appeared to eliminate any chance of changing one's social and political position through radicalism. Radicalism was not only anti-American but impractical. Many who still espoused radical ideals were deported, imprisoned, or black-listed.[6] With the thaw in the cold war mentality during the 1960s, radicalism among minorities returned, but in a different form.

The Black Panthers

When Huey Newton taunted the police on the courthouse steps in Oakland, when he stood there with his gun and challenged them and called them pigs, most people saw only his swaggering bravado. I cannot pretend to read his thoughts, but I believe that, in part at least, this same frenetic desperation was seizing him, as it seizes all who seek release from terror in a final convulsive claim to manhood. This is the point where persecution breaks down, where it backfires: when it drives the victim beyond fear. (Tucker, 1971: 59)

The Black Panthers were one of the most startling and dramatic developments of the late 1960s. Yet it was natural for the threads of radicalism, sewn into the black community years before, to appear again, woven into a different cloth. The Black Panthers, mainly organized in ghetto communities, claimed at their peak over 100 chapters throughout the country. The Panthers accepted violence; they did not advocate it. (This assertion is open to question, depending on one's ideological perception. However, this was the Panther point of view.) Violence had been forced upon them by the outside community, whose representative was the police. In the ghetto community, the police generally represented the political power of the state. It had been known for years that ghetto communities were especially abused by police. Ghettos contained poor people; poor people commit more violent crimes than middle-class or upper-class people; therefore, more police are needed in ghetto areas. Since the vast majority of police are white, they are starkly visible in any nonwhite community.

Huey Newton and other Black Panther leaders felt that violence was legitimate because blacks were in effect a third-world people and had been denied rights because of that status. The denial had not come about peacefully, but had resulted from intense violence against the minority group. However, the Panthers were not advocating a race war or racial distinctions:

We see it as a necessity for us to progress as human beings and live on the face of this earth along with other people. We do not fight racism with racism. We fight racism with solidarity. We do not fight exploitative

---

6.   A number of cold war documentaries are available through the federal catalog; for example, *Red Nightmare*, narrated by Jack Webb, and Woody Allen's not so funny *The Front*, an excellent film with insight into the fear of this era.

capitalism with black capitalism. We fight capitalism with basic socialism. And we do not fight imperialism with more imperialism. We fight imperialism with proletarian internationalism (Seale, 1970: 71).

The majority would be confronted with minority peoples who were willing to die for their cause.

Whether this is rhetoric or reality is beside the point. One importance of the Black Panther movement is that it acted as a model and organizational framework for the black community. It had programs such as free breakfasts for children in Oakland, California, and other communities. Interestingly, the Panthers supported voter registration drives. They also forced city governments to reevaluate the types of police services provided in minority communities. We do not judge the Panthers bad or good; we merely state that they apparently filled the radical void in the black community.

An even more important aspect of the Black Panthers is that they provided a model for other minority communities. Many minority groups emulated their organization and strategies, notably the Chicano Brown Panthers, the Asian-American Political Alliance among Japanese-American students, and the re-formed Young Lords in the Puerto Rican community of New York. Radical student groups abroad used the Panther model, as did the Dahlit Panthers, an organization among the untouchable class in India. Will the Panther model have any long-lasting impact, or will it simply disappear? It is too early to tell. But no matter what happens to this particular form of radicalism, it appears certain that radicalism will continue as a form of minority political activity.

Minority socialism.   The history of radicalism in the United States extends from the American Revolution to the present. Minorities have also used radicalism to form political movements, but with greater frequency in this century. Unions were the most powerful form of radicalism during this early period. Radicals used Marxist and socialist terms extensively and believed that the economy determines one's social and political situation. They tried to organize in ways which would either significantly change the capitalist system or overthrow it. Although it would be incorrect to suggest that all radical movements were violent, violence is usually seen as a legitimate tool against political structures which oppress the minority. The Black Panthers, one of the most influential of contemporary radical groups, played a vital role model for many other minority groups in this country and abroad.

Nationalism

One of the most intense types of minority political movements is nationalism. First, nationalists demand a profound commitment to the sanctity of their culture. Second, nationalism generally condones violence as a legitimate method of advancing goals. Third, nationalists often support their beliefs with religion or a religious fervor. The last point is crucial, because almost any act can be justified if it is divinely ordained.

Land.   Nationalism usually takes two forms: either land and autonomy within the state, or a mass return to a homeland. Although both desires seem simple, they are actually complicated. Disagreement over what constitutes the foundation of a state's existence often causes factionalism among organizations within minority groups that apparently have the same goals. The important unifying factor is *land* as a symbol that a group exists politically and has political importance. Such use of land is a symbolic device correlating somewhat with the rise of nationalism over the past three hundred years.

Nationalism is often successful.   Minorities often use nationalism because it has been so successful. Modern history is full of examples of the use of violent methods to wrest massive areas of land away from one state to form another. (One of the most notable examples is the United States.) Because so many nationalist revolutions have succeeded, it is often impossible for a minority group to believe that nationalism may not work for them.

Nationalist revolutions do not come about peacefully:

> *I cite these various revolutions, brothers and sisters, to show you that you don't have a peaceful revolution. There's no such thing as a non-violent revolution. The only kind of revolution that is non-violent is the Negro revolution. The only revolution in which the goal is loving your enemy is the Negro revolution. It's the only revolution in which the goal is a desegregated lunch counter, a desegregated theater, a desegregated park, and a desegregated public toilet; you can sit down next to white folks—on the toilet. That's no revolution. Revolution is based on land. Land is the basis of all independence. Land is the basis of freedom, justice and equality. . . . (Breitman, 1965: 9)*

That is Malcolm X's critique of the nonviolent movement, as well as a stirring insight into the importance of land to minorities. Minorities often use their demands for land to highlight the history of exploitation of their group at the hands of the majority. For example, American Indians were forced to live on reservations, which (especially in Oklahoma and Texas) were later found to contain valuable resources. So the Indians were forced off the reservations and given smaller tracts of land. Since they were given no tools, seed, or other supplies, the first county tax levy would force them to sell the property— which they had not been intended to keep in the first place. The violent take-over of Indian land, and the subsequent subtle swindling of other lands from the Indians, were highlighted in November 1969 by the seizure of Alcatraz Island in San Francisco Bay by the first pan-tribal effort of American Indians in the twentieth century. The "Proclamation to the Great White Father" lists the ironies of American land dealings with the Indians.

Proclamation:
To The Great White Father and All His People

We, the native Americans, re-claim the land known as Alcatraz Island in the name of all American Indians by right of discovery.

We wish to be fair and honorable in our dealings with the Caucasian inhabitants of this land, and hereby offer the following treaty:

We will purchase said Alcatraz Island for twenty-four dollars ($24) in glass beads and red cloth, a precedent set by the white man's purchase of a similar island about 300 years ago. We know that $24 in trade goods for these 16 acres is more than was paid when Manhattan Island was sold, but we know that land values have risen over the years. Our offer of $1.24 per acre is greater than the $.47 per acre that the white men are now paying the California Indians for their land.

We will give to the inhabitants of this island a portion of that land for their own, to be held in trust by the American Indian Movement and by the Bureau of Caucasian Affairs to hold in perpetuity—for as long as the sun shall rise and the rivers go down to the sea. We will further guide the inhabitants in the proper way of living. We will offer them our religion, our education, our life-ways, in order to help them achieve our level of civilization and thus raise them and all their white brothers up from their savage and unhappy state. We offer this treaty in good faith and wish to be fair and honorable in our dealings with all white men.

We feel that this so-called Alcatraz Island is more than suitable for an Indian Reservation, as determined by the white man's own standards. By this we mean that this place resembles most Indian reservations in that:

1. It is isolated from modern facilities, and without adequate means of transportation.
2. It has no fresh running water.
3. It has inadequate sanitation facilities.
4. There are no oil or mineral rights.
5. There is no industry and so unemployment is very great.
6. There are no health care facilities.
7. The soil is rocky and non-productive; and the land does not support game.
8. There are no educational facilities.
9. The population has always exceeded the land base.
10. The population has always been held as prisoners and kept dependent upon others.

Further, it would be fitting and symbolic that ships from all over the world, entering the Golden Gate, would first see Indian land, and thus be reminded of the true history of this nation. This tiny island would be a symbol of the great lands once ruled by free and noble Indians.

The United States and colonialism.   The heated debate over the Panama Canal treaty in 1978 was a remarkable experience for many American academics. Most scholars had thought that the ten-year agony of Americans in Vietnam had cured their desire to control other nations politically, economically, or socially. Yet the vote on the Panama Canal treaty, which would end American control of a colony, was very close; most political scientists feel that if the question had been put to a public vote, the treaty would have been rejected. It is important to realize that there are external minorities—that is, colonies—with important interests in American politics.

Besides the Panama Canal Zone, the United States still has colonial control over Samoa, the Virgin Islands, and Puerto Rico. Especially in Puerto Rico there has been growing nationalist sentiment (interestingly, complemented by a growing desire for statehood). Such nationalist movements parallel the sentiments of internal nationalist groups. In fact, in 1962 a delegation from Puerto Rico asked the United Nations to decide whether Puerto Rico ought to be free; a significant majority of the delegates voted in favor of the Puerto Rican proposal. The United States was placed in the embarrassing position of vetoing the measure.

The danger of acculturation.   From the nationalist viewpoint, the most dangerous direction a minority can take is to become like the majority. Nationalists feel that all other movements involve fundamental compromise with the majority culture, in effect stripping away the minority's culture so that the minority individual becomes a white-Indian, a white-black, or a Christian-Jew. Other movements seem to offer cultural genocide. Especially, nationalists judge power advocates naive for believing that cutural separation from the majority is possible without physical separation. Here is a statement of the black nationalist position:

> The "accepted" Negro, the "integrated" Negro are mere euphemisms which hide a cruel and relentless cultural destruction that is sometimes agonizing to the middle-class Negro but is becoming intolerable to the black masses. A Negro who refuses to yield his identity and to ape the white model finds he can survive in dignity only by rejecting the entire white society, which most ultimately means challenging the law and the law enforcement mechanisms. . . .
>
> A formal partitioning of the United States into two totally separate and independent nations, one white and one black, is the only solution. Many will condemn it as a defeatist solution . . . [but] a society is stable only to the extent that there exists a basic core of value judgments that are unthinkingly accepted by the bulk of its members. (Browne, 1968: 56)

Many other militant nationalist organizations have also attacked individuals who would try to be part of the larger society. In a very real sense, nationalists are correct when they suggest that complete assimilation would lead to the destruction of the minority group as an entity in society. But they do not believe that the minority group will ever be accepted; rather, a few token members will be given what appear to be significant positions, while the vast majority of members will suffer discrimination. This is the position of groups like the rabidly nationalist Jewish Defense League.

For the nationalist group, culture takes on the character of an ideology; that is, one's culture is not merely *one* way of seeing the world, but the *only* way. This ideology is useful because it teaches the nationalist the role he or she must play in the overall drama of liberation, the end product of any nationalist movement. Attacking acculturation with the majority and developing a cultural world view are the basis of nationalist political action.

Other political movements endanger the minority.   The nationalist feels that other types of political movements, especially nonviolence and radicalism, undermine the minority individual's ability to identify with a group, as well as minority group power in society. This loss of power occurs because minorities, no matter whether they are acculturated or not, have no political input into society. As one Jewish nationalist commented,

> *the black American is the first to openly abjure the idea of assimilation, to recognize the inherent lie in the concept of the melting pot. Through black nationalism he has developed a new black pride and hence the ticket to liberalism.*
>
> *The young American Jew is a good deal slower. He desperately craves assimilation; the very idea of "Jewishness" embarrasses him. If you tell him that he doesn't "look Jewish," he will invariably take it as a compliment. The concept of Jewish nationalism, Israel notwithstanding, he finds laughable. . . . He scrapes along ashamed of his identity and yet is obsessed with it. He goes so far as to join black nationalist organizations, not as a Jew, but as a white. He does not and will not understand that his relevance is as a Jew, a fellow victim, and that his only effectiveness is as such. His destiny is that of the Jews but he denies what is apparent to the rest of us; he wants to be an "American," a leftist American talking liberation and an aspiring WASP. (Rosenberg, 1973:6)*

Nationalists resent other types of movements. Although all political movement members think their particular form of political action is the right path, none are so vehement as the nationalists. In fact, in the late 1960s an open war developed between the nationalist Black Muslims, led by Ron Karenga, and the Black Panthers; several people were killed and dozens injured. More recently there has been fighting between nationalist groups in both the black and the Chicano communities.

The religious basis of political actions.   One of the most fascinating aspects of nationalism is that most such movements have a strong religious basis. That is, such movements are based not only on secular interests, but on divine command or inspiration. This has been true of Chicano, Jewish, and Italian nationalist movements, among others, at various times throughout American history. One consequence of tying nationalist movements so closely to religion is that strict rules and organization can be maintained, as well as zeal and commitment to group goals that could not be expected from groups that emphasize individuality and freedom. For example, anyone who knows any of Reverend Sun Myung Moon's followers cannot help but be impressed (positively or negatively) by their commitment.

The pre-eminent nationalist leader of this century, both a brilliant political strategist and a religious leader, was probably Malcolm X. He and the Black Muslim movement epitomized minority nationalism in the 1960s. A juvenile delinquent and ex-convict who was converted to the "fruit of Islam" in prison, Malcolm became one of the most outspoken social critics of the early 1960s. He was particularly condemned when he suggested that "the chickens had come home to roost" after the assassination of President John F. Kennedy. Malcolm split with the Black Muslims shortly after returning from his *hadj* (a trip to Mecca required of all faithful Moslems). He said that his eyes had been opened by the intermingling of races in Mecca to the possibility of blacks and whites existing in harmony. Malcolm formed a separatist Muslim group and was gunned down, allegedly by Muslim traditionalists, in 1965.

The religion Malcolm X preached was a natural foundation for his politics. All such movements use religion as ultimate justification for their political actions. (In some ways, it is accurate to suggest that religion is always a precursor to violence and subjugation. The late Jomo Kenyatta of Kenya was fond of saying that when the missionaries landed in Africa, they had the Bible and the Africans had the land. After a long sleep the Africans had the Bible and the missionaries had the land.) Inevitably, the liturgy portrays the group as being tested by God, who will ultimately deliver them with a strong hand. This is true of the Black Muslims, as is shown by the following simplified rendition of their view of their origins.

In the beginning there was only the black tribe of Shabbaz. A great scientist became incensed because he could not make all the people speak the same language. Trying to blow up the earth, he "blasted out" the moon. (At one time all of the planet was called the moon; this is why the peoples of Africa call themselves the people of the moon.) Fifty thousand years after this event the black people left their homeland in Asia and traveled to Africa. Six thousand years ago Yakub, one of the geniuses of the black race, developed a mutation; after 600 years he finally developed the white man. His invention was the devil, and Yakub is the man the Bible refers to as Adam. God punished the Muslim people by allowing the "devils" to rule for 6,000 years, to test the mettle of the black nation. The 6,000 years ended with the birth of the prophet W. F. Fard, the Mahdi, who was born in 1877 and will live for 444 years. He was born of a Caucasian "devil" woman (known as Baby Gee) and Alphonso, "a jet black man from the Tribe of Shabbaz." Fard formed the Nation of Islam and named Elijah Muhammad (for whom Malcolm X acted as prophet) the infallible leader of the Muslims, to lay the foundation for the end of the rule of the white devil (Udom, 1962: ch. 5).

Obviously, Muslim religious beliefs suggest the ultimate separation and success of the black race. Many people find these beliefs ludicrous, yet there are similar stories in both the Old and the New Testaments that would seem just as ludicrous to those of other faiths. The point is that nationalist movements often use religion, calling on followers to make tremendous sacrifices.

Nationalists as patriots.   Nationalism seeks either the separation or the segregation of minorities. Marcus Garvey started the back-to-Africa movement, while Black Muslims wanted a group of southern states to become the new black nation. Chicanos want the return of Aztlán (California, New Mexico, Arizona, and Texas), on which to build their nation. American Jews want the United States government to guarantee the safety of the state of Israel and thereby insure their dual identity with both countries. The forms of nationalism are endless, yet its goals are generally clear. Land is the crucial element, supported by identity and usually by religion. Nationalists are also prone to condone violence, which has been an effective tool. One of the most famous and successful nationalist (although in no way minority) movements was the rebellion of the American colonies against Great Britain. It is ironic that the American Revolution is often the model of action for nationalist minority groups in America.

CONCLUSION AND SUMMARY

As we said earlier, in most cases many different types of political action groups exist simultaneously, addressing the same grievances. They ebb and flow with internal and external social pressures. Minority political action groups in various forms have existed since the beginning of American history. Their success has little to do with the form they take. Although William Gamson suggests that violent groups tend to be more successful than nonviolent groups, it is also true that social movements have had little direct success (Gamson, 1975). Most successes have been due to circumstances beyond the group's control, such as war, economic recession or expansion, or the election of a sympathetic president.

The most fascinating thing about all political movements, and especially about minority political movements, is their long-term effect. In general, minorities obtain partial fulfillment of the goals of the movements, usually long after the movements have left the scene. Such movements leave a legacy through which the minority, and the entire nation, can begin to deal with ethnic and racial problems. This tradition adds to our understanding of history and also makes us realize that the social and political issues we confront today have a foundation that surpasses our limited view. Given the economic and political nature of American society, it is highly likely that such minority movements will arise again within our lifetimes and have a profound impact on our future.

Minority groups organize for political action because of both political and psychological pressures. Minority political organization occurs in societies that are perceived as vertical. If a society distributes its goods unequally according to minority status, and if individuals perceive their relative deprivation in that society, then various types of political movements will be formed. These movements will break with the accommodationists, who generally feel that they benefit more from the present situation than they would if they were to organize and oppose the whole society. Minority political movements tend to organize along one of the following lines: advocating nonviolence, advocating rebellion, wanting to develop the identity or cultural power of the group, espousing radicalism, or advocating some sort of separation through nationalism. These forms of political action groups tend to coexist, with one type of movement ascending to dominance because, at a particular time, it seems the most legitimate approach.

Chapter

Power and Discrimination: The Sociology of Dominance

SEVEN

THE POSITION OF DOMINANCE

In this chapter we shall look at the role of the dominant ethnic group, the people at the top. In the United States these people are largely Protestant, of northwest European ancestry, and white. Because of the power and privilege that come with upper-class position, anything they think or do greatly affects society. Without the actions of the dominant group there would be no minority groups, for it is the actions of the dominant group that form and maintain ethnic stratification.

In his 1948 article, "The Sociology of Majorities," sociologist Robert Bierstedt pointed out that sociologists tend to study minority groups but ignore the dominant (or majority) group. Four years earlier, Gunnar Myrdal's book *The American Dilemma* had provided a model for this new perspective. In *The American Dilemma*, Myrdal analyzed the "Negro problem" from the nontraditional perspective of white behavior, emphasizing the white-created discrimination that blacks faced. Responding to Myrdal and Bierstedt, American social science slowly changed direction in its effort to understand minority groups, beginning to focus on dominant groups as well. The result was a more complete picture of the minority situation.

The dominant group came to be viewed as an ethnic group, like the minority, only separated from it by the gulf of power and privilege. By using its power, the dominant group becomes the architect, caretaker, and principal beneficiary of the society. The structure it builds and benefits from is some form of ethnic stratification, such as we outlined in Chapter 3. Specifically, then, this chapter will focus on the role of the dominant group in a system of ethnic stratification. For example, we shall learn why and how relatively powerful ethnic groups seek to establish ethnic stratification systems, and how dominant groups maintain ethnic stratification over time. The latter issue includes the question of discrimination. First we shall take a general look at the position of the dominant group in a system of ethnic stratification.

Ethnic Identity at the Top:
The Experience of Dominance

One of the many luxuries of dominance is that individuals in that position can choose whether to be concerned with their ethnicity. Ethnicity may become a source of pride, leading to the tracing of famous family trees and to the forming of organizations based on select ancestry. In the United States the Daughters of the American Revolution is such an organization; Great Britain's elaborate system of royalty, with its many titles, serves the same purpose. The purpose, of course, is to build boundaries between "us" and "them" to emphasize "our" shared ethnicity. On the other hand, an individual from a dominant ethnic group may ignore his or her ancestry, choosing instead to identify as "American" or "British." This is a luxury that black-Americans and Mexican-Americans cannot afford; their experience of discrimination against their ethnic minority constantly calls attention to the hyphen.

Discrimination is not the only factor that calls attention to ethnicity. Simply knowing individuals of different ethnicity calls attention to one's own ethnicity, through the contrast. Choosing whether to know such people, or even to have contact with them, is another luxury of dominance. When an ethnic minority is physically segregated, contact with the dominant ethnic group becomes highly unlikely. The reservation system for American Indians and the housing and educational segregation of American blacks tend to keep both of these groups outside the spheres of activities of most white Americans. As we saw in Chapter 5, social segregation can keep people from knowing each other, even though they have contact. Social segregation involves rigid rules of social interaction; these rituals allow people to get along with each other without really knowing each other. The slave owner, for example, could say (and really believe) that his slaves were loyal and happy, for as far as he knew, they were. By setting the rules of both physical and social segregation, the dominant group can provide itself with the luxury of minimal contact with other ethnic groups.

However, the position of dominance in an ethnically stratified society does not totally insulate its members. The fact that one is in a position to dominate others is not easily overlooked, and it is this particular aspect of dominance that sets apart the sense of ethnicity that grows from being in the dominant group. To a minority, ethnicity may be something to cling to or a source of pride to be fought for, but the dominant group may step into pride in its ethnicity as easily as one steps into a pair of comfortable old shoes. The minority experience teaches the individual how ethnicity, and especially pride in ethnicity, are subject to change with the minority's fortunes in the ethnic stratification system. (Even the most oppressed minority has memories of the past before oppression; American blacks know of the slave trade, and American Indians are well aware of who used to own the land.) The dominant experience, on the other hand, gives the individual a much more stable sense of ethnic pride. By design, there is far less change at the upper end of the stratification system. The dominant individual comes to think of the dominant culture as one and the same with dominance itself, which in turn colors the culture.

The white man's burden: the dominant group as caretaker.   The over-lapping of ethnicity and the sense of dominance is a distinctive feature of dominant groups. Ethnic stratification creates similar perceptions among minority groups (as they come to see their class and their ethnicity as related), but nowhere is the phenomenon more clear than in the dominant group.

> *People in most dominant groups conceive of themselves as valuable objects; their ascendancy is believed to be due to their inherent superiority. In ethnic stratification these qualities are assumed to be inherited genetically; people of good "stock" are the bearers of highly valued characteristics —dependability, honesty, intelligence, and courage. Those who have ruled for many generations are so convinced of their superiority that they do not even discuss it. During the hey-day of the British Empire, for example, many Englishmen would have regarded boasting of their paramount attributes as being in poor taste. This did not mean, however, that they had any doubts about the virtues of Englishmen. (Shibutani and Kwan, 1965: 257)*

On its face, dominance seems to turn pride in one's culture into outright conceit. But when one ethnic group maintains a position of dominance for several generations, they come to take for granted their assumption of superiority. For example, it is difficult to label any human being conceited for feeling superior to the family dog, since dogs have served humans as long as any of us can remember. And though it may seem insulting to extend this example to minority-group humans, it nevertheless suggests how being in the position of master can go to one's head.

One of the best historical examples of the conceit of dominance also provides a label for the phenomenon. That example is Rudyard Kipling's poem "The White Man's Burden," written in 1899. The "burden" of the white man was, of course, the nonwhite who lived in the white man's colonies. While colonization is generally viewed today as European exploitation of the rest of the world, it was seen quite differently in Kipling's day. The European was considered (by other Europeans, of course) not an exploiting businessman but rather a concerned and often exasperated father figure, trying to do his best for unlearned and unappreciative children. Kipling speaks of serving "your captives' need." He clearly understands that the colonized peoples had not chosen their captivity (again, much like children), but that they were nevertheless being "served" by the whites. Kipling's description of these colonized peoples as "half devil and half child" makes it clear why they need guidance. The childlike theme continues as Kipling speaks of "sloth and heathen folly" and the "blame of those ye better." The lazy nonwhite "children" are unfortunately unable to appreciate the European "parental sacrifice" being made in their interests. We emphasize the parent–child analogy, because social scientists often refer to this attitude of the dominant group toward the dominated as paternalism. It tends to occur in stable, noncompetitive societies in which the dominant group is very powerful and ethnocentric.

THE WHITE MAN'S BURDEN
1899

Take up the White Man's burden—
Send forth the best ye breed—
Go bind your sons to exile
To serve your captives' need;
To wait in heavy harness
On fluttered folk and wild—
Your new-caught, sullen peoples,
Half devil and half child.

Take up the White Man's burden—
In patience to abide,
To veil the threat of terror
And check the show of pride;
By open speech and simple,
An hundred times made plain.
To seek another's profit,
And work another's gain.

Take up the White Man's burden—
No tawdry rule of kings,
But toil of serf and sweeper—
The tale of common things.
The ports ye shall not enter,
The roads ye shall not tread,
Go make them with your living,
And mark them with your dead!

Take up the White Man's burden—
And reap his old reward:
The blame of those ye better,
The hate of those ye guard—
The cry of hosts ye humour
(Ah, slowly!) toward the light: —
"Why brought ye us from bondage,
Our loved Egyptian night?"

Take up the White Man's burden—
Ye dare not stoop to less—
Nor call too loud on Freedom
To cloak your weariness;
By all ye cry or whisper,
By all ye leave or do,
The silent, sullen peoples
Shall weigh your Gods and you.

Take up the White Man's burden—
Have done with childish days—
The lightly proffered laurel,
The easy, ungrudged praise.
Comes now, to search your manhood
Through all the thankless years,
Cold-edged with dear-bought wisdom,
The judgment of your peers!

Ethnocentrism.   An ethnocentric individual believes in the inherent superiority of his or her ethnic group. Its culture is the only decent, reasonable, and practical way of living; all other cultures are at best silly and at worst evil. In this sense, then, an ethnocentric individual is centered upon one ethnic lifestyle to the exclusion of all others. All other cultures are ranked according to their degree of similarity to the culture of the ethnocentric individual.

As ethnic groups encounter each other in a given society, they must come to terms with the cultural differences among them. In such situations, people are ethnocentric not just because their ethnic groups may well be in competition (although that helps), but also because it is natural to be ethnocentric. The belief that one's culture is the best is inherent in culture. As we said in Chapter 1, cultures live in humans just as much as humans live in their cultures. Growing up in a culture gives one a strong emotional attachment to it. This emotional attachment comes to the fore only when cultures come into contact; observing someone else's lifestyle calls attention to one's own for the first time.

The concept of ethnocentrism helps us understand the reactions of all ethnic groups, whether minority or dominant. It is especially useful in studying dominant groups, however, for their power allows them to express their ethnocentrism more strongly. A dominant group, largely able to control the society, often weaves its ethnocentrism right into the fabric of that society. For example, the Judeo-Christian heritage in the United States is unfavorable to polygamy (having more than one spouse); most Americans think it natural that a marriage should contain one man and one woman only. As a result of this cultural practice among the dominant group, laws have been passed prohibiting everyone from engaging in polygamy. The practice became an issue when Utah entered the Union, because the then polygamist Mormons had to give it up. In the hands of the dominant group, ethnocentrism requires conformity.

The Job of Dominance: Privilege or Responsibility?

Belonging to the dominant group in a society is clearly preferable to belonging to a minority group; the privilege of upper-class membership and a high-status ethnicity are among the most sought after rewards in any society. That privilege brings with it power, wealth, and respect. However, in addition to these advantages, dominance also entails limits and, in particular, responsibilities.

While the dominant group is the primary beneficiary of a system of ethnic stratification, it is also the primary caretaker of that system. Though it can "take care" of the society to its own advantage, it must also see to it that the society continues to operate—which involves keeping many people in the lower classes working for the system. This is best expressed by Richard A. Schermerhorn:

> They (the dominant group) cannot press their advantage too far without raising serious opposition, trouble, and disorder from those in lower echelons. Even in order to exploit them, the privileged must see to it that those in subordinate positions not only subsist, but are motivated to continue playing their roles in a system to which both upper and lower groups contribute, though in functionally different ways. (Schermerhorn, 1970: 23)

We have already seen how a sense of responsibility for society can develop among the dominant group; recall the idea of the "white man's burden." Coupled with this responsibility are limits. Before enjoying their privileges, the dominant group must first insure that the society keeps functioning. The minority group or groups in the society must either be happy enough or under control enough to keep working. In practice, they must usually be a little of both, and both can be arranged by the dominant group.

Human happiness is complicated. What makes one person happy may not make the next person happy, especially if the two people differ in class or ethnicity. Since in a system of ethnic stratification people differ in both ways, the things that make people happy (money, prestige, power, and so on) must be distributed accordingly. A stable system of ethnic stratification resembles a finely tuned machine in which the right rewards are distributed to the right people at the right time, keeping everyone at least a little bit happy. But, since all machines get out of tune over time, a stable system is one that can change as people's desires change. The things that keep parents happy may not satisfy the children.

In addition to keeping the lower classes relatively happy, the dominant group must also be in a position to control their behavior, should they become unhappy. We use the word *control* for lack of a better general term; keep in mind that we are speaking of a wide range of methods for control. For example, the dominant group's ability to make a given minority work at a certain job is one facet of control. This kind of control was exerted over the Irish immigrants whose labor was not needed in Boston but was needed in digging canals and laying railroad track. The institution of slavery provided a similar kind of control over American blacks. When the alternative is starvation or worse, people will generally work, regardless of whether they are happy.

A more obvious form of control is raw force. Whatever else the dominant group may control, it must control force. Not only is direct force necessary from time to time, but many other forms of control depend upon it. From the minority group's perspective, the knowledge that force may follow if orders are not obeyed can be a prime motivation.

Finally, the dominant group may control the thoughts of minority group members. This complicated form of control is difficult to see in practice. It consists primarily in the dominant group's using its position to direct certain kinds of information at minority groups while withholding other kinds. For example, information about agricultural methods and domestic duties was transmitted to the slaves; information about reading and writing was withheld. Because they could not read, slaves had no access to other information such as abolitionist literature. The purpose of thought control is to make the minority group a more enthusiastic part of society, regardless of its low status. In this sense, even the happiness of an individual minority group member may be partly under the control of the dominant group.

In short, the dominant group is inseparable from matters of power and control. It is the principal architect, caretaker, and beneficiary of ethnic stratification. In all of those roles, the dominant group becomes largely responsible for both the form of its society and its future. The following section explores how powerful ethnic groups use their strength to form ethnic stratification, and how they continue to use it to maintain their dominant position. Basically, these processes boil down to the question of how the dominant group discriminates.

POWER AND DISCRIMINATION: THE CONTROL
OF SOCIETAL INSTITUTIONS

Just as power is the most distinctive feature of a dominant group, discrimination is its most distinctive act. A group gains a position of dominance through power and then maintains that position through discrimination against the minority groups it creates. Discrimination, as we said earlier, is behavior that hinders the competitive ability of a group, preventing that group from improving its position in the stratification system. There are two broad forms of discrimination: overt discrimination and institutional (or covert) discrimination.

Overt discrimination is those forms of discrimination that directly affect *all* members of a given group without affecting any members of other groups. For example, not allowing black people to vote but offering the vote to all white people would be overt discrimination. *Institutional (covert) discrimination* is indirect forms of discrimination that affect a particular group because of certain attributes or abilities most of that group's members have (or lack). An example of institutional discrimination would be not allowing people to vote whose net worth is less than $40,000; this would prevent *most* black people from voting, since ethnic stratification keeps most of them in the lower income brackets. Such a rule, however, would also prevent a large number of white people from voting. This is a characteristic of institutional discrimination: it affects minority groups at the expense of many members of the dominant group.

Most people use the word *institution* to refer to a physical structure such as a prison or a mental hospital. Social scientists, however, use the term in a much more general and abstract way. An *institution* is a cluster of interrelated roles or activities in society. Thus, the family (not *a* family but *the* family) is an institution; it has many roles or activities (mothers, fathers, children, socializing the young, and so on) that are interrelated. Interrelation means that roles make sense only in terms of each other; it is impossible to define "mother," for example, without also defining "child." Societies tend to develop in such segments; a human concern (such as having and bringing up children) develops over time into a variety of activities sharing a tie with the same concern. At the same time, these activities seem, *as a group,* to be somewhat set apart from other groups of activities.

In the United States today, for example, there is an invisible boundary between the institution of the family and the institution of education. A child relating to its brothers, sisters, and parents is a very different person from the same child relating to its teacher and peer group at school. "Family matters" are somehow different from "school matters," even though one affects the other. The fact that one affects the other brings us to a very important point: while there are boundaries between institutions, there are nevertheless important interrelations between and among them. For example, a child's upbringing affects how that child does in school, and the child's experiences in school affect how he or she responds to the family. If the child attends a religious school, three institutions are closely tied. Beyond that, political institutions run schools (and insist that they be attended), while economic institutions fund them. All of these in turn affect the family.

Why bother with the concept of institution, in view of all these interrelationships? Because trying to understand all of society at once is an overwhelming task. The concept of institution allows us to approach it piece by piece. Since there are boundaries between institutions, they are logical pieces to work with.

Institutions are the major social arenas within a society. As such, they are important not only in how they direct the overall society but also to the individuals who must interact within them. For example, a political institution that protects the right of an individual to own private property is of great importance both to the individual who owns property and to the individual who does not; it affects both their lives. As this example suggests, one of the most significant questions about institutions concerns the use of power in society: who controls the institutions, and how? This question is very important in the area of dominant–minority relations. We shall next explore the relationship between power and societal institutions, to learn more about (1) how dominant groups come to control institutions (or how they form ethnic stratification), and (2) how dominant groups maintain their control over time. We shall also explore in more detail some of the forms of discrimination, including overt discrimination, institutional discrimination, and the extreme form of discrimination called exploitation.

The Formation of Ethnic Stratification

Ethnic stratification is not an inevitable occurrence when two or more ethnic groups share the same society. It occurs only at the instigation of a particularly powerful ethnic group in that society. That group's power must be considerable and it must be focused, if the ethnic group is to establish itself in a continuing position of dominance within a system of stratification. What motivates a powerful ethnic group to use its power in this way, and what are the social conditions under which the group will be successful? These two questions appear to be independent from each other, but in practice they are highly interrelated. Social conditions favorable to the creation of ethnic stratification can help motivate an ethnic group to work toward it; conversely, a strong motivation can direct an ethnic group to work at creating favorable social conditions when none exist. While neither the motivations nor the conditions operate the same way every time ethnic groups come together, social scientists have made some tentative generalizations.

The role of the nation state.   A beginning condition for the formation of ethnic stratification is the modern nation state. Since the minority–dominant relationship exists only when two or more ethnic groups share the same political boundaries, we must first have those political boundaries; the dominant group becomes dominant by its very control over the government of a nation state, because it can patrol the activities of all within the boundaries of that state.

C. Wagley and H. Harris point out the importance of the growth of the state in the historical development of dominant–minority relations. Small kingdoms governed by local leaders may have had their share of conflict, but the ethnicity of the population was in most cases homogenous enough to rule out dominant–minority group conflict. The rise of the nation state, however, provided the arena in which such conflict could occur. And the same historical and technological changes that led to the nation state also gave rise to an assortment of wars and revolutions (leading to many boundary changes), plus opportunities for large-scale population shifts; both occurrences resulted in multi-ethnic societies (Wagley and Harris, 1958: 140–43).

As the nation state evolved, many new sources of conflict also developed, not the least of which was (and still is) the difference between "nation" and "state." A nation is generally thought of as a group of people who share not only government but also culture and tradition; a state is simply a political arrangement that affects a body of people. A major source of conflict in the modern nation state can be the efforts of a powerful ethnic group to turn their multi-ethnic state into a nation. The culture and tradition they have in mind, of course, are their own; such demands on a minority ethnic group often lead to conflict (Wagley and Harris, 1958: 241–43).

The importance of the first contact between ethnic groups.   Ethnic stratification can occur only when two or more ethnic groups share political boundaries. For this to happen, either the boundaries or the ethnic groups must move (see Chapter 1). Thus, for any two ethnic groups, it is possible to locate the historical point of first contact between them. The circumstances under which this first contact occurs are very important for the groups' future relations.

Stanley Lieberson approached the question of first contact between ethnic groups by focusing on their relative power. In particular, in looking at the movement of people, he was concerned with whether the "host" ethnic group or the "migrant" ethnic group was stronger. His historical analysis found that a stronger migrating group led to more rigid forms of ethnic stratification characterized by conflict between the ethnic groups, to a numerical decline of the host population, to radical transformation of the host culture, and to unlikely prospects for assimilation of the host population into the dominant migrating group (Lieberson, 1961: 904–5). An example of this situation in the United States is the relationship between the strong migrating Europeans and the host American Indian population. The opposite case, in which a strong host allowed a weaker ethnic group to immigrate, created a situation of considerably less conflict, and a much higher probability of assimilation for the migrating group (Lieberson, 1961: 905–6). Examples of this situation are the immigration of the Catholic Irish and the southeast

Europeans into an American society by then dominated by Protestants of northwest European background.

When the immigrant is subordinate, there are far fewer ways for the ethnic groups to threaten each other. However badly the immigrant may be treated, his situation may still be an improvement over the conditions that initially motivated immigration. This was clearly true in the case of the Catholic Irish, who faced considerable discrimination in the United States but would have starved in Ireland during the 1840s. The dominant group is also in a position to curtail immigration, should the immigrant group become a threat.

However, when the host population is subordinate there are many ways in which the groups might threaten each other. Because it is numerically smaller, the strong migrating group will be wary of the larger host population; at the same time, it will need to control the host population to make its way economically and to make its migration worthwhile. This condition of ethnic contact is generally referred to as colonization (see Blauner, 1972).

The role of racism.   Racism is an ethnic group's belief in their genetic superiority to another ethnic group. Their attitude and resulting behavior toward that other ethnic group can be described as racist. The belief develops somehow in the course of ethnic contact; once developed, it can influence the future course of those ethnic relations.

Pierre van den Berghe examined the role of racism in the formation and evolution of ethnic stratification. He noted that racism tended to develop when physical differences between two ethnic groups coincided with vast differences in status and culture. This dual occurrence often led the stronger group to assume that the physical differences (or biological differences in general) were responsible for the cultural differences. As ethnocentrism by the stronger group led them to believe the other group's culture to be inferior, that same ethnocentrism could define the other group's biological heritage as inferior (van den Berghe, 1967: 13).

In terms of ethnic stratification, racism invites the stronger group to exploit the weaker group. Whatever ethics the dominant group lives by are pushed aside by their belief in the racial inferiority of the group they exploit (van den Berghe, 1967: 16–17). Racism thus provides an excellent rationalization for exploitation. In the United States, racism was used to justify slavery. As racism continues over time in the relations between two ethnic groups, it is an effective obstacle to the assimilation of the subordinate ethnic group. The resulting rigid ethnic stratification system takes on many of the characteristics of a caste society.

The role of competition.   The threat of another ethnic group in competition for scarce goods and resources provides an excellent motivation for a stronger ethnic group to discriminate against it, thereby forming and maintaining ethnic stratification. *Direct* competition, however, is not necessary; the stronger group might discriminate against and exploit the labor of the weaker ethnic group in hopes of improving its abilities in competition with a third, equally strong group. For example, white farmers in the pre–Civil War South exploited black slaves so that they might be more competitive with other white businessmen within their own society.

Donald Noel points out the singular importance of competition (as one of the factors that encourages strong ethnic groups to exploit weaker ones) in forming ethnic stratification. He develops this theme with the example of slavery in the United States. His historical analysis observes the particular competitive demands for wealth and presitge that were characteristic of the frontier society of the pre–Civil War South (Noel, 1968: 165–71). American blacks, the most defenseless of all ethnic groups present at the time, were ripe for exploitation through the developing institution of slavery.

The role of industrialization: a decreasing variety of arrangements.
Industrialization is usually accompanied by many of the phenomena we have already discussed, such as the nation state, racism, and competition. But the number of possible arrangements two ethnic groups might form decreases with the demands of an industrial economy.

The term *industrialization* summarizes many of the major changes in the Western world over the last two centuries, focusing on economic changes. The most significant economic change was the relative decline of agricultural work and traditional crafts coupled with the rise of factories and manufactured goods. Many other changes accompanied this shift: the new economic system required new forms of government for security (the rise of the nation state), new economic systems (the rise of capitalism), and urbanization (which allowed for the easy movement of workers, goods, and services). The importance of industrialization to our discussion of ethnic stratification is that industrialization feeds on expansion (bringing new groups of people into the system) and requires systematic patterns of dominance (often placing those new people in a minority situation).

Schermerhorn notes that ethnic contacts that lack patterns of dominance between groups tend to occur in nonindustrial societies, for instance, between a nomadic ethnic group and an agricultural ethnic group. In such a situation, the two groups could enjoy a symbiotic relationship, each providing goods and/or services for the other. But as Schermerhorn also points out, the industrial world makes equality between ethnic groups the *least* likely possibility when ethnic groups come into contact (Schermerhorn, 1970: 68).

The role of industrialization is examined in greater depth but with the same result by Tamotsu Shibutani and Kian Kwan, who followed the movement of Europeans and their economic system around the world. In particular, the mobility of capital (which is much more easily transported than valuable goods) made it possible for corporations to become international. It seemed a natural step for the Europeans to supply the capital and for native populations around the world to supply the labor. This business arrangement succeeded, however, in joining ethnic groups into ongoing patterns of dominance and subordination and promoted drastic changes in the native cultures involved (Shibutani and Kwan, 1965: 170–97).

In short, industrialization created a number of motivations for powerful ethnic groups to form ethnic stratification systems. The development of capitalism and an industrial economy in Europe provided not only the incentive for ethnic stratification (through the competition inherent in the system), but also the means for forming ethnic stratification systems (technological advances and the higher levels of social organization, such as bureaucracies and the nation state, that accompany an industrial economy).

Overt Discrimination

Once an ethnic stratification system is formed, its survival depends on the attention the powerful ethnic group gives it. Like all other caretakers, the dominant ethnic group must be concerned with maintenance. Much of this maintenance takes the form of acts of discrimination, as the dominant group simultaneously seeks to keep the minority group clustered in the lower classes and to maintain its own position in the upper classes. Overt discrimination is the most powerful form for this purpose; it affects all members of the minority at which it is directed, without affecting any members of the dominant group.

Overt discrimination has existed worldwide both in the past and today; its popularity is explained by its effectiveness. It is as American as hot dogs, having been adapted to fill the particular needs of dominant groups throughout the 200-year history of the United States. As we saw in Chapters 1 and 2, acts of discrimination have remained fairly much the same, the only change being the substitution of one minority ethnic group for another. For instance, Catholic Irish in the United States can today find the kind of employment and housing that 100 years ago was closed to them. Other minority ethnic groups, such as blacks, Mexican-Americans, and American Indians, have been substituted for the Irish; today they face the kinds of discrimination that were so effective against the Irish earlier. It is as if signs had been made long ago that read, "No _____ need apply," complete with a selection of extra letters for filling in the blank with the names of different ethnic groups as times and the needs of the dominant group changed.

In the United States today, most European ethnic groups have surmounted the barriers of overt discrimination and either have succeeded in climbing out of the bottom of the ethnic stratification system or are doing so. Past discrimination leaves handicaps, however; for example, there is still not full equality between individuals of northwest and southeast European descent. Nonetheless, contemporary American discrimination is directed mainly at black Americans, Mexican-Americans, and American Indians. Technically, many past forms of overt discrimination against these groups are now against the law. But as the desire to discriminate remains, overt discrimination still occurs, coupled now with less obvious, institutional discrimination.

The Current State of Ethnic Stratification in the United States

At the time of the 1970 census, the population of the United States was slightly over 200,000,000. Of that number, 22,500,000 were black; 11,000,000 were of Spanish origin (and 60 percent of those were Mexican-American); and 800,000 were American Indian. Those three groups attract the attention of social scientists in relation to their size; we therefore have the most information about black Americans and the least about American Indians. It is nevertheless clear that all three groups are currently ethnically stratified in the United States, as a result of past and present discrimination.

The census data in figure 8 allow us to compare the two larger of these three minority groups to the white population in terms of a variety of socioeconomic circumstances. Figure 8 compares these groups in terms of extremes. For example, in comparing the education attained by persons 20 to 24 years old, we can see that only approximately 15 percent of white young people drop out of high school, while around 45 percent of them go on to at least some college. A higher percentage of black young people (around 28 percent) drop out of high school, and a lower percentage (around 27 percent) go on to college. Among Americans of Spanish origin, a still higher percentage drop out of high school and a still smaller percentage go on to college.

Education is clearly important in the United States; educational diplomas and degrees have become closely associated with employment. Groups such as black Americans and Americans of Spanish origin, who have less education than the white population, are at a competitive disadvantage when seeking employment. Looking at the other criteria in figure 8, we see similar relationships among the three groups. White Americans are much less likely to be unemployed; when employed, they are much more likely to hold white-collar as opposed to blue-collar jobs. White-collar jobs as a rule bring more prestige to their occupants. As we see from the last three items in the figure, they also tend to bring higher incomes. White American families are much more likely to be in the higher income brackets, and much less likely to be below the poverty level, than either of the other two groups. Finally, white Americans tend to have smaller families—so whatever income there is goes farther.

Figure 8 gives us various kinds of information, but it actually measures only one thing: poverty. All the individual characteristics it measures rise and decline together. It is not always easy to discover which characteristic "causes" the others—more education does not always lead to more income, for instance—but it is apparent that the characteristics are highly interrelated in American society. In terms of ethnic stratification, therefore, we could gain a fairly accurate picture of the ranking system by looking at any one of the characteristics listed in figure 8.

Figure 9, which portrays only differences in income, reveals the same basic relationships as figure 8, adding a few more ethnic groups to the comparison.

FIGURE 8.   Socioeconomic Characteristics of White, Black, and
Spanish-Origin Population, 1975

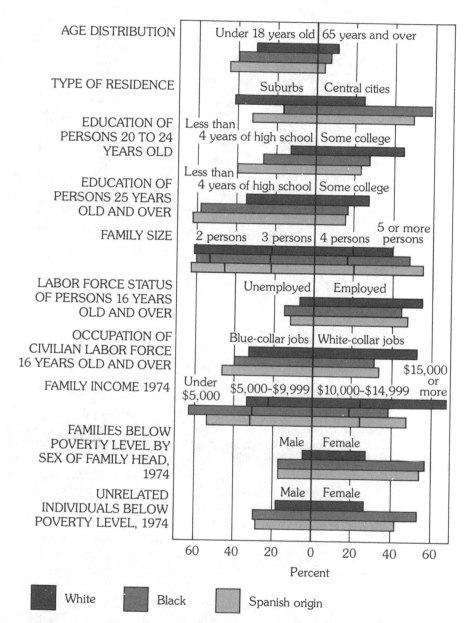

SOURCE: Social Indicators (Washington, D.C.: U.S. Dept. of Commerce, 1976).

Perhaps most important for our purposes, figure 9 includes American Indians
and indicates their inferior position to both the white and black populations of

FIGURE 9.   Median Income of Persons 14 Years Old and Over, by
Race, 1949 and 1969

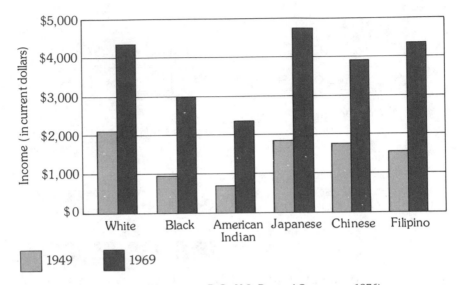

SOURCE: Social Indicators (Washington, D.C.: U.S. Dept. of Commerce, 1976).

the United States. It is not surprising that American Indians have correspondingly low educational levels and high unemployment rates. Figure 9 also
shows how little change has occurred between 1949 and 1969. While each of
the five minority ethnic groups made gains during that period in relation to the
white population, the overall distribution of wealth changed very little. Finally,
both figures 8 and 9 indicate why we are focusing on black Americans,
Mexican-Americans, and American Indians in this section on discrimination.
Each of those three groups lags behind in terms of any socioeconomic
characteristic measured. Former minority groups from southeast Europe, on
the other hand, have just about reached economic parity with the rest of the
European (or white) population, as have minorities from Asia. We do not
suggest that all these groups have achieved total *acceptance* in the United
States; Asian ethnic groups and, among Europeans, the Jews in particular still
face discrimination, particularly in terms of social acceptance. However,
economic parity is the first and most important goal for any minority. For that
reason we focus on the three groups whose confrontation with discrimination
most directly affects their economic position.

We have described ethnic stratification as the fruit of past and present
discrimination against the specific groups in question. By itself, however,
stratification does not prove the existence of discrimination; it is conceivable,
for instance, that an ethnic group would reject economic opportunities for
cultural reasons. While such an explanation would reassure some members of
the dominant group, it is certainly not adequate for explaining the degree and

persistence of poverty among American blacks, Mexican-Americans, and American Indians. We examined some of the early forms of discrimination against these groups in Chapters 1 and 2. The following four sections of this chapter will examine some recent forms of discrimination. Discrimination tends to affect all aspects of a group's existence; we shall divide it into four basic categories: discrimination in (1) health and medical care, (2) income and occupational attainment, (3) education, and (4) housing.

Discrimination in Health Care

Discrimination against ethnic minorities in the area of medical treatment is largely ignored by social scientists. Their lack of interest seems all the more unusual when we consider that discrimination in medical care can lead to the deaths of minority individuals. Thus, to the affected individuals and their families, other forms of discrimination cannot possibly be of equal importance.

Most of the research in this area focuses on the medical treatment received by the different social classes. Not surprisingly, upper-class people generally receive better treatment than lower-class people. Thus, if we study an ethnic minority found disproportionately in the lower classes, any difference in treatment that is related to social class will also affect that group disproportionately.

The strongest evidence of discrimination in medical treatment is the different life expectancies and infant mortality rates in white and nonwhite populations in the United States. It is apparent from figures 10 and 11 that health care has improved in recent years in the United States. It is also apparent that those advances in health care are distributed disproportionately to the white and nonwhite populations, so that the gap between the two groups has remained roughly the same. (The gap in infant mortality among nonwhites has decreased but the gap in life expectancy has narrowed little.) It appears, then, that being nonwhite shortens one's life about five years. This difference is actually the general product of ethnic stratification rather than of specific discrimination. Nonwhites die sooner than whites because a higher percentage of nonwhites are found in the lower classes; *within* each social class, there is very little difference in life expectancy between whites and nonwhites. Nevertheless, some discrimination in medical care *is* specific to certain ethnic groups, as we shall see.

Discrimination in medical care is caused by a wide range of factors. Simply being poor closes many doors: the poor often have inferior (or no) medical insurance; less access to doctors (and often less qualified doctors, when they find them); and less access to hospitals (and, again, often poorer hospitals and/or inferior treatment) (see Newman et al., 1978: 187–235; Ehrenreich and Ehrenreich, 1970; Sudnow, 1970). Some of this inferior care is directly due to poverty (people in private hospital rooms receive more attention than the less well-heeled in the wards); some of it is due to ethnic differences. As an

FIGURE 10.   Life Expectancy at Birth, by Sex and Race, 1929–1974

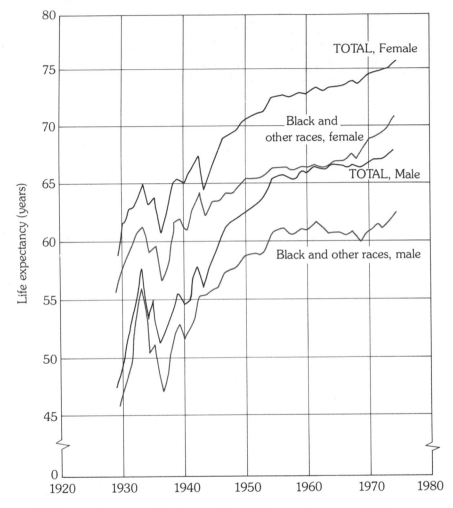

SOURCE: Social Indicators (Washington, D.C.: U.S. Dept. of Commerce, 1976).

example of ethnic discrimination in medicine we point to segregated medical facilities for blacks and whites, common in the not too distant past (Newman et al., 1978: 194–95). Also, ethnic groups such as Mexican-Americans often encounter language discrimination when seeking medical care, and any ethnic group that differs culturally from the middle-class medical professional may encounter more general communication problems (Strauss, 1970: 19; Hollingshead and Redlich, 1958).

Discrimination in Employment

From the information in figures 8 and 9 it is clear that there is presently a gap in income between white Americans, on the one hand, and black

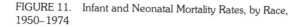

FIGURE 11.   Infant and Neonatal Mortality Rates, by Race,
1950–1974

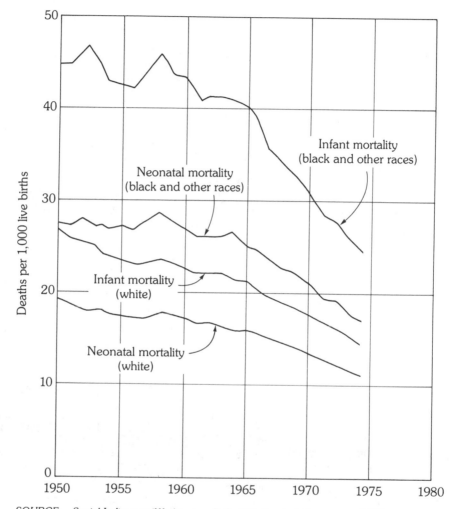

SOURCE: Social Indicators (Washington, D.C.: U.S. Dept. of Commerce, 1976).

Americans, Mexican-Americans, and American Indians, on the other. For all but the very wealthy, income is a direct result of occupation; therefore, it is safe to suggest that the income gap reflects an occupational gap. The income gap could be caused by minority individuals holding more poorly paying jobs, or by their being unemployed more frequently than the rest of the population. As we shall see, both possibilities play a part in maintaining the poverty of minority ethnic groups, and both are products of occupational discrimination against these groups.

Unemployment rates are strong evidence of employment discrimination against minority groups. "The last hired and the first fired" applies equally to

FIGURE 12.   Unemployment Rates by Race, 1948–1975

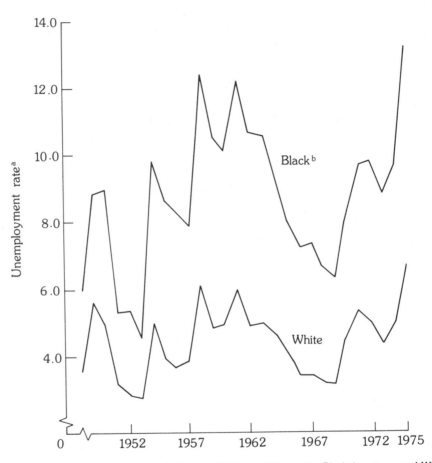

SOURCE: Dorothy Newman et al., Protest, Politics and Prosperity: Black Americans and White Institutions 1940–75 (New York: Pantheon, 1978), p. 43. Reprinted by permission.

[a] Percentage of the civilian labor force.
[b] Negro and other nonwhite races.

black Americans, Mexican-Americans, and American Indians. Figure 12 illustrates its operation with regard to blacks over the last three decades: black and white unemployment rates both reflect general economic trends, yet the employment gap has remained relatively constant. The civil rights legislation of the 1960s has had little effect. Unemployment is equal if not greater for the other two minorities; a 1969 survey of the ten largest Indian reservations, for example, found unemployment rates from 23 percent to 52 percent (Gomez et al., 1974: 126). Such rates alone would be enough to lower the average income of an ethnic group dramatically. But in addition, when members of these minorities do find work, either they work at more poorly paid jobs or they are simply poorly paid.

FIGURE 13.   Percentage Distribution of American Workers by Ethnic
Group and Occupation

Ethnic Origin	Professional/ Technical	Managers	Clerical and Sales	Crafts	Operatives	Other*
Total Population	14%	10%	24%	13%	16%	23%
German	16%	11%	23%	14%	14%	22%
Irish	12%	10%	27%	15%	16%	20%
Italian	12%	11%	26%	15%	17%	19%
Polish	17%	10%	25%	15%	17%	16%
Blacks and Other Nonwhite	10%	4%	17%	9%	21%	39%
American Indians	10%	6%	10%	22%	24%	29%
Mexican Americans	6%	5%	17%	13%	27%	33%

SOURCE: Derived from Current Population Reports (U.S. Bureau of the Census), Series P-20,
No. 249, "Characteristics of the population by ethnic origin"; CPR, Series P-23, No. 46, "The
social and economic status of the black population in the United States, 1972"; CPR, Series P-20,
No. 310, "Persons of Spanish origin in the United States: March 1976"; Subject Report: American
Indians (from 1970 population census) (U.S. Bureau of the Census).

* Includes laborers, farmers and farm managers, service workers, and private household workers.

American blacks, Mexican-Americans, and American Indians disproportionately fill the low-status/low-income jobs. The census data summarized by
figure 13 give a clear picture of ethnic stratification in the occupational world.

Blacks, Mexican-Americans, and Indians are much more likely than whites to be operatives, general laborers, farm laborers, or service workers (including private household workers). Since more of them work at these occupations, few of them, of course, work at the higher-status/higher-income occupations. Of particular interest is the relative absence of these ethnic groups in managerial, clerical, and sales positions; 34 percent of the overall work force occupies these positions, but only 21 percent of blacks, 16 percent of Indians, and 22 percent of Mexican-Americans fall into those categories. As a group, those occupations are generally labeled white-collar; they are the occupations of most middle-class Americans. Even though the three ethnic groups are moving closer to parity with other Americans in professional and technical occupations, there still appears to be a major barrier against the attempts of most ethnic group individuals to move into the middle class. Thus, since 1940 the overall gap in occupations between whites and nonwhites in the United States has narrowed only a little (Newman et al., 1978: 36).

In addition to higher unemployment rates and more poorly paid occupations, the three ethnic minorities face a third problem: even within the same occupations, they are paid less than dominant group members. Paul Siegal (1965) determined that black workers receive an average of $1,000 less per year than white workers who do the same work and have the same job qualifications. Using the same statistical technique, Dudley Poston and David Alvirez (1976) found that Mexican-American workers are penalized about $900 yearly for their ethnic background. In short, there is a "cost" to the worker attributable to discrimination against his or her ethnic group; either employers are not willing to pay equal wages to ethnic minorities, or (more probably) they can pay minority workers less because minority individuals have few other options.

The fact of occupational discrimination is more easily determined than its source. An apparent conspiracy of past history and present social structure seems to maintain this discrimination. For instance, their history of slavery and inferior education, coupled with today's emphasis on education and skills in most forms of employment, has handicapped many blacks. A similar tale could be told about Mexican-Americans and their years of rural residence and farm work.

We will turn now to a brief discussion of discrimination by American labor unions in hopes of illustrating the process of discrimination as it affects employment. During most of this century, labor unions have been a major route to employment for American workers. As unions grew in power, they came to have increasing say over which people worked at which jobs, leaving employers to choose only among workers provided by the unions. The major American labor union federations have always supported the principle of labor organization without regard to race or religion (Kain, 1969: 19). Union locals, on the other hand, often differed from these principles; particularly in the craft unions there was considerable discrimination against blacks. Not until the Congress of Industrial Organizations (which organized by industries, not skills) was formed did significant numbers of American blacks enter integrated unions.

Discrimination by the early craft unions took up where direct employer discrimination had left off. The white union official often operated with the same prejudices as the employer. Thus, blacks were often kept out of the unions' apprenticeship programs (Friedman, 1975: 391–92). Some discrimination was unintentional: union leaders tended to favor their own children or the children of friends and acquaintances for apprenticeship programs; thus, the social segregation of American life led to economic discrimination. In addition, informal hiring practices discriminated against blacks through the same social segregation, because blacks were seldom in the chain of communication along which news of employment might pass (Crain, 1975: 206–7). The result of all this is clearly indicated in figure 13: only 9 percent of black workers are in craft occupations—the lowest percentage of any ethnic minority.

Occupational discrimination can both result from and cause other forms of discrimination. Educational discrimination, for example, can deprive ethnic minorities of the skills they need to get certain jobs. Similarly, housing discrimination can lead to occupational discrimination. A study of employment and residence in the San Francisco Bay Area revealed that 83 percent of the new jobs created between 1958 and 1968 were located outside the central-city areas where blacks were forced to live (Friedman, 1975: 397–98). Viewing occupational discrimination as a cause rather than as an effect, we might note the lowered income associated with occupational discrimination and the many limitations that poverty creates. For example, the minority consumer is often easy prey for high-interest lending operations and "easy payment" retail outlets that make their money through the repossession and resale of furniture, cars, and televisions whose owners cannot make payments (Jones, 1972: 135–36). When discrimination pervades a society, it begins to appear that a conspiracy exists to stop the minority individual at every turn.

Discrimination in Education

Educational institutions are an increasingly important social arena in any industrial nation, and particularly in the United States. They take over the task of providing each new generation with the knowledge and skills of the last generation. As industrialized nations require increasing numbers of skilled workers (along with fewer and fewer unskilled workers), educational institutions become a very important way station on the road to a good job. Education has an additional role: its rites of passage (diplomas, degrees, and the like) have come to be valued and required in many jobs. No country in the world sends a higher proportion of its daughters and sons to college as does the United States. As a result the majority of occupations require higher levels of education than are really required for the job (Newman et al., 1978: 71–76). Such requirements make educational institutions doubly important: they dispense "union cards" as well as knowledge and skills. Having the knowledge and skills (however acquired) may be useless unless they are accompanied by official recognition in the form of a diploma or degree. Clearly, when schools discriminate, the effects of that discrimination are far-reaching.

Perhaps ironically, the present elaborate system of public education in the United States was begun in part as a response to the vast ethnic diversity caused by massive immigration around 1900. The hope was that schools could "Americanize" all of the foreign-born children; the practice of pledging allegiance to the flag was begun with this in mind. As one educator of the time put it,

> These southern and eastern Europeans are of a very different type from the north Europeans who preceded them. Illiterate, docile, lacking in self-reliance and initiative, and not possessing the Anglo-Teutonic conceptions of law, order, and government, their coming has served to dilute tremendously our national stock, and to corrupt our civic life. . . .
>
> Our task is to break up these groups or settlements, to assimilate and amalgamate these people as a part of our American race, and to implant in their children, so far as can be done, the Anglo-Saxon conception of righteousness, law and order, and popular government, and to awaken in them a reverence for our domestic institutions and for those things in our national life which we as a people hold to be of abiding worth. (Cubberley, 1909: 15–16)

Public schools did not solve all the problems, as educators like Elwood Cubberley hoped, but in the course of learning a "reverence for our democratic institutions," the immigrant children also picked up something of reading, writing, and arithmetic. The great emphasis placed on this free education by two immigrant groups of this period, the Jews and the Japanese, opened many doors for their children later on. However, the schools proved considerably less useful to other minorities.

One of the worst failures of American education was the attempt of the Bureau of Indian Affairs to provide schools for American Indians. For the most part, those schools neither "Americanized" nor taught skills effectively. In 1969 the average American Indian under federal supervision had completed only five years of school; 27 percent of the adult Indian population was illiterate (Gomez et al., 1974: 126). Typically, Bureau schools were underfinanced and structured to fit the dominant Anglo culture that ran them rather than the individual American Indian cultures whose members attended them.

Similar cultural conflicts occurred with the education of Mexican-American children. Like the BIA schools on the reservations, public schools for Mexican-American children reflected the Anglo culture that organized them. In particular, Mexican-American children faced a language problem: they were expected to learn strange ideas in what was to them a foreign language. Until fairly recently, Mexican-American children were generally forbidden to speak Spanish anywhere on school grounds and were punished if they did. While many European immigrant children had faced similar language and general cultural conflicts at school, at least they lived mostly in urban areas where they were exposed to English and Anglo culture elsewhere than in school. American Indians on reservations and Mexican-Americans were typically rural; school was one of the few places they encountered the dominant culture. As of 1976, 24 percent of Mexican-Americans had completed fewer than five years of school; only 33 percent had finished high school (U.S. Government Bureau of the Census, 1977: 5). Although Mexican-American children attend school, it is clear that most schools do not serve them well. In California in 1970, twice as many Mexican-American children were placed in classes for the mentally retarded than would be expected from their overall numbers in the school system (Moore, 1976: 83). Assuming that there are no biological differences between these children and the rest of the school population, it appears that teachers have as much trouble understanding the children as the children have understanding the teachers.

The history of education for black Americans is longer and more involved than for Mexican-Americans or Indians but no more successful. White slave owners believed that uneducated slaves could be more easily controlled. (In this case schools are viewed—even in their absence—as a means of control.) The emancipation of blacks after the Civil War began a long history of separate and unequal educational facilities. The results of this inequality first surfaced on a large scale during World War I, when large numbers of young men were tested by the Selective Service System. Of whites, 25 of every 1,000 were rejected for failing the written examination. For blacks, the rates were 50 per 1,000 in the northern and western states and 180 per 1,000 in the southern states (Kain, 1969: 16). As recently as 1951–52 in Mississippi, the school budget expenditure for white students was $147 per pupil per year; for black students, it was only $32 per pupil (Kain, 1969: 16). Although the Supreme Court found such school segregation unconstitutional in 1954, most of the racial separation in school systems has continued because of housing segregation. The 1966 study *Equality of Educational Opportunity* (generally known as the Coleman Report) found that the vast majority of American schools were still largely segregated; in addition, black students lagged far behind white students as measured by standardized tests (Coleman et al., 1966). The courts could do little about the difference in test scores, but they could do something about segregation; their answer was busing.

Compared to the 1960s, the 1970s were relatively quiet in terms of ethnic conflict. Amid that quiet, the numerous disputes over busing in American cities stand out. For all the turmoil it caused, busing is a simple process. It is a direct means of moving some blacks to predominantly white schools and some whites to predominantly black schools. The role of the school bus in ethnic conflict was nothing new in American society; buses had been used in the past to bus black students *out* of white school districts, to maintain segregation. But busing in the 1970s also affected white students. It is too soon to know what (if any) effect busing will have on the educational achievement of the students involved. However, we can examine the disputes over busing.

For roughly the last two decades, American cities have been growing poorer as the more affluent white population has been moving to the suburbs. Because court-ordered busing tends to affect only the various schools within a given district (within a certain city, for instance), the white students involved tend to be from middle-class and working-class families who are not able to move to more affluent neighborhoods. Busing disputes therefore shape up as battles between two ethnic groups that are very similar in social class, one white and the other black. The structure of ethnic stratification becomes even more apparent in cities like Boston, in which those middle-class whites tend to be European ethnic groups like the Irish or the Italians, who are still struggling up the ladder of social stratification. The following statement about busing, by an Irish-American factory worker in South Boston, indicates something of the "war with two fronts" that groups located in the middle of the ethnic stratification system feel they must fight.

> I graduated from South Boston High School and there was a time I thought my children would graduate from there, and my grandchildren, though I don't know about that now; and I'll tell you, the kids from Southie don't go to Harvard and don't go South to fight for the colored people, and don't try to protest against their own government by calling it every name in the book, and glorifying the dictatorships we're opposed to. The kids from Southie have to work during high school, and they try to get jobs, if they can, as soon as they graduate, if they do. Some just drop out. We're poor here, a lot of us. This is no suburb. This is no Beacon Hill or Back Bay. This is no Brattle Street, off Harvard Square.
>
> My brother says the people near Harvard, the professors and doctors and lawyers and fat-cat businessmen, their kids, a lot of them, don't go to the Cambridge public schools, they go to fancy private schools and they have nice summer homes and all the rest. Well, who has the money to afford those private schools? Not us. And if we even mention trying to form our own private schools here in South Boston, then they tell us we're trying "to evade the federal court order" and we're "racists." But if rich people send their children to private school, they're not trying to "evade" anything. Or anybody, like us people here. Oh, no. They're just trying to give their children the "best education possible," that's what my brother hears them say—and he's no professor, but he can listen with his ears and he can figure out what he hears. (Ford, 1975: 459)

The ultimate irony of busing and of educational discrimination in general is that education helps blacks find better jobs only if they get a lot of it (four years of college or more). In other words, the less education a black has, the more likely he or she will face occupational discrimination, losing jobs to whites with the same or less education (Newman et al., 1978: 98). Earlier we said that blacks do better in comparison with whites in the professional and technical fields, while they fall far behind the middle-level occupations. For blacks, education leads to advancement in highly specialized fields requiring much training. In general, education is not nearly the predictor of occupational status and income for blacks that it is for whites (Duncan, 1968; Thurow, 1969: 111–12). In short, occupational discrimination is ultimately far more important than educational discrimination. Education may be wonderful, but it is no guarantee of upward mobility if you are black.

Discrimination in Housing

The quality of housing directly affects the quality of life. The location of one's home is also important: the community can provide certain activities and experiences but deny other activities and experiences. Ethnic minorities face discrimination in both quality and location of their housing. Quality is important in its own right, but discrimination in location prevents affected minorities from living near desirable jobs and schools, and thus leads to other forms of discrimination. When minorities face residential segregation, they generally must pay more for their housing. This is because of increased demand: all minority individuals must live in a restricted area, which raises prices. Mexican-Americans, moving increasingly to cities, find themselves restricted to certain neighborhoods (barrios) in which prices are high in relation to the housing quality (Glick, 1974: 346). The segregation of blacks in American cities similarly raises prices for them (Rapkin, 1969). Blacks pay from 3 percent to 20 percent more for their housing, depending on the city and whether they rent or buy (Newman et al., 1978: 137). Because segregation forces minorities to pay more for poorer quality housing, it appears that the discrimination minorities face in *where* they live is also a major factor in determining *how* they live.

Of all American households, 81 percent are located in segregated neighborhoods (Newman et al., 1978: 142). That figure has remained largely unchanged since the 1940s. It is not totally a reflection of choice, nor can it be explained by the economic limitations on many minority individuals in their search for housing. It is largely the result of past and present discrimination by real estate brokers and lending institutions. This discrimination, carried out with the acceptance and often the encouragement of the dominant community, can be viewed as "good business"; the perpetrators were and are appealing to a majority of the market they hoped to attract. Housing discrimination can also lead to higher profits for real estate brokers, if scare tactics accompanying the move of a black family into a white neighborhood artificially (and temporarily) lower housing prices while raising the volume of business. Minority individuals can become pawns in the larger game of dominant group individuals attempting to make money from each other. The minority individual does not "pay" until he or she moves into the newly segregated neighborhood and finds the prices higher than ever.

The real estate business has long promoted housing discrimination. In 1924 the National Association of Realtors Code of Ethics endorsed discrimination:

> *A Realtor should never be instrumental in introducing into a neighborhood a character of property or occupance, members of any race or nationality, or any individuals whose presence will clearly be detrimental to property values in that neighborhood. (Newman et al., 1978: 149)*

That goal was enforced through the use of the restrictive covenant, a restriction attached to a piece of property that excluded "non-Caucasians" from ownership. Until invalidated by the Supreme Court in 1948, the restrictive covenant was legally enforceable. Partly in response to the 1948 Supreme Court decision, the National Association of Realtors altered its code:

> *A Realtor should not be instrumental in introducing into a neighborhood a character of property or use which will clearly be detrimental to property values in that neighborhood (Newman et al., 1978: 151).*

Even though the formal statement was altered and the restrictive covenant invalidated, practices of discrimination continued in a more informal but nonetheless effective manner.

There are numerous options open to the realtor who wants to discriminate; if they are not all entirely legal, they are nevertheless difficult to document and prosecute. A realtor may unofficially limit the houses shown to a minority buyer, quote different sales terms, show less enthusiasm in pursuing financing, or simply declare a house to be sold when it is still on the market (see Friedman, 1975: 393–94; Newman et al., 1978: 152–53; Rothman, 1969; and Gomez et al., 1974: 347). Similar forms of discrimination occur with rental housing, either through a realtor or directly by the landlord (Johnson et al., 1975).

The prospective minority home owner faces an even larger obstacle in the form of discrimination by banks and other lending institutions. As table 8 shows, blacks are denied loans 25 percent of the time, compared with a 15 percent rejection rate for prospective white borrowers. The difference in rejection rates continues even when income or years at their present occupation are held constant. Part of the reason for this is redlining, the practice by lending institutions of drawing imaginary lines around areas within which they will not issue home loans (Newman et al., 1978: 155–59). These are often the only areas of the city open to the minority individual.

In sum, both the quality and the location of housing for the minority individual are under the control of dominant group members, who maintain it through a variety of discriminatory actions. Legal efforts to end this discrimination have, for the most part, only increased the creativity of the dis-

Table 8.   *Percentage of Loan Applications Denied in Six Metropolitan Areas by Income Class, Years at Present Occupation, and Amount of Loan Requested, and by Race, June–November 1974*

Characteristic	Black[a]	White
All borrowers	25	15
Gross annual income		
Less than $5,000	40	34
$5,000–9,999	33	22
10,000–14,999	27	16
15,000–24,999	21	14
25,000 and over	23	12
Years at present occupation		
Less than 1 year	31	17
1 year	23	15
2 years	24	15
3–5 years	26	14
Over 5 years	23	14
Amount of loan requested		
Less than $5,000	26	11
$5,000–$15,000	34	17
15,001–25,000	23	15
25,001–45,000	22	14
45,001–60,000	15	17
Over $60,000	35	19
Number of cases	320	1,693

SOURCE: Dorothy Newman et al., Protest, Politics, and Prosperity: Black Americans and White Institutions 1940–75 (New York: Pantheon, 1978), p. 180. Reprinted by permission.

[a] Negro and other nonwhite races.

criminators in their efforts to circumvent the law. Like discrimination in health care, employment, and education, discrimination in housing has become less overt in response to these laws. For example, in the case of discrimination by lending institutions, the discrimination appears to be no longer the work of a single discriminator but rather built into the system of the institution. As we shall see in the following section, this kind of institutional (or covert) discrimination is somewhat less effective against minority individuals, but at the same time it is more difficult for them to combat.

Institutional (Covert) Discrimination

Earlier we defined institutional discrimination as those indirect forms of discrimination that affect a certain group because of certain attributes or abilities most of that group's members have (or lack). More often than not, institutional discrimination operates through the situation already provided by ethnic stratification: that is, since minority group members are disproportionately poor, institutional forms of discrimination that affect the poor disproportionately affect minorities. In this case, poverty becomes the "attribute" possessed by the minority that leads to their being affected by discrimination. To the extent that they are culturally different from the dominant group, minorities often have different kinds of skills and abilities from the dominant group. Should the dominant group decide to discriminate on the basis of certain abilities, the minority group might easily be disproportionately affected. As we shall see, the use of intelligence tests (which measure similarity to the dominant group in knowledge and style of thinking) has prevented minorities from obtaining jobs and education. This is because their different cultural background makes it difficult for them to pass the tests, and passing the tests is the key that opens the door to such opportunities.

Institutional discrimination that affects minorities because of their cultural background can be intentional or unintentional. The dominant group employer, for instance, may insist that a prospective employee have a certain body of abilities because the employer knows that a given minority is not likely to possess them. On the other hand, the employer might simply value that body of abilities for their own sake, with no intention of discriminating. Unlike overt discrimination, intent is not inherent in the act of institutional discrimination, and it cannot be proved by the existence of the discrimination. For that reason it is a tempting alternative for members of the dominant group who wish to discriminate in the face of laws prohibiting such actions.

Dominant groups are in a position to organize social relations; not surprisingly, they tend to shape social relations to their benefit. Thus, social institutions develop along lines that emphasize and reward the values and abilities of dominant group members; simultaneously, those institutions de-emphasize and do not reward the values and abilities of other ethnic groups that share the society. For example, all major institutions in the United States today operate in (and reward the speakers of) Standard American English. Individuals who speak other languages or other dialects of English are at a disadvantage, whether they are going to school, to court, to work, or to vote, or are attempting to fill out an income tax return.

For the minority group individual, institutional discrimination seems to be a conspiracy that places barriers at every turn. There is seldom a single discriminator who can be held personally responsible, and institutional discrimination, from whatever source, cannot be proved. As black leader Whitney Young describes it,

> I go to the employer and ask him to employ Negroes, and he says, "It's a matter of education. I would hire your people if they were educated." Then I go to the educators and they say, "If Negro people lived in good neighborhoods and had more intelligent dialogue in their families, more encyclopedias in their homes, more opportunity to travel, and a stronger family life, then we could do a better job of educating them."

And when I go to the builder he says, "If they had the money, I would sell them the houses"—and I'm back at the employer's door again, where I started to begin with. (Young, 1964: 18)

As we have seen, blacks encounter overt forms of discrimination in employment, education, and housing that intensify their problems. But unintentional institutional discrimination by itself (which we might call the cycle of poverty) accounts for a good number of the barriers against them. For ethnic groups, this discrimination results from a lack of structural assimilation.

As we defined it in Chapter 5, structural assimilation refers to the acceptance of the minority group by the dominant group. Acceptance can occur at the institutional level (such as in education, housing, or employment), and/or at the social level, which suggests total acceptance. Structural assimilation does not occur until the minority first attempts to assimilate behaviorally (or acculturate), by conforming to the culture of the dominant group. But a minority group can behaviorally assimilate only so far without some structural assimilation. If the minority group is kept out of contact with the dominant group in institutional settings, it is also cut off from learning how those settings operate. In short, there is a closed circle: you cannot get the job without the knowledge and you cannot get the knowledge without the job. Lack of structural assimilation tends to keep the minority away from both the money and the skills they need to overcome discrimination. We will better understand this process after looking more closely at one such barrier, the use of intelligence (IQ) tests in education and employment.

A case in point: the IQ test.   Intelligence tests were developed in the early part of this century to measure differences in intelligence among individuals. The assumption behind the tests was that intelligence is separate from knowledge and experience. Intelligence, it was assumed, is inherited and should remain constant throughout one's life, regardless of the experiences to which it is applied and the knowledge acquired. The problem is that intelligence can be observed only when an individual is being intelligent *about something*—and whether that something is a mechanical or an intellectual problem, it cannot be divorced from an individual's knowledge and experience. In short, one *learns* to be intelligent and will appear to be more intelligent about things one has encountered previously.

From the outset, the kinds of problems included in intelligence tests bias them. An individual who is familiar with the kinds of problems in a test will appear to be more intelligent than another individual who is unfamiliar with them. Not surprisingly, the people who have developed intelligence tests also happened to be members of the dominant group. Naturally, the kinds of problems and their style of presentation were geared to the culture of the dominant group. Individuals from different ethnic groups therefore appeared to be less intelligent according to the tests. That outcome does not constitute institutional discrimination, however; the test results discriminated only by the way in which they were used.

Educators came to use IQ tests to place students in classes with others of like intelligence. Schools developed college preparatory programs (as distinguished from "high school terminal" programs), and placement in one or the other could clearly affect the options open to the individual student later. If dominant group members were the ones who scored high on the test, they became the students destined for college; as minority individuals failed, they were routed elsewhere, sometimes into classes for the mentally retarded (see Moore, 1976: 83). The IQ test became the gatekeeper at the door of educational opportunity.

Employers have also used intelligence tests to screen job applicants. The gatekeeping role of the intelligence test is even clearer in this context. To the extent that minority applicants are unfamiliar with the items on the intelligence test, they are deprived of jobs, regardless of whether they are capable of doing the job. The employer, of course, cannot be accused of racial or ethnic discrimination, since the test verifies that only the "unintelligent" face discrimination.

Affirmative action: a remedy?   Affirmative action is any program designed to get minority group individuals past the barriers of institutional discrimination that would normally stop them. Such programs exist in educational institutions, employment, and in other situations where such barriers exist. For example, a minority student who had been placed in high school terminal classes and who lacked the skills needed to pass a college entrance examination might be lifted over that barrier and given a chance that would otherwise be denied. The basic logic behind such programs is this: if there is a cycle of discrimination that affects the minority individual, it is necessary to break that cycle manually. If poor education leads to poor jobs, which lead to poor housing, which leads back to poor education, then it should be possible to improve the whole chain by improving one link of it. A better job should lead to better housing, a middle-class lifestyle, and better schools, which lead to better education and, it is hoped, a new generation that will not need the help of affirmative action. In short, affirmative action is an attempt to force structural assimilation.

It is difficult to evaluate the effect of affirmative action programs. So far, such programs appear to be helping those members of minority groups who were already doing fairly well to do still better, without having much impact on those minority individuals locked in the lower class (see Lester, 1975; and Friedman, 1975: 404–5). Affirmative action programs have also opened a political can of worms; dominant group members counter them with cries of reverse discrimination and assaults on the courts to have them invalidated.

Most of the institutional barriers against minorities affect them because they are lower-class, not because they are ethnically different from the dominant group. Thus, these barriers are also confronted by lower-class individuals who are ethnically of the dominant group. They, too, do poorly on IQ tests, for example, because of the difference in lifestyle between classes in American society. The problem of institutional discrimination therefore comes down to a matter of political definition: if lower-class individuals could gain official recognition of themselves as members of minority groups, then they too could acquire the benefits of an affirmative action program. To the white Anglo-Saxon Protestants of Appalachia, who have been poor, isolated, and exploited for almost two centuries, such a demand does not seem very different from the demands of ethnic minorities. Most useful to our discussion is the overriding importance of social class in the dynamics of discrimination; we must understand the interrelationship between class differences and ethnic differences if we are to understand the social situations and political actions of the individuals involved.

Minority Exploitation

Those who occupy the lower positions in the social stratification hierarchy work under the direction of those who occupy the higher positions. Members of different classes have different (often opposite) interests; each class can gain only at the expense of the other. Thus, discrimination is not only a means of protection but also a means of limiting the gains of a lower class to increase the gains of the higher class. Effective discrimination limits the options of the affected group, giving them little choice in their lives. The lack of choice no doubt includes an inability to achieve upward mobility, but discrimination is often designed also to limit the affected group to a particular activity useful to the dominant group. (The best example of this process in United States history is the institution of slavery.) When the discrimination of ethnic stratification so limits the options of a subordinate group that they are forced into activities advantageous to the dominant group, we may describe the situation as exploitation.

Blacks: the system of slavery.   The Africans who became enslaved were not placed in that position because they were an already existing threat to other groups in the United States. Rather they were imported to the United States, first as servants and later as slaves, for the purpose of bringing wealth to those who brought them here. The institution of slavery denied slaves the fruits of their labor, giving them instead to the slave owner, who could become wealthy through the efforts of the slaves. The one-sidedness of this relationship required that the individual slave have no other options, for those options would certainly have been taken, had they been available. It was necessary for the slave owner to establish the overwhelming discrimination of slavery, to maintain the situation of exploitation. Although some discrimination was motivated by fear of a future threat from the slaves, that fear would not have existed had not Africans been brought to the United States in the first place. Slavery is an excellent example of ethnic stratification motivated by the hope of gain on the part of the dominant group.

Mexican-Americans: farm workers in the Southwest.   A less obvious but nonetheless pertinent example of minority exploitation is the history of

Mexican-Americans in the United States (Moore, 1976: 18–30). This ethnic group initially entered the United States upon annexation of Mexican land after the Mexican War in the 1840s. Those relatively small settlements were later overshadowed by immigrants from Mexico who began coming, both legally and illegally, in the early 1900s. Those early immigrants left Mexico because of economic and political upheavals; it is their reception in the United States that interests us, however.

Economic changes in the American Southwest resulted in a shortage of farm laborers in the early 1900s. The situation became even more critical a decade later, as the labor demands of World War I further depleted the local work force. Mexican farm laborers were sought to fill this void. Many Mexicans immigrated during this period in the status of temporary farm workers; those Mexicans would be of no use if they desired any other kind of work, and their designation as temporary indicates that the United States foresaw a time when they might be less welcome. That time came during the depression of the 1930s, when the demand for farm workers decreased dramatically. Many of the "temporary" workers who had decided to stay wound up on the welfare rolls in California. Local leaders in California determined that it would be less expensive to ship these people back to Mexico than to provide for their welfare in the United States (Moore, 1976: 25, 41–42). Accordingly, mass deportation began.

Following the depression, the cycle occurred a second time for almost the same reasons. The economic boom and labor shortage caused by World War II created a shortage of farm laborers in the Southwest. To fill this occupational need, the *bracero* program was organized; once again, "temporary" Mexican farm workers were brought to the United States. Again the war's end saw an overabundance of farm workers, and a second deportation of Mexicans began in the 1950s. In 1954 alone, over 1,000,000 Mexicans were deported (Moore, 1976: 43).

The message in the history of Mexican-Americans is clear: Mexicans are welcome only if their activities can be controlled so as to be useful to the already extablished upper classes. When farm workers were needed, Mexicans were not only welcome but were actually brought into the United States; when farm workers were not needed, those same Mexicans were removed from the economy. Like the slaves before them, Mexicans were useful only in particular exploited activities, and considerable effort was expended to see that they had no other options.

Exploitation of other minorities.   Similarities exist in the histories of almost every other ethnic group in the United States. The Chinese were welcome as laborers to build the western branch of the Transcontinental Railroad; after the railroad was completed, racial violence broke out against them in the West, and ultimately all further immigration from China was ended in 1882 (Lyman, 1975). The Irish faced employment discrimination in all eastern cities, but their services were much sought after by labor contractors for canal building in the East and, later, for the building of the eastern branch of the Transcontinental Railroad (see Duff, 1971). Again and again, the same picture emerges: ethnic groups find themselves in specific lower-class activities not by their choice but because dominant groups limit their options. In each case—plantation owner, farm owner in the Southwest, and railroad company—the dominant group accumulated considerable wealth by exploiting minority groups. Just as the modern American citizen cannot patronize a rival telephone company if his present service is unsatisfactory, many minority group members must be content to pass on the value of their labor to others if their only choice is to do that or starve.

SUMMARY

This chapter has focused on the unique position of the dominant ethnic group. Individuals in such groups tend to associate their dominance with their culture. This association is expressed as ethnocentrism or as racism; because of the power of the dominant group, such feelings tend to be reflected in the society itself.

This chapter answered the major questions of how and why powerful ethnic groups establish ethnic stratification in the first place and, once it is established, how they maintain it. We saw that ethnic stratification tends to be associated with the more general process of industrialization, particularly with the competitive economic situation brought about by industrialization. We explored a range of ways in which dominant groups maintain ethnic stratification, focusing on overt discrimination, institutional (or covert) discrimination, and exploitation. These types of discrimination were examined focusing on their effects on American blacks, Mexican-Americans, and American Indians.

Chapter

Ideology and Legitimacy: The Politics of Dominance

EiqHT

THE POLITICAL POWER OF THE MAJORITY

So far our major emphasis in the political arena has been on how minorities deal with the kinds of environments that majorities provide for them. Now we want to know the majority's view of this process, and what sort of political atmosphere exists in the United States because of tension between the majority and minorities. This chapter will deal with four major issues: (1) the use of ideology to legitimize minority status, (2) minority voting behavior and its impact, (3) the use of social science to justify the majority position, and (4) problems in understanding equality. Equality is the major thread woven throughout this chapter. Equality is not absolute; rather we shall always speak of equality *of* some criterion or other. In this chapter we are most interested in understanding the social and political processes that give minorities equal power in some instances but blatantly unequal power in other instances.

Introduction to Political Power

In any society political equality is always tempered by political power. Indeed, the political power arena appears to be the crucible in which minorities and majorities engage each other. A political sociology professor once wrote on the blackboard 24 different definitions of political power, and claimed that there were at least 100 additional definitions for the term.[1] We shall define *political power* here as *the authoritative allocation of meaning*. That is, to hold political power a group must be able to define what is good and bad, what is important and unimportant, as well as what is valuable and what is

---

1. For the best overview of the implications of defining political power, see Stephen Lukes, *Power: A Radical View* (New York: Macmillan, 1974).

worthless in a society. Any group of individuals that controls the "defining" power in a society has political dominance.

We are not suggesting that *Webster's Dictionary* is the most important political authority in society! Rather, we are talking about laws, norms, social mores, and policy decisions that are determined—defined—by society. To say that possessing marijuana in any quantity is punishable by a five-year prison sentence is to define the possession of marijuana as bad (and, conversely, to define the nonpossession of it as good). Such a definition, authoritatively allocated by the police, the courts, or even the universities, is political power.

Who Constitutes the Majority in America?

To ask who constitutes the majority in the United States unfortunately begs the question of who holds political power. In an age without dominating figures such as John D. Rockefeller, Andrew Mellon, and Jay Gould, it is difficult to designate any small group of individuals who hold sway over the entire American population. Some social scientists, such as C. Wright Mills (1956), have argued that an elite group of individuals controls American society. Elaborating on this view, Marc Pilisuk and Thomas Hayden (1965) have attempted to demonstrate that American society as a whole tends to foster an elite, through the social and economic systems. An example of such an elite is the so-called military-industrial complex. (Remember that it was not a vociferous voice of the new left that coined the term *military-industrial complex*, but the staid grandfather of the Republican party, Dwight D. Eisenhower.) Of course, the concept of the power elite is only one perspective on American social relationships; we shall discuss other views below.

Assuming that there is some group in society that holds more power than others, we want to know how it uses its power in relationship to the minority. The notions of numerical majority and minority are not necessarily what is meant here. We use *majority* to mean *a group or groups that hold the majority of power in society.* Such a group or groups might be a numerical majority, but that is not a necessary condition.

Given the interrelationship of class and the ideas of race noted throughout this book, it is clear that one great advantage upper-class persons usually have is that their position, economic resources, and subsequent political advantages tend to give them control over the majority of power in their society. This is especially true in the United States. The upper classes find that it is often to their advantage to construct formal (political) and informal (social) rules that distinguish between themselves and other (minority) groups. Distinctions among races might be made consciously or according to pragmatic rules, such as market mechanisms. For instance, a typewriter company manager might refuse to hire a black typewriter salesman, not (at least, so he says) because he is prejudiced, but because most of the people the salesman would be selling to would be white secretaries, who would feel threatened by a black male (Franklin and Resnick, 1973). Such discrimination is merely one aspect of political power as it is used to determine economic and social relationships.

Contemporary upper-class individuals in a vertical society, or in a society tending toward vertical construction, would feel less responsible for such discrimination than individuals in other types of societies. If we concede that there is indeed a majority that holds power, reinforcing discrimination against minorities in American society, then we have a much more complex problem than that implied by the simple discrimination of one individual against another. Given current economic conditions in the United States, there are very few individuals who actually control companies. You might be the president, a member of the board of directors, or the senior manager of a large corporation, yet feel that you are only a cog in the wheel. There is a general feeling that institutions tend to run by themselves.

> What is being said is that these institutions have lives and purposes of their own. No single person, not even the president or chairman, can be said to have made a critical corporate decision. If the man at the top sits at the controls, the car rides on rails he cannot move. The reason, of course, is that our corporate institutions are too large for a single individual to impress with his personality. Moreover the typical chief executive, sitting at the top for only a few years, spends much time in carrying out policies he did not himself inaugurate. His job is to organize his subordinates so that decisions will be carried out. He must, however, share the task of making those decisions, and it is hard to affix responsibility even at the top. The time has come when the institution in fact directs the man who in theory presides over it. (Hacker, 1969: 78)

The typewriter company manager probably refused to hire a black salesman because he felt he had no power over the institutions with which he was dealing, not because he was prejudiced.

Of course, people—not institutions—make decisions, or enforce decisions that have already been made. But the idea of "institution as power holder" is important to understanding how the majority perceives itself. Social and political groups in the nation as a whole and even within individual communities often feel themselves powerless to do anything, even though they hold the majority of political power. This paradox is bewildering, since most Americans also believe that they live in a democracy. For our purposes, the "powerless powerful majority" is a social myth that allows these people not to confront the issue of prejudice because it endangers the status quo. The status quo is important, for it insures the social and political position the majority enjoys. In a sense this attitude reflects a subconscious recognition that any gains made by individuals in lower social classes have an immediate cost in terms of status, economic resources, or power. Because many minority groups represent either a different class or a different race, or both, those who control the majority of political power find it convenient to enjoy their position yet shoulder no responsibility for inequities experienced by minorities.

Minority and Majority Interactions

Ethnic and racial minority groups must continually deal with the majority. Because the majority holds the largest amount of power in society, by definition it controls the authoritative allocation of meaning. Ethnic and racial distinctions are socially defined as *negative*, but we do not mean to suggest that the group that controls such meanings (the majority) consciously defines particular minorities as undesirable. Rather, forces such as the market, class attitudes, and perceived self-protection tend to make people who hold power believe stereotypes about minorities. Therefore, they use their majority status formally or informally to define such people out of certain jobs, businesses, positions, or even neighborhoods. The process is very subtle, but its impact is often severe and long-term. We shall use the example of the American Indians' relationship with white society.

The Experience of the American Indian

Gunpowder gave Europeans a decided advantage over the Indians almost from the moment they set foot on North American soil. Certainly, the Indians could have adopted the use of gunpowder, but European technology and economic attitudes would still always place them in an inferior competitive position. When the whites first arrived on this continent, notably at Jamestown and Plymouth, they were treated well by some Indians and made war on by others. Friendly natives taught the whites skills needed to survive the harsh American winters and how to adapt to the environment. The one economic notion the Indians did not possess—the idea of owning land—would force a confrontation with most whites. English settlers could not understand the Indians' difficulty grasping the notion of ownership. As pressures for land increased along the Atlantic shore, land shortages developed. (Remember that it was almost 100 years after the founding of Jamestown before whites moved away from the major bodies of water.) The need for land, as well as the Indians' rather brutal methods of warfare, tended to develop a series of racial stereotypes.

Certainly, the warlike American Indians were brutal by contemporary standards, but the seventeenth century British were no less so. It was commonplace for condemned prisoners in the Tower of London to be flogged, hung by the neck until almost dead, cut down, then castrated while their intestines were torn out and burned. Finally they were drawn and quartered. Other unfortunate prisoners were forced to watch these atrocities. The point is that the notion of the bloodthirsty Indian was actually more a social myth than a relevant way of distinguishing between peoples.

By the late seventeenth century, on the eastern shore of Virginia and Maryland, Indians were hunted like wolves, with a bounty on their heads, as a menace to society. Whites who had originally bought land from the Indians found it much cheaper to take it by gunfire. During the French and Indian Wars, the French taught the Indians a device for counting dead warriors:

scalping. From the scalps the French could keep track of the number of British the Indians had killed for them. Thus was created a social image that later contributed to ideas about how distinct the Indians were from civilized whites.

As more and more Indians were displaced by the white westward migration, it became apparent that something had to be done about the Indians who surrendered. Defined as pariahs, they were no longer acceptable within white society. Usually they were forcibly removed to lands considered uninhabitable by whites—desolate desert country or mosquito-infested swamps. The resettlements caused confusion in geographic names across America. For example, in the rolling hills of southwestern Ohio is Miami University, nestled between the Big Miami and Little Miami Rivers. Why Miami in Ohio, when everyone knows it is in Florida? Because the Miami Indians were forced off their land in Ohio and resettled in what was then the most desolate place imaginable, southern Florida. Other Indians were removed along the infamous trail of tears (the route of the Cherokee expulsion to Oklahoma), or to desert reservations in Arizona and New Mexico or the Badlands of North and South Dakota.

Once the stereotype of the Indian was developed it was almost impossible to change, even assuming that people would have liked to do so. By the early twentieth century few Indians were left, and they were generally isolated in poverty on reservations. The American Indian had ceased to be a problem because American society, through violence and social policies, had decimated the Indian population.

We relate the history of the Indians not to condemn the actions of the majority or to elicit guilt. Our purpose is to show the tremendous impact of ideological points of view on minorities. We need to study not only the situation of minorities, and their perception of themselves, but also the majority's perception of the minority.

IDEOLOGY AND LEGITIMACY: LIBERALISM AND CONSERVATISM

The term *ideology* often has negative connotations, such as Nazism or Communism, thereby limiting the concept of ideology to a specific time or place. But the United States is also under a dominant ideology—capitalism. For that matter, most societies during the past several hundred years have had dominant ideologies. Briefly, an ideology is a world view, or a perspective on how the world works, that inculcates certain values and goals and an idea of how to achieve those goals (Dolbeare and Dolbeare, 1976). For example, many Americans believe that the capitalist "free market" is how the world works; that we have free choices among goods and services; that competition is good; and that by keeping government more or less out of the marketplace we will progress toward a better life.

A world view (or ideology) tends to define our cultural values and will ultimately have an impact on how we treat minorities and minority demands.

However, it would be incorrect to suggest that ideologies remain fixed and stable. On the contrary, they change according to internal and external social pressures. For instance, as table 9 shows, there have tended to be certain dominant and progressive belief systems (ideologies) about American blacks, which have changed according to the political and social structure of oppression. Note the impact of culture on the social ideology of the time; it is clear that contemporary values are important determinants of such abstract ideas as justice, equality, and fairness.

Value systems also tend to change the flavor and intensity of certain ideologies. Certainly, the dominant perspectives within American capitalism are the ideologies of conservatism and liberalism.[2] Each of these ideologies sees the minority question in a different light. The next sections will explore the differences between the two viewpoints.

The Liberal Approach to Majority Rule

Liberals believe that equal opportunity before the law is the cornerstone of American democracy. Although they firmly believe in the competitive market, they understand that certain groups have historically been disadvantaged. How is such a problem redressed? By providing jobs and employment opportunities, say liberals. Their view of American capitalism is that government and business operate hand in hand. Because of this, changes cannot be made that might endanger government's relationship with the private sector. Private investment, confidence in government, and cooperation are essential elements of the social and political system. Liberals also assume that all individuals and groups have at least the potential to participate in the economy.

Everyone gets a piece of the pie.   The liberal's ultimate belief is that everyone can get a piece of the pie; that is, American society gives all groups the opportunity to vie for goods, services, and opportunities. Liberals supported ending legal racial segregation, but were far less amenable when blacks demanded their own organizations, separate from whites, and attacked the free market system as unjust and racist. (Of course, in the 1960s and early 1970s Indians, Chicanos, Orientals, and women also attacked the ideology of capitalism as the foundation of discrimination against them.)

From the liberal point of view, such attacks on the capitalist system were sheer ingratitude. Decades had been spent providing minorities with equal opportunities, and now the minorities were criticizing the system that the liberals were trying to protect by providing these opportunities. No longer were there laws segregating blacks and other minorities in education, jobs,

---

2. Conservatism and liberalism are simply types of capitalism. Both support the free enterprise ideal and believe in the value of competition. In fact, they have more similarities than differences. Do not confuse American conservatism and liberalism with the European types. For example, most European conservatives (in England, France, and Germany) support various forms of socialism, which even American liberals would be loath to do.

Table 9. Summary of the Structure of Racial Oppression and Racial Beliefs in American History

PERIOD[a]	STRUCTURE OF OPPRESSION	DOMINANT BELIEFS	"PROGRESSIVE" BELIEFS
English heritage –1650	1. Colonial expansion 2. Indentured servant system	1. Blacks are uncivilized heathens. 2. Blackness is evil, a curse of God. 3. Blacks are bestial by nature.	
Colonial America 1650–1760	1. Slave trade 2. Institutionalization of slavery	1. Black bestiality, especially sexual aggressiveness, requires control.	
Revolutionary era 1760–1820	1. Abolition of slave trade 2. Confinement of slavery	1. Slavery is a necessary evil. 2. Blacks are ill-suited or unprepared for freedom	1. Slavery is inconsistent with revolutionary ideology. 2. While culturally deprived and debased by slavery, blacks are capable of betterment.
Ante-bellum 1820–1860	1. Further institutionalization of slavery in face of ideological challenges and North–South economic and political competition	1. Slavery is a positive good that protects the interests of masters and slaves alike. 2. Slavery harnesses the savage nature of blacks, civilizing them as much as possible. 3. The childlike dependency of blacks requires white protection. 4. Northern stereotype defines blacks as ignorant, lazy, and immoral.	1. There are "racial" differences. 2. Blacks' "childlike simplicity" reveals a basic Christian nature. 3. Slavery is morally wrong; it corrupts and takes advantage of a naturally submissive people.

Table 9.   Summary of the Structure of Racial Oppression and Racial Beliefs in American History (continued)

PERIOD[a]	STRUCTURE OF OPPRESSION	DOMINANT BELIEFS	"PROGRESSIVE" BELIEFS
Civil War and Reconstruction (1861–1877)			
Post-Reconstruction to World War I 1877–1914	1. Dismantling of Radical Reconstruction 2. Growing legalized segregation in all institutional spheres 3. Relegation of blacks to menial farm-factory occupations 4. Enforcement of segregation and relegation through white violence 5. Legalized and de facto segregation	1. Black corruption in Reconstruction confirms their inherent inferiority. 2. Blacks have failed to take advantage of "equal" opportunities; in accordance with social Darwinism, they should be left to find their social niche. 3. Without the supervision and compulsion of slavery, blacks have degenerated to their natural state, where they are lazy, prone to crime, and lust for white women. 4. The traits of blacks that make them different from and inferior to whites require separation of the races.	1. The black race is less advanced than the white because it has not progressed as far on the scale of evolution. 2. Blacks are potentially useful citizens. Their natural docility and kindness can be channeled through education, industrial training, and white guidance 3. Racial purity and the instinct of race prejudice necessitate racial segregation.
World War I to World War II 1914–1941	1. Northern migration of southern blacks and their confinement to ghettos 2. Last hired and first fired policy 3. Union exclusion and confinement to low-scaled occupations 4. Segregation and disenfranchisement backed by violence, formal law, and de facto practices	1. Black inferiority is an indisputable scientific fact, backed by evolutionary theory and intelligence testing. 2. Segregationist doctrine continues to be affirmed: racial segregation is natural and instinctive, for the good of and desired by both races; blacks are permanently inferior beings; segregation is needed to control their criminality and lust and to guard against amalgamation.	1. All apparent social, cultural, and intellectual differences between the races are the result of the environment. 2. Blacks are the victims of an oppressive environment that creates discontent, frustration, and a fatalistic sense of powerlessness.

Table 9. Summary of the Structure of Racial Oppression and Racial Beliefs in American History (continued)

PERIOD[a]	STRUCTURE OF OPPRESSION	DOMINANT BELIEFS	"PROGRESSIVE" BELIEFS
World War II (1941–1948)			
Second Reconstruction 1948–1968	1. Efforts to increase opportunity without alteration of basic institutional and community patterns	1. Rejection of legal segregation 2. Blacks have been discriminated against in the past. 3. Blacks are not inherently inferior to whites and are capable of change. 4. Change is best accomplished by improving substandard schools and renovating black ghettos; in other words, by providing "equal opportunities."	1. Black appearances of inferiority reflect cultural deprivation and the impact of undesirable environments. 2. Complete social integration is the only viable means to racial harmony. 3. Forced integration of schools is essential to any program of change.
1968–Present	1. Continued de facto residential segregation 2. White violence and protest of educational integration 3. Decreased political and legal efforts to enforce civil rights legislation, even in the face of "affirmative action" policies	1. Blacks' inferior status is largely attributable to blacks themselves, especially their lack of motivation. 2. The pace of change in race relations has been too fast. 3. Enough has been done—reverse discrimination and forced integration measures such as open housing laws and busing are wrong.	1. Racism is generic to the social structure of American society. 2. The "equal opportunities" doctrine has failed—there is need to redress past wrongs. 3. Immediate integration is not possible —community control and group power are more practicable.

[a] Dates correspond to the following historical events:

1650: roughly marks the beginning of the distinction, soon recognized in law, between indentured servitude for whites and lifetime servitude for blacks
1760: first serious antislavery crusade gets into full swing
1820: height of debates leading to the Missouri Compromise; re-emergence of strong antislavery sentiment
1860: election of Abraham Lincoln; beginning of Southern secession
1877: election of Rutherford B. Hayes; withdrawal of federal troops from the South
1914: World War I
1941: World War II
1948: Harry Truman establishes the Commission on Civil Rights, issues an executive order desegregating the armed forces
1968: Assassination of Martin Luther King; publication of the Kerner Report; election of Richard Nixon

SOURCE: Adapted from Jonathan H. Turner and Royce Singleton, "A theory of ethnic oppression: toward a reintegration of cultural and structural concepts in ethnic relations theory." Social Forces 56, no. 4 (June 1978), pp. 1001–18. Copyright © 1978 The University of North Carolina Press. Used by permission.

restaurants, hotels, and the like. The liberals believed that this was the limit to which government could go if it was to protect not only minorities but the free market economy.

The problem with the liberals' idea of how minorities, notably blacks, would obtain full equality is that once segregation had been outlawed, unequal treatment had to be resolved through market mechanisms. Is that a situation of full equality? Let us use an analogy, a cross-country race. If one runner has been superbly trained to run and another has been put into leg chains (by law) and denied proper training, is it reasonable to consider the race fair? Most people would not. Now assume that the race has begun and the first runner is just passing the two-mile mark. The second runner, still in leg chains, is approaching the quarter-mile mark. The judges of the race run up to him, bemoan the unfairness of the race, remove the chains from his ankles, and tell him that he can now run fairly. Then the judges return to their observation post, satisfied that the race is now fair.

Although the analogy is overdrawn, it demonstrates the common liberal position and indicates why liberals significantly split over programs like lateral entry into jobs and affirmative action. The liberals believe that each runner has the potential to win the race; this is what they mean by "everyone being able to get a piece of the pie." Minorities generally object that the rules of the game—the free market economy—are rigged against them, but liberals feel that there is little they can do. If they tamper with the market economy, especially with notions of class and the right of class advantage, then the entire economic system might be in danger of collapsing. In an interesting sense, they are correct.

Poor and middle-class whites objected to the idea that racial minorities should be given an advantage over them. After all, many of them were poor and were not given advantages. This feeling led white ethnics—such as Italians, Jews, and Poles—to organize because they were not given the advantage of "class jumping." That is, it was generally impossible, especially in areas of high ethnic concentrations, to make the kinds of jumps that federal programs were suggesting. Additionally, blacks, Chicanos, and Indians were apparently going to be competing directly with them for jobs and economic security. Civil rights conflicted with self-interest. This is not to suggest that such groups are selfish; rather they recognized the reality of having to live in a society dominated by the liberal emphasis on the market economy. If they were laid off, liberals might support public assistance or even federally sponsored jobs, but would do nothing to alleviate the larger problem by tampering with the private sector.

Benign neglect.   By 1970 the pressure of white ethnic groups, as well as a significant shift toward conservative politics, allowed policy makers to deemphasize the role of government in helping minorities. Although some government programs for minorities continue to function, in general they have helped only those minorities and women who probably would have succeeded without them (Newman et al., 1978). The beginning of this change in government's stance was probably a memo to then President Richard Nixon by Daniel Patrick Moynihan. Its importance is not so much that Moynihan was the president's urban advisor, but rather that he was a policy maker articulating the position of most members of the American majority. "Benign neglect" became the federal policy toward minorities in the 1970s:

> The time may have come when the issue of race could benefit from a period of "benign neglect." The subject has been too much talked about. The forum has been taken over by hysterics, paranoids, and boodlers on all sides. The Administration can help bring this about by paying close attention to such progress—as we are doing—while seeking to avoid situations in which extremists of either race are given opportunities for martyrdom, heroics, histrionics or whatever. . . .
>
> There is a silent black majority as well as a white one. It is mostly working-class, as against lower- and middle-class. It is probably moderate. . . . This group has been generally ignored by government and the media. The more recognition we can give to it, the better we shall all be. (Moynihan, 1970: 69)

The memo implicitly recognizes the importance of exploiting class to insure the smooth running of American politics. Benign neglect was not only the de-emphasis of civil rights; it was also an attempt to split black movements along class lines.

Emphasizing the judiciary. Techniques such as benign neglect have always been the policy of liberal government in the United States. They are necessary for liberals to balance public good with private interest. The liberal conviction is that if a balance is maintained between competing sectors of American society, then the country will have periods of progress. To achieve this, individuals must identify as individuals, not along racial or ethnic lines. If race and ethnicity were emphasized, it would be very difficult to propose a policy such as tax cuts for the wealthy, because individuals with ethnic or racial identity would quickly conclude that as members of their minority group, they would be unlikely to benefit, if for no other reason than that few members of their group are wealthy.

Liberals ultimately turn to the courts to resolve minority grievances, for several reasons. First, the courts are a much less visible arena in which to resolve public policy issues. Second, the courts have consistently refused to tamper with social class relationships. Last, most Americans feel that the present judicial system is fair. Thus, the courts can dispose of sticky political issues out of the spotlight of presidential policy or congressional debate. For example, the *Rodriguez* case (see Chapter 4) did away with an issue that was almost unresolvable by the executive branch of government. The *Bakke* case was a convenient means to nullify most affirmative action programs without sullying the executive or legislative branches.

The Conservative Approach to Majority Rule

On the issue of race, liberals and conservatives differ little over policy positions. Very few conservatives actually supported segregation laws; even arch-conservative Senator Barry Goldwater of Arizona did not support such laws—although he did not want the federal government involved in ending them. Goldwater's emphasis on states' rights is rather archaic in a nation of some 220,000,000 people, but the point is that only the most rabid southern racists (such as Harry Byrd of Virginia, Strom Thurmond of South Carolina. and George Wallace of Alabama) opposed the end of segregation by law. Most conservatives felt that segregation laws should end, but by state discretion.[3] Neither conservatives nor liberals were willing to address the issue of class.

Liberals may be somewhat more embarrassed by class distinctions in American society than conservatives, but not much. Most conservatives argue that racial distinctions do not exist in American society. Instead, what we see as racial distinctions are really class distinctions. Conservatives argue that "the poor will always be with us." Since conservatives appear to have growing support among Americans, it is important to understand their position.

Edward Banfield's unheavenly city.   The most provocative conservative American social scientist is Edward Banfield of Harvard University. Like generations of conservative social scientists before him at Harvard, including William Graham Sumner and Walter Bagehot, Banfield emphasizes the inevitability of social class in the United States. He says that racial prejudice "is not the main obstacle" for blacks today:

> The other minority groups once lived in the oldest parts of the inner city—and the Negro lives in them now—not so much because they were looked down on (although, of course, they were) as because they had low incomes. It was because they were poor that they had to come to the city, and being poor they could not afford good housing. . . .
>
> Today the Negro's main disadvantage is the same as the Puerto Rican's and the Mexican's: namely, that he is the most recent unskilled, and hence relatively low-income migrant to reach the city from a backward rural area. (Banfield, 1974: 78)

Banfield theorizes that the lower classes are locked into their situation; government programs will not alleviate the problems of the poor. This is because the lower classes are present-oriented while the middle classes are future-oriented. Although such definitions present significant problems for psychologists (see Franklin and Resnick, 1973: 164–72) as well as for other social

---

3.   One might argue that this is a small distinction, that falling back on states' rights means that there was no practical way to end segregation. This might be true, if one considers legal segregation the most heinous form of segregation. However, the liberal approach also allows segregation in the form of de facto segregation. Which is worse for minorities?

scientists, they do fit the popular American notion of why poverty exists. If one saves money, delays gratification by working all year for a two-week vacation, and buys life insurance, one is considered a valued member of society. All of these activities are future-oriented. People who do not participate are not merely culturally different, they also deny our values.

But Banfield is merely playing a variation on the liberal theme. Where liberals are ashamed to mention words like *class* for fear that they might make American society look elitist, conservatives face the issue squarely. In fact, most conservatives, including Banfield, feel no embarrassment at all about the elite nature of American society and politics. Thus, the problem with blacks is that they take the issue of race too seriously. The blacks fail to recognize their ability to take advantage of the American pluralist perspective to drag themselves out of the squalor and degradation of the culture of poverty. There is no real problem in the inner city, for blacks live better now than ever before; their problem is that they are unable or unwilling to plan for the future. Thus, if the American political system attempts to make significant social changes to help the poor (read "blacks"), such attempts are not only doomed to failure but may endanger the American economic, social, and political system.

Minorities endanger the political system.   Banfield's social analysis is interesting. For conservatives the free market economy is the *sine qua non* of a democratic nation; therefore, there can be nothing wrong with class relationships. The American racial problem is not really a problem, but causes difficulties only because minorities believe it is a problem. One social scientist has called this view "blaming the victim" (Ryan, 1976), because it suggests that racial groups create and are responsible for their own situation. It is curious that Banfield writes about a "non-problem"; from his point of view there is nothing unnatural or immoral about poverty or slums for large majorities of racial groups. The problem he is concerned with is the danger such groups represent for the larger society. The horrible conditions of urban ghettos do not concern him as much as "huge enclaves of people of low skill, income, and status." Such people are a threat; there is "political danger in the presence of great concentrations of people who feel little attachment to the society" (Banfield, 1974: 13).

At bottom, both conservatives and liberals have vested interests in the established order; they want to avoid changes that might make individuals question the distribution of goods and services in American society. The majority of Americans either have benefited from the economic system or believe, given the status quo, that they will potentially benefit from it. The white majority must strongly resist changes that would benefit minorities. For if minorities get their way, not only will the contradictions of the system become apparent, but other groups (white ethnics, white Appalachians, even low-level white-collar workers) might begin to question the justice of the American economic and political order. Whatever the causes of discrimination, there is a recognition that major changes will not take place without changes in the economic system.

Such instability would be intolerable to both conservatives and liberals. Liberals, however, tend to ignore this tension, shifting the burden to the courts and believing that racial problems can be resolved by minimal adjustments to the present economic and social system. The conservatives see blacks and other racial minorities not as victims of the system, but rather as holding a position that is justly theirs for being last in line in the great urban centers. Neither liberals nor conservatives question the basic economic order, for the free market is the foundation for both ideologies.

The Crisis of Capitalism: Protecting the Free Market

Most economists argue that the free market ended in the United States with the erection of the Rockefeller oil monopoly in 1837. Yet most Americans think that the United States is a free market capitalist system. Is it? Most economists describe our economy as oligopolistic; that is, a small group of producers controls the market in any given commodity. As table 10 shows, the top 25 companies control a significant amount of all sales, profits, and assets in the United States. One hundred companies in the United States have sales equal to 39 percent of our total gross national product, almost 34 percent of all profit, and well over half of all assets owned in this country. Of course, few of these companies control monopolies in individual industries; rather, they diversify. Like the little fish that is eaten by the larger fish that is devoured by the huge fish, companies grow through take-overs.

The tangle of take-overs and stock deals has become so complex that it is questionable whether such ventures are legal. For example, there are many interlocking directorates (arrangements by which a few people control the stocks of hundreds of corporations), but to prove them would take millions of dollars in accountants' fees and access to documents that might not be available. Table 11 elaborates on the implication of table 10: that most such companies are on an economic par not only with other such companies, but also with other countries in the world. It is no surprise that companies with such a strong position in both the United States and the rest of the world do not want to shake the market foundations on which they are built. Multinational corporations often rise above nationalism, supplying both sides in war. International Telephone and Telegraph had substantial holdings in both the United States and Nazi Germany during World War II. In 1967 ITT received a $27,000,000 settlement from the United States government for the company's German plants bombed during the war—many of which were manufacturing munitions (Sampson, 1973).

Symbolism versus reality: capitalism in the 1980s.   Because of most Americans' vested interest in the notion of the free market, it is important to differentiate between the myth and the reality of the free market. This is especially important if we are to understand the role minorities play in such a

Table 10.   The Largest United States Industrial Firms, 1974 (in millions of dollars)

	Sales	Profits	Assets
Exxon	$ 42,061	$ 3,142	$ 31,332
GM	31,550	950	20,468
Ford Motor Co.	23,621	361	14,174
Texaco	23,256	1,586	17,176
Mobil Oil	18,929	1,048	14,074
Standard Oil of California	17,191	970	11,640
Gulf Oil	16,458	1,065	12,503
General Electric	13,413	608	9,369
IBM	12,675	1,838	14,027
ITT	11,154	451	10,697
Chrysler	10,971	52	6,733
U.S. Steel	9,186	634	7,718
Standard Oil (Indiana)	9,085	970	8,916
Shell Oil	7,634	621	6,129
Western Electric	7,382	311	5,240
Continental Oil	7,041	328	4,673
E. I. duPont de Nemours	6,910	404	5,980
Atlantic Richfield	6,740	474	6,152
Westinghouse Electric	6,466	28	4,302
Occidental Petroleum	5,719	281	3,326
Bethlehem Steel	5,381	342	4,513
Union Carbide	5,320	530	4,883
Goodyear Tire & Rubber	5,256	158	4,242
Tenneco	5,002	322	6,402
Phillips Petroleum	4,981	402	4,028
TOTAL (top 25)	313,382	17,879	238,697
(top 100)	539,084	28,844	403,406
Top 100 as percent of total economy	39.0[a]	33.9	56.6

SOURCE: Richard C. Edwards, Michael Reich and Thomas E. Weisskopf, The Capitalist System, 2nd ed. (Englewood Cliffs, N.J.: Prentice-Hall, © 1978) p. 131. Reprinted by permission.

[a] Corporate sales as a percentage of GNP.

high stakes situation. The myth of the free market is that everyone can play. Presently only one of every twenty businesses started in the United States in any given year lasts to celebrate its fifth birthday. To test that statistic, find out how many students in your class have parents who own a business. Unless you are studying at an upper-middle-class, private, predominantly white institution, fewer than one in five will. And most of their businesses are service-related — doctor, plumber, lawyer, or television repair — not manufacturing.

The chance that an individual can move up through the class structure by buying a business and making it a success is presently very slim. In other words, blacks and other racial minorities, *even if their race were not a factor,*

Table 11.   Nations and Corporations Ranked by Size of Annual Product, 1971

Rank	Economic Entity	Product[1] (billions of dollars)	Rank	Economic Entity	Product (billions of dollars)
1	United States	1,068.1	46	Pakistan	8.2
2	USSR	343.1	47	*Chrysler*	8.0
3	Japan	223.0	48	Nigeria	7.9
4	West Germany	196.8	49	Thailand	7.8
5	France	172.0	50	Chile	7.6
6	United Kingdom	135.8	51	*Texaco*	7.5
7	China	128.1	52	U.A.R.	7.5
8	Italy	100.6	53	*Unilever*[2,3]	7.5
9	Canada	89.4	54	*ITT*	7.4
10	India	60.6	55	Portugal	7.1
11	Poland	44.1	56	Bulgaria	7.0
12	Brazil	43.9	57	New Zealand	6.9
13	Spain	37.4	58	Peru	6.7
14	Mexico	36.7	59	Israel	6.6
15	Australia	36.4	60	Taiwan	6.4
16	Netherlands	34.6	61	*Western Electric*	6.1
17	East Germany	34.5	62	*Gulf Oil*	5.9
18	Sweden	34.3	63	Algeria	5.2
19	Czechoslovakia	30.7	64	*British Petroleum*[2]	5.2
20	Argentina	29.0	65	*Philips Gloeilampen*[3]	5.2
21	Belgium	28.7	66	*Standard Oil (California)*	5.1
22	*General Motors*	28.3	67	Puerto Rico	5.1
23	Switzerland	22.9	68	*Volkswagen*[4]	5.0
24	*Standard Oil (New Jersey)*	18.7	69	*U.S. Steel*	4.9
25	South Africa	18.4	70	Bangladesh	4.7
26	Denmark	17.2	71	*Westinghouse*	4.6
27	Austria	16.5	72	Malaysia	4.5
28	*Ford Motor Co.*	16.4	73	Ireland	4.5
29	Rumania	15.2	74	North Korea	4.4
30	Yugoslavia	15.1	75	Cuba	4.4
31	Iran	13.4	76	South Vietnam	4.3
32	*Royal Dutch/Shell*[2,3]	12.7	77	*Nippon Steel*[5]	4.1
33	Hungary	12.4	78	*Standard Oil (Indiana)*	4.1
34	Turkey	12.3	79	Morocco	4.0
35	Norway	12.2	80	*Shell Oil*	3.9
36	Finland	12.0	81	*du Pont*	3.9
37	Greece	11.3	82	*Siemens*[4]	3.8
38	Venezuela	11.2	83	Saudi Arabia	3.8
39	Indonesia	9.5	84	*Imperial Chemical Industries*[2]	3.7
40	*General Electric*	9.4	85	*RCA*	3.7
41	Philippines	9.1	86	*Hitachi*[5]	3.6
42	South Korea	8.3	87	*Goodyear*	3.6
43	*IBM*	8.3	88	Hong Kong	3.6
44	Colombia	8.3	89	Iraq	3.6
45	*Mobil Oil*	8.2	90	*Nestlé*[6]	3.6

SOURCE: Richard C. Edwards, Michael Reich and Thomas E. Weisskopf, The Capitalist System, 2nd ed. (Englewood Cliffs, N.J.: Prentice-Hall, © 1978) p. 479. Reprinted by permission.

1.   Gross national product for countries and gross sales for corporations.
2-6.   Corporations based outside the United States, in: (2) the United Kingdom; (3) the Netherlands; (4) West Germany; (5) Japan; or (6) Switzerland.

have come upon the national scene at the wrong time. The emphasis on black capitalism would have been important in 1900, but today, when almost any business success story is covered in *Time* or *Newsweek* (testifying to the rarity of such events), the American dream of owning a business is more myth than reality. It is reasonable to predict that in the 1980s fewer and fewer individuals will have the market sovereignty so important to achievement in modern capitalism. However, because we as a nation believe so strongly in the benefits of the free market, the myth will persevere.

To the victors go the spoils: justifying the minority position.   A myth like that of the free market always protects those who benefit from the status quo. According to the myth, since blacks and other racial minorities are no longer fettered by legal restraints, they themselves are at fault if they do not make progress. This will be the predominant theme of the 1980s, assuming that no major economic disaster interrupts the myth. The reality is that minorities will fall further and further behind the majority in economic and political clout. Although small inroads will be and have been made by blacks, Chicanos, and women, for the most part economic arrangements will force political and social situations to remain about the same.

It is important to the majority in American society to justify the situation of minorities. And the higher up the socioeconomic ladder you climb, the more situations you must account for. The Polish steel worker in Buffalo, New York, usually needs to justify only the black whose position is beneath him. The white college senior at Radcliffe has to justify both the black and the Polish positions, as well as many others. This process of justification is political power: defining why Poles, blacks, or any other group deserve their positions in American society. The majority believes that the blame for minorities' lower positions lies not with those who hold the ability to politically define these ethnics, but with the minorities (the victims) themselves.

The political economy of minority status.   In a sense, sociologists like Edward Banfield are right when they suggest that the problem of race in the United States is a class problem. Most people cannot see the need for a poor social class, much less the necessity to insure that blacks, Chicanos, or other ethnic groups comprise such a large share of the lower class. They fail to recognize that there is a political economy of minority status, and that minority groups play a vital role in the modern American political economy. However, this role is buried under a host of myths, prescriptions, and presuppositions.

The major purpose of a lower class in the United States is to maintain the belief in scarcity. That is, for the economy to work effectively, people must not only buy goods; they also must believe that certain goods and services are more scarce than others. For example, the United States buys grain (as well as many other commodities) from farmers to keep the price of grain up. The federal government has enough grain in storage now to feed the entire world for a year, and literally to wipe out starvation. However, if we gave away our grain, the prices would drop so low that no one would want to grow grain. More and more farmers would go out of business (which is happening already, despite a massive federal effort), and agribusinesses—huge farms controlled by large corporations—would take over. The point of this example is that without the notion of scarcity, and sometimes the reality of scarcity, our economy would collapse. For instance, the lower-class person insures that people will believe color televisions are scarce (they cost so much that the poor cannot afford them), as well as creates a ready-made clientele for used cars, without whose trade-in few in the middle class could afford new cars.

Having specific racial groups to dominate lower-class status bolsters the myth of the market economy in several ways. First, racism helps some lower-class whites survive in a world that would otherwise define them as failures. Their logic is simple: at least I am not black. Second, blacks and other minorities are consumers of items that most lower-class whites would find objectionable. Third, division of the lower classes into racial or ethnic categories avoids any objection to the creation of scarcity, and deflects attention from the few people who control the vast majority of wealth in the United States. This is not meant to suggest that the rich manipulate society; rather, if one is a multimillionaire, it is in one's self-interest to do nothing about racial discrimination in the United States. One can thus ignore class, hire individuals who are less a direct challenge because of their culture or values, and simultaneously ignore any blame for one's actions.

In sum, racism has several benefits to the majority. It insures that society sees the advantages of present economic circumstances and that other groups take the blame for economic problems. Racism also provides a clientele for less desirable and used items that otherwise would have no consumers. Race is not only the means of accomplishing those purposes, but racial categories are convenient. Economic considerations necessitated that some group fill such roles. American blacks, all but unprotected after Reconstruction and the infamous Civil Rights Cases, were very convenient candidates. Blacks, Chicanos, and Indians "arrived" (that is, were allowed to enter the marketplace) when American industrialization was by and large complete. Most of the economic expansion behind the free market myth had ended by 1900; in fact, Robert Blauner argues that there has been a substantial slowdown in economic expansion since World War I (Blauner, 1972). That is precisely when blacks, Chicanos, Indians, and women became a factor in the industrialized labor force. It is apparent that economic forces encourage the social position of contemporary minorities.

The Converts: Accommodation and Its Benefits

It is true that individual members of minorities have succeeded: Sammy Davis, Jr., and Reggie Jackson are successful blacks, Bobby Vinton and Tony Kubek successful Americans of Polish descent. But what do such notables prove? Not much. One hundred years ago, one of the most visible Americans was Booker T. Washington, yet his status was by no means indicative of the social or political position of most black Americans in the late 1800s. There are exceptions to every rule, and although groups do become assimilated into American society, the successful individual is not a good indicator of such assimilation.

The commitment of the converts.   A much better indicator of assimilation is individual commitment to the American system. It is an old saying that the most fanatical believers in any religious movement are the converts to that movement, not those born into it. In much the same way, members of ethnic or racial groups in the United States who feel they have a significant stake in American Society are its most vocal defenders. As we saw in Chapter 6, members of a minority movement who perceive that they have been successful will become accommodationists. Most feel an intense loyalty to society because they see themselves as successful, and they credit their success to the opportunities available in society.

Although success is relative, many individuals do reach personal goals and do feel a warm, abiding commitment to society for providing them with opportunities to do so. Of course, the reliability of these individuals' judgments depends not on their good fortunes, but on how representative they are of their ethnic or racial group. It is not difficult to find a successful American black, but how typical is that person of the black community? Does his or her success point to a de-emphasis of race in American society? We need to understand the role such people play in determining our view of their group's situation. We also need to know why they resent other ethnic or racial groups and their claims that government should compensate them for prejudice.

White ethnics.   "We made it, so why can't they?" is a common theme in ethnic communities today. Although the question is most often asked by white second- and third-generation Americans referring to blacks, it is also asked by Japanese-Americans criticizing Chinese-Americans as well as in many other interethnic situations. As we have seen, the economic realities that confronted eastern European immigrants are substantially different from those that face other minorities. Nevertheless, the longer-established ethnic communities resent the other minorities, and their resentment has blunted government efforts to help groups such as blacks and Chicanos.

Most white ethnics initially supported the black civil rights movement against southern segregation, not merely because it was evidently just, but also because it did not threaten their own social and political position. David Danzig of the American Jewish Committee points out:

> There are great differences between the civil rights movement and the "Negro Revolution," and these differences papered over so long by certain historical exigencies are now surfacing into full view. The civil rights movement was and is essentially concerned with the structure of law and social justice: its goals were equality before the law and equality of individual opportunity. As a movement it was begun by people whose aim was not to aid the Negro as such but to bring American society into closer conformity with constitutional principle. For the greatest part of its history, civil rights was the white liberal's cause. Liberals expounded the moral basis of human rights in religion and politics, developed the theory of human equality in the physical and social sciences, led the intellectual offensive against racism, and took the initiative in founding the civil rights organizations. . . .
>
> What changed civil rights almost overnight from a peripheral moral issue to our major domestic movement was the emergence of the Negroes themselves as a nationwide bloc. (Quoted in Barbero, 1974: 612)

Blacks had always perceived themselves as a bloc, but it took the civil rights movement to focus their energy into a viable political force. As such a force, blacks were a significant threat to the lower-middle-class (or new middle-class) individuals who were just one rung above them on the social class ladder, notably Jews, Italians, Poles, and Irish.

An underlying dimension of conflict has existed throughout the twentieth century between ethnic and ethnic, ethnic and racial, and racial and racial groups. For example, anti-Semitism was common in the black community 40 years ago; early in the Second World War blacks were known to say, "Well, Hitler did one good thing: he put those Jews in their place" (Weisbord and Stein, 1970: 59). Conversely, anti-black sentiment has a long history among Jews. The tension erupted in the 1960s, when it appeared that blacks and other minorities were endangering the economic and political advantages of newly entrenched European minority groups. The most notable battle was fought by the predominantly Jewish New York City teachers' union and blacks, over neighborhood control of schools.

It would be wrong to assume that because of economic competition, white ethnics—especially Catholics and Jews—tend to be more racist than other people. Andrew R. Greeley's recent studies suggest otherwise: "Monitoring of national attitudes on racial integration show that Irish Catholics are the most pro-integration of Gentile religio-ethnic groups in the North, and that Italian and German Catholics fall right on the northern mean in their sympathy for racial integration" (Greeley, 1974: 218). Although Slavic Catholics fell slightly below the mean, Jews tended to rank far higher than any Christian ethnic group. These religious distinctions do not hold across political issues, but break down ethnically. Nevertheless, even in the competitive economic, social, and political atmosphere in which ethnic and racial groups coexist, such groups still have considerable sympathy for the problems of other groups in dealing with the majority in American society.

WRESTLING FOR POWER: THE VOTING BEHAVIOR OF MINORITIES

It is an old political wives' tale that Republicans are Protestants and Democrats are Catholics and Jews. Although there is some truth to this adage, it conceals more than it explains. This section will explore ethnic and racial voting patterns, which often ignore religion, and the impact of ethnic and racial voting on American politics.

Patterns of Minority Voting Behavior

American mythology has it that the question of who holds power in the United States is decided in the voting booth. Although it is debatable whether significant power shifts ever occur because of the ballot, it is certain that if the door to power is ever to open for minority groups, the ballot box is the means to unlock that door.

Ethnic and racial individuals tend to vote largely according to their group affiliations. However, these groups (notably blacks, who make up a large proportion of the southern electorate) do not hold much political power. The reason is that they tend not to vote. Studies reveal that economic background tends to determine voter turnout; lower-class individuals do not vote as often as members of the middle class or upper middle class. Since high percentages of many minorities are in the lower or working class, minorities tend not to vote as heavily as the majority. There are a number of reasons for not voting, not necessarily including apathy. Lewis Lipsitz suggests that nonvoters, especially those in the lower or working class, are generally vitally concerned with issues, but do not believe that voting is an effective means of causing change in the United States (Lipsitz, 1974: 273–87).

Of course, not all ethnic and racial minorities are lower- or working-class people. Yet, especially among racial groups, there is an increasing tendency not to vote. As we saw in Chapter 4, the political impact of race has class overtones, no matter to what socioeconomic class a person belongs. Additionally, social scientists have found that within religious groups there tends to be a much greater diversity of voting behavior, if they merely control for ethnicity. For example, we usually view Catholics as a monolithic group; yet table 12 demonstrates that there are significant differences among Catholics depending on their ethnicity. Abraham Miller's study, conducted in New Haven, Connecticut, still suggests that party loyalty among Catholics, Protestants, and Jews breaks down much as we would guess. However, other studies (Ladd and Hadley, 1978: Greeley, 1974), using larger, nationwide

Table 12.   *Ranking of Ethnic Groups by Percent Identifying with the Democratic Party*

Group	Percent Democratic	N
American Jews	92	48
Irish Catholics	81	63
Negroes	76	238
Polish Catholics	75	110
European Jews	71	147
Austrian Catholics	70	27
American Catholics	69	693
Eastern European Catholics	68	73
Italian Catholics	64	193
British Catholics	62	13
Eastern European Protestants	61	31
Western European Catholics	55	29
German Catholics	51	39
Austrian Protestants	44	9
German Protestants	44	137
Scandinavian Protestants	42	112
American Protestants	39	2,286
Western European Protestants	38	40
Irish Protestants	36	14
British Protestants	31	65

SOURCE: Abraham Miller, "Ethnicity and party identification: construction of a dialogue."
Western Political Quarterly (Vol. 27, September 1974, 474–490). Reprinted by permission.

samples, suggest, for example, that both Polish Protestants and Polish Catholics are heavily Democratic, and that German Catholics, Protestants, and Jews tend to be less than 50 percent Democratic. Ethnicity is a crucial concept in understanding voting behavior in the United States.

Historical overview.   It is important not to lose sight of the gross impact of race and ethnicity: if we lump all ethnic and racial groups together, they tend to vote for the Democratic rather than the Republican party. But they have not always voted in this way. In fact, not until the New Deal of Franklin D. Roosevelt did black Americans begin voting heavily for Democrats. Before 1930, most blacks (when they were allowed to vote) cast their ballots for Republicans, the party of Abraham Lincoln. Ethnic Americans, primarily those of Catholic and Jewish backgrounds, did not begin to vote heavily Democratic until 1928.

As early as 1900 blacks had felt deserted by both the Republican and the Democratic parties, who all but ignored them when political payoffs were handed out to other groups (Du Bois, 1963). Although Woodrow Wilson invited Booker T. Washington to the White House, he did more than almost any other president to segregate the federal government. Offices were segregated or Negro employees' desks were curtained off; commissions to the military were denied to blacks; separate eating places were arranged in cafeterias. Wilson refused to speak out against the numerous lynchings of his time. He felt that the mass segregation of the federal government was rendering blacks "more safe in their possession of office and less likely to be discriminated against." Additionally, his cabinet officers and appointees fired massive numbers of well qualified black civil servants. The Georgia collector of internal revenue declared, "There are no government positions for Negroes in the south. A Negro's place is in the cornfield" (Kluger, 1975: 90–91).

Blacks generally recognized that the Democrats were not going to help them, no matter which way they voted. In the South blacks had been all but disenfranchised by the 1920s. Until 1900 blacks had turned out to vote in massive numbers; then Jim Crow laws made them ineligible. And when the laws did not work, white violence or threats did. Outside the South blacks could not turn to the Republicans, for in other regions of the country the Ku Klux Klan allied itself with the Republican party (Ladd and Hadley, 1978: 48–49). Although some scholars argue that the black affiliation with the Democratic party began in 1924, because of the anti-Klan stand of its candidate, James W. Davis, the black voting shift did not really occur until the 1928 nomination of Catholic Al Smith. Black identification with the Democratic party was solidified by Smith's nomination and the subsequent election of Franklin D. Roosevelt in 1932.

Other ethnic groups have also vacillated between the two political parties during the past 100 years. Jews have been politically active since the early years of the republic. Although the last state law limiting the Jewish vote (in New Hampshire) was not repealed until 1876, Jews played an active electoral role in most states. They flocked early to the Jeffersonian party (soon to be called Democratic), after the Federalists attempted to pass a constitutional amendment "to prohibit naturalized citizens from serving in Congress." After apparently anti-Semitic foreign agreements were made between Whig President Millard Fillmore and Switzerland, and after the next president, Democrat James Buchanan, refused to end the treaty, Jews drifted into Abraham Lincoln's new Republican party.[4]

Jews had a close relationship with the Republicans during this period. American Jews' concern for the plight of Jews in Russia is not a new phenomenon. As early as 1879 President Rutherford B. Hayes, at American Jewish urging, warned the Rumanians not to persecute Jews. Both President Chester A. Arthur and President Benjamin Harrison urged the Russian government to end the pogroms. Teddy Roosevelt was the darling of the Jewish community in the United States; his presidency marked the zenith of Jewish support for the Republican party. President William Howard Taft alienated

---

4. Although Jews remained loyal to the Republican party for the next 50 years, the relationship was rocky. For example, General Ulysses S. Grant alienated large numbers of Jews during the Civil War when he ordered all Jews in Tennessee to leave the area within 24 hours. President Lincoln rescinded the order when he heard about it.

the Jewish vote by reneging on his promise to end a discriminatory trade treaty with Russia, leaving Woodrow Wilson to pick up the lion's share of Jewish support. Yet both Warren G. Harding and Calvin Coolidge carried the Jewish vote; not until the candidacy of Al Smith in 1928 did Jews shift to the Democratic camp. They have been there in overwhelming numbers ever since (Levy and Kramer, 1972: 95–121).

Do not assume from the discussion that Jews always vote in a bloc. In fact, a number of Jewish candidates have failed to win overwhelming Jewish support, such as Arthur Goldberg in his 1970 race against Nelson Rockefeller for the governorship of New York. In states like Ohio, Jews tend to be far less loyal to the Democrats. A number of forces within the state account for this, but a primary factor, especially in the Cincinnati area, is the predominantly German background of many Jews.

The impact of minorities on political campaigns.   Although politicians today eat blintzes, tacos, and chitterlings to win support, it would be inaccurate to suggest that ethnic and racial considerations dominate American politics. The impact of ethnic groups is still concentrated in the Northeast and Midwest. For example, in Boston any politician running for office still needs the support of the large Irish ethnic community; in Cleveland almost 80 percent of the populace identifies itself with ethnic groups. In Orleans Parish (the city of New Orleans) politicians must contend not only with the large black population, but also with sizable Irish and Italian communities. However, in most of the United States ethnic groups have been assimilated and racial groups generally isolated, in the ghettos or on the reservations.

The ethnic vote can be helpful to candidates who elicit massive support from individual groups. Senator Edmund Muskie of Maine received strong support from Polish communities when he ran with Hubert Humphrey as the vice-presidential nominee in 1968, as well as in the 1972 primaries. But ethnicity and religion can also backfire. Not only will large numbers of white Protestants suspect someone who appeals to or comes from an ethnic, non-Protestant religious, or racial community, but the candidate also risks alienating other ethnic communities. For instance, in 1960 John F. Kennedy won tremendous support from the Irish Catholic community, but he alienated large numbers of black voters. Certainly, he won a majority among black voters, but not as many of their votes as either Lyndon Johnson or Humphrey. In fact, Kennedy received less than 60 percent of the black vote in Georgia, Kentucky, and Massachusetts; Johnson and Humphrey received over 95 percent of the black vote in those states in 1964 and 1968 (Levy and Kramer, 1972).

This emphasizes the contemporary impact of the minority and ethnic vote as the greater or lesser support of these groups for Democratic candidates. Republicans have fielded so many presidential candidates unattractive to minorities (this is now less so, although it is still true in many senatorial races) that most minorities feel they have no choice when they vote. For this reason,

Table 13. *Racial and Religious Vote, by Percent, 1964–1976*

	1964		1968			1972		1976	
	Johnson	Goldwater	Humphrey	Nixon	Wallace	McGovern	Nixon	Carter	Ford
Black	97	3	94	5	1	87	13	83	17
White	59	41	38	47	15	30	70	48	52
Protestant	55	45	35	49	16	31	69	46	54
Catholic	75	25	59	33	8	40	60	55	45
Jewish	90	10	83	15	2	63	37	68	32

SOURCE: Adapted from Gerald Pomper (ed.), The Election of 1976 (New York: David McKay, 1976), p. 61; Mark R. Levy and Michael S. Kramer, The Ethnic Factor: How America's Minorities Decide Elections (New York: Simon & Schuster, 1972), statistical index; and The American Institute of Public Opinion (the Gallup Poll).

the minority vote is often taken for granted. This leads to low voter turnout and reduces the impact of minority party loyalty. However, loyalty is still important in coalition building. For example, in 1972, 87 percent of black voters voted for George McGovern.

> *But, in 1976, black citizens generally did no more than maintain their previous record of high support for Democratic candidates, and their contribution to the Carter victory was neither more substantial nor more distinctive than had been their contribution to the candidacies of other recent Democratic contenders for the presidency. Furthermore, the short-term data indicate that* if black citizens made a disproportionate contribution to the votes for any recent candidate, that candidate was George McGovern, not Jimmy Carter. *(Miller and Levitin, 1976: 206)*

Democratic candidates must build a voting coalition including the ethnic and racial groups. As table 13 shows, Jimmy Carter's candidacy made religious groups—Jews and Catholics—highly suspicious; they gave him substantially fewer votes than they had given Johnson and Humphrey.[5] Blacks and other racial minorities still contributed to the Democratic victory, but they did not provide the margin of Carter's victory.

Most Republicans have ignored ethnic and racial groups, with the exception of Richard Nixon's ethnic strategy in 1972 (Phillips, 1970). However, there are signs that many Republicans are trying to include ethnics in much broader based coalitions, as did Representative Jack Kemp in his impressive 1978 showing in very ethnic Buffalo, New York. The 1978 congressional elections suggest that moderate Republicans, who also tend to be more sympathetic to ethnic and racial groups, may regain significant influence in their party, for the first time since 1964. If moderates like Senators Charles Percy, Mark Hatfield, Nancy Kassebaum, and Howard Baker are successful, there is a good chance that the Republicans will again be wooing ethnic and racial groups.

The causes of voting trends are complex, and most of those we have mentioned are individual or personal. Another cause, depicted in figure 14, is the group dimension: that is, how much better off a group would be with one presidential candidate than another. Obviously, the classic division—blacks and the poor versus business interests—remains. But the data in figure 14, derived from the 1976 presidential election, show that a large number of people perceived *neither* candidate as better for their group. Women, the old, and the young appear especially alienated from the political choices presented by the national political parties. This could have important consequences for voting behavior, and subsequently for minority rights, throughout the 1980s.

---

5. Carter won more Jewish and Catholic votes than had George McGovern, but the nature of McGovern's candidacy in 1972 does not make that fact meaningful as part of a long-term trend.

FIGURE 14. Group Members' Perceptions of Which 1976 Candidate for President Would Be Better for Group

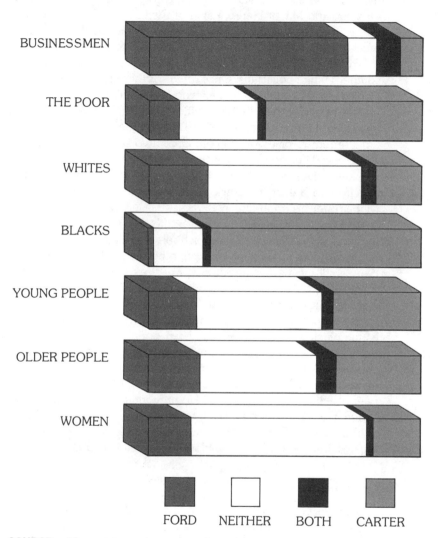

BUSINESSMEN

THE POOR

WHITES

BLACKS

YOUNG PEOPLE

OLDER PEOPLE

WOMEN

FORD   NEITHER   BOTH   CARTER

SOURCE: "Group interests have major electoral impact." ISR Newsletter (Institute for Social Research, The University of Michigan) (Winter 1979): 3.

The changing face of southern politics.   The most important change wrought by means of groups using the vote has come in the states of the old Confederacy. The reenfranchisement of blacks in the South from 1954 to 1972 has created a substantial new political force, if for no other reason than the size of the black population. Influential blacks have been elected to represent regions in which they would not even have been able to vote 20 years ago. The most noteworthy among this group are former United Nations

Ambassador Andrew Young, former Congresswoman Barbara Jordan, former State Senator Julian Bond of Georgia, Mayor Ernest Morial of New Orleans, and Mayor Henry Marsh of Richmond, Virginia. As we said earlier, these offices are sometimes not as great a gain as they seem; for example, most black mayors have few or no resources to develop their decaying cities.

The mark of the southern black vote is most distinct on the character of southern white politicians. Once rabid southern racists such as Senator Strom Thurmond of South Carolina, who were openly hostile to desegregation, have changed, at least in their political strategies. Today they openly court the black vote in their states. In 1978 Thurmond even supported a constitutional amendment to give Washington, D.C., two senators and a representative in Congress. Thurmond, and everyone else on Capitol Hill, knew that these representatives would be black and liberal; he supported the amendment in an effort to attract the black vote in South Carolina. And he was a clear winner over his opponent in 1978.

The South, especially the rural South, has changed politically. It has seen the most effective integration of schools as well as a substantial improvement in the standard of living of whites and blacks (Wainscott, 1978). The Ku Klux Klan is still active in the South (as well as the North), but it tends now to organize more in urban and suburban areas. Metairie, Louisiana; Chamblee, Georgia; and Henrico County, Virginia, are the main areas of concentration for the Klan. But such groups apparently do not have as much political weight as the black voters. No candidate can openly express racism in the contemporary South and expect to win. Even in conservative Virginia, when Senate candidate John Warner mentioned in a 1978 television interview that he had been responsible for slowing down integration efforts while secretary of the navy, he did everything he could to prevent the broadcasting of the interview. When it was broadcast anyway, he argued that his statement had been a slip of the tongue. This is a long way from the massive resistance campaign (against integration) of Harry Flood Byrd in the 1950s.

Long-Term Voting Trends

The most marked political change of the 1980s will be the complete shift in voting divisions from Catholic versus Protestant to black versus white (Miller and Levitin, 1976; Ladd and Hadley, 1978). For almost 100 years voting patterns have been decided by issues that were considered either Protestant or Catholic, including prohibition, isolationism, and welfare. In the 1960s this classification began to shift; issues are now characterized as black or white. The Catholic vote has tended to melt (although there are still significant ethnic pockets), and the vast majority of issues are couched in terms of race, from welfare expenditures to military costs. These shifts are reflected in table 14.

The importance of the shift is that it will determine the policy issues of the next decade. We will hear more about racial issues than ethnic ones, not because ethnics have disappeared or even assimilated, but rather because

Table 14.   *Summary of the Partisanship and Opinion Profiles of Groups in the 1950s and 1970s*

Group	1950s		1970s	
	Issues	*Party*	*Issues*	*Party*
Middle and upper status native white southerners	Quite a bit to the right	Strongly Democratic	Move further right	Move away from Democratic party, more Independent
Lower status native white southerners	Moderately right	Strongly Democratic	Move further right	Move away from Democratic party, more Independent
High status northern WASP	Moderately right	Strongly Republican	Move a bit left and splits	Less Republican, more Independent
Middle and lower status northern WASP	Center	Slightly Republican	Move a bit right	More Independent and more Democratic
Blacks	Strongly left	Strongly Democratic	Move even further left	Even more Democratic
Catholics	Moderately left	Strongly Democratic	Move to center	A bit more Independent
Jews	Strongly left	Strongly Democratic	Move further left	A bit more Independent
Border South	Moderately right	Strongly Democratic	Move a bit further right and split a bit	More Independent

SOURCE: Norman H. Nie, Sidney Verba and John R. Petrocik, The Changing American Voter (Cambridge, Mass.: Harvard University Press, 1976), 268. Reprinted by permission.

they fall on the "white" side of the cleavage. "Virtually all Republican votes come from whites," writes Robert Axelrod. "Even in 1960 when a quarter of the black vote went to Nixon, 97 percent of Nixon's votes came from whites, while in 1968, 99 percent of Nixon's votes came from whites" (Axelrod, 1972: 11). This is not to suggest that all issues will be black or white (no pun intended), but rather that issues will be articulated along these lines. Many whites will still lean toward the "black" side on issues such as welfare, education, and taxation. And, of course, a few blacks will find themselves on the "white" side of policy questions.

The trend has been accelerated by the American ideological swing toward conservatism. Conservatives have captured a number of institutions, notably the "Nixon" Supreme Court. More importantly, party identification is dissolving rapidly. Fewer Americans align themselves with one of the major political parties now than at any time in the last 100 years. As Arthur Gunlicks has commented, the United States really has a "no-party system." The implications for minorities are profound. They will have to seek new coalitions to support any policy they see as crucial to their group. Ethnics will generally be less willing than before to join with racial groups in supporting such legislation.

The decline of parties and the rise of single-issue interest groups will make the federal government less likely to help minorities that have not yet succeeded in American society, at least through the 1980s. The taxpayers' revolt of the late 1970s had many causes, but chief among them was the resentment the majority of Americans felt toward programs to aid minorities. The majority was reacting not to government spending for defense or agricultural price supports, but to spending for programs designed to help minorities. Thus, while blacks, Chicanos, and other minorities might benefit by electing their own political representatives, it is highly unlikely—at least through the 1980s—that such representatives will be successful in promoting policies and programs to help their communities.

THE USE OF SOCIAL SCIENCE TO JUSTIFY THE MAJORITY POSITION

By and large, academics are a conservative force, justifying the present society by lending credibility to the institutions of government. They suggest that if the system is open enough to allow critics, then the political institutions must be fair. In a way some academics directly contribute to the control of the majority, by developing theories or carrying out studies that tend to legitimize the public policies of the majority.[6] In this section we shall explore the work of these scholars, and its implications.

The Politics of Sociology and Psychology

It may seem strange to suggest that sociologists and psychologists are involved in important political activities. Yet we know that the research many of them do is crucial to the workings of the American social and political system. For instance, children who are tested early in their elementary school careers find their test scores to be either a crown or an albatross. If they happen to do well, they are placed in advanced classes with better teachers, experimental materials, and the intangible factor that everyone (teachers, peers, parents, and administrators) thinks they will do well. If the student does poorly on the tests the reverse is true, but teachers will still pass him on exams

---

6.   In this discussion we purposely avoid the issue of objectivity in the social sciences. Additionally, we do not intend to suggest that all social scientific studies that justify the majority position are by definition wrong. What we are interested in is the impact of such studies—and their impact is usually detrimental to minorities. On the question of objectivity in the social sciences, see Michael Weinstein, Philosophy, Theory and Method in Contemporary Political Thought (Glenview, Ill.: Scott, Foresman, 1971); A. R. Louch, Explanation and Human Action (Berkeley: University of California Press, 1969); John O'Neill, Sociology as a Skin Trade (New York: Harper & Row, 1972); Stanislav Andreski, Social Science as Sorcery (New York: St. Martin's Press, 1972); Richard Bernstein, Restructuring of Social and Political Theory (New York: Harcourt Brace Jovanovich, 1976).

or promote him to the next class no matter whether he has mastered the material or not, because they believe he cannot do any better. Every year such students find their disabilities multiplied, which somewhat explains the massive numbers of high school graduates who are illiterate.

It has been suggested that the entire field of psychology, as well as psychiatry, creates indicators that force political decisions. The most provocative case for this argument is made by Thomas Szasz, a professor of psychiatry at Syracuse University Medical School:

> *For some time now I have maintained that commitment —that is, the detention of persons in mental institutions against their will —is a form of imprisonment; that such deprivation of liberty is contrary to the moral principles embodied in the Declaration of Independence and the Constitution. . . .*
>
> *Existing social institutions and practices, especially if honored by prolonged usage, are generally experienced and accepted as good and valuable. For thousands of years slavery was considered a "natural" social arrangement for the securing of human labor; it was sanctioned by public opinion, religious dogma, church, and state. . . . Since its origin, approximately three centuries ago, commitment of the insane has enjoyed equally widespread support; physicians, lawyers, and the laity have asserted, as if with a single voice, the therapeutic desirability and social necessity of institutional psychiatry. (Szasz, 1970: 113)*

Szasz argues that insanity is a social myth, an excuse for removing from our presence people with whom we do not feel socially comfortable. In the United States the vast majority of institutionalized people, feels Szasz, should not be in institutions.

How does all of this affect minorities? Sociology and psychology, as well as the rest of the social sciences, are processes of classification. People are classified and implicitly or explicitly ranked according to their status, problems, or culture. For example, black Americans are overrepresented not only in American prisons, but also in mental institutions. Many others besides Szasz have suggested that this is caused by our methods of classifying people and by environmental pressures (such as being lower-class), rather than by any pathological psychiatric tendency within the group. The roots of present problems are often found in earlier classifications, and in the tendency for psychological tests and the perception of teachers, both black and white, to classify blacks as slower learners.

Sociologists' methods ultimately create or reinforce stereotypes of minorities. For example, the Moynihan Report (Moynihan, 1965) has probably had a profound impact on your image of blacks. It concludes that the black family is weak and generally dominated by the mother, and that the roots of this weakness lie in the experience of slavery. This distortion has been both continued and magnified by black unemployment, which has shaped children, particularly boys, who are so damaged that they cannot take advantage of educational or employment opportunities. Moynihan concludes that better ghetto schools and antidiscriminatory employment practices will have no effect until the black family structure is changed.

For the most part the notion of the weak black family is a myth. Admittedly there are great numbers of broken homes among blacks, but there is also more emphasis on relationships outside the nuclear family, such as with aunts and uncles. Additionally, recent historical studies have demonstrated that the slave system did not destroy the black family, and that family structure may be even more important to the black community than to the white (Guttman, 1976). The discussion always returns to economic issues. The poor have more broken homes and their children generally do not do as well in school as those of other people. This has nothing to do with the family — but by placing the blame on the family structure, Moynihan shifted responsibility from the political arena back to the black family. As the urban policy advisor for the Nixon administration and a senator from New York, he has had a profound impact on our ideas about black Americans.

Arthur Jensen and the New Conservatives.   A political movement that began in the 1970s to reestablish the legitimacy of majority political policies is the New Conservatives (Coser and Howe, 1976). Comprised mostly of academics from various fields, and spearheaded by the journal *The Public Interest,* the New Conservatives have become one of the most provocative and important forces defending the status quo in contemporary American society. Many important social scientists are included in this group, including Daniel Patrick Moynihan, James Coleman, James Q. Wilson, Nathan Glazer, and Irving Kristol. Perhaps the most important is Arthur Jensen. In a highly controversial article on IQ and its racial implications, Jenson (1969) suggested that 80 percent of a person's IQ is inherited. Subsequently he claimed that the differences between black IQ and white IQ indicate that blacks are biologically inferior to whites.

We shall discuss the legitimacy of Jensen's "findings" below; what is most important to the present discussion is their political impact. By again raising the specter of racial inferiority to the level of legitimate intellectual discourse, Jensen and others have influenced policy makers. Armed with such "information," a federal appointee learns the tremendous expense of a headstart program for preschoolers and concludes that the program is a waste of money. If IQ is biologically inherited, why squander taxpayers' money to support such programs? During the Nixon and Ford administrations many such programs were dismantled or simply allowed to die of lack of attention or resources. Belt-tightening economic policies under Carter have meant that the programs are not faring much better.

The IQ controversy.   The use of IQ to justify discrimination against groups, or lack of action on behalf of groups, did not begin with Jensen. Since its invention, the IQ test has been used to justify political policies directly affecting minorities. Although it would be unfair to suggest that Alfred Binet, the originator of the test, had any such applications in mind, the tests were first used in the United States expressly for that purpose. Lewis Terman, Robert Yerkes, and Henry Goddard were among the first American psychologists to use the test; they were also leaders of the American eugenics movement. They believed that the American breeding stock was being diluted by genetically inferior people from eastern Europe. In Terman's words, "If we would preserve our state for a class of people worthy to possess it, we must prevent, as far as possible, the propagation of mental degenerates . . . the increasing spawn of degeneracy" (Terman, 1917).

Who were the degenerates? Henry Goddard, using his test to examine immigrants on Ellis Island, discovered that 80 percent of all eastern Europeans were feebleminded, including 89 percent of all Poles, 83 percent of all Jews, 79 percent of all Italians, 87 percent of all Russians, and so on. Eugenicists and geneticists used Goddard's data to argue in favor of the Johnson Immigration Act of 1924, which until 1965 sharply limited the number of eastern European immigrants to the United States. Because of this law the government turned down the applications of hundreds of thousands of Jews between 1939 and 1945 for sanctuary in the United States; most of them died in Nazi concentration camps.

What is this powerful instrument, IQ, which determines the implicit worth of individual life and—in the extreme—a person's very right to live? How can psychologists use this measure to argue that blacks are genetically inferior to whites, or that truck drivers' and factory workers' children are genetically inferior to business executives' and physicians' offspring, or that the Irish are genetically inferior to the English? Such claims were not made 100 years ago; all of the conclusions listed above were still being published in major psychology journals within the past 20 years.

Nature versus nurture.   The political issues of why these studies have had such a profound impact center around the *nature vs. nurture* controversy among social scientists (notably psychologists, anthropologists, and geneticists). The point of this controversy is whether individuals are affected more by their genetic background or their environment. Although no one would argue that either environment or genetics contributes 100 percent of a person's makeup, it has become commonplace to suggest that 80 percent, 90 percent, or 92 percent of individual makeup depends on genetics or environment.

Even though IQ stands for Intelligence Quotient, we do not know whether IQ actually measures intelligence. What *is* intelligence? Most of us have at some time taken a standardized test, and we know that a number of factors influence our scores, such as how tired or nervous we are, whether we are comfortable in the test surroundings, and whether the test is geared to middle-class standards. An additional problem is the ambiguity inherent in all objective-type exams. Look at the following example:

Which of the following sports is most different from the other three?

1.   Baseball
2.   Field hockey
3.   Football
4.   Pool

The "correct" answer is pool, because it is the only indoor sport. But what about the others? Baseball is different because it has no goal, such as an end zone, goal, or pocket. Field hockey is the only one of the sports played predominantly by women. Football is the only one played with a ball that is not round. In fact, most objective questions are ambiguous, and researchers have demonstrated that the brighter someone is, the more likely he or she is to choose a wrong answer!

The major drawback of any intelligence test is its cultural bias. Cultural bias is amplified if researchers average people together according to racial or ethnic "types," a process that assumes that the researchers expect to find differences—and academics such as Jensen do. However, an examination of black–white differences reveals an interesting fact. Tangentially, researchers studying stroke victims found that geography has a much greater impact on IQ than do most other indicators, even genetics. Among subjects from Boston and Philadelphia, whites in Boston had an average IQ of 104, blacks an average of 100. This finding appears to bear out genetic determination of IQ, although four points is a statistically meaningless margin. But among subjects in Philadelphia, the average white score was 95 and the average black score 91 (Nichols and Anderson, 1973). Does this mean that Boston blacks are genetically better than any Philadelphians? Of course not. We do not know that a higher IQ means "better" in any sense of the word, except if society defines it to be better.[7]

We do know that IQ is a strong predictor of scholastic achievement, if we confine the meaning of scholastic achievement to current American cultural standards. Intelligence tests tell us how well one conforms to being a white middle-class American; if this is what we mean by intelligence, then of course IQ measures intelligence.

The importance of the nature versus nurture controversy is its political impact. *Whether or not Jensen and the New Conservatives are right* (and we do not suggest that they are), the most important effect of their work is in the area of public policy. Their research directly affects individuals in minority

---

7.   On the impact of environment on IQ, see S. Scarr-Salapatek and R. A. Weinberg, "When black children grow up in white homes," Psychology Today, 9: 80; R. Heber, H. Garber, S. Harriston, C. Hoffman, and C. Falendar, "Rehabilitation of families at risk for mental retardation," Progress Report of the Rehabilitation Research and Training Center in Mental Retardation, University of Wisconsin–Madison, December 1972; Richard C. Lewontin, "Biological determinism as a social weapon," in Biology as a Social Weapon (Minneapolis: Burgess Publishing, 1977).

groups, especially racial groups, in the United States. If one accepts the validity of their work, one apparently has no choice but to accept the native inferiority of blacks and other lower-class people. The ultimate effect of that acceptance would be to legitimize the social and political status of minorities, justifying the superior position of the present majority in society.

Sociobiology and equality.   Some people tend to accept the work of the New Conservatives because it appears to parallel, and thereby gain legitimacy from, the "new" discipline of sociobiology. Sociobiology studies the physical origins of social behavior. The most prominent sociobiologist is Edmund Wilson, whose book *Sociobiology* has warranted a cover story in *Time Magazine* and lengthy articles in *Newsweek*. Wilson argues that behavior such as indoctrinability, spite, male dominance, reciprocal altruism, blind faith, genocide, warfare, xenophobia, entrepreneurship, religion, language, and homosexuality is biologically caused. For instance, altruism is biologically based, according to Wilson; an individual will risk his life to dive into freezing water to save another (relative, friend, or stranger) because he is trying to insure the optimal survival of the gene pool. That is, in preserving life (or even in taking it, for war is also argued to be biologically specific), one is trying to insure the survival of the maximum number of genes. Wilson emphasizes that he is not suggesting any eugenic or racial preference in nature. Rather, the greatest scope of genetic diversity will lead to the "emergence of really outstanding individuals."

Clearly—Wilson's disclaimer notwithstanding—such notions are easily transformed into rationalizations for racial or class differences. We believe that such conclusions cannot legitimately be made from current theories of sociobiology. First, even if we knew the role of genes in influencing IQ, we would not know anything about the plasticity of the trait, that is, how and why it varies (Lewontin, 1977). Second, we often assume that we know who are the biologically successful individuals. But in the Middle Ages epileptic seizures were considered a sign of royalty, and certainly—given the cultural values of the time—an indicator of success. Surely, few of us would agree with that definition today. Yet sociobiologists often succumb to such cultural biases, and this problem is compounded if we make any conclusions about social classes and ethnic or racial groups.

The more sensitive sociobiologists appreciate the apparent trap: if one believes that people are biologically determined, does that belief preclude political or social equality? Many sociobiologists, unlike the New Conservatives, conclude that this is not necessarily the case. Biology might provide greater urges in certain behavioral directions, but nothing dictates that these types of behaviors are determined and incapable of change by human volition. Richard Dawkins writes in *The Selfish Gene*:

> I am not advocating a morality based on evolution. I am saying how
> things have evolved. I am not saying how we humans morally ought to
> behave. I stress this, because I know I am in danger of being misun-

*derstood by those people, all too numerous, who cannot distinguish a
statement of belief in what is the case from an advocacy of what ought
to be the case. My own feeling is that a human society based simply on
the gene's law of universal ruthless selfishness would be a very nasty
society in which to live. . . . Be warned that if you wish, as I do, to build
a society in which individuals cooperate generously and unselfishly
towards common good, you can expect little help from biological nature.*
(Dawkins, 1976: 3)

Discrimination: Normative versus Empirical Criteria

By now it must be clear that most of the issues we have discussed
concerning minority and ethnic communities hinge on one crucial concept:
equality. Equality has been a vital issue in political philosophy since the time
of the pre-Socratics and the Old Testament. Thomas Jefferson wove it irrevocably into the American polity by stating that it was a self-evident truth
that "all men are created equal." (Actually, the emphasis on equality in
America goes even further back, to Roger Williams and the Puritan epoch.)
What do we mean by equality?

Interpretations of equality: the majority position.   Americans often assume that we can measure equality, that it is a precise notion. Obviously, laws
that make individuals unequal in rights are clear violations of any notion of
equality. Discriminatory laws have created tensions since the very beginning
of our nation. Mr. Jefferson condemned the king of England for committing,
among the many other dreadful acts mentioned in the Declaration of Independence, a "cruel war against human nature itself, violating its most sacred
rights of life and liberty in the persons of a distant people who never offended
him, captivating and carrying them into slavery in another hemisphere, or to
incur miserable death in their transportation thither." Unfortunately, this
section was deleted from the final draft of the Declaration in a political
compromise. When the Constitution was being written in 1787, the greatest
compromise was again over the slavery issue—not, as some would have it,
over plans for large and small states (Lowi, 1977: 74–78). Thus, the first 170
years of the nation's history were devoted to dealing with de jure questions of
political equality. Only during the past generation have Americans had to deal
with de facto questions of equality, that is, equality sanctioned by society and
by implicit political provisions, not by law.

Equality has both normative and empirical dimensions. By normative we
mean simply that equality is a value, and not necessarily an absolute value,[8]
for there are many types of equality that even the most egalitarian person

---

8.   There is a tradition of absolute equality in the United States. The "locofocists" during the
heyday of Jacksonian democracy demanded absolute equality in everything: dress, economic
background, and political power. See A. J. Beitzinger, *A History of American Political Thought*
(New York: Dodd, Mead, 1972), pp. 332–33.

might not sanction. For example, short people have legitimate complaints against tall people, but would limiting the height of human beings help make a society more equal?

The most sensible definition of equality emphasizes the ability of human beings to reach their full potential without hindrance from external social, economic, or political norms. It is not reasonable to try to satisfy our desire for empirical evidence of equality, because no one upon sincere reflection would want a perfectly equal society (see Pennock and Chapman, 1967). Indeed, it is the *variety* of human existence that appears to make equality sensible.

If we try to use empirical measures we run into significant problems, for which measures of equality do we select? For example, many people argue that the average woman is not physically as large as (and therefore not equal to) the average man. But what do we mean by average? One of the authors of this book is 5'7" tall and weighs 140 pounds soaking wet. He has a woman friend who is 5'11" tall and weighs 170 pounds. Would it make sense to hire him over her to load trucks because the average woman is not able to lift as much as the average man? No. Although there are useful indicators of what makes individuals more or less equal, we often assume that these make absolute sense. Subsequently we pass laws, or develop cultural norms, that define individuals as more or less equal.

Equality of opportunity and beyond.   The majority has tried to address the changing notions of equality forced upon it by minorities during the 1960s by practicing equality of opportunity. Equality of opportunity implies that once society has removed all legal restraints on individuals, it is up to the individuals to catch up with the rest of society. Any inequalities still existing after this are due to natural differences over which the state has no control. For example, it is argued that time will ultimately remove the major differences between whites and blacks in American society. This argument has little appeal to minorities, who are still under the onus of de facto norms, beliefs, and practices that discriminate against them. Returning to the foot race we described early in this chapter, blacks would argue that they have been shackled for 200 years, that the race for society's goods has started, but that they were not allowed to run until whites were well out in front. If such a race is unfair, then so is equality of opportunity as a policy (Schaar, 1968).

Blacks, women, and other minorities generally demand *equality of result*. They feel that to catch up to the majority of society, they must have *preference* for jobs, positions, or power if their qualifications are equal to those of majority applicants. Such treatment is justified, they feel, because it is the only way in which folkways will be broken. The busing issue is a good example because it is one approach to eliminating inequality of educational backgrounds. Although many minority and majority members have opposed busing, it is apparently the easiest way to accomplish racial desegregation of public schools. The problem has been that white parents who must send their children to integrated schools have decided instead to move to the suburbs or to establish private academies. Even parochial schools, especially Catholic schools, have become havens for parents who do not wish their children to attend school with substantial numbers of black children. So, although busing seems to be the easiest road to integration, it has in effect created many more segregated school systems. Busing per se is not necessarily a bad policy; rather, the prejudices of whites in American society run far deeper than federal and state policy advisers have assumed.

Affirmative Action: Just Recompense or Reverse Discrimination?

The most serious confrontation between majority and minority positions—equality of opportunity versus equality of result—has occurred over the issue of affirmative action. There are major difficulties with affirmative action, including arguments over its implementation and its results. We shall concentrate on its political impact, especially given recent Supreme Court decisions. In the legal arena the issues surrounding the meaning of equality become most clear. And, as we pointed out at the beginning of this chapter, those who define that meaning, or who control its interpretation, are exercising political power.

Since the passage of the 1964 Civil Rights Act and President Lyndon Johnson's Executive Order 11246 (Gilman, 1980), great controversy has surrounded the idea of affirmative action and its implementation. The major affirmative action lawsuits have concerned hiring and admission to colleges and universities. This concentration is logical; these are generally the "gatekeepers" to status in American society. Contrary to popular belief, affirmative action does not require employers or universities to hire or admit minorities or women no matter what. Rather, it suggests that if a minority individual or a woman applies for a position in an area where such persons have previously been discriminated against, and that individual is equal to other candidates, he or she ought to be given preference for the position.

The rather simple idea of affirmative action became caught up in the mechanisms of the federal bureaucracy. The Equal Employment Opportunity Commission (EEOC) demanded that employers develop affirmative action goals or targets, but these goals did not have the effect of creating quotas, except in a small number of cases. Interestingly, quotas were effectively created in areas where women and blacks had been least discriminated against, in higher education and technical employment. Certainly, there had been discrimination in these areas, but for the most part the people involved were well able to take care of themselves without the weight of government behind them. As Phillip Slater succinctly states, "If you empty a sack of money into a crowd, the greediest will get the most and no matter how many nipples a government puts out for the poor, it always seems to find a middle-class mouth fastened around every one" (Slater, 1976: 112). Affirmative action has not helped those who sought jobs in the lower- or middle-class economy: truck driver, store managers, and the like. At these levels discrimination still forces many women and minorities out of competition.

Another question about affirmative action is whether the two categories of women and minority groups ought to be treated alike. Some people argue that including women in affirmative action programs has hurt blacks and other minorities. First, because blacks have on the whole become less vocal than women, they tend to lose out in competition with them. Second, it is much easier to find qualified women for a position than to find qualified blacks. Third, treating women and blacks alike assumes that they have equivalent experiences of discrimination. It seems wrong to suggest that the white daughter of a corporate lawyer ought to be treated the same as the son of a black tenant farmer, yet even though women have not been victims of "generations of economic deprivation," they are considered for purposes of affirmative action to be in the same position as blacks, Chicanos, or Indians (Goldman, 1975: 289–306).

We do not argue that women lack a legitimate claim to just and equal treatment. Rather, we mean to show the tremendous difficulty of attempting to define equality and to develop public policy remedies for inequalities. Obviously there must be some type of program for all groups if de facto inequality and institutional discrimination are to be ameliorated. Without such a program, tension will inevitably lead to a great deal of political and social instability in American society.

Supreme Court decisions.   The strength of those who argue that affirmative action is reverse discrimination, as well as the gist of recent Supreme Court cases, suggests that the majority in American society has won a major victory. Most Americans feel that affirmative action is unfair and has resulted in many qualified whites not obtaining positions or appointments they deserved. The *Bakke* case gave an air of legitimacy to that complaint.

The facts of the earlier *DeFunis* case are that Marco DeFunis, a white, in 1970 was denied admission to the University of Washington Law School; DeFunis argued that his application had been denied because of a minority admissions program.[9] The Court avoided confronting the issue because

---

9.   The question would not even have arisen 30 or 40 years ago, when there were more than enough places available for any candidate with minimal qualifications. Today high LSAT scores and high grade points are prerequisites for law school; other exams are required by other professional schools. Even in the 10-year period from 1966 to 1976, the median LSAT score required for law school admission rose 90 points, and undergraduate grade averages rose from 2.8 to 3.4. The problem with professional exams is that they are used to distinguish between persons very similar in ability, a task of which they are not capable. In many European countries students who meet minimal qualifications for professional schools have their names drawn at random to fill the classes. In the United States, however, we believe there is a great difference between a student with a 3.0 undergraduate average and a 580 LSAT score and a student with a 3.2 grade point and a 600 LSAT score. Perhaps that is why one of our colleagues has suggested that Princeton, New Jersey, is the real center of political power in the United States: it is the home of both the Gallup Poll and the Educational Testing Service.

DeFunis had eventually been admitted elsewhere, making the case apparently moot.

Justice Lewis F. Powell's decision in Bakke.   The Supreme Court finally dealt with the issue of affirmative action in the case of Allan Bakke. The decision was not typical: only one justice, Lewis F. Powell, wrote the majority opinion; several concurring and dissenting opinions were also filed (Sindler, 1978). Although this pattern has occurred in other Supreme Court cases, very few have the potential impact and magnitude of *Bakke*. Justice Powell decided that Allan Bakke had been discriminated against by the University of California at Davis Medical School because it had not admitted him but had reserved several slots for (less qualified) culturally deprived and/or minority applicants. The Davis plan, requiring a reserved pool or quota for minorities, was ruled unnecessary to achieve the goal of greater numbers of minority physicians. But Justice Powell also suggested that race could be used under some circumstances to remedy past abuses. The use of race as one determinant *among others,* such as geographical diversity or being the offspring of an alumnus (the system employed by Harvard University), would be acceptable. The problem with the Harvard plan is that it includes an implied bias that can work for or against a student. Although there are no quotas, a study of Harvard's previously admitted classes indicates that there are some definite parameters for the number of minorities and women admitted.

The Supreme Court vote in favor of Allan Bakke was five to four, with a majority of the Nixon appointees voting with Justice Powell; the separate vote to allow race to be taken into account by the schools was also five to four, with the majority of Nixon appointees opposed. The shift of one vote could have drastically changed the outcome of the case and its impact on racial minorities and women in the United States.

Many will argue that the recent *Weber* case (*United Steelworkers of America, AFL-CIO-CLC* v. *Weber et al.* [47 lw 4851]) does not fit within the interpretation we have laid out here. After all, the Weber case did approve of affirmative action programs for minorities in industry. Actually, even a cursory reading of the case demonstrates that it is far from a ringing approval of such programs. The plan at the Kaiser Aluminum plant near New Orleans admitted black and white workers to a training program on a 50–50 basis. The program was designed to increase the number of black craft workers in the plant. (Blacks comprised only 1.83 percent of all craft workers even though they comprised 39 percent of the work force.) Even Justices Burger and Rehnquist, who placed dissenting votes, thought the Kaiser plan was fair, but not in keeping with the 1964 Civil Rights Act.

First, it must be noted that the decision was *very* narrow. Justice Brennan, who wrote the decision for the Court, began the second section of the brief by stating: "We emphasize at the outset the narrowness of our inquiry." It was argued that the Kaiser plan was voluntary, which means that any federal coercion by EEOC or other agencies would warrant the disqualification of other programs. Second, the decision appears to ground the fairness of the plan on the fact that no such program would exist at all if it were not for affirmative action. That is, 50 percent of the participants in the program were white, and would not have had any chance whatsoever if Kaiser had not agreed to the plan. Moreover, the plan did not require the discharging of whites and was designed as a temporary measure only. Third, the majority opinion suggests that there are illegal affirmative action plans, which invites further challenges. "We need not today define in detail the line of demarcation between permissible and impermissible affirmative action plans. It suffices to hold that the Kaiser-USWA affirmative action plan falls on the permissible side of the line" (47 lw50: 4855). The most important aspect of this case was that it was decided by only five of the nine justices. One vote could swing a comparable decision in the opposite direction. The importance of court decisions is that they follow a discernible direction or pattern, giving guidance to the lower courts. Bakke and Weber will only add confusion.

Because these decisions were so close, individuals on both sides of the issue will continue to press the Supreme Court over the question of affirmative action. Since neither *Bakke* nor *Weber* firmly resolved the issue one way or the other, many individuals will feel that their special situation (all reverse discrimination cases are special, by definition) requires litigation. Until there is a clear trend in such cases or an end to the fence straddling, the fate of affirmative action programs will be unknown.

Taking rights seriously.   Justice Powell's rather narrow view of the equal protection clause in *Bakke* is not easily adaptable to cases outside education and training. Since the majority of affirmative action/reverse discrimination cases appealed to the Court will be outside the area of education, it appears that in industry and business, where they are needed most, affirmative action programs will be phased out (Dworkin, 1978). Justice Powell sees a broad difference between an exclusionary program, such as a quota, and allowance for a handicap, such as considering race as one element in college admissions. But that opinion does not resolve the issue for the white applicant, who is interested not in the method that excludes him, but rather in how much any program reduces his ability to be admitted.

The problem is not one of method, although the Court has said that method is the essence of the issue. Rather, the question is one of rights. The present economy requires a decreasing number of workers, and layoffs (or a failure to create new jobs) always victimize the minorities last to arrive. Many white Americans argue that it is unfair to penalize whites; they are actually asking, Should they or we be disadvantaged? No one suggests that giving veterans preference violates individual rights, although it certainly injures nonveterans. And we use the same rationale for veterans' benefits as for affirmative action: GI's were removed from the general population at the time when they could compete most effectively, and therefore when they return to civilian life they should receive preference in schools and hiring.

According to Ronald Dworkin, in this era of de facto inequality we have not yet come to grips with what are rights in American society. Rights are the government's institutionalization of equality. They are designed to protect minorities from the majority. This was certainly the vision of the framers of the Constitution, who insisted on a Bill of Rights as its first ten amendments. Yet today there is significant public sentiment that demand for rights is out of control. The Great Silent Majority must retake command.

There is also confusion over who is the majority. Many ethnic groups who perceive themselves as only marginally outside (because they are not black) count themselves part of the majority. What does this majority define as the common good? Will it exclude those people who see themselves as bare participants in society?

> The institution of rights is therefore crucial, because it represents the majority's promise to the minorities that their dignity and equality will be respected. . . . The institution requires an act of faith on the part of minorities, because the scope of their rights will be controversial when-ever they are important, and because the officers of the majority will act on their own notions of what these rights really are. Of course these officials will disagree with many of the claims that a minority makes. That makes it all the more important that they take their decisions gravely. . . . The Government will not re-establish respect for law with-out giving the law some claim to respect. It cannot do that if it neglects the one feature that distinguishes law from ordered brutality. If the Government does not take rights seriously, then it does not take law seriously either. (Dworkin, 1977: 205)

THE SITUATION OF MINORITY COMMUNITIES

As we have seen, the majority brings an impressive array of political tools to any conflict with minorities. The considerable pressure brought to bear by the majority results in many failures and few successes; it is no wonder then how easily minority groups can become disenchanted with political activity. Because of this, minority activity tends to occur in cycles, and some people even suggest that such cycles have occurred every 30 years since 1860. Whether or not there has been a regular pattern, there have been trends of minority activity. Sometimes it has taken a cultural form, others the form of political activism, and still other periods have seen violence. Minorities some-times make the majority bend on policy issues; at other times they face absolute disaster, such as in the 1890s. The case of Plessy v. Ferguson (1896) was purposely appealed by Louisiana blacks to the Supreme Court because very few Americans, North or South, thought that the Court would support segregation. In fact, as late as 1898 southern newspapers were making fun of Jim Crow laws:

> If there must be Jim Crow cars on the railroads, there should be Jim Crow cars on the street railways. Also on all passenger boats. . . . If there

are to be Jim Crow cars, moreover, there should be Jim Crow waiting saloons at all stations, and Jim Crow eating houses. . . . There should be Jim Crow sections of the jury box, and a separate Jim Crow dock and witness stand in every court—and a Jim Crow Bible for colored witnesses to kiss. (Woodward, 1966: 68) .

Ironically, with the exception of the Jim Crow witness box, all of these suggestions were instituted within a decade. Where does the current ebb in the equal rights struggle leave the racial minorities who were fighting for equality?

Political Ways Cannot Change Folkways

William Graham Sumner believed that no matter what government did, it could not affect the folkways of society. On the surface Sumner's assessment might appear accurate. In the case of busing, many whites avoided it by moving to the suburbs, and the Supreme Court supported them in *Rodriguez*. Most "social experiments" attempted in the United States have been short-lived. According to one pundit, the War on Poverty was "one of the shortest wars in American history and the most completely surrendered."

If minorities who are substantially excluded from political and social opportunities do not catch up in the next decade, what will happen? Optimists have always believed that minorities will catch up. In the landmark Civil Rights Cases, the Court concluded little more than ten years after the end of slavery that blacks must "cease to be a special favorite of the laws" —and all the protections of the federal government were stripped away in the belief that blacks would eventually catch up. Justice Thurgood Marshall's passionate dissent in *Bakke* suggests that the majority is coming full circle, back to the Civil Rights Cases, and that we are again abrogating rights.

EXCERPT FROM JUSTICE THURGOOD MARSHALL'S DISSENT IN *BAKKE*

While I applaud the judgment of the court that a university may consider race in its admissions process, it is more than a little ironic that, after several hundred years of class-based discrimination against Negroes, the Court is unwilling to hold that a class-based remedy for that discrimination is permissible. In declining to so hold, today's judgment ignores the fact that for several hundred years Negroes have been discriminated against, not as individuals, but rather solely because of the color of their skins. It is unnecessary in twentieth century America to have individual Negroes demonstrate that they have been victims of racial discrimination; the racism of our society has been so pervasive that none, regardless of wealth or position, has managed to escape its impact. The experience of Negroes in America has been different in kind, not just in degree, from that of other ethnic groups. It is not merely the history of slavery alone but also that a whole people were marked as inferior by the law. And that mark has endured. The dream of America as the great melting pot has not been realized for the Negro; because of his skin color he never even made it into the pot.

These differences in the experience of the Negro make it difficult for me to accept that Negroes cannot be afforded greater protection under the Fourteenth Amendment where it is necessary to remedy the effects of past discrimination. In the *Civil Rights Cases,* . . . the Court wrote that the Negro emerging from slavery must cease "to be the special favorite of the laws." . . . We cannot in light of the history of the last century yield to that view. Had the Court in that case and others been willing to "do for human liberty and the fundamental rights of American citizenship, what it did . . . for the protection of slavery and the rights of the masters of fugitive slaves," . . . we would not need now to permit the recognition of any "special wards."

Most importantly, had the Court been willing in 1896, in *Plessy* v. *Ferguson,* to hold that the Equal Protection Clause forbids differences in treatment based on race, we would not be faced with this dilemma in 1978. We must remember, however, that the principle that the "Constitution is color-blind" appeared only in the opinion of the lone dissenter. . . . The majority of the Court rejected the principle of color blindness, and for the next sixty years, from *Plessy* to *Brown* v. *Board of Education,* ours was a Nation where, *by law,* an individual could be given "special" treatment based on the color of his skin.

It is because of a legacy of unequal treatment that we now must permit the institutions of this society to give consideration to race in making decisions about who will hold the positions of influence, affluence, and prestige in America. For far too long, the doors to those positions have been shut to Negroes. If we are ever to become a fully integrated society, one in which the color of a person's skin will not determine the opportunities available to him or her, we must be willing to take steps to open those doors. I do not believe that anyone can truly look into America's past and still find that a remedy for the effects of that past is impermissible.

It has been said that this case involves only the individual, Bakke, and this University. I doubt, however, that there is a computer capable of determining the number of persons and institutions that may be affected by the decision in this case. For example, we are told by the Attorney General of the United States that at least twenty-seven federal agencies have adopted regulations requiring recipients of federal funds to take "*affirmative action* to overcome the effects of conditions which resulted in limiting participation . . . by persons of a particular race, color, or national origin" . . . (emphasis added). I cannot even guess the

number of state and local governments that have set up affirmative
action programs, which may be affected by today's decision.

I fear that we have come full circle. After the Civil War our
government started several "affirmative action" programs. This Court in
the *Civil Rights Cases* and *Plessy* v. *Ferguson* destroyed the
movement toward complete equality. For almost a century no action
was taken, and this nonaction was with the tacit approval of the courts.
Then we had *Brown* v. *Board of Education* and the Civil Rights Acts of
Congress, followed by numerous affirmative action programs. *Now,* we
have this court again stepping in, this time to stop affirmative action
programs of the type used by the University of California.

The United States has consistently failed to test fairly the question of
whether political ways can change folkways. If this failure persists, then the
issues of equality and the rights of minorities will be with us, as well was with
our grandchildren. They will continue to be a divisive, and potentially destruc-
tive, factor in the American polity.

White Flight

White flight to the suburbs has reshaped American society more than any
phenomenon since the influx of immigrants from 1890 to 1910. Because
whites have been taking a good deal of tax revenue with them, as well as forcing
businesses and industries to join them in the suburbs, core cities now face
potential economic disaster. Not only are urban schools more segregated
(although there are notable exceptions), but the tax base to support these
schools has eroded dangerously. The doughnut cities, which we mentioned in
Chapter 2, promise fewer opportunities for minorities.

Even in the area of higher education there has been an increasing tendency toward segregation, because of both black and white pressures. Cherish-
ing their new-found racial identity, blacks want to maintain mostly black
schools, or to associate mostly with other black students in integrated school
systems. Whites are happy not having large influxes of blacks, although for
the next 20 years blacks will comprise a larger and larger percentage of
college-age students. Parallel school systems will continue to exist in states like
Louisiana and Virginia, with Grambling, Southern, Norfolk State, and Virginia
State for blacks and LSU, the University of New Orleans, Old Dominion
University, and the University of Virginia for whites. Most Americans will have
to deal with segregation for their lifetimes.

Economic Inequality

The *Bakke* case will substantially slow economic gains by minorities,
because it is being read as a rebuff of equality programs. Although the federal
government maintains that it will still enforce such programs, most of their
teeth are missing in the post-*Bakke* era. The economic gap between blacks,

Chicanos, and Indians on one hand and white society on the other, which has tended to grow since 1952, will begin to widen more rapidly. Will these minorities come to feel relatively deprived and again take social or political action?

The Future

In the atmosphere of self-concern of the late 1970s and early 1980s, most Americans have forgotten the divisive issues of the 1960s, especially civil rights. This tendency has existed throughout most of American history; we assume that if we cannot see a problem, it does not exist. We hide slums under expressways or move them to less visible areas through urban redevelopment. Only in times of crisis do we suddenly *realize* that what we thought was all right, what is suddenly so pressing, was there all the time.

SUMMARY

This chapter has covered a great deal of ground, yet a great deal more is left uncovered. We have discussed the impact of major ideologies, conservatism and liberalism, on minorities, yet we have not explored how these ideologies use the electronic and print media as well as political institutions to further their aims. We have disucssed the importance of our economy to the minority situation, but we have not examined fully the impact of multinational corporations. We learned how minorities and ethnics vote to try to change society, but we ignored a rule of thumb in American politics: that elections change very little. For the most part incumbents are returned to office; even in the "shake-ups" of 1974 and 1978, most of those elected to Congress were veteran legislators. We discussed the political force of academics, and their ideas and theories, but we barely touched upon the power of science and social science and how the majority brings them to bear.

The last part of the chapter discussed the issue of equality and the New Conservatives. Their view that those who have deserve what they have tends to justify the majority position. The question whether the majority must continue programs to benefit minorities was all but decided in the *Bakke* case. Although the ruling might be interpreted as favorable to minorities, its ambiguity and the arguments upon which it rests suggest that the movement to try to provide minorities with rights is, if not over, substantially curtailed.

Some questions never arise in discussions of equality. We rarely ask whether the existence of private institutions of higher learning violates our sense of equality by providing the wealthy with greater advantages than they already have. We seldom question a university admissions committee that admits the son of a wealthy alumnus even though his grade point and other qualifications are substantially below those of the average entering student. All of these are clearly class issues; the issues we dealt with in this chapter are those created by the tension between race and class.

The context and scope of equality far exceed what we have dealt with in this chapter. Although minorities are the major focus of this book, remember that they exist in the larger context of social class. The politics of the majority usually operate at both class and racial/ethnic levels.

Chapter

Minority Politics in the Future

NINE

ASSIMILATION VERSUS PLURALISM: CONFORMITY OR THE RIGHT TO BE DIFFERENT?

Americans have always been proud of their country for being both a nation of immigrants and a home for individual liberty. But along with our recognition of diversity and individual rights, we have a strong concern for conformity. We expect the many immigrant groups that made this nation to become, in due course, Americans in at least their behavior and hopefully in their hearts. Individual rights are protected until they conflict with the needs of the group. For example, Chinatown may be a good place to eat Chinese food, but you may not want to live there. An eccentric individual is regarded as eccentric only as long as he or she bothers no one; should that individual become too pushy, he or she may become defined as mentally ill or even criminal. In short, in American society there is much disagreement over how much difference is to be tolerated and how much conformity is to be demanded.

In terms of ethnic relations, conformity is generally referred to as acculturation (see Chapter 5). A culturally different ethnic minority is often expected to conform culturally to the lifestyle of the dominant group in return for social acceptance from that dominant group. The processes of conformity and acceptance lead to assimilation, the route taken by many ethnic minorities in America. The demand to be different, in ethnic relations, is the demand for cultural pluralism (again see Chapter 5). The ethnic minority insists on its right to continue being different but also demands that it not be penalized for doing so. The black power movement, for instance, emphasizes both pride in being black and the need for group power in the black community; the power is necessary to protect and support the right to be different.

The conflicting demands for conformity and difference have great meaning for American society in general, and specific importance for ethnic relations within that society. Other, nonethnic groups that have felt oppressed because of their "differences" have looked to ethnic minorities as models of political response. The association of older people known as the Gray Panthers, for example, is based on the Black Panthers. This section will explore the conflict between conformity and difference, focusing primarily on the issues of assimilation and cultural pluralism and secondarily on the wider society and the growth of "new minorities." The history of this conflict is varied. Around the time of World War I, for example, the Americanization movement demanded cultural conformity from new immigrant groups and encountered little protest. During the 1970s, on the other hand, increasing numbers of people demanded the right to be different. Because each option has significant economic and social costs, the conflict is seldom taken lightly.

The Americanization Movement

The masses of southeast European immigrants streaming into American cities in the 1890s provided the initial incentive for the Americanization movement. These immigrants lived in ethnic enclaves, were poor, and tended to be culturally very different from the developing culture of the United States. The first efforts to help them adjust came from the social settlements, the most notable of which was Jane Addams's Hull House, in Chicago. Early social workers tried to teach the immigrants the cultural skills needed to cope with their new environment; simultaneously they encouraged immigrants to take pride in their old cultures, to ease the process of adjustment (Higham, 1955: 236). Meanwhile, other groups (such as the Daughters of the American Revolution) were developing another brand of Americanization, which included teaching cultural skills but replaced the glorification of the old cultures with glorification of the "new culture" —America. This combination of cultural information and indoctrination (the winning of minds and hearts, so to speak) was the basis for the Americanization movement.

The second (and overriding) incentive for the growth of the Americanization movement was World War I (see Higham, 1955: 242–44; Fairchild, 1926: 156–62). People began to be particularly concerned with the hearts (and loyalties) of immigrants, and with the hyphen in, for example, German-American. World War I caused a somewhat disorganized nationwide attempt to instill patriotism as quickly as possible. The following list of goals stated by the National Americanization Committee indicates the wide range of behaviors considered important in becoming an American.

> The interpretation of American ideals, traditions, and standards and institutions to foreign-born peoples.
> The acquirement of a common language for the entire nation.
> The universal desire of all peoples in America to unite in a common citizenship under one flag.

The combating of anti-American propaganda activities and schemes and the stamping out of sedition and disloyalty wherever found.

The elimination of causes of disorder, unrest, and disloyalty which make fruitful soil for un-American propagandists and disloyal agitators.

The abolition of racial prejudices, barriers, and discriminations, of colonies and immigrant sections, which keep people in America apart.

The maintenance of an American standard of living including the use of American foods, preparation of foods, care of children.

The discontinuance of discriminations in housing, care, protection, and treatment of aliens.

The creation of an understanding of and love for America and the desire of immigrants to remain in America, have a home here, and support American institutions and laws. (National Americanization Committee, 1918: 20)

The primary means of achieving these extensive goals was usually some form of education. Immigrant children attended public schools, where they learned about American government and how to salute the flag; their parents were learning roughly the same things in night school or in classes associated with their work. In view of the demands of the wartime economy, most business people saw these classes as a means of creating more productive and more cooperative workers (Higham, 1955: 244–45). One of the more creative businessmen of the period, Henry Ford, originated some colorful attempts at Americanization. His compulsory English school included a pantomime in which the immigrant workers dressed in "foreign looking" clothing and carried signs bearing the names of foreign countries. They then marched into a large "pot" (labeled "melting pot") at center stage, while another group of immigrants, dressed alike in American clothing and waving small American flags, marched out the other side of the pot (Higham, 1955: 248).

The group of programs comprising the Americanization movement did not last long into the 1920s. The passage of the National Origins Act in 1924, which cut off most immigration from southeast Europe, made many of the movement's concerns academic (see Chapter 1). But the ideal of conformity promoted by the Americanization movement programs survived the movement. Many of the antiforeign feelings of the 1920s surfaced again (perhaps understandably) during World War II, and still again during the McCarthyism of the 1950s, as the United States marched into the cold war. Such demands for conformity may well occur in cycles, as we move from periods of greater to lesser tolerance and back again.

In a society of ethnic stratification, demand for conformity becomes translated into demand for assimilation. The dominant group attempts to turn the "state" it controls into a "nation," based on the dominant culture. The patriotism and sense of "we-ness" characteristic of a nation can exist only if the minority ethnic groups conform to the culture of the dominant group.

Despite dominant group demands for conformity, compliance is not always forthcoming; minority groups may insist on cultural differences. The 1960s and 1970s witnessed demands for difference from a variety of groups that felt ignored, disliked, handicapped, or oppressed; conformity is becoming less popular.

The Growth of Pluralism

We documented the growth of cultural pluralism among ethnic minorities in Chapter 5, focusing on Jews, blacks, and Mexican-Americans, As an ideology, cultural pluralism has recently found varying popularity with almost every other ethnic group in the United States. American Indians have organized and begun fighting for tribal land; Japanese-Americans recall the years of internment during World War II as they learn to speak Japanese in night school; and perhaps most interestingly, some eastern European ethnic groups, such as Polish-Americans and Italian-Americans, are rediscovering roots well covered by years of assimilation. In terms of ethnic identity and goals, cultural pluralism was clearly the most visible if not the dominant ideology of the 1970s.

If further evidence is needed for presenting pluralism as a trend, we need only look outside the world of ethnic politics. The variety of movements comprising feminism and women's liberation all suggest a pluralistic basis. There are separate magazines intended for women only, and women's legal and social services (rape counseling centers and organizations to help abused wives, for example). In short, many women demand the right to be different from men and to have the society recognize and support that difference.

Similarly, many homosexual rights organizations that proclaim gay liberation have a pluralistic emphasis. Many homosexuals in the past chose to keep their lifestyles as private as possible while "passing" as heterosexuals. But it is more common today for that homosexuality to be stated openly, coupled with the demand that homosexuals be accorded all the rights that heterosexuals enjoy. One important goal of gay liberation is to convince everyone (especially homosexuals) that homosexuality is perfectly normal and that individuals have a *right* to that lifestyle. As with many efforts toward pluralism, gay liberation has been met with demands for conformity. Several local elections in the 1970s have indicated a desire that certain kinds of discrimination against employing homosexuals continue, particularly with regard to teachers and other educators.

Along with "Sister Power" and "Gay Power" (not to mention the earlier white, black, brown, red, and yellow forms) we now have "Gray Power." This new minority is made up of old people who feel that American society has a negative stereotype about the nature and abilities of old people, and that American society constantly discriminates against old people. Probably the most colorful of the political organizations which represent the interests of old people is the Gray Panthers, organized by Maggie Kuhn (see Hessel,

1977). The Gray Panthers condemn American society for putting its old people out to pasture and emphasize the virtues of being old, particularly the right of old people to be free from discrimination based on their age. Those organizations which have been labeled Gray Power or the Gray Lobby have taken on the task of protecting the special interests of old people, working against discrimination ranging from individual acts of discrimination to the acts of Congress. Once again, we see political organizations defending the right to be different, while insisting that American society be altered so as not to abridge those rights.

Organizations of the physically handicapped also use pluralism as the basis for their political action. Such groups initially formed to eliminate the kinds of discrimination faced by their members due to particular disabilities. People confined to wheelchairs, for example, could not engage in activities that occurred in buildings with stairs. The Architectural Barriers Act of 1968 and the Rehabilitation Act of 1973 were passed in response to those needs; federal funds can now be withheld if structural accommodations are not made for the physically handicapped. In addition, the Rehabilitation Act of 1973 mandates the creation of affirmative action programs for the benefit of the physically handicapped (*Newsweek*, 1976: 74–75). However, such programs often encounter the sense of pride in difference that is characteristic of pluralism. For example, Jim Gashel of the National Federation of the Blind, assessing the supposedly model program for the handicapped at the Unviersity of Illinois, Champagne-Urbana, criticized its "medical model" aspect. Just as early black power advocates hated being "taken by the hand" by whites who wanted to help them, Gashel criticized programs for the handicapped that focus only on their physical disabilities while ignoring their strengths (*Science*, 1976: 1400–1401).

Among the physically handicapped, the most striking parallel with ethnic pluralistic politics is found among the deaf. In the past, deaf people were encouraged to learn lip reading, which can be considered an effort at assimilation by conforming to the mode of communication favored by hearing people. Recently, however, many deaf people favor the use of sign language and take pride in its use. Institutions such as Gallaudet College in Washington, D.C., which accepts only students with serious hearing impairment, have become centers for the development of group pride. The touring National Theater of the Deaf (in which the actors communicate in sign language coupled with spoken "subtitles" for people with communication impairment in understanding sign language) has helped turn sign language into an art. In short, there is a growing pride among the deaf based on the strengths inherent in their difference from those who can hear.

Such examples of organizations that form to build group pride and to work for the right of the group to be different, in whatever way, suggest a reevaluation of conformity among Americans. Instead of viewing differences in sex, sexual preference, age, ethnicity, or physical ability as unfortunate, many Americans now call attention to those differences and challenge the rest of society to accept them. Acceptance often entails a number of costs for the dominant group, as they reorganize their means of coping with the minority.

The Problems of a Pluralistic Society

When groups form for the purpose of defending their difference from the norm, they must always fight to gain acceptance from the dominant group. In many cases, however, they must first fight for recognition; some groups face discrimination not because they are disliked or feared but simply because they (or their particular difference, which creates the discrimination) have been overlooked. For instance, stairs are not constructed to frustrate people in wheelchairs, but for the convenience of the majority of the population, with functioning legs. Thus, a first goal of many groups is to gain recognition of their particular difference, so as to eliminate acts of discrimination that we might label inconsideration.

Acts of inconsideration result from oversight by the dominant group; ideally they cost nothing to alter. By that we mean that there are no economic costs involved and—perhaps more importantly—no significant loss of power for the dominant group. Many such forms of discrimination can be classified as unintended offensive treatment: the dominant group acts upon its stereotypes of the group in question, and in so doing acts in a manner offensive to that group. For example, the program for the handicapped at the University of Illinois seemed to treat blind people as sick, which was offensive to blind people. The organizers of the program undoubtedly had no intention of offending anyone; they could be moved to stop their offense simply by having their attention called to it.

A second type of inconsiderate act of discrimination is the unintended lack of facilities. This type of discrimination occurs through oversight, as does unintended offensive treatment, but it can have more important consequences for the affected group because it creates very real barriers between them and the institutions of the dominant group. Again, ideally, this type of discrimination should cost nothing (or practically nothing) to eliminate. Providing multilingual information at public facilities adds only minor printing expenses for signs and causes no significant loss of power to the dominant group. But let us recall the example of stairs and wheelchairs. The construction of ramps alongside stairs adds to the financial costs of constructing a building; when elevators must be included even in two-story buildings, the added cost is significant. Imagine how many groups might want public facilities altered so as to be more accommodating to them; there would be great monetary costs and, in some cases, potential decreases in dominant group power. We must turn from the simple *recognition* of group differences by the dominant group, to their willingness to *accept* those differences.

If the dominant group accepts others' differences, it is willing to alter its institutions to make them more accessible to the group demanding the change. In some cases these changes may be minor, involving only the correction of an oversight. In other cases, however, the changes may be major and the costs beyond what the dominant group wants to accept. We can divide these costs into two types: economic costs and social costs. *Economic costs* are simply the added expenses involved in altering a facility. *Social costs* are a much more general category, all relating to the degree of dominance possessed by the dominant group. As we have seen throughout this book, the dominant group maintains its position through its control of societal institutions, and it uses that control to make those institutions operate in its best interests. Major alterations in those institutions can lessen that control, and accepting the alterations proposed by a minority group may be a greater social cost than the dominant group wishes to bear.

How realistic is the wish for a pluralistic society? In the area of economic costs, we must determine how much money is needed to provide equal treatment for how many people. A fairly major institutional change might be justified if enough people will benefit from the change. Presumably, legislation guaranteeing the rights of the physically handicapped was based on the assumption that there were enough physically handicapped people to justify the expense; a handicap suffered by only one person probably would not result in such widespread changes. In addition to the numbers of people involved, there is the factor of how much money is needed for a change. An institutional change that threatened to deplete the treasury would probably not be funded under any circumstances. Such decisions are made in the political arena, where real needs and values can be established.

A fundamental question involves the social costs to the dominant group of increasing pluralism. How much diversity can a major industrial nation like the United States absorb and still function? The ultimate national model of pluralism is Switzerland, where three distinct ethnic groups live peacefully under one government. But Switzerland is unique; the very fact that there are few (if any) examples of working pluralism besides Switzerland calls into question its feasibility. Canada faces the problem of the political demands of Quebec. When the predominantly French-Canadian province legislated that all business activities must take place in the French language rather than in English, many businesses chose to leave rather than to change to cope with the added diversity. Although few such dramatic confrontations have occurred in the United States (largely because we lack such a large and concentrated minority), many groups' political activities are designed to lead in that direction. Again, the question is basically political and the answers will be determined through political processes.

The gains of minorities in the United States in their efforts to remain separate *and* equal come through the exercise of power and result in an equalization of power among various segments of the society. But while the days of the Americanization movement are over, its characteristic demands for conformity are still very much alive in the political arena. Perhaps minorities engaged in pluralistic politics seek only an end to ethnic stratification, and will disband if they gain that end. On the other hand, we may see increasing pluralistic demands in the future if people continue to search for identity based on their difference from the norm.

PERSPECTIVES ON POLICY: THE FUTURE OF POLITICAL PLURALISM

Does this emphasis on political pluralism show a hidden bias by academics toward the American political system as it is presently constructed? Several social scientists feel that significant prejudices are inherent in *any* pluralistic perspective. Political pluralism emphasizes that groups (for our purposes, minorities) can and do have an input into the political system. Yet we find that our political system does not focus on issues that are of vital concern to the majority of Americans. The status quo orientation of pluralism tends to make the political system ignore out-groups until a crisis develops; reforms are not initiated *within* organizations to insure representation of changing attitudes (Connolly, 1969: 18–19).

There are several indications that the political system in the United States is not focusing on issues of major concern to the population. First, massive pessimism found by recent public opinion polls shows that many Americans are becoming increasingly disenchanted with economic and social circumstances in this country. A more important indicator is voting turnout. There has been a sharp decline in the percentage of eligible voters who go to the polls. In 1976 fewer than 54 percent of all eligible voters voted, and the "large" turnout surprised many analysts (Pomper, 1976: 72). In most off-year elections, when a presidential election is not being held, less than 35 percent of the voters in many states cast ballots. Some political scientists argue that low voter participation is a stabilizing factor, but there have been periods of very high voter turnout in the United States without instability. In the 1896 election between William McKinley and William Jennings Bryan, over 80 percent of those eligible voted.[1]

As we said above, out-groups are ignored until a crisis develops. William Gamson's research contradicts many classical views of political pluralism. Gamson argues that the majority of groups that are *effective* in changing the political system do not work within it, but commit violent or illegal acts (Gamson, 1975). Social scientists are often blind to underlying social turbulence until it erupts around them. One respected political scientist, in the introduction to his 1960 textbook, noted that "the era of war [is] over in the United States" and, because of the *Brown* v. *Board of Education* decision by the Supreme Court, "an era of racial harmony and peace is at hand." This just before the war in Vietnam, race riots, and the Black Panthers!

Pluralism often does not allow groups and organizations to foster reforms within themselves. Such changes are difficult to institute, especially in political

---

1. The large numbers of disenfranchised blacks (and others) were not included in calculating the percentage, but the large turnout supports our point nonetheless.

parties. We have in the United States what one observer has called a "no-party" system, with no ongoing party organization and no platform; the political parties try to incorporate every ideological perspective represented in this nation. Even within interest groups, internal reform—forcing the leadership to catch up with the membership—is almost impossible. For example, the leadership of the American Medical Association has been out of touch with its members for years. Within the past decade thousands of doctors have quit the association in disgust. Yet legislators and the American public still see it as the institution representing medicine in the United States (Christenson, 1976). The National Rifle Association still stymies passage of legislation to regulate hand guns, even though a 1976 Gallup poll showed not only that the vast majority of Americans favor hand gun control, but that 52 percent of the NRA's membership also favor it.

Clearly, political pluralism has dangerous biases, especially since most of us believe "it is the way the system works." It is important to suggest another political possibility, although not a pleasant one: political revolution. The likelihood seems remote that violence would become so extreme as to overthrow the present form of government. However, we shall touch upon it, because minorities would play a crucial role in any such scenario. They are the most likely to conclude that the political system is rigged against them. (Again, as we said in Chapter 6, this perception can be an accurate or inaccurate interpretation.) Therefore, minority groups are the most ready arena of instability in American politics. However, minorities are probably more likely to enter into illegal protest or violence than into outright rebellion.

Keeping the limitations of pluralism in mind, we shall suggest some probable changes and problems concerning minority groups that will arise, assuming that pluralism remains the dominant mode of politics.

The Role of Government Intervention

The American polity has been evolving toward a more and more centrally controlled government. The cause of this development is not a federal power grab, but the impossibility of dealing with modern problems at state and local levels. Additionally, state governments have been notoriously arbitrary in dealing with minorities, and they have had a greater tendency to abrogate civil rights. Although we should not dismiss state and local governments' impact on minorities, it appears that in the future there will be continuing gravitation toward federal government to resolve even the most mundane political issues.

The federal government is the most important center of political authority because it can intervene in the economy on behalf of groups. The courts' current interpretation of the interstate commerce clause all but excludes state and local governments in these matters. The government has had to consistently intervene on behalf of the economy since 1932. Although many Americans disparage President Franklin D. Roosevelt for beginning socialism and the welfare state, it is more likely that he saved the United States from a socialist or fascist revolution. Capitalism has been ailing around the world for over a century. Today in the United States we have a modified form of socialism, rather than pure capitalism. Social security, unemployment compensation, Medicare, and retirement benefits are all socialist modifications of the American economic system. Economic instability throughout the 1970s made many Americans uneasy; given the pressures of external competition, especially from Japan and Western Europe, and the power imbalance in favor of the oil-producing countries, the stability of the American economy will not improve.

Government intervention in the economy has a profound impact on minorities in the United States. The federal government has had to interfere to protect large numbers of unemployed people who face difficult economic choices. They can exist deprived (starvation is still part of the American scene), go on welfare, or become involved in illegal activities. Many Americans believe that the welfare life is an easy one; actually, it is not only degrading but marginal. Few welfare programs in this country provide a reasonable standard of living, much less the booze and Cadillac lifestyle middle-class Americans envision (Ryan, 1976). Some jobs do go unfilled; either they require substantial skills or education, or they pay the minimum wage, which is a poor living if one must support a spouse and three children.

In the United States, most "racial" minorities (blacks, Chicanos, Indians, and others, depending on the section of the country) find themselves in the lowest social class. For that reason, even the present modified capitalistic system does not benefit minorities as much as it does the middle and upper middle classes, who have a significant chance for social mobility. Many minorities are trapped in the lower classes by the slowdown in industrialization as well as by the increasing emphasis on specialization. One hundred years ago an uneducated immigrant could find menial work and have at least an outside chance of working his way up, although the Horatio Alger myth is a great exaggeration even for the nineteenth century. Today menial labor is either eliminated by technology or it pays so poorly that people cannot afford to take such jobs. This leads to many paradoxes, one of which involves the minimum wage. When the government raises the minimum wage, a great number of marginal employees lose their jobs, usually to be replaced by machines. However, if the minimum wage is not raised, the same workers face starvation by inflation.

Education.   Government can intervene, sometimes effectively, on behalf of minorities. One area where government impact has been clearest is education. In the 1960s the federal government, especially the Justice Department, effected profound changes in educational institutions. The large-scale desegregation plans developed for communities throughout the United States gave the impression that major changes were occurring across the country.

However, several factors reversed that trend, leading to circumstances reminiscent of the mid-1950s. Richard Nixon's election and his commitment to end busing, Daniel Moynihan's benign neglect policy (see Chapter 8), and white flight into the suburbs all contributed to regression for minorities in education.

Segregated schools are harmful in many ways. City tax bases are eroding because of white flight to the suburbs and the tendency of businesses to follow. Accordingly, funds are inadequate to support school systems in the inner cities. Students who are already handicapped by lower-class backgrounds[2] attend inferior schools often with poorly qualified teachers. More importantly, their environment does not encourage academic achievement. If such students drop out of high school or are so poorly prepared that they cannot gain admission to college or trade school, the cycle will repeat itself yet again.

If society returns completely to segregated educational patterns, pressures from minorities will be immense. (Paradoxically, some of the impetus to maintain segregation comes from black institutions of higher education. Many blacks feel that such black institutions are needed to maintain their group identity.) Segregated educational institutions will reinforce segregation, because such institutions are always underfunded. It takes little digging to note the inequities in funding between the University of Texas and Texas A and I, Louisiana State University and Grambling, and the University of Virginia and Virginia State University. Given white-dominated state legislatures, equal funding for white and black state colleges is unlikely; even if it were accomplished, it would take a generation to improve the dismal facilities and faculty of some black institutions. Even more important is the ability of these colleges to break the economic ties between businesses and corporations, and certain institutions of higher education. Most economic institutions prefer to hire graduates of "name" institutions of higher education, a category that does not include most black colleges. Many would argue that this description is biased because it seems to ignore the redeeming cultural features of some black institutions. But this unflattering perspective is accurate from the viewpoint of political pluralism, and assuming that pluralism continues as the dominant mode of American politics, the description will continue to be accurate.

Housing.   Although stable, integrated neighborhoods exist in many cities in the United States, this does not appear to be a long-term trend. In 1980 the average cost of a new house in a metropolitan area was $80,000; prices of older houses were rising commensurately. If a minority buyer put 10 percent down (close to $10,000, including closing costs), he would have monthly

---

2.   This is not a value judgment, but a cultural reality. American society is geared toward the middle-class background. For example, a college dean pretended that he had no son, because the boy was not especially bright and pumped gas at a local filling station—something that apparently violated the dean's middle-class norms.

payments of over $700 for 30 years if he had a 9.5 percent loan. Although his budget would be extremely tight, assume that he could spend half of his monthly wage before taxes for his home. At that rate his absolute minimum yearly salary would be almost $17,000 (or almost $9 per hour). Certainly, he could buy a cheaper home, but it would probably be in a racially segregated neighborhood. For example, in Richmond, Virginia, the Regional Development and Planning Commission built houses in the $50,000 range in the previous slum area of Fulton. There are a few wealthy black applicants, but no whites are willing to move into an area with such a bad reputation. Before conscious discrimination ever takes place, the market eliminates the vast majority of minority buyers.

Integrated housing might solve some of the problems of minority education. Rather than supporting forced busing, perhaps we should argue for forced integration of housing. Such a proposal obviously goes against the very grain of the American belief in property rights. Making major changes in housing patterns will be enormously difficult, because Americans believe that a person's home is his castle. Realtors are active participants in this process (Newman et al., 1978); they generally want not to alienate groups of people or to create unstable neighborhoods. Unstable conditions, although they might benefit individual real estate agents, tend to hurt most realtors when masses of whites begin leaving a neighborhood.

Pluralism will tend to maintain the status quo in housing. The foreseeable future seems to hold not improving housing conditions for minorities, but an increasing gap between the housing of the majority and the minorities. Inflation (which, like our system of taxation, operates regressively against poorer individuals) will widen the gap. Minorities will remain largely in ghettos, isolated from mainstream middle-class lifestyles.

Affirmative action.   The tidal wave of public sentiment will all but end affirmative action programs. Many now exist on paper only; certainly in the next 20 years fewer and fewer will have any effect. The *Bakke* case could be reversed, but it is unlikely that the Court will do so. At any rate, such programs have not helped those who need them most. Black high school graduates still have more difficulty finding jobs than white high school dropouts. The shift toward the political right has put greater value on individuality, but the economic rules of the system are still weighted against some people because of their race, sex, or ethnicity. Women presently seem to benefit most from affirmative action programs, but it is too early to conclude this firmly; blacks were given preference by such programs before women were, and it may be that a reaction will occur against giving preference to women.

The point of this discussion is to note the importance of political culture. In the 1960s Americans appeared to have a broad commitment to equality; during the '70s the pendulum swung back toward the Lockean notion of freedom.[3] Americans have apparently given up the attempt to obtain equality, a shift that will continue to affect minority groups. If such groups are to work within the pluralistic system, they must find ways to challenge the dominant notion of freedom: the right to sell one's house to whomever one chooses, the right to hire whom one likes, the right to send one's children to school with the children of those with whom one has most in common. Although most of our laws suggest that these are not basic American rights (see Chapter 4), the "Nixon" Supreme Court seems increasingly to be deciding issues as if they were.

Race and Politics in the 1980s

Minority political activity may not be as volatile in the 1980s as it was in the 1960s and early '70s, for several reasons. There is a tendency to blame federal government "overregulation" for most of our ills. Rather than being seen as fostering equality or fair treatment, Washington is viewed as overburdening private enterprise and initiative. Minorities sense this lack of efficacy in government and feel stalemated by these majority interests.

There has been a parallel change in the attitudes of college students from the early 1970s to the present. Subjects of discussion in a recent freshman government class were Ralph Nader, groups like Common Cause, and their effect on American politics. The students criticized Nader for seeing "something wrong everywhere." They held him responsible for higher automobile prices because of the safety devices he had fought for; they also criticized him for pointing out the health hazards of asbestos roofs on buildings like the school gymnasium. They did not blame the manufacturers, but Nader, for being the cause of government interference. In the 1970s Eugene McCarthy, erstwhile presidential candidate in 1968 and 1976, pointed out that activism had caused many changes: "In the 1950s if all the front right wheels fell off of every Oldsmobile, it was simply a bad year for buying Oldsmobiles." However, it seems that much of the American public would like to rid itself of government regulation on behalf of the consumer, and return to the era of *caveat emptor* (buyer beware).

Today most minorities feel that their causes have been shoved aside in favor of attention to the economy. There has always been a delicate balance between government and business in America. Now business is becoming more dependent on government to purchase its products and to regulate its

---

3. There are two different forms of freedom in modern political thought. Dominant in the United States is Lockean freedom (derived from the writings of John Locke), which emphasizes individual freedom—my right to do what I please as long as I do not harm my neighbor. The other notion of freedom was expressed by Jean Jacques Rousseau, who argued that one is free only in society, and that individual freedom is absurd. Therefore, freedom is the right to do things that better the community. Rousseau even argued that people ought to be forced to be free. Compare Rousseau's *The Social Contract* with Locke's *Two Treatises on Government*.

practices. Most businesses would be ill equipped to handle mass deregulation; in most cases huge monopolies would form, eliminating competition. The result would be further racial stratification and the inability of minority groups even to approximate the average majority standard of living.

It is unlikely that minorities will act violently or illegally in the 1980s. Economic circumstances, however, may either catalyze action in the latter part of the decade or set the stage for massive protest in the early 1990s. In an inflationary economy, although the middle classes complain most, the lower- and working-class people feel the greatest pinch. And in the United States, members of these classes tend to be members of certain minority groups.

Stanislav Andreski argues that the degree of minority group suffering depends on the relative depth of racial and ethnic cleavage as compared to class divisions:

> When goods are growing scarce men will fight for the shares, but whether they will divide themselves on class lines, or according to religious or ethnic or racial distinctions, depends on the relative strength of the various kinds of social bonds: a fissure occurs along the line of least cohesion. The difficulty of harmonizing conflicting interests will be greatest if more than one distinguishing mark coincides: if, for instance, class positions correspond to differences of religion, language, culture, and physical traits. (Andreski, 1963: 201)

When the dimensions of the current economic struggle become clear, the ebb in minority activity will be over; there will be a reemphasis on equality to regain the ground minorities are presently losing.

Social and political trends.   The back-to-the-fifties trend in American culture and politics will probably last at least until the mid-1980s. At that time American blacks will still be in a position of economic inferiority, and women will also be experiencing a push "back to the kitchen" (although that force will be blunted by the economy, because few households will be able to maintain their standard of living without two wage-earners). American Indians will be under increasing pressure to assimilate, because reservations, which protect community cultures, do not fit well into an individualistic society. The Eisenhower policy of termination will not return; instead, more massive yet subtle pressures will be applied (Deloria, 1974).

The case of the American Indians is a good model for understanding the retrenchment of political and social activity. As early as 1832, in *Worcester* v. *State of Georgia,* the Supreme Court recognized the autonomy and sovereignty of the American Indian. Not until 1924, however, were Indians given United States citizenship. The federal and state governments consistently took what they wanted from the Indians, ignoring treaties and often the law. Today many Indians are filing suit for the return of their lands; some land in New Mexico, Oregon, and Washington has been returned to Indian trust. It is economically impossible for states to pay for illegally confiscated Indian land. One third of the state of Maine, for example, belongs by treaty to two Indian tribes. The states have appealed to Congress to abrogate all treaties made with the Indians; Congress will do so, if for no other reason than the large number of states that otherwise face bankruptcy. On a smaller scale, many states have taken back fishing rights granted to the Indians by treaty, even though fishing is often the Indians' only livelihood. People who fish for sport have more political clout than Indians, in most states.

In the current cultural and political climate in the United States, the tendency is for the majority to act against the interests of most minorities. The majority justifies its actions and believes them to be correct. For example, although many of us sympathize with the American Indians, we do not feel that we owe them large sums of money; after all, why should we pay for our grandparents' sins? Most of us believe in equal rights for blacks, but even if a black person is equal to us, why should he or she receive preference for a job? After all, we need jobs also. Cultural values are changing; although equality is desirable, it must not come at our expense. (Of course, in any society that institutes equality, those who had *more* will by definition come to have *less*.)

Minorities will tend increasingly to be isolated in urban ghettos. Presently 80 percent of Chicanos—who are most noted as migrant workers—live in urban areas. Most of the racial minorities live in deteriorating inner cities, often ruled by organized crime and by street gangs. If decent housing developments exist in these cities, they still tend to isolate minorities. The increasing numbers of minority mayors and other politicians has not led to a commensurate increase in power. Most political power has evaporated into the suburbs, accompanied by economic power. This trend has been paralleled by a vast increase in transportation facilities. Little more than 50 years ago only a lunatic would have lived more than a few blocks from his place of employment; today many people travel 20 to 50 miles to work. Expressways may help commuters, but they also insure that racial and economic problems will not be solved within cities. It is far easier to leave for the suburbs than to solve these problems. Ironically, the energy crisis—the nightmare of the average citizen—could have beneficial consequences if it forces people back into the cities. (There is also potential for disaster: employers may decide to relocate their businesses in the suburbs for the convenience of the executives, which would have the effect of starting an entirely new urban environment.)

Democraphics and politics.   It is an adage that Republicans tend to sleep either in separate beds or in separate rooms, which explains why there are more Democrats than Republicans. The adage contains a hint of truth. Democrats do tend to be poorer and less educated than Republicans. Birth control information is not readily available to most poor people, nor can they readily afford abortions. More importantly, poor people tend to be more religious and to judge birth control and especially abortion as sinful. For instance, recent studies of American Catholics suggest that while upper-middle-class Catholics all but ignore the Church's prohibitions, lower-class Catholics feel bound by them (Ryan, 1976; Greeley, 1977). The point is that although today more voters see themselves as independents, many future voters are being born into Democratic families. Assuming that socialization factors remain consistent, children born to two Democratic parents are 80 percent likely to affiliate with the Democratic party when they grow up.

However, these people will also tend to be poor, and therefore they will not vote as often as wealthier adults. Most will also be from minority families—black and Chicano, and lower-middle-class Catholics. They will be isolated in urban areas, and their votes will more than likely challenge the status quo. Economically less stable than the rest of society, they will be caught in the economic decline forecast for the United States during the rest of the twentieth century. Their full voting impact will not be felt until the 1990s.

A general overview.   What is the source of our projections? If we simply examine the birth rates of blacks and whites, poor people and middle-class people, in the late 1960s and early '70s, we can easily project who the new voters will be and who will fill the schools in 20 years. Demographic predictions for this country suggest a substantial growth of minority groups, especially compared to the growth of the majority. The pressures accompanying such growth are evident. The greater the number of people in a minority group that experiences social, economic, or political prejudice, the thinner will be spread the already limited available goods and services. If the political system remains pluralistic during the 1980s, then political pluralism—because it discourages the artificial redistribution of economic and political power—will increase social pressures.

We do not necessarily predict an outbreak of riots or even of violent political activism, although both are possible. A viable alternative is massive change *within* the American government structure, such as occurred in 1932. Theodore Lowi argues that the United States has had four or five types of government since its founding, and suggests that we are in the fifth or sixth republic. Although he probably would not agree with this interpretation of his thesis, it is possible that the increasing numbers of minority group members in this country may force a peaceful yet monumental change in American institutions.

Education.   The growth in minority population will have consequences in other areas besides politics. In education, although white children will still be a majority, there will be a sharp increase in the number of minority students of college age by the year 2000 (see table 15). The data in table 15 assume a fertility rate of 2.1 children for both black and white families. Studies suggest that this is far from realistic. In 1970 whites averaged 2.3 children, blacks averaged 3.0. Thus, the number of minority children graduating from high school could reach 40 percent of the total graduating class by the year 2000. Of course, that is the extreme projection, but it suggests some potential problems.

Table 15.   *Population and Population Projections, by Race, 15- to 29-Year-Olds*

Year	(in thousands) Whites	Blacks	Black Percentage of Total
1910	23,235	2,972	13
1920	24,662	3,048	12.5
1930	28,606	3,526	12.3
1940	31,262	3,645	11.6
1950	30,502	3,707	12.2
1960	30,635	3,883	12.7
1970	42,464	5,666	13.3
1980	51,346	7,837	15.3
1990	45,412	7,853	17.3
2000	45,014	8,044	17.9

SOURCE: Derived from table 1/3, Social Indicators 1976 (Washington, D.C.: U.S. Department of Commerce, December 1977), 23.

Parenthetically, these differences are not *race* differences as much as *class* differences. If we control for class—that is, compare upper-class whites and blacks, middle-class whites and blacks, and working-class whites and blacks—the birth rate differences between races disappear. Working-class people tend to produce more children than middle- and upper-class people. In fact, black female college graduates actually have a lower birth rate than white female college graduates. Thus, although we appear to be emphasizing racial differences in this chapter, remember the thesis woven throughout this book: *at base, all political and social racial differences are economically caused, and can be explained using the concepts of social class and social stratification.*

The presence of large numbers of minority children in our school systems will continue, if not intensify, racial segregation. Violence in the schools will increase, for there will be more lower- and working-class students, and fewer black and white middle-class students. Racial difficulties appear bound to increase.

Colleges and universities also face dilemmas. If projections hold, the class of 2000 could well be more than one-quarter minority. Most minority students will be poorly prepared, because of the current resegregation of most schools. The institutions of higher learning will also not be prepared for their influx. Programs will not be able to adjust to the change in students' background—assuming the colleges can even attract working-class students. Also, between the years 2000 and 2010, more than 27 percent of all college professors teaching today will retire. With tuition in private colleges already climbing beyond the reach of most of the middle class, and because they will have to pay qualified teachers far more in a highly competitive market, private institutions will find that they have too few students to fund them. The result will be a massive change in higher education.

More importantly, the United States will be forced again into affirmative action, because of the large numbers of educated minority persons competing for positions of power. Assuming that political pluralism persists, it is unlikely that these graduates will be integrated into the political and economic power structure without some sort of social or political activism.

International pressures on American politics.   International events increasingly influence American politics. Even the casual observer of Capitol Hill has noted the tremendous increase in numbers of foreign lobbyists. Nations such as Algeria, West Germany, and Syria pay people like Clark Clifford (former secretary of defense) and William Rogers (former secretary of state) million-dollar fees to represent them to the executive branch and to Congress. Also important is the growing number of foreign investors in American business and industry. This development has raised an outcry in the United States, although Americans have been encouraged to invest abroad for more than 50 years. To understand American politics and minority politics in the future, we must evaluate the impact of foreign money.

As American investors have done in other parts of the world, foreign investors may make American businesses insensitive to workers' needs. Most investors are interested in profits; local issues or problems be damned. If Japanese, European, and Middle Eastern investors express such attitudes, instability will likely increase in the United States. However, disregard for local problems is not attributable only to foreign investors. Increasing dominance by multinational corporations is a growing concern. Many of these conglomerates' sales far outstrip most countries' gross national product, as table 11 pointed out (see Chapter 8).

Another source of international pressure is the Communist nations, which tend to view many minorities in this country as third world peoples exploited by the American economic system. Whether or not this is true, Communist ideology is a persuasive alternative to political pluralism for many minority group members. For years minorities have used Marxist perspectives to analyze and attempt to change their situation. These individuals do not want socialism as much as they see a "radical" ideology as an effective tool to end economic and social discrimination against them.

Conflict and accommodation in the twenty-first century.   Alexis de Tocqueville, one of the most astute observers of the American scene, in the early 1830s grasped the implications of racial discrimination on the American continent. His observations on American Indians and women are worthwhile; his comments on black Americans are prophetic:

> *Those same abuses of power which now maintain slavery would then become the sources of the greatest dangers facing the southern whites. Nowadays only descendants of Europeans own the land and are absolute masters of the whole labor force; they alone are rich,*

educated and armed. The black man has none of these advantages, but being a slave, he can manage without them. When he has become free and responsible for his own fate, can he be deprived of all these things and not die? What gave the white man his strength in times of slavery would expose him to a thousand dangers once slavery is abolished.

As long as the Negro is kept as a slave, he can be held in a condition not far removed from that of a beast; once free, he cannot be prevented from learning enough to see the extent of his ills and to catch a glimpse of the remedy. (de Tocqueville, 1969: part 2, ch. 10)

Minority politics has been a dominant theme from this country's very inception, and it is unlikely that the issues that concern blacks, Chicanos, Indians, women, or even the handicapped will be resolved within the next 20 years. W. E. B. Du Bois said that the issue of the twentieth century is the colorline; we suggest that it will also be *the* issue of the *next* century—sometimes eclipsed by other issues, but always lurking behind the social and political relationships of Americans.

PARABLE: THE CONTEXT OF MINORITY SOCIOLOGY AND POLITICS

Once upon a time there was a man who sought escape from the prattle of his neighbors and went to live alone in a hut he had found in the forest. At first he was content, but a bitter winter led him to cut down the trees around his hut for firewood. The next summer he was hot and uncomfortable because his hut had no shade, and he complained bitterly of the harshness of the elements.

He made a little garden and kept some chickens, but rabbits were attracted by the food in the garden and ate much of it. The man went into the forest and trapped a fox, which he tamed and taught to catch rabbits. But the fox ate up the man's chickens as well. The man shot the fox and cursed the perfidy of the creatures of the wild.

The man always threw his refuse on the floor of his hut and soon it swarmed with vermin. He then built an ingenious system of hooks and pulleys so that everything in the hut could be suspended from the ceiling. But the strain was too much for the flimsy hut and it soon collapsed. The man grumbled about the inferior construction of the hut and built himself a new one.

One day he boasted to a relative in his old village about the peaceful beauty and plentiful game surrounding his forest home. The relative was impressed and reported back to his neighbors, who began to use the area for picnics and hunting excursions. The man was upset by this and cursed the intrusiveness of human beings. He began posting signs, setting traps, and shooting at those who came near his dwelling. In revenge groups of boys would come at night from time to time to frighten him and steal things. The man took to sleeping every night in a chair by the window with a loaded shotgun across his knees. One night he turned in his sleep and shot off his foot. The villagers were saddened by this misfortune and thereafter stayed away from his part of the forest. The man became lonely and cursed the unfriendliness of his former neighbors. And all these troubles the man saw as coming from outside himself, for which reason, and because of his technical skills, the villagers called him the American. (Slater, 1976: xiii–xv)

Minority social and political relationships must be understood in the context of the larger American society. Phillip Slater's book *The Pursuit of Loneliness,* from which the parable above is taken, suggests that the culture and values of American society are at the breaking point. Although we agree with Slater's analysis of the disease, we are not sure how soon it will become terminal. The United States definitely has problems, but very few Americans see it on its death bed.

Most Americans are lonely and frustrated. They feel no need for their neighbors, no sense of community, nor even a sense of control over their own lives. Most feel trapped within the bureaucracy. What happens to other people is not their responsibility and certainly does not warrant their doing something about it.

Although technically they live in a democracy, few Americans believe that they have any voice in what happens to them. Few even understand what a democracy is. In a freshman government class held two months after President Nixon's resignation over Watergate, the students were involved in heated debate over his ouster. One student tearfully said, "Who are we to criticize the president of the United States?" How does an instructor answer such a question in a country whose people are supposedly the sovereign? It appears that most Americans feel that they receive the bounty of their land by divine providence and luck and have no control over the circumstances of their neighbors, much less over the plight of minority people in this nation. Minorities do not agree with this attitude, nor can minorities and the majority agree over who has control. The majority believes that no one has control over the society, that an "invisible hand" guides us. Minorities see unfair advantages granted to certain members of society because of where they were born, their race, or their sex. We fail to answer with one voice the question, who controls America?

SUMMARY

In this chapter we have discussed various dimensions of social pluralism as well as the impact of political pluralism on minorities. New categories such as the handicapped and the aged have coalesced as minority groups challenging the social and political organization of society. These groups and the traditional minorities will have a continuing effect on our society. The questions of equal education and housing and of affirmative action were not resolved in the 1970s; they were merely postponed. Were they postponed indefinitely, or only held off until the next decade—or perhaps until the twenty-first century? The future of minority groups is irrevocably intertwined with the nature of American society, future social and political demographics, and international economic and political pressures. The question is, who has—and who will have—control in America?

Bibliography

Abrahamson, Mark, Ephraim Mizruchi and C. Hornung
   1976   Stratification and Mobility. New York: Macmillan.
Acuña, Rudolf
   1972   Occupied America: The Chicano's Struggle for Liberation. New York: Can-
           field Press.
Adorno, T. W., E. Frenkel-Brunswik, Daniel Levinson and R. Nevitt Sanford
   1950   The Authoritarian Personality. New York: Harper & Row.
Alba, Richard D.
   1976   "Social assimilation among American Catholic national-origin groups."
           American Sociological Review 41: 1030–46.
Allport, Gordon
   1954   The Nature of Prejudice. Reading, Mass.: Addison-Wesley.
Andreski, Stanislav
   1963   "An economic interpretation of antisemitism," The Jewish Journal of Sociol-
           ogy 5, no. 2: 201–13.
Axelrod, Robert
   1972   "Where the votes came from: an analysis of electoral coalitions, 1952–
           1968." American Political Science Review, March 1972.
Bachrach, Peter
   1971   Political Elites in a Democracy. New York: Atherton.
Banfield, Edward
   1974   The Unheavenly City. Boston: Little, Brown.
Banton, Michael and Jonathan Harwood
   1975   The Race Concept. New York: Praeger.
Barbaro, Fred
   1974   "Ethnic resentment." Society 2, no. 3.
Barth, Fredrik (ed.)
   1969   Ethnic Groups and Boundaries. Boston: Little, Brown.
Becker, Howard S.
   1963   Outsiders: Studies in the Sociology of Deviance. New York: Free Press.
Bell, Robert R.
   1976   Social Deviance: A Substantive Analysis. Homewood, Ill.: Dorsey.
Bennett, Lerone, Jr.
   1966   "Stokeley Carmichael: architect of black power." Ebony, September 1966.

Berger, Peter and Thomas Luckmann
   1966   The Social Construction of Reality. Garden City, N.Y.: Doubleday.

Berkowitz, Leonard
   1962   Aggression: A Social Psychological Analysis. New York: McGraw-Hill.

Bertzinger, A. J.
   1972   A History of American Political Thought. New York: Dodd, Mead.

Bettelheim, Bruno and M. Janowitz
   1950   Dynamics of Prejudice. New York: Harper & Brothers.

Bierstedt, Robert
   1948   "The sociology of majorities." American Sociological Review 13: 700–710.

Blalock, Hubert M., Jr.
   1967   Toward a Theory of Minority-Group Relations. New York: John Wiley.

Blauner, Robert
   1972   Racial Oppression in America. New York: Harper & Row.
   1975   "Colonized and immigrant minorities." In Norman Yetman and Hoy Steele
           (eds.), Majority and Minority: The Dynamics of Racial and Ethnic Relations.
           Boston: Allyn & Bacon.

Blaustein, Albert P. and Robert L. Zangrando
   1968   Civil Rights and the Black American. New York: Simon & Schuster.

Bogardus, Emory S.
   1925   "Measuring social distances." Journal of Applied Sociology 9: 299–308.

Bosmajian, Haig
   1974   The Language of Oppression. Washington, D.C.: Public Affairs Press.

Breitman, George (ed.)
   1965   Malcolm X Speaks. New York: Grove Press.

Breton, Raymond
   1964   "Institutional completeness of ethnic communities and the personal relations
           of immigrants." American Journal of Sociology 70: 193–205.

Brotz, Howard
   1959   "Social stratification and the political order." American Journal of Sociology
           64: 575–85.

Browne, Robert S.
   1968   "The case for two Americas—one black, one white." New York Times
           Magazine, August 11, 1968.

Carmichael, Stokely
   1971   "What we want." In Gary Marx (ed.), Racial Conflict: Tension and Change in
           American Society. Boston: Little, Brown.

Cazden, Courtney, Vera John and Dell Hymes (eds.)
   1971   The Functions of Language in the Classroom. New York: Teachers College
           Press.

Christenson, Reo
    1973   Heresies Right and Left: Some Political Assumptions Reexamined. New York:
            Harper & Row.
    1976   Challenge and Decision. New York: Harper & Row.
Cleaver, Eldridge
    1968   Soul on Ice. New York: McGraw-Hill.
Cohen, Sanford
    1970   Labor in the United States, 3rd ed. Columbus, Ohio: Charles E. Merrill.
Coleman, James S. et al.
    1966   Equality of Educational Opportunity. Washington, D.C.: U.S. Office of
            Education.
Connolly, William
    1969   The Bias of Pluralism. New York: Atherton.
Coser, Lewis and Irving Howe
    1976   The New Conservatives: A Critique from the Left. New York: New American
            Library.
Cox, Oliver C.
    1948   Caste, Class and Race: A Study in Social Dynamics. Garden City, N.Y.:
            Doubleday.
Coxon, A. P. M. and C. L. Jones (eds.)
    1975   Social Mobility. Baltimore: Penguin Books.
Crain, Robert L.
    1975   "School integration and occupational achievement of Negroes." In Thomas
            F. Pettigrew (ed.), Racial Discrimination in the United States. New York:
            Harper & Row.
Crèvecoeur, J. Hector St. John
    1974   "What Is an American" (from letters from an American farmer–1782). In
            Richard J. Meister (ed.), Race and Ethnicity in Modern America. Lexington,
            Mass.: D. C. Heath.
Cubberley, Ellwood P.
    1909   Changing Conceptions of Education. Boston: Houghton Mifflin.
Cuber, John F. and William Kenkel
    1954   Social Stratification in the United States. New York: Appleton.
Dahrendorf, Ralf
    1959   Class and Class Conflict in Industrial Society. Stanford, Ca.: Stanford Univer-
            sity Press.
Daniel, Pete
    1972   The Shadow of Slavery: Peonage in the South 1901–1969. New York:
            Oxford University Press.
Davidson, Basil
    1961   The African Slave Trade. Boston: Little, Brown.

Davies, James D.
1969   "The J-curve of rising and declining satisfactions as a cause of some great revolutions and contained rebellion." In Hugh Davis Graham and Ted Robert Gurr (eds.), Violence in America, vol. 2. Washington, D.C.: National Commission on the Causes and Prevention of Violence.

Davis, James A.
1966   "The campus as a frogpond: an application of the theory of relative deprivation to career decisions of college men." American Journal of Sociology 72: 17–31.

Davis, Kingsley and Wilbert E. Moore
1945   "Some principles of stratification." American Sociological Review 10: 242–49.

Dawkins, Richard
1976   The Selfish Gene. New York: Oxford University Press.

Deloria, Vine
1974   Behind the Trail of Broken Treaties. New York: Dell.

de Tocqueville, Alexis
1969   Democracy in America. Garden City, N.Y.: Anchor Books (Doubleday).

Deutsch, Martin
1969   "Happenings on the way back to the forum: social science, IQ, and race differences revisited." Harvard Educational Review 39: 1–35.

Deutsch, Martin, Irwin Datz and Arthur Jensen (eds.)
1968   Social Class, Race, and Psychological Development. New York: Holt, Rinehart and Winston.

Deutsch, Morton
1973   The Resolution of Conflict. New Haven, Conn.: Yale University Press.

Dolbeare, Kenneth M. and Patricia Dolbeare
1976   American Ideologies: The Competing Beliefs of the 1970s. Chicago: Markham.

Dollard, John, Neil Miller, Leonard Doob, O. H. Mowrer and Robert Sears
1939   Frustration and Aggression. New Haven, Conn.: Yale University Press.

Dreyer, June Teufel
1976   China's Forty Millions: Minority Nationalities and National Integration in the People's Republic of China. Cambridge, Mass.: Harvard University Press.

Du Bois, W. E. B
1963   An ABC of Color. New York: International Publishers.

Duff, John B.
1971   The Irish in the United States. Belmont, Ca.: Wadsworth.

Dumont, Robert and Murray Wax
1969   "Cherokee school society and the intercultural classroom." Human Organization 28: 217–26.

Duncan, Otis Dudley
1968   "Inheritance of poverty or inheritance of race?" In Daniel Moynihan (ed.), On Understanding Poverty. New York: Basic Books.

Dworkin, Ronald
1977   Taking Rights Seriously. London: Gerald Duckworth.
1978   "The Bakke decision: did it decide anything?" The New York Review, August 17, 1978.

Edwards, Richard C., Michael Reich and Thomas E. Weisskopf
1978   The Capitalist System. Englewood Cliffs, N.J.: Prentice-Hall.

Eells, Kenneth et al.
1952   Intelligence and Cultural Differences. Chicago: University of Chicago Press.

Ehrenreich, Barbara and John Ehrenreich
1970   The American Health Empire: Power, Profits, and Politics. New York: Vintage Books.

Ehrlich, Howard J.
1973   The Social Psychology of Prejudice. New York: John Wiley.

Eisenstadt, S. N.
1971   Social Differentiation and Stratification. Glenview, Ill.: Scott, Foresman.

Eisinger, Peter K.
1974   "Racial differences in protest participation." American Political Science Review, June 1974, p. 603.

Elkins, Stanley M.
1963   Slavery. New York: Grosset & Dunlap.

Enloe, Cynthia H.
1973   Ethnic Conflict and Political Development. Boston: Little, Brown.

Fairchild, Henry Pratt
1926   The Melting Pot Mistake. Boston: Little, Brown.

Fanon, Frantz
1967   Black Skins, White Masks. New York: Grove Press.

Ford, Maurice DeG.
1975   "Busing in Boston." Commonweal 102 (October 10, 1975): 456–60.

Foster, George M.
1960   Culture and Conquest: America's Spanish Heritage. Chicago: Quadrangle Books.

Franklin, John Hope
1967   From Slavery to Freedom, 3rd ed. New York: Vintage Books.

Franklin, Raymond and Solomon Resnick
1973   The Political Economy of Racism. New York: Holt, Rinehart and Winston.

Frazier, E. Franklin
  1957   Race and Culture Contacts in the Modern World. Boston: Beacon Press.
  1962   Black Bourgeoisie. New York: Collier Books.
Friedman, Robert
  1975   "Institutional racism: how to discriminate without really trying." In Thomas
          F. Pettigrew (ed.), Racial Discrimination in the United States. New York:
          Harper & Row.
Gamson, William A.
  1974   "Violence and political power: the meek don't make it." Psychology Today,
          July 1974, pp. 35–36.
  1975   The Strategy of Social Protest. Homewood, Ill.: Dorsey.
Geschwender, James A.
  1977   Class, Race and Worker Insurgency. New York: Cambridge University Press.
  1978   Racial Stratification in America. Dubuque, Iowa: Wm. C. Brown.
Gilman, Stuart C.
  1972   "The color-line and humanism: an ethical study of W. E. B. Du Bois." The
          Journal of Human Relations, December 1972.
  1975   "A review essay on social terrorism: Dreiser's Harlan Miner's Speak revi-
          sited." Mountain Review, Fall 1975.
  1980   "Affirmative action: equality gained, equality lost." Virginia Social Science
          Journal 14, no. 1, April 1980.
Glazer, Nathan
  1950   "The dynamics of ethnic identification." American Sociological Review 23:
          31–40.
  1954   "Ethnic groups in America: from national culture to ideology." In Monroe
          Berger, Theodore Abel, and Charles H. Page (eds.), Freedom and Control in
          Modern Society. New York: Van Nostrand Reinhold.
Glazer, Nathan, and Daniel Moynihan
  1963   Beyond the Melting Pot. Cambridge, Mass.: MIT Press.
Glick, Lawrence B.
  1974   "The right to equal opportunity." In Rudolph Gomez et al. (eds.), The Social
          Reality of Ethnic America. Lexington, Mass.: D. C. Heath.
Goffman, Erving
  1959   The Presentation of Self in Everyday Life. Garden City, N.Y.: Doubleday.
Goldman, A. H.
  1975   "Limits to the justification of reverse discrimination." Social Theory and
          Practice, Spring 1975.
Goldsby, Richard A.
  1977   Race and Races (2nd ed.). New York: Macmillan.
Gomez, Rudolph, Clement Cottingham, Russell Endo and Kathleen Jackson (eds.)
  1974   The Social Reality of Ethnic America. Lexington, Mass.: D. C. Heath.

Gordon, Milton
  1964a   Assimilation in American Life. New York: Oxford University Press.
  1964b   "Social structure and goals in group relations." In Morroe Berger, T. Abel and C. Page (eds.), Freedom and Control in Modern Society. New York: Octagon Books.
  1978   Human Nature, Class, and Ethnicity. New York: Oxford University Press.
Grant, Joanne
  1968   Black Protest: History, Documents and Analyses. New York: Fawcett.
Grant, Madison
  1916   The Passing of a Great Race. New York: Charles Scribner's Sons.
Greeley, Andrew M.
  1974   Ethnicity in the United States: A Preliminary Reconnaissance. New York: John Wiley.
  1977   The American Catholic: A Social Portrait. New York: Basic Books.
Gregory, Dick
  1968   The Shadow That Scares Me. Garden City, N.Y.: Doubleday.
Guttman, Herbert G.
  1976   The Black Family in Slavery and Freedom, 1750–1925. New York: Vintage Books.
Hacker, Andrew
  1969   "Power to do what?" In William Connolly (ed.), The Bias of Pluralism. New York: Atherton.
Handlin, Oscar
  1957   Race and Nationality in American Life. Boston: Little, Brown.
Harris, Louis
  1977   "Races deeply split over 'black neglect' issues." Richmond News Leader, September 14, 1977.
Hartley, E. L.
  1946   Problems in Prejudice. New York: Kings Crown.
Heisler, Martin O. (ed.)
  1977   Ethnic Conflict in the World Today. Issue of The Annals of the American Academy of Political and Social Science 433, September 1977.
Henry, Andrew F. and James F. Short, Jr.
  1954   Suicide and Homicide. Glencoe, Ill.: Free Press.
Herberg, Will
  1960   Protestant–Catholic–Jew. Garden City, N.Y.: Anchor.
Herskovits, Melville J.
  1941   The Myth of the Negro Past. Boston: Beacon Press.
Hessel, Dieter
  1977   Maggie Kuhn on Aging. Philadelphia, Pa: The Westminster Press.
Higham, John
  1955   Strangers in the Land: Patterns of American Nativism 1860–1925. New York: Atheneum.

Hill, Herbert
    1967   "The racial practices of organized labor—the age of Gompers and after." In
            Arthur M. Ross and Herbert Hill (eds.), Employment, Race and Poverty. New
            York: Harcourt, Brace & World.

Himes, Joseph S.
    1966   "The functions of racial conflict." Social Forces 45: 1–10.
    1974   Racial and Ethnic Relations. Dubuque, Iowa: Wm. C. Brown.

Hollingshead, August and Fredrick Redlich
    1958   Social Class and Mental Illness: A Community Study. New York: John Wiley.

Hovland, Carl I. and Robert Sears
    1940   "Minor studies of aggression: correlation of lynchings with economic indices."
            Journal of Psychology (Winter): 301–10.

Hsu, Francis L. K.
    1971   The Challenge of the American Dream: The Chinese in the United States.
            Belmont, Ca.: Wadsworth.

Humphreys, Laud
    1972   Out of the Closets: The Sociology of Homosexual Liberation. Englewood
            Cliffs, N.J.: Prentice-Hall.

Jackson, George
    1970   Soledad Brothers. New York: Bantam Books.

Jaco, E. Gartley (ed.)
    1972   Patients, Physicians and Illness: A Sourcebook in Behavioral Science and
            Health. New York: Free Press.

Jacobs, Paul and Saul Landau (eds.)
    1971   To Serve the Devil. New York: Random House.

Jensen, Arthur
    1969   "How much can we boost IQ and scholastic achievement?" Harvard Edu-
            cational Review 39: 1–123.

Johnson, Daniel, Richard Porter and Patricia Mateljan
    1975   "Racial discrimination in apartment rentals." In Thomas F. Pettigrew (ed.),
            Racial Discrimination in the United States. New York: Harper & Row.

Jones, James M.
    1972   Prejudice and Racism. Reading, Mass.: Addison-Wesley.

Jones, Maldwyn Allen
    1960   American Immigration. Chicago: University of Chicago Press.

Josephy, Alvin, M., Jr.
    1975   "Freedom for the American Indian." In Norman Yetman and Hoy Steele
            (eds.), Majority and Minority: The Dynamics of Racial and Ethnic Relations.
            Boston: Allyn & Bacon.

Kain, John F. (ed.)
    1969   Race and Poverty: The Economics of Discrimination. Englewood Cliffs, N.J.:
            Prentice-Hall.

Kallen, Horace M.
    1915   "Democracy versus the melting pot." The Nation 100: 190–194, 217–222.

    1924   Culture and Democracy in the United States. New York: Liveright.

Kaufman, Walter
    1957   "Status, authoritarianism, and anti-Semitism." American Journal of Sociology (January): 379–82.

Kennedy, Ruby Jo Reeves
    1944   "Single or triple melting pot? Intermarriage in New Haven, 1870–1940." American Journal of Sociology 49: 331–39.

    1952   "Single or triple melting pot? Intermarriage in New Haven, 1870–1950." American Journal of Sociology 58: 56–59.

Killian, Lewis and Charles Grigg
    1964   Racial Crisis in America. Englewood Cliffs, N.J.: Prentice-Hall.

King, M. L., Jr.
    1967   Where Do We Go from Here? New York: Harper & Row.

Kitano, Harry H. L.
    1976   Japanese American: The Evolution of a Subculture. Englewood Cliffs, N.J.: Prentice-Hall.

Kluger, Richard
    1975   Simple Justice. New York: Vintage Books.

Knowles, Louis L. and Kenneth Prewitt
    1969   Institutional Racism in America. Englewood Cliffs, N.J.: Prentice-Hall.

Koestler, Arthur
    1976   The Thirteenth Tribe. New York: Random House.

Kolenda, Pauline
    1978   Caste in Contemporary India: Beyond Organic Solidarity. Menlo Park, Ca.: Benjamin/Cummings.

Kramer, Judith
    1970   The American Minority Community. New York: Appleton.

Krauss, Irving
    1976   Stratification, Class and Conflict. New York: Free Press.

Ladd, Charles E., Charles Hadley and Lauriston King
    1971   "A new political realignment." The Public Interest, no. 23, pp. 46–64.

Ladd, Everett and Charles D. Hadley
    1978   Transformation of the American Party System, 2nd ed. New York: W. W. Norton.

Lam, Margaret M.
    1936   "Racial myth and family tradition—worship among part-Hawaiians." Social Forces 14, no. 3.

Laumann, Edward O.
    1973   Bonds of Pluralism. New York: John Wiley.

Leggett, John
    1968   Class, Race and Labor. New York: Oxford University Press.

Lenski, Gerhard E.
  1966   Power and Privilege: A Theory of Social Stratification. New York: McGraw-Hill.

Lester, Julius
  1975   "The current state of black America." In Norman Yetman and Hoy Steele (eds.), Majority and Minority: The Dynamics of Racial and Ethnic Relations. Boston: Allyn & Bacon.

Levin, Jack
  1975   The Functions of Prejudice. New York: Harper & Row.

Levy, Mark R. and Michael S. Kramer
  1972   The Ethnic Factor: How America's Minorities Decide Elections. New York: Simon & Schuster.

Lewontin, Richard C.
  1977   "Biological determinism as a social weapon." In the Ann Arbor Science for the People Editorial Collective. In Biology as a Social Weapon. Minneapolis: Burgess Publishing.

Lieberson, Stanley
  1961   "A societal theory of race and ethnic relations." American Sociological Review 26: 902–10.

Lieberson, Stanley, Guy Dalto and Mary Ellen Johnston.
  1975   "The course of mother-tongue diversity in nations." American Journal of Sociology 81: 34–61.

Lipsitz, Lewis
  1970   "On political belief: the grievances of the poor." In Phillip Green and Sanford Levinson (eds.), Power and Community: Dissenting Essays in Political Science. New York: Random House.
  1974   "On political belief: the grievances of the poor." In Allen R. Wilcox (ed.), Public Opinion and Political Attitudes. New York: John Wiley.

Little Horn, Annette
  1971   "An Indian review of *Stalking Moon*." In Paul Jacobs and Saul Landau (eds.), To Serve the Devil, vol. 1. New York: Random House.

Lowi, Theodore
  1977   American Government: Incomplete Conquest. Hinsdale, Ill.: Dryden.
  1979   The End of Liberalism, 2nd ed. New York: W. W. Norton.

Lukes, Stephen
  1974   Power: A Radical View. New York: Macmillan.

Lyman, Stanford M.
  1975   "Contrasts in the community organization of Chinese and Japanese in North America." In Norman Yetman and Hoy Steele (eds.), Majority and Minority: The Dynamics of Racial and Ethnic Relations. Boston: Allyn & Bacon.

Mack, Raymond (ed.)
  1963   Race, Class and Power. New York: Van Nostrand Reinhold.

McNeill, William H.
 1976   Plagues and Peoples. Garden City, N.Y.: Anchor Press/Doubleday.
Makielski, S. J.
 1973   Beleaguered Minorities. San Francisco: W. H. Freeman.
Marx, Karl
 1956   Selected Writings in Sociology and Social Philosophy, T. B. Bottomore
         (trans.). New York: McGraw-Hill.
 1973   Capital, vol. 1. New York: International Publishers.
Marx, Karl and Frederick Engels
 1947   The German Ideology, R. Pascal (ed.). New York: International Publishers.
Mayer, Milton
 1955   They Thought They Were Free. Chicago: University of Chicago Press.
Meier, August and Elliot Rudwick
 1976   "The origins of non-violent deviant action in Afro-American protest." In
         Along the Color-Line. Urbana, Ill.: Univ. of Illinois Press.
Memmi, Albert
 1968   Dominated Man. New York: Orion Press.
Michelman, Frank I.
 1969   "Foreword: on protecting the poor through the Fourteenth Amendment."
         Harvard Law Review 83: 7.
Miller, Abraham
 1974   "Ethnicity and party identification: continuation of a theoretical diaglogue."
         Western Political Quarterly 27: 479–90.
Miller, Neal E. and Richard Begelski
 1948   "Minor studies of aggression: the influence of frustrations imposed by the
         in-group on attitudes expressed toward out-groups." Journal of Psychology
         25: 437–42.
Miller, Warren E. and Theresa E. Levitin
 1976   Leadership and Change: Presidential Elections 1952–1972. Cambridge,
         Mass.: Winthrop.
Mills, C. Wright
 1956   The Power Elite. New York: Oxford University Press.
Moore, Joan W.
 1976   Mexican Americans. Englewood Cliffs, N.J.: Prentice-Hall.
Moore, Joan and Alfredo Cuellar
 1970   Mexican Americans. Englewood Cliffs, N.J.: Prentice-Hall.
Morner, Magnus
 1967   Race Mixture in the History of Latin America. Boston: Little, Brown.
Morse, Stanley and Kenneth J. Gergen
 1970   "Social comparison, self-consistency, and the concept of self." Journal of
         Personality and Social Psychology 16: 145–56.
Mosse, George L.
 1968   Nazi Culture. New York: Grosset & Dunlap.

Moynihan, Daniel P.
   1965   The Negro Family: The Case for National Action. Washington, D.C.: U.S. Department of Labor.
   1968   On Understanding Poverty. New York: Basic Books.
   1970   "Memo to Nixon on the status of Negroes." New York Times, January 16, 1970.
Myrdal, Gunnar
   1944   An American Dilemma. New York: Harper & Row.
National Americanization Committee
   1918   "What you can do for Americanization."
Nava, Julian
   1973   Viva La Raza! New York: D. Van Nostrand.
Navarro, Armando
   1974   "The evolution of Chicano politics." Aztlan 5, no. 1, no. 2.
Neiburg, H. L.
   1969   Political Violence. New York: St. Martin's Press.
Newman, Dorothy, Nancy Amidei, Barbara Carter, Dawn Day, William Kruvant and Jack Russell
   1978   Protest, Politics, and Prosperity: Black Americans and White Institutions, 1940–75. New York: Pantheon.
Newman, William M.
   1973   American Pluralism: A Study of Minority Groups and Social Theory. New York: Harper & Row.
Newsweek
   1958   "Indian raid." January 27, 1958, p. 27.
   1976   "The next minority." December 20, 1976, pp. 74–75.
   1977a "Britain: race pays off." May 9, 1977, pp. 48–49.
   1977b "English spoken here." May 9, 1977, p. 63.
Nichols, P. and E. V. Anderson
   1973   "Intellectual performance, race and socioeconomic status." Social Biology 20: 367.
Noel, Donald L.
   1968   "A theory of the origin of ethnic stratification." Social Problems 16: 157–72.
Parenti, Michael
   1967   "Ethnic politics and the persistence of ethnic identification." American Political Science Review 61: 717–26.
Park, Robert E.
   1950   Race and Culture. New York: Free Press.
Pease, Jane and William Pease
   1968   "Black power—the debate in 1840." Phylon 20, Spring 1968, pp. 19–26.
Pennock, J. Roland and John W. Chapman (eds.)
   1967   Equality. Chicago: Atherton.

Pettigrew, Thomas F.
  1964   A Profile of the Negro American. Princeton, N.J.: D. Van Nostrand.
Pettigrew, Thomas F. (ed.)
  1975   Racial Discrimination in the United States. New York: Harper & Row.
Phillips, Kevin P.
  1970   The Emerging Republican Majority. New York: Anchor Books.
Pilisuk, Marc and Thomas Hayden
  1965   "Is there a military-industrial complex which prevents peace? Consensus and
          countervailing power in pluralistic systems." Journal of Social Issues, 21: 3.
Pinkney, Alphonso
  1975   Black Americans. Englewood Cliffs, N.J.: Prentice-Hall.
Pomper, Gerald
  1974   Elections in America. New York: Dodd, Mead.
  1976   The Election of 1976. New York: David McKay.
Poston, Dudley, L., Jr. and David Alvirez
  1976   "On the cost of being a Mexican-American worker." In Carrol A. Hernandez
          et al. (eds.), Chicanos: Social and Psychological Perspectives. St. Louis:
          C. V. Mosby.
Poussaint, Alvin F.
  1974   "Minority group psychology: implications for social action." In Rudolph
          Gomez et al. (eds.), The Social Reality of Ethnic America. Lexington, Mass.:
          D. C. Heath.
Rapkin, Chester
  1969   "Price discrimination against Negroes in the rental housing market." In John
          F. Kain (ed.), Race and Poverty: The Economics of Discrimination. En-
          glewood Cliffs, N.J.: Prentice-Hall.
Rendon, Armando B.
  1974   "Four declarations of independence." In Rudolph Gomez, et al. (eds.), The
          Social Reality of Ethnic America. Lexington, Mass: D. C. Heath.
Riordon, William L.
  1963   Plunkitt of Tammany Hall. New York: E. P. Dutton.
Rolle, Andrew F.
  1972   The American Italians. Belmont, Ca.: Wadsworth.
Röpke, Wilhelm
  1964   "South Africa: an attempt at a positive appraisal." Reprinted from Schweizer
          Monatshefte, 44th year, no. 2, May 1964.
Rose, Peter I.
  1974   They and We: Racial and Ethnic Relations in the United States. New York:
          Random House.
Rosenberg, M. J.
  1973   "To Uncle Tom and other Jews." In Jack Nusan Porter and Peter Dreier (eds.),
          Jewish Radicalism: A Selected Anthology. New York: Grove Press.

Rosenthal, Robert and Lenore Jacobson
  1968   Pygmalion in the Classroom. New York: Holt, Rinehart and Winston.

Rossides, Daniel W.
  1976   The American Class System: An Introduction to Social Stratification. Boston: Houghton Mifflin.

Rothman, Jack
  1969   "The ghetto makers." In John F. Kain (ed.), Race and Poverty: The Economics of Discrimination. Englewood Cliffs, N.J.: Prentice-Hall.

Royko, Mike
  1971   Boss. New York: E. P. Dutton.

Ryan, William
  1976   Blaming the Victim. New York: Random House.

Sagarin, Edward (ed.)
  1971   The Other Minorities. Waltham, Mass.: Ginn.

Sampson, Anthony
  1973   The Sovereign State of I.T.T. New York: Stein & Day.

Sanders, William B.
  1976   Juvenile Delinquency. New York: Praeger.

Schaar, John
  1968   "Equality of opportunity and beyond." In J. Roland Pennock and John W. Chapman (eds.), Equality. Chicago: Atherton.

Schermerhorn, Richard A.
  1961   Society and Power. New York: Random House.
  1970   Comparative Ethnic Relations: A Framework for Theory and Research. New York: Random House.

Schopenhauer, Arthur
  1928   Schopenhauer: Selections, DeWitt H. Parker (ed.). New York: Charles Scribner's Sons.

Schultz, John
  1962   "An interview with Robert F. Williams." Studies on the Left, vol. 2, no. 3, 1962.

Schur, Edwin M.
  1971   Labeling Deviant Behavior: Its Sociological Implications. New York: Harper & Row.

Schutz, Alfred
  1970   On Phenomenology and Social Relations. Chicago: University of Chicago Press.

Science
  1976   "The handicapped: HEW moving on civil rights in higher education." Science 194, December 24, 1976, pp. 1399–1402.

Seale, Bobby
    1970   Seize the Time. New York: Vintage Books.

Shibutani, Tamotsu
    1962   "Reference groups and social control." In Arnold Rose (ed.), Human Behavior and Social Processes. Boston: Houghton Mifflin.

Shibutani, Tamotsu and Kian Kwan
    1965   Ethnic Stratification. New York: Macmillan.

Siegel, Paul M.
    1965   "On the cost of being a Negro." Sociological Inquiry 35: 41–58.

Simmel, Georg
    1950   The Sociology of Georg Simmel, Kurt Wolff (ed. and trans.). New York: Free Press.

    1955   Conflict and the Web of Group Affiliations. New York: Free Press.

Simon, James F.
    1973   In His Own Image. New York: David McKay.

Simpson, George and J. Milton Yinger
    1972   Racial and Cultural Minorities: An Analysis of Prejudice and Discrimination, 4th ed. New York: Harper & Row.

Sindler, Alan
    1978   Bakke, Defunis and Minority Admissions. New York: Longman.

Slater, Phillip
    1976   The Pursuit of Loneliness. Boston: Beacon Press.

Smith, Elmer Lewis
    1958   The Amish People. New York: Exposition Press.

Sochen, June
    1974   Herstory: A Woman's View of American History. New York: Alfred.

Sorenson, Anemette, Karl E. Taeuber and Leslie J. Hollingsworth
    1974   Indexes of Racial Segregation for 109 Cities in the United States 1940–1970. Madison, Wisconsin: Madison Institute for Research on Poverty.

Sowell, Thomas
    1972   Black Education: Myths and Tragedies. New York: David McKay.

Stampp, Kenneth M.
    1956   The Peculiar Institution: Slavery in the Ante-Bellum South. New York: Vintage Books.

Steiner, Stan
    1969   La Raza: The Mexican Americans. New York: Harper & Row.

Stevens, William K.
    1978   "Since the 1967 riots, Detroit has moved painfully toward a modest renaissance." The New York Times, March 1, 1978, sec. C, p. C-15.

Storing, Herbert J. (ed.)
    1970   What Country Have I? King "Letters from the Birmingham jail." New York: St. Martin's Press.

Strauss, Anselm
1970   "Medical ghettos." In Anselm Strauss (ed.), Where Medicine Fails. New Brunswick, N.J.: Transaction Books.

Sudnow, David
1970   "Dead on arrival." In Anselm Strauss (ed.), Where Medicine Fails. New Brunswick, N.J.: Transaction Books.

Szasz, Thomas
1970   Ideology and Insanity. Garden City, N.Y.: Doubleday.

Szymanski, Albert
1978   The Capitalist State and the Politics of Class. Cambridge, Mass.: Winthrop.

Tannenbaum, Frank
1946   Slave and Citizen. New York: Vintage Books.

Teal, Donn
1971   The Gay Militants. New York: Stein & Day.

Terman, Lewis
1917   The Measurement of Intelligence. Boston: Houghton Mifflin.

Thurow, Lester C.
1969   Poverty and Discrimination. Washington, D.C.: Brookings Institution.

Tribe, Laurence H.
1978   The Constitutional Protection of Individual Rights: Limits on Government. Mineola, N.Y.: The Foundation Press.

Tucker, Sterling
1969   Black Reflections on White Power. Grand Rapids, Mich.: W. B. Eerdmans.
1971   For Blacks Only. Grand Rapids, Mich.: W. B. Eerdmans.

Turner, Frederick Jackson
1920   The Frontier in American History. New York: Henry Holt.

Turner, Jonathan H. and Royce Singleton
1978   "A theory of ethnic oppression: toward a reintegration of cultural and structural concepts in ethnic relations theory." Social Forces 56, no. 4, June 1978.

Udom, E., V.
1962   Black Nationalism. New York: Dell.

Uhlman, Fred
1977   Reunion. New York: Farrar, Straus & Giroux.

United Nations
1973   "Population distribution, internal migration and urbanization." In The Determinants and Consequences of Population Trends, vol. 1. New York: United Nations.

U.S. Government Bureau of the Census
1970   International Migration and Naturalization. Washington, D.C.
1977   "Persons of Spanish origin in the United States: March, 1976." Current Population Reports P–20, no. 310, July 1977.

U.S. News and World Report
   1975   "Chavez vs. the Teamsters: farm workers' historic vote." 79: 82–83.
van den Berghe, Pierre L.
   1967   Race and Racism: A Comparative Perspective. New York: John Wiley.
   1970   Race and Ethnicity. New York: Basic Books.
Vander Zanden, James W.
   1972   American Minority Relations, 3rd ed. New York: Ronald Press.
Veeder, William H.
   1974   "Federal encroachment on Indian water rights and the impairment of reserva-
           tion development." In Rudolph Gomez et. al. (eds.), The Social Reality of
           Ethnic America. Lexington, Mass.: D. C. Heath.
Vose, Clement E.
   1969   Caucasians Only: The Supreme Court, The NAACP, and the Restrictive
           Covenant Cases. Berkeley: University of California Press.
Wagley, C. and H. Harris
   1958   Minorities in the New World. New York: Columbia University Press.
Wagner, Roy
   1975   The Invention of Culture. Englewood Cliffs, N.J.: Prentice-Hall.
Wainscott, Stephen A.
   1978   "Performance vs. potential in southern school desegregation 1967–1972."
           Presented at the Southern Political Science Association meeting, Atlanta,
           November 1978.
Warner, Wm. Lloyd and Leo Srole
   1945   The Social System of American Ethnic Groups. New Haven, Conn.: Yale
           University Press.
Weinstein, Michael, and Kenneth W. Grundy
   1974   The Ideology of Political Violence. Columbus, Ohio: Chas. Merrill.
Weisbord, Robert and Arthur Stein
   1970   The Bittersweet Encounter. Westport, Conn.: Negro Universities Press.
White, Ralph K. and Ronald O. Lippitt
   1960   Autocracy and Democracy. New York: Harper & Brothers.
Winslow, Ola E.
   1974   A Destroying Angel: The Conquest of Smallpox in Colonial Boston. Boston:
           Houghton Mifflin.
Wirth, Louis
   1928   The Ghetto. Chicago: University of Chicago Press.
   1945   "The problem of minority groups." In The Science of Man in the World Crisis,
           edited by Ralph Linton. New York: Columbia University Press.
Woodward, C. Vann
   1966   The Strange Career of Jim Crow. New York: Oxford University Press.
Wu, Ching-Tsu
   1972   Chink. New York: World.

Yinger, J. Milton
    1961   "Social forces involved in group identification or withdrawal." Daedalus 90: 247–62.

    1965   A Minority Group in American Society. New York: McGraw-Hill.

Young, Whitney
    1964   To Be Equal. New York: McGraw-Hill.

Zangwill, Israel
    1909   The Melting Pot. New York: Macmillan.

Glossary

Accommodation   Political inaction by a minority group that chooses to work within current social and political circumstances.

Acculturation   *See* Assimilation, behavioral.

Affirmative action   A government program designed to move subordinate group members past discriminatory barriers (particularly in employment) that would normally limit their advancement.

Amalgamation   *See* Melting pot.

Americanization   *See* Assimilation.

Apartheid   Legal separation of races, as practiced in South Africa.

Assimilation, behavioral (acculturation)   The aspect of assimilation that involves the behavior of individuals in the minority group. When their behavior conforms to the general cultural patterns of the dominant group, they may be described as behaviorally assimilated.

Assimilation, structural   The dominant group's social, economic, and political acceptance of a minority group. Such acceptance generally depends upon prior behavioral assimilation by the minority group.

Caste (closed) society   A society with a system of social stratification characterized by no social mobility of societal members.

Category   A collection of people who share at least one important social characteristic (such as sex, race, or social class).

Class (open) society   A society with a system of social stratification characterized by frequent social mobility of societal members.

Co-optation   Raising the social class (real or imagined) of subordinate group members for the purpose of increasing or creating loyalty to the dominant group. This technique is often applied to minority group political leaders. (Related slang: bought off, sold out, Uncle Tom.)

Cultural pluralism   1. A society in which two or more ethnic groups maintain their separate ethnic identities while sharing political power. 2. The conscious political effort of a minority group to maintain its ethnicity (through promoting its culture) while simultaneously working to acquire political influence and economic advantages within a society.

Culture   The complex whole that includes knowledge, belief, art, morals, law, custom, and any other capabilities and habits acquired by humans as members of society.

Discrimination   Any act that hinders the competitive abilities of a group so as to limit their upward social mobility. (*See* Overt discrimination; Institutional discrimination.)

Dominant (majority) group   A social group whose members dominate the major institutions of a society by controlling the most important positions in those institutions. Generally, dominant group members share or conform to a common ethnicity.

Elitism   A perspective on political power that argues for the existence of an ongoing elite group that controls decision making in economic and political arenas.

Ethnic group   A group of people who share a cultural background and maintain elements of that culture in their daily lives.

Ethnic stratification   The clustering of ethnic group members at certain class levels of social stratification. As a result of ethnic stratification, members of certain groups will be found disproportionately in certain social classes.

Ethnicity   *See* Culture.

Ethnocentrism   An individual's belief in the inherent superiority of his or her ethnic group.

Ethnophaulism   Negative, slang term for an ethnic group (such as wop, nigger).

Exploitation   Profiting from minority group individuals who have little choice in their activities because of discrimination against them; for example, slavery.

Expulsion   The physical removal of most or all members of a subordinate group from within the boundaries of a nation state.

Genocide   Actions by the dominant group that cause the deaths of most or all members of a given subordinate group.

Group   A collection of people who think of themselves as having something significant in common. In addition, they generally engage in regular social interaction.

Horizontal ethnic differentiation   The existence of parallel ethnic communities and stratification hierarchies within a society.

Ideology   A world view that inculcates certain values and goals, including some idea about how one can achieve those goals.

Institutional (covert) discrimination   Any discriminatory act that indirectly limits social mobility through the establishment of standards that most members of an affected minority group find difficult to meet. Generally, such standards require skills, abilities, or experiences denied to most minority group members, because of either their social isolation or their ethnic stratification, or both.

Issei   Japanese immigrant to the United States.

Majority group   *See* Dominant group.

Melting pot (amalgamation)   The mixing and blending of cultures by means of a corresponding mixing of people through intermarriage.

Minority (subordinate) group   A social group that faces discriminatory treatment from a more powerful dominant (majority) group. Generally, the minority group is found disproportionately in the lower classes as a result of that discrimination. (*See* Ethnic stratification.)

Nationalism   A separatist political movement based on ethnic identity.

Nisei   American-born child of Japanese immigrant to the United States.

Nonviolence   Legal or illegal nonviolent political activity that attempts to arouse the conscience of dominant group members by calling attention to the plight of the minority group.

Overt discrimination   Any discriminatory act that directly limits social mobility solely on the basis of minority group membership.

Pluralism   A perspective on political power that argues for the existence of a multiplicity of groups in a society, each having input into political decision making.

Political movement   Any group that uses purposeful action in trying to change the political definition of itself or of society as a whole.

Political power   The authoritative allocation of meaning in a society.

"Power" political movements   Ethnic political movements that attempt to recapture the essential cultural values and styles inherent in their history.

Prejudice   A negative attitude toward a specific social group.

Racial group   A group of people who are socially defined as having a common and distinctive genetic heritage. *See* Racism.

Racism   Prejudice and discrimination directed against a minority group, accompanied by the belief in the genetic inferiority of that minority.

Radicalism   Political attempt to overthrow the present political system, violently or peacefully.

Rebellion   Open or determined defiance of or resistance to any authority or controlling power.

Relative deprivation   The idea that deprivation is felt by an individual in terms of his or her perceptions of what he or she should have.

Restrictive covenant   A legal attachment to a piece of property limiting the social groups (ethnic, racial, or the like) that may purchase it.

Segregation, physical   The physical separation of a minority group from a dominant group; for examples, in a prison or on an Indian reservation.

Segregation, social   The social separation of a minority group that is in physical contact with the dominant group. This separation is maintained through highly formalized interaction patterns that maintain social distance; for example, the master–slave relationship.

Separatism   The conscious political effort of a minority group to separate itself politically from the dominant group. This effort may take the form of (1) physically removing the members of the minority group from the political boundaries of the dominant group, or (2) setting up new political boundaries (to be governed by the minority group) within the old political boundaries of the dominant group.

Social class   A collection of activities that share a relatively common position on the hierarchy of social stratification.

Social mobility   The movement of an individual (or group) from one social class to another.

Social stratification   A social ranking of human activities into a hierarchy, ranging from those activities considered the most important or valuable to those activities considered the least important or valuable. The occupants of those activities receive amounts of social power, prestige, and money according to their place in the hierarchy.

Stereotype   A belief that members of a specific social group all share attributes as a result of their group membership.

Subordinate group   *See* Minority group.

Vertical ethnic differentiation   Near-perfect ethnic stratification in which different ethnic groups occupy different social classes.

Acknowledgments

Beacon Press — for the excerpt on pages 297–298 from *The Pursuit of Loneliness* by Philip Slater. Copyright © 1970 by Philip Slater. Revised edition copyright © 1976 by Philip Slater. Reprinted by permission of Beacon Press.

Commonweal Publishing Company — for the excerpt on page 220 from "Busing in Boston" by Maurice DeG. Ford. Reprinted by permission of Commonweal.

McGraw-Hill, Inc. — for the excerpt on pages 167–168 from *Soul on Ice* by Eldridge Cleaver. Reprinted by permission of McGraw-Hill, Inc.

Macmillan Publishing Co., Inc. — for the excerpt on pages 147–148 from *Chicano Manifesto* by Armando B. Rendon. Copyright © 1971 by Armando B. Rendon. Reprinted by permission of Macmillan Publishing Co., Inc.

The Native Nevadan — for the excerpt on page 179 from the review of the movie *Stalking Moon* by Annette Little Horn. Reprinted by permission of *The Native Nevadan*, Reno, Nevada.

Social Forces — for the excerpt on pages 168–169 from "Racial Myth and Family Tradition — Worship Among the Part-Hawaiians" by Margaret M. Lam. Reprinted by permission from *Social Forces*, vol. 14, no. 3, March 1936. Copyright © The University of North Carolina Press.

Ziff-Davis Publishing Company — for the excerpt on pages 98–99 from "Violence and Political Power: The Meek Don't Make It" by William Gamson. Reprinted by permission from *Psychology Today* magazine. Copyright © 1974 by Ziff-Davis Publishing Co.

Index